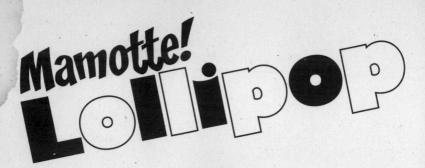

Mamotte! Lollipop

3

Michiyo Kikuta

Translated and adapted by
Elina Ishikawa

Lettered by
North Market Street Graphics

Ballantine Books · New York

A Del Rey Trade Paperback Original

Mamotte! Lollipop volume 3 copyright © 2004 by Michiyo Kikuta
English translation copyright © 2007 by Michiyo Kikuta

Published in the United States by Del Rey Books, an imprint of The Random House Publishing Group, a division of Random House, Inc., New York.

Publication rights arranged through Kodansha Ltd.

First published in Japan in 2004 by Kodansha Ltd., Tokyo

ISBN 978-0-345-49667-6

Printed in the United States of America

www.delreymanga.com

9 8 7 6 5 4

Translator and adapter—Elina Ishikawa
Lettering—North Market Street Graphics

Contents

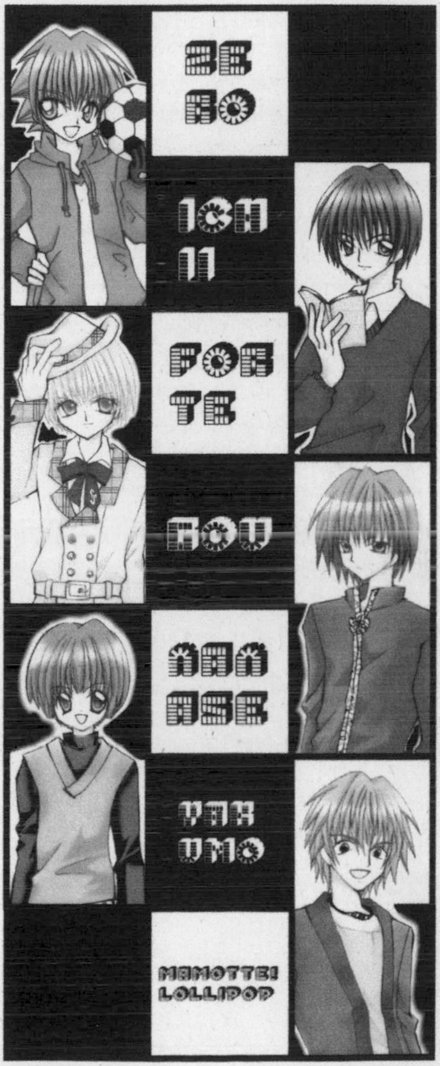
ZE
RO
ICH
II
FOR
TE
NOV
NAN
ASE
YAK
UMO
MAMOTTE!
LOLLIPOP

Honorifics Explained

Throughout the Del Rey Manga books, you will find Japanese honorifics left intact in the translations. For those not familiar with how the Japanese use honorifics and, more important, how they differ from American honorifics, we present this brief overview.

Politeness has always been a critical facet of Japanese culture. Ever since the feudal era, when Japan was a highly stratified society, use of honorifics—which can be defined as polite speech that indicates relationship or status—has played an essential role in the Japanese language. When addressing someone in Japanese, an honorific usually takes the form of a suffix attached to one's name (example: "Asuna-san"), is used as a title at the end of one's name, or appears in place of the name itself (example: "Negi-sensei," or simply "Sensei!").

Honorifics can be expressions of respect or endearment. In the context of manga and anime, honorifics give insight into the nature of the relationship between characters. Many English translations leave out these important honorifics and therefore distort the feel of the original Japanese. Because Japanese honorifics contain nuances that English honorifics lack, it is our policy at Del Rey not to translate them. Here, instead, is a guide to some of the honorifics you may encounter in Del Rey Manga.

-san: *This is the most common honorific, and is equivalent to Mr., Miss, Ms., or Mrs. It is the all-purpose honorific and can be used in any situation where politeness is required.*

-sama: *This is one level higher than "-san" and is used to confer great respect.*

-dono: *This comes from the word "tono" which means "lord." It is an even higher level than "-sama" and confers utmost respect.*

-kun: This suffix is used at the end of boys' names to express familiarity or endearment. It is also sometimes used by men among friends, or when addressing someone younger or of a lower station.

-chan: This is used to express endearment, mostly toward girls. It is also used for little boys, pets, and even among lovers. It gives a sense of childish cuteness.

Bozu: This is an informal way to refer to a boy, similar to the English terms "kid" and "squirt."

Sempai/
Senpai: This title suggests that the addressee is one's senior in a group or organization. It is most often used in a school setting, where underclassmen refer to their upperclassmen as "sempai." It can also be used in the workplace, such as when a newer employee addresses an employee who has seniority in the company.

Kohai: This is the opposite of "sempai" and is used toward underclassmen in school or newcomers in the workplace. It connotes that the addressee is of a lower station.

Sensei: Literally meaning "one who has come before," this title is used for teachers, doctors, or masters of any profession or art.

[blank]: This is usually forgotten in these lists, but it is perhaps the most significant difference between Japanese and English. The lack of honorific means that the speaker has permission to address the person in a very intimate way. Usually, only family, spouses, or very close friends have this kind of permission. Known as yobisute, it can be gratifying when someone who has earned the intimacy starts to call one by one's name without an honorific. But when that intimacy hasn't been earned, it can be very insulting.

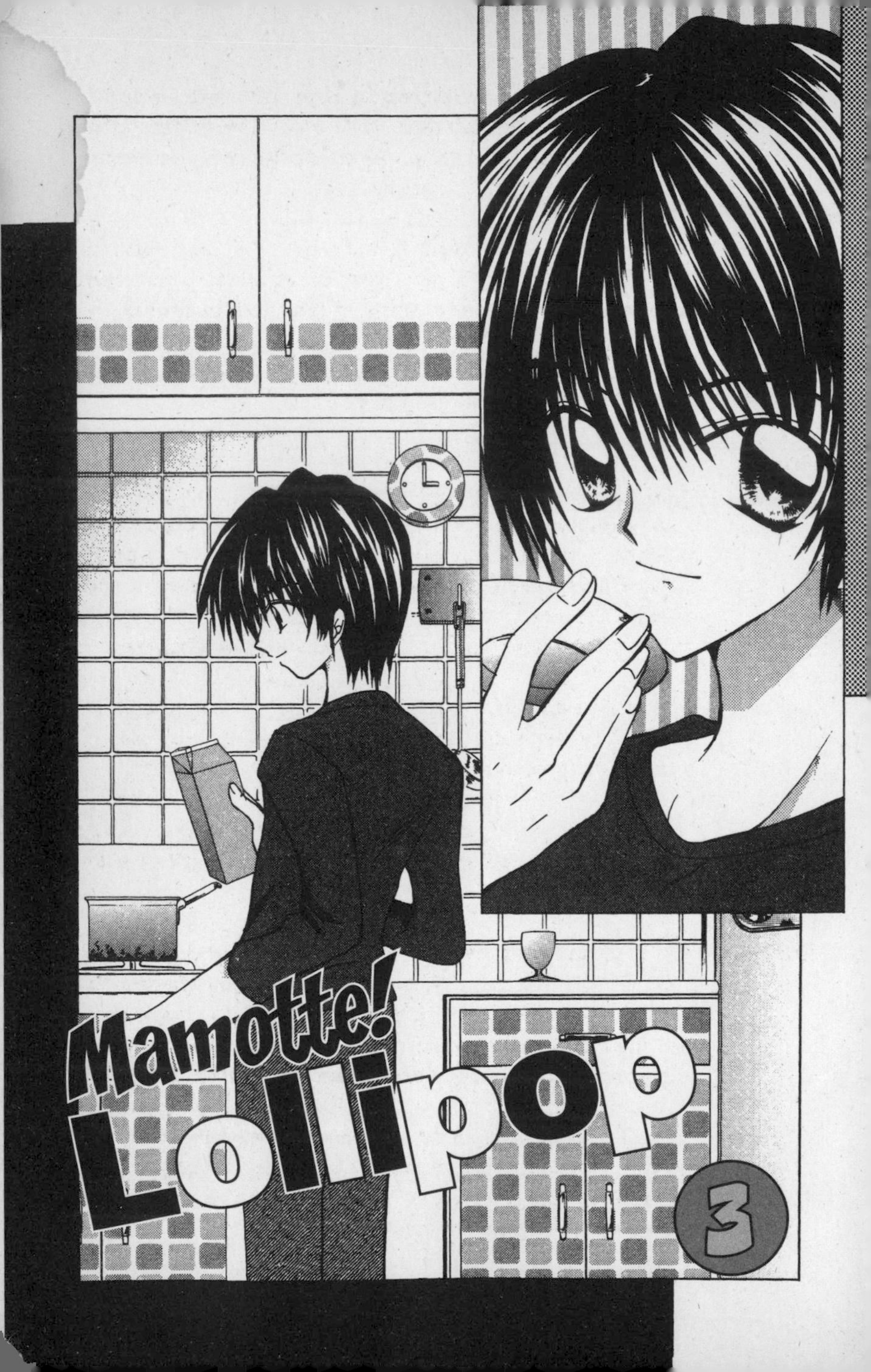
Mamotte!
Lollipop
3

CONTENTS

MAMOTTE! LOLLIPOP:

BONUS STORIES:

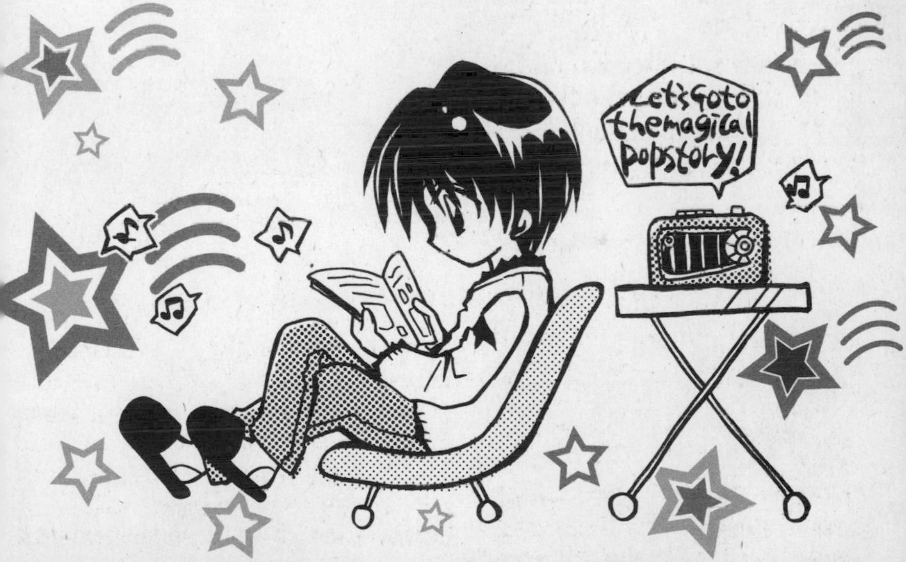

Let's go to the magical popstory!

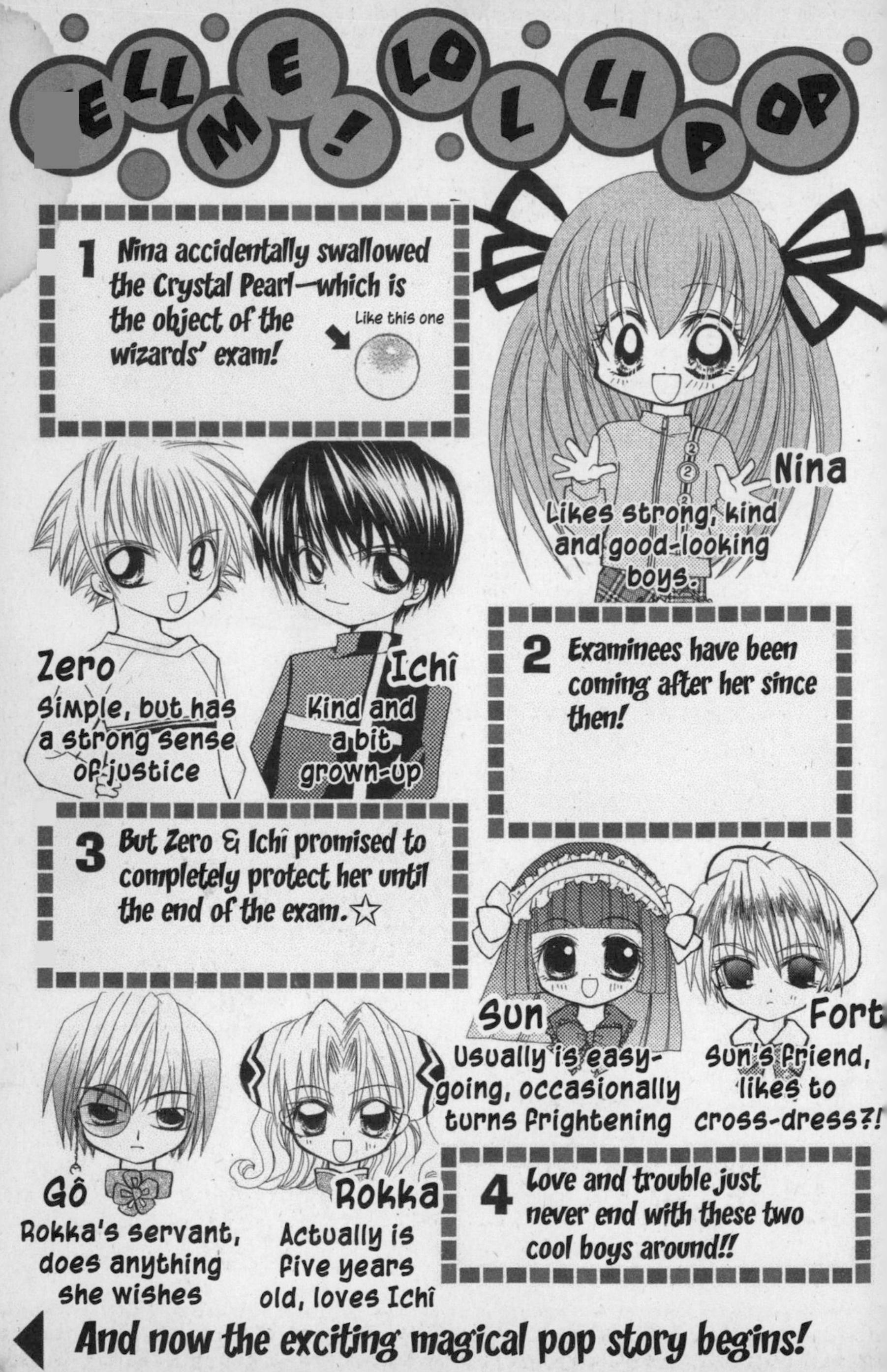
ELL ME! LOLLIPOP
1 Nina accidentally swallowed the Crystal Pearl—which is the object of the wizards' exam!
Like this one
Nina
Likes strong, kind and good-looking boys.
2 Examinees have been coming after her since then!
Ichî
Kind and a bit grown-up
Zero
Simple, but has a strong sense of justice
3 But Zero & Ichî promised to completely protect her until the end of the exam.☆
Fort
Sun's friend, likes to cross-dress?!
Sun
Usually is easy-going, occasionally turns frightening
4 Love and trouble just never end with these two cool boys around!!
Rokka
Actually is five years old, loves Ichî
Gô
Rokka's servant, does anything she wishes
And now the exciting magical pop story begins!

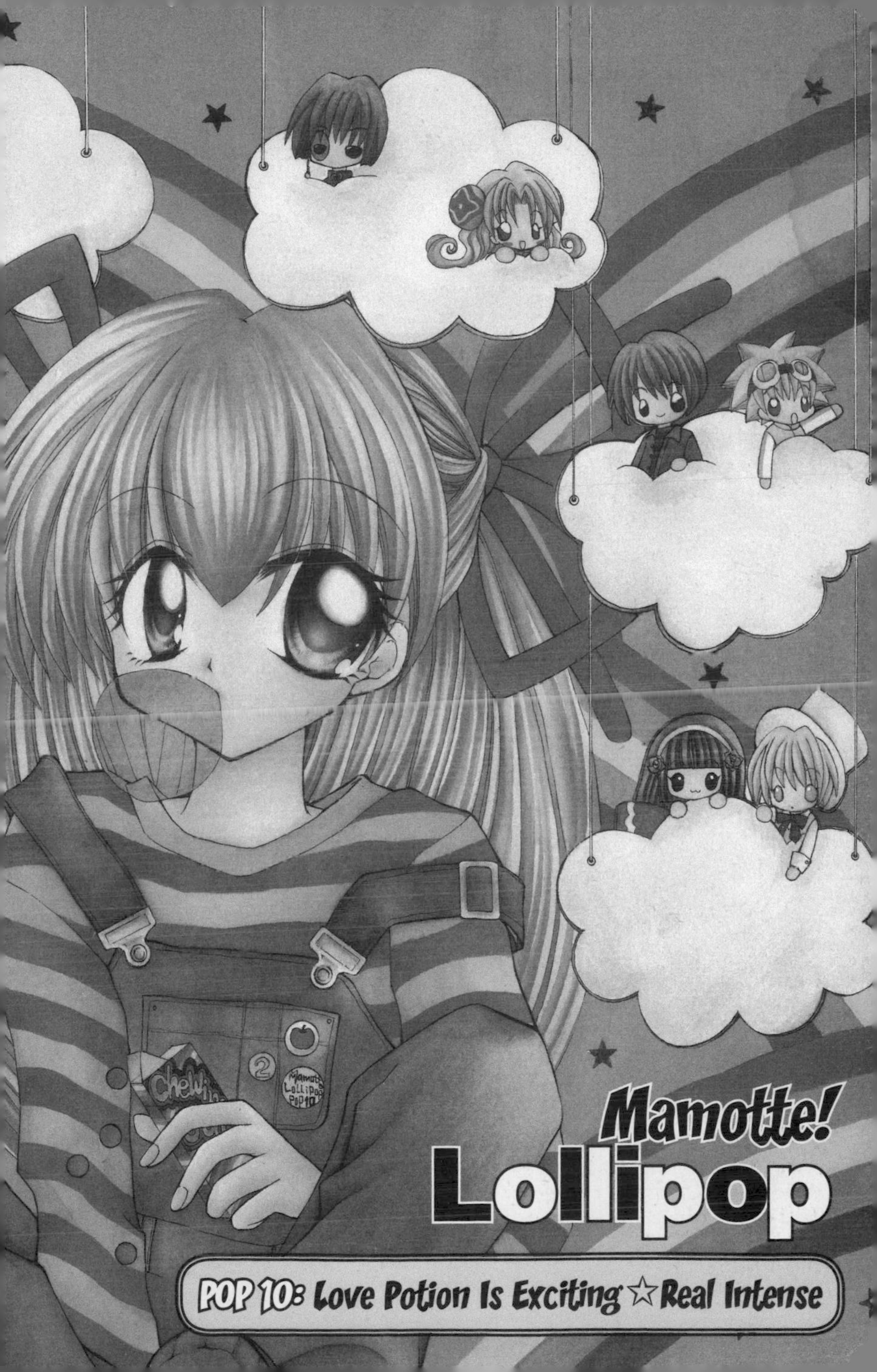
Mamotte!
Lollipop
POP 10: Love Potion Is Exciting☆Real Intense

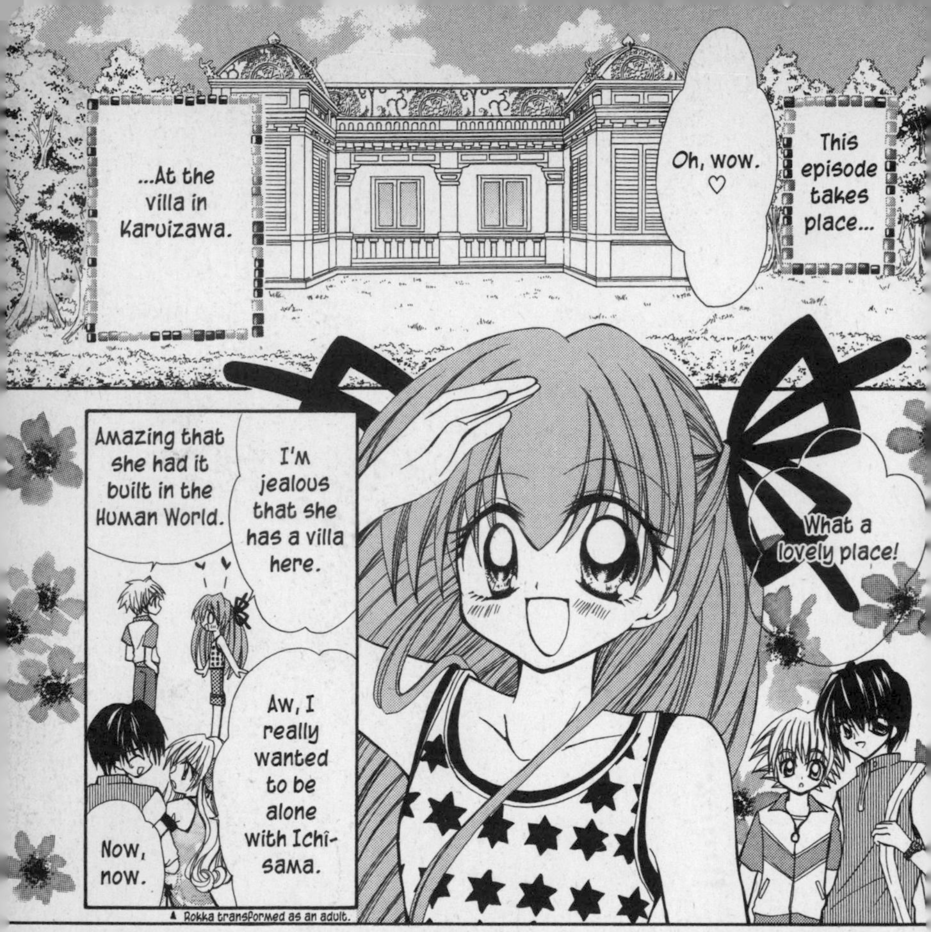
This episode takes place...
Oh, wow. ♡
...At the villa in Karuizawa.
What a lovely place!
I'm jealous that she has a villa here.
Amazing that she had it built in the Human World.
Aw, I really wanted to be alone with Ichi-sama.
Now, now.
▲ Rokka transformed as an adult.

Pop10 Love Potion Is Exciting ☆ Real Intense

I really had a great time creating this episode! It was fun being able to draw a lot of little Rokka. (Since she doesn't show up often . . .) I got a chance to do close-up shots of other characters, too. My assistants (goddesses) actually designed everyone's outfits in this episode. There are some I redesigned to my taste, but I think they look good and fit the characters' personalities well. Thank you to my assistants.

I like the cover page as well. I drew it with an idea of the NHK education program . . .(Maybe?) But it turned out kind of off-season. It looks too much like in the early summer for the December issue of the magazine . . .It was perfect for this book's release.

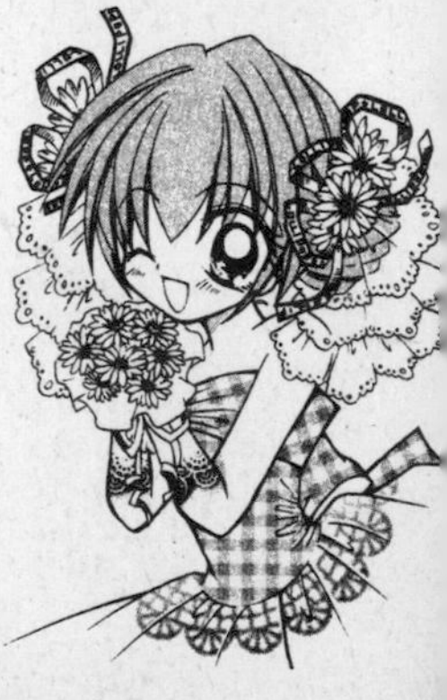

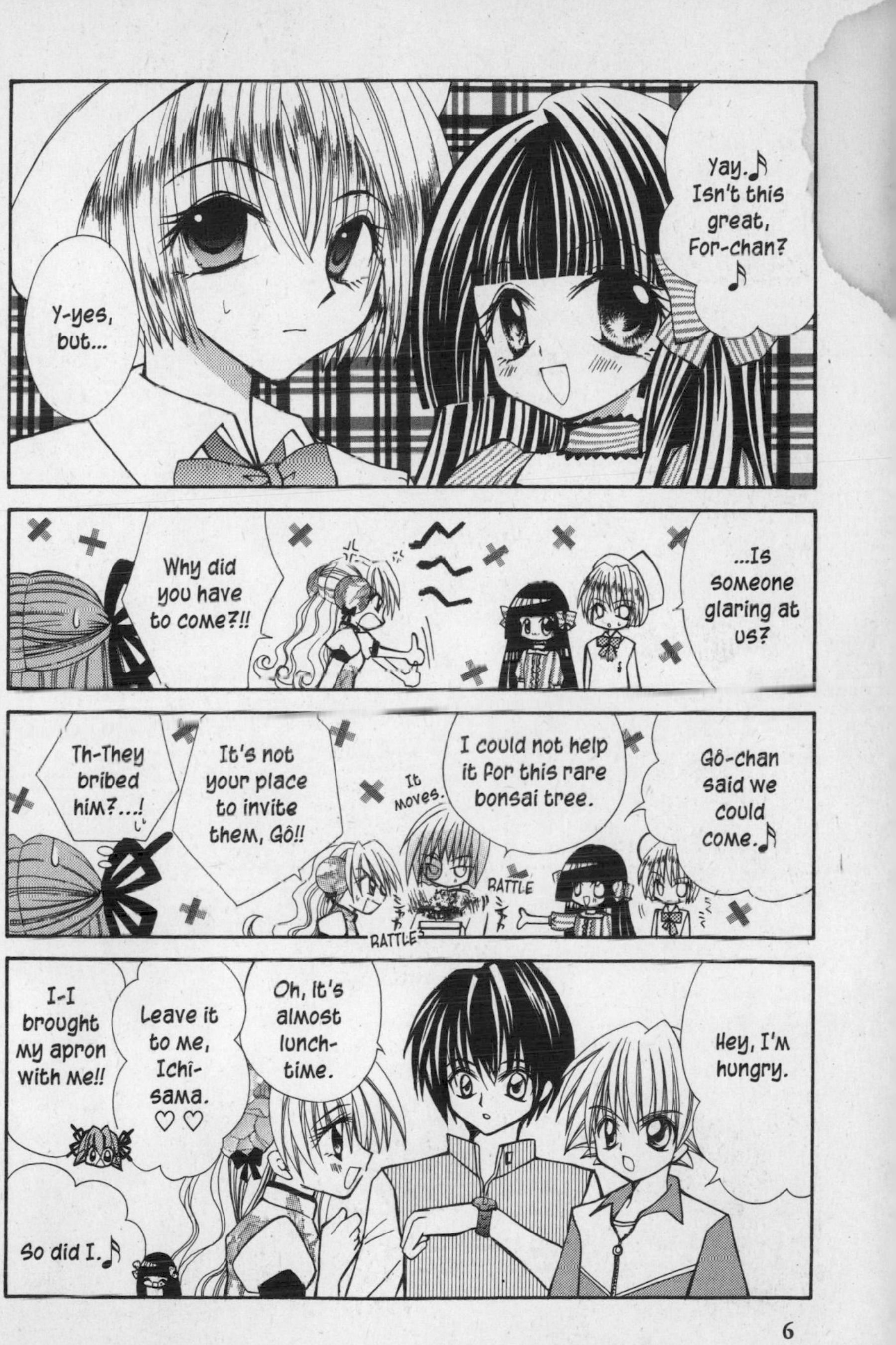

Yay.♪ Isn't this great, For-chan?♪
Y-yes, but...
...Is someone glaring at us?
Why did you have to come?!!
Gô-chan said we could come.♪
I could not help it for this rare bonsai tree.
It moves.
RATTLE
It's not your place to invite them, Gô!!
Th-They bribed him?...!
RATTLE
Hey, I'm hungry.
Oh, it's almost lunch-time.
Leave it to me, Ichi-sama. ♡♡
I-I brought my apron with me!!
So did I.♪

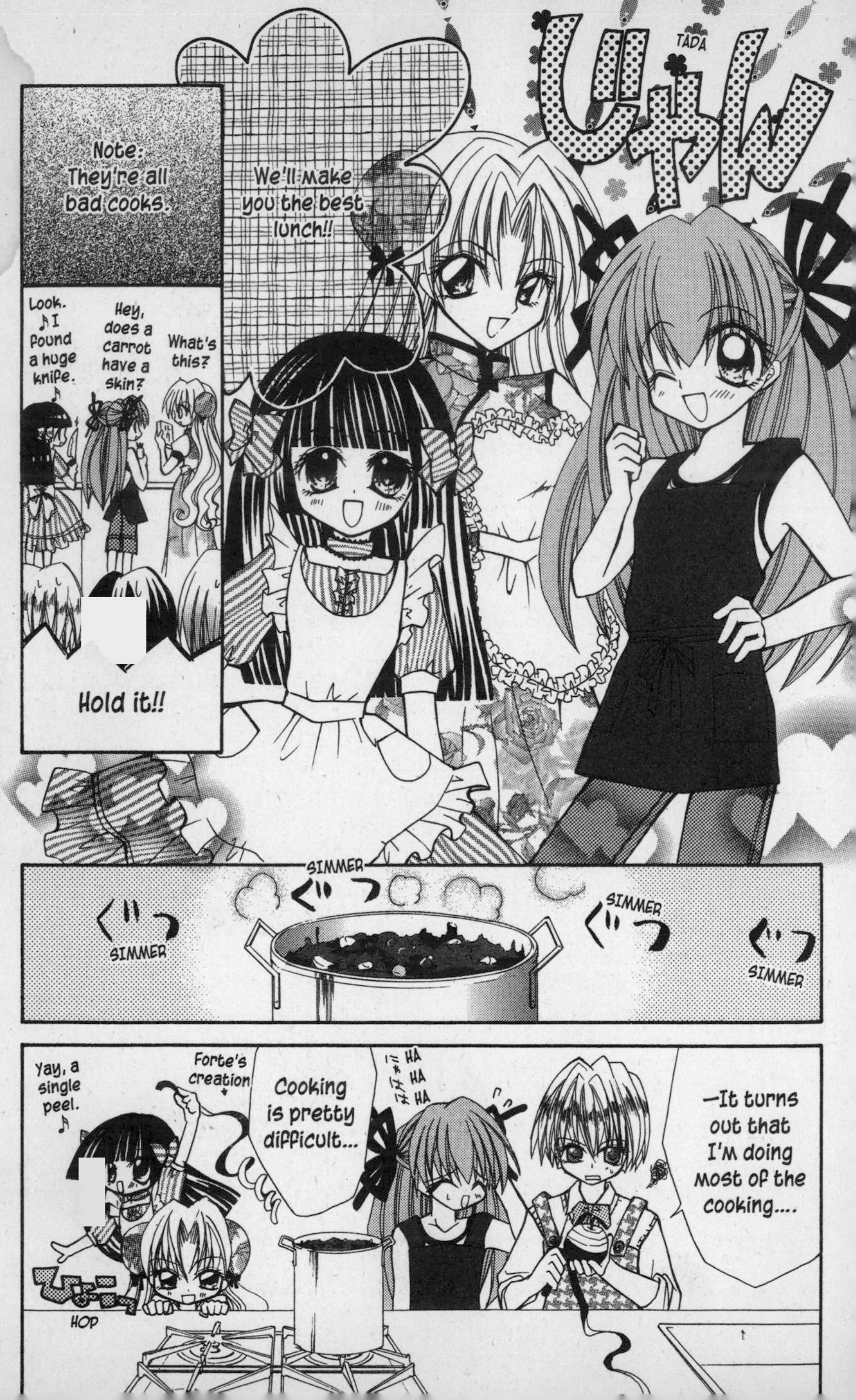
じゃん
TADA
We'll make you the best lunch!!
Note: They're all bad cooks.
What's this?
Hey, does a carrot have a skin?
Look. ♪I found a huge knife. ♪
Hold it!!
ぐつ
SIMMER
ぐつ
SIMMER
ぐつ
SIMMER
ぐつ
SIMMER
—It turns out that I'm doing most of the cooking....
にはは
HA HA HA
Cooking is pretty difficult...
Forte's creation
Yay, a single peel. ♪
HOP

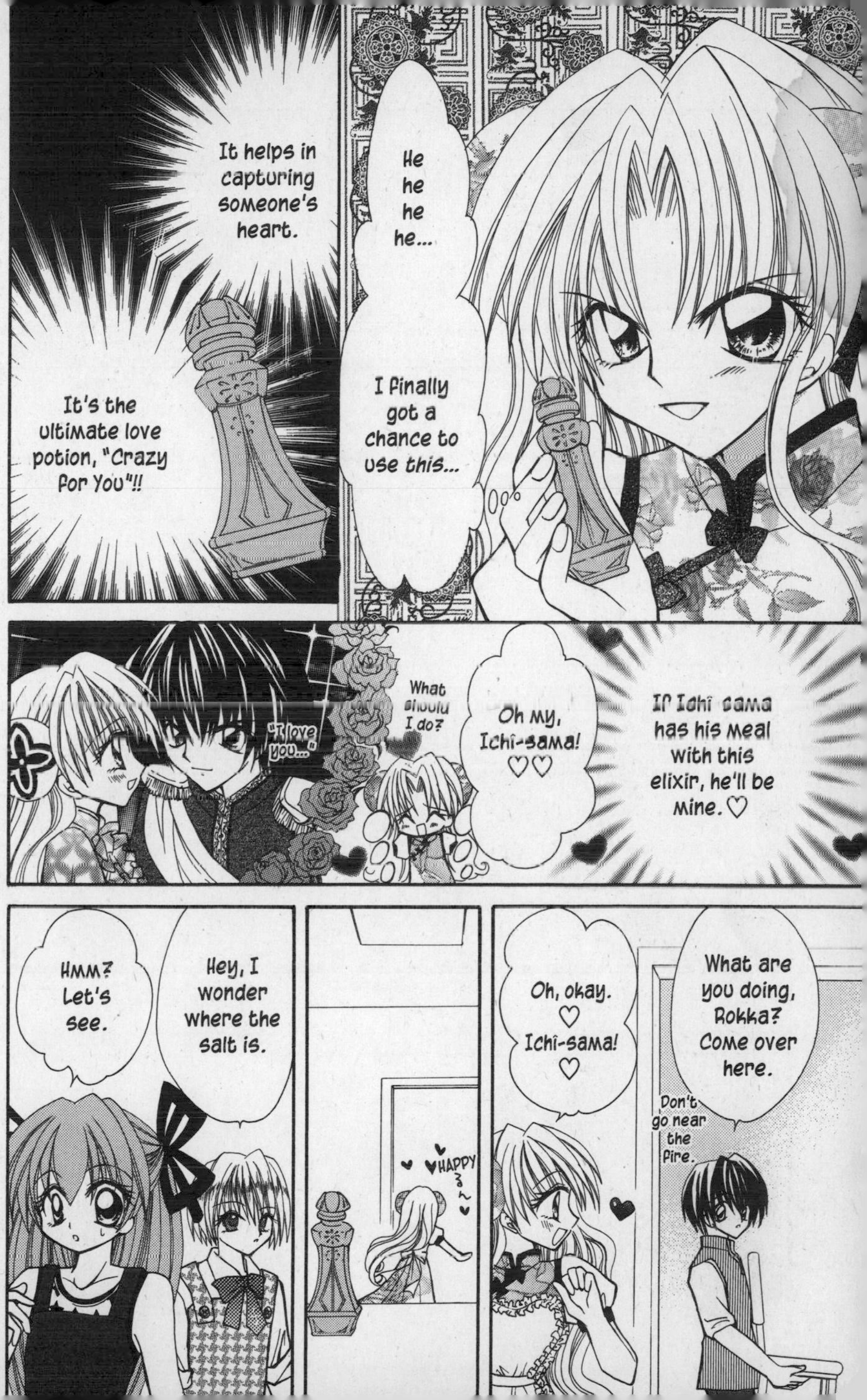
He he he he...
I finally got a chance to use this...
It helps in capturing someone's heart.
It's the ultimate love potion, "Crazy for You"!!
If Ichî-sama has his meal with this elixir, he'll be mine. ♡
Oh my, Ichî-sama! ♡♡
What should I do?
"I love you..."
What are you doing, Rokka? Come over here.
Don't go near the fire.
Oh, okay. ♡ Ichî-sama! ♡
♥ ♥HAPPY るん ♥
Hey, I wonder where the salt is.
Hmm? Let's see.

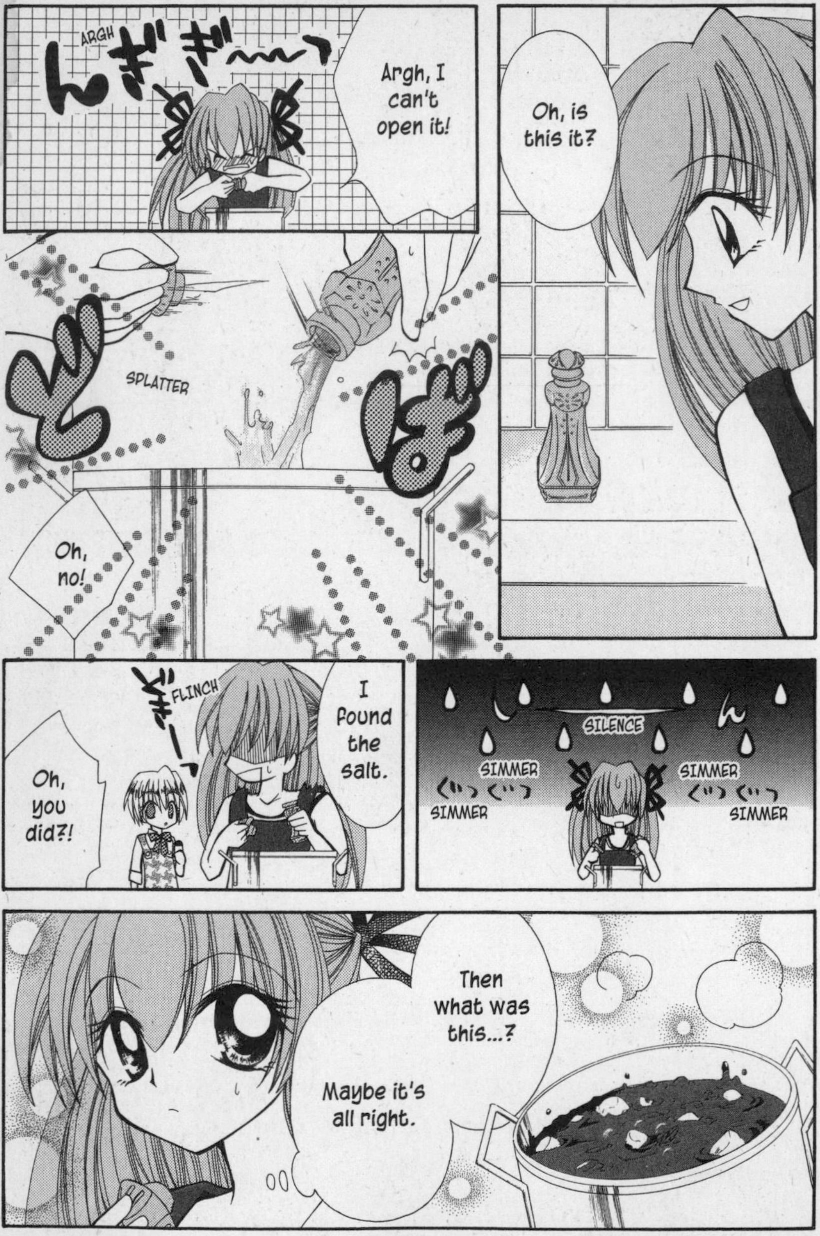

Oh, is this it?
ARGH
Argh, I can't open it!
SPLATTER
Oh, no!
SILENCE
SIMMER
SIMMER
SIMMER
SIMMER
FLINCH
I found the salt.
Oh, you did?!
Then what was this...?
Maybe it's all right.

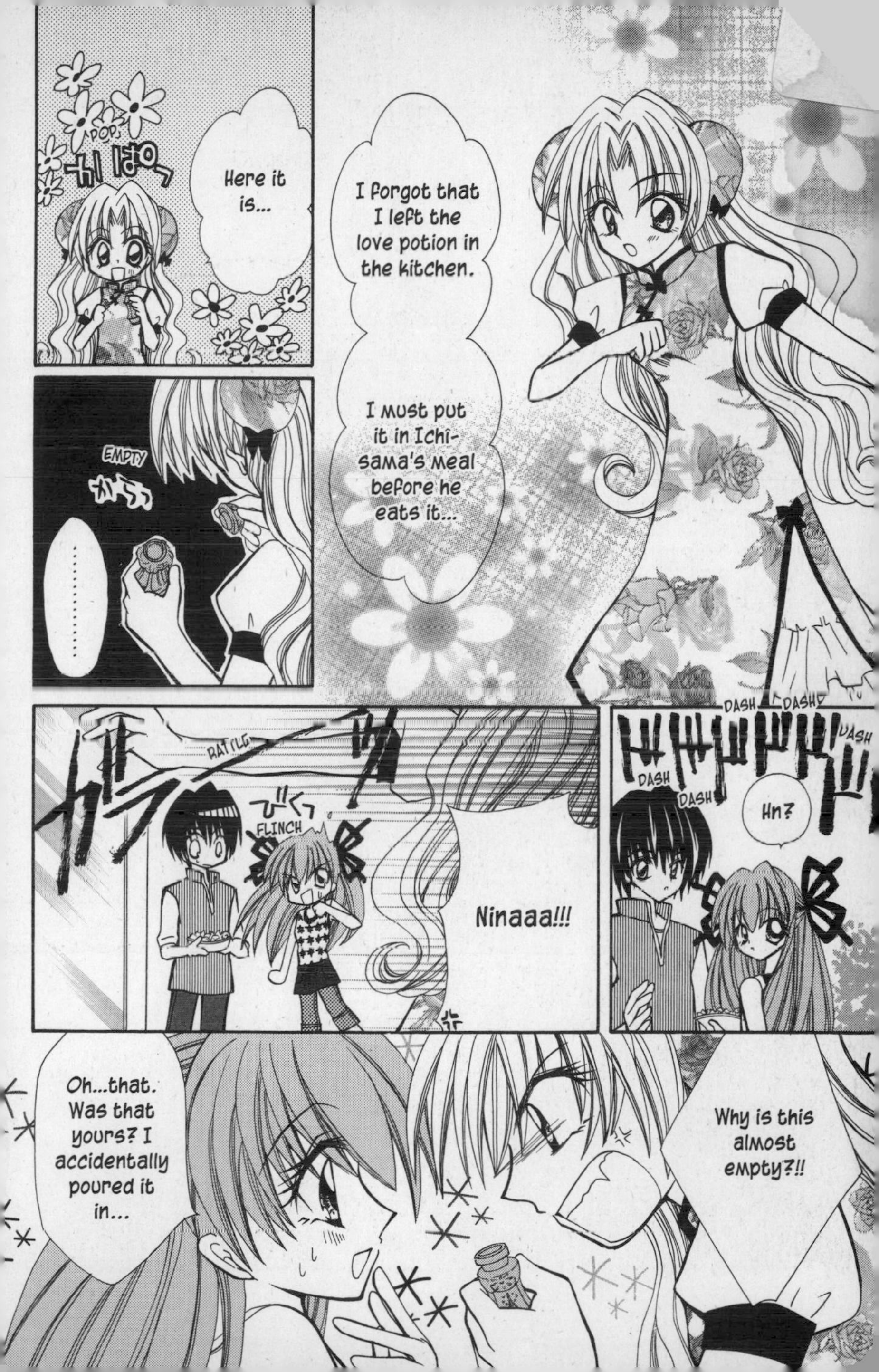
I forgot that I left the love potion in the kitchen.
I must put it in Ichi-sama's meal before he eats it...
POP
Here it is...
EMPTY
......
DASH DASH DASH DASH DASH
Hn?
RATTLE
FLINCH
Ninaaa!!!
Why is this almost empty?!!
Oh...that. Was that yours? I accidentally poured it in...

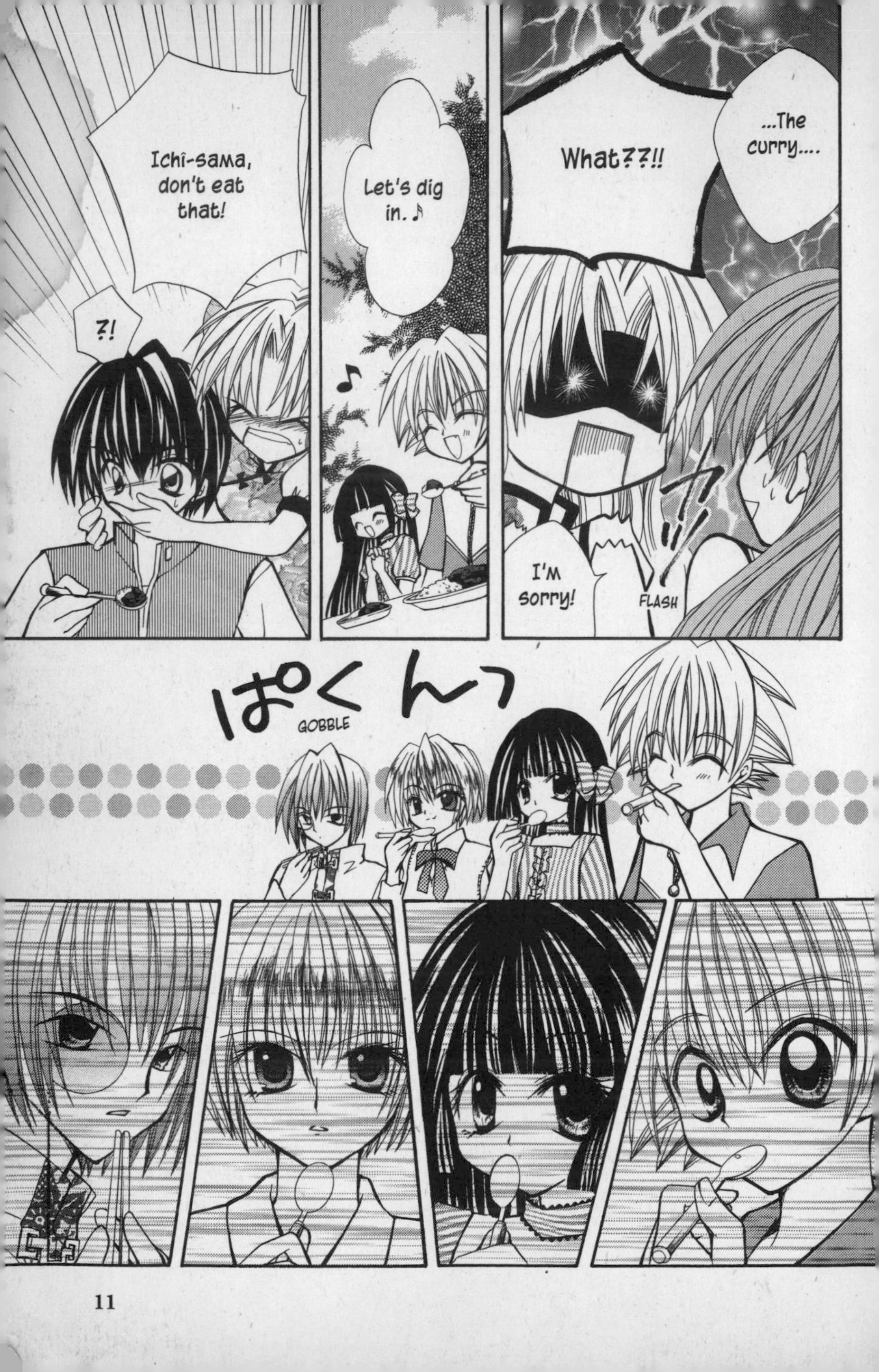
...The curry....
What??!!
I'm sorry!
FLASH
Let's dig in. ♪
Ichi-sama, don't eat that!
?!
ぱくんっ
GOBBLE

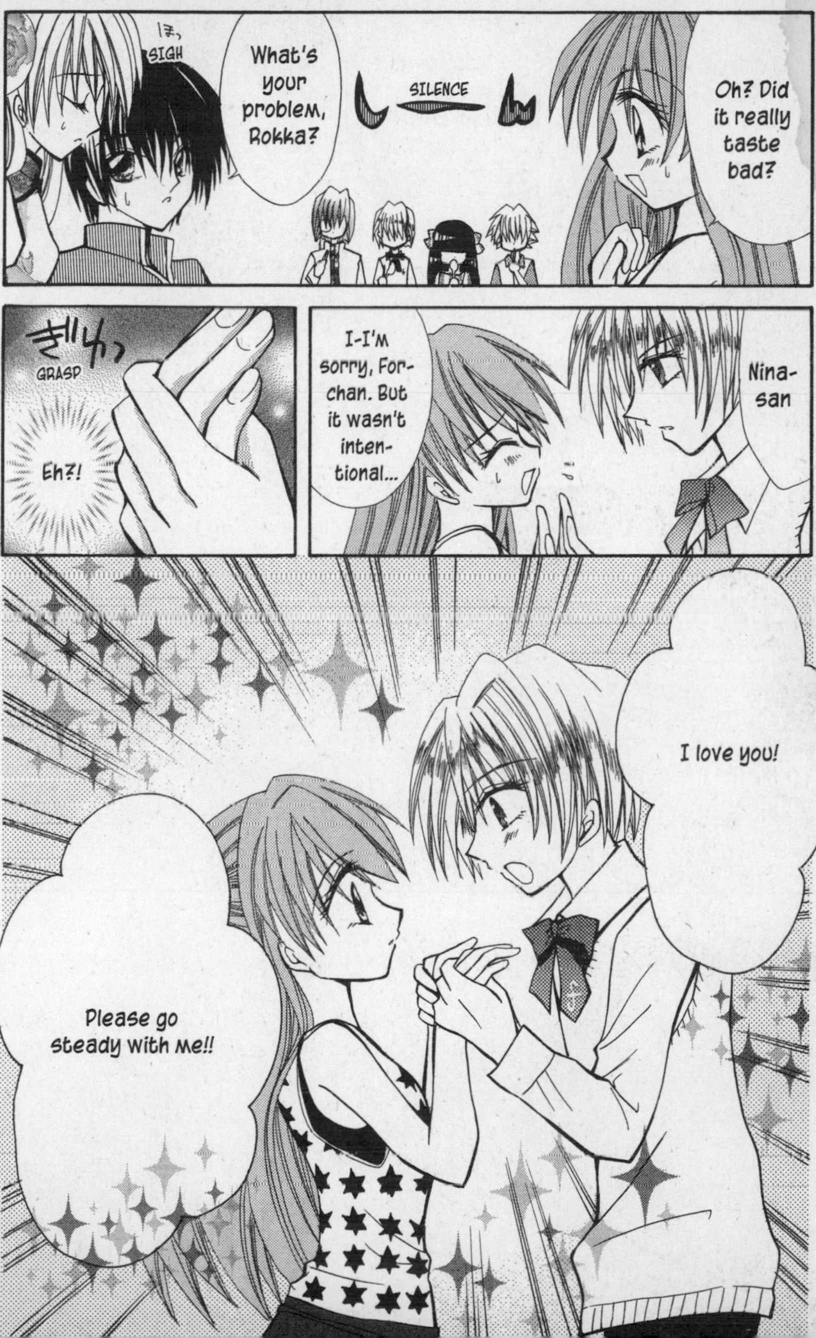
Oh? Did it really taste bad?
SILENCE
What's your problem, Rokka?
ほっ
SIGH
Nina-san
I-I'm sorry, For-chan. But it wasn't inten-tional...
ぎゅっ
GRASP
Eh?!
I love you!
Please go steady with me!!

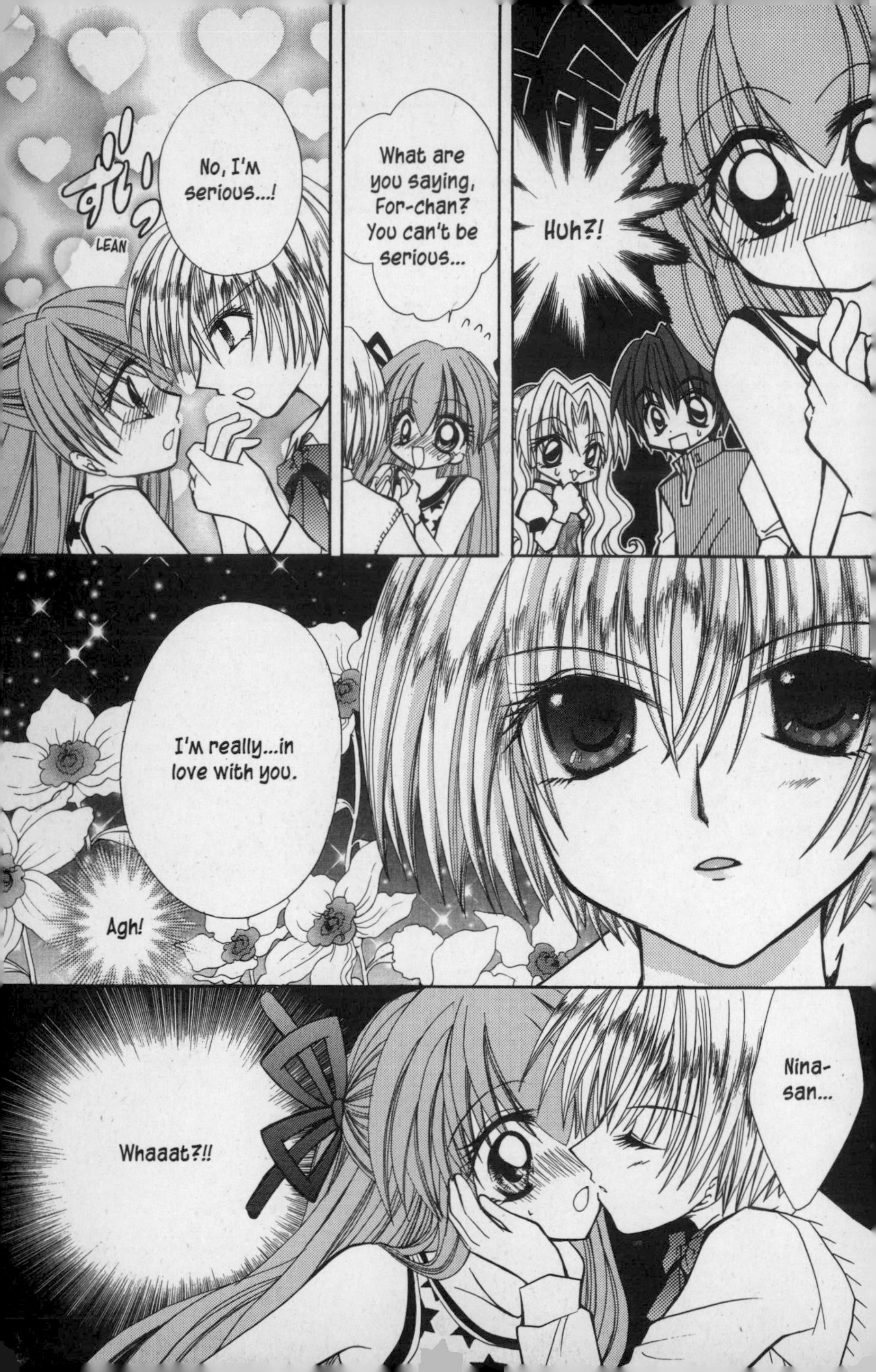
Huh?!
What are you saying, For-chan? You can't be serious...
No, I'm serious...!
LEAN
I'm really...in love with you.
Agh!
Nina-san...
Whaaat?!!

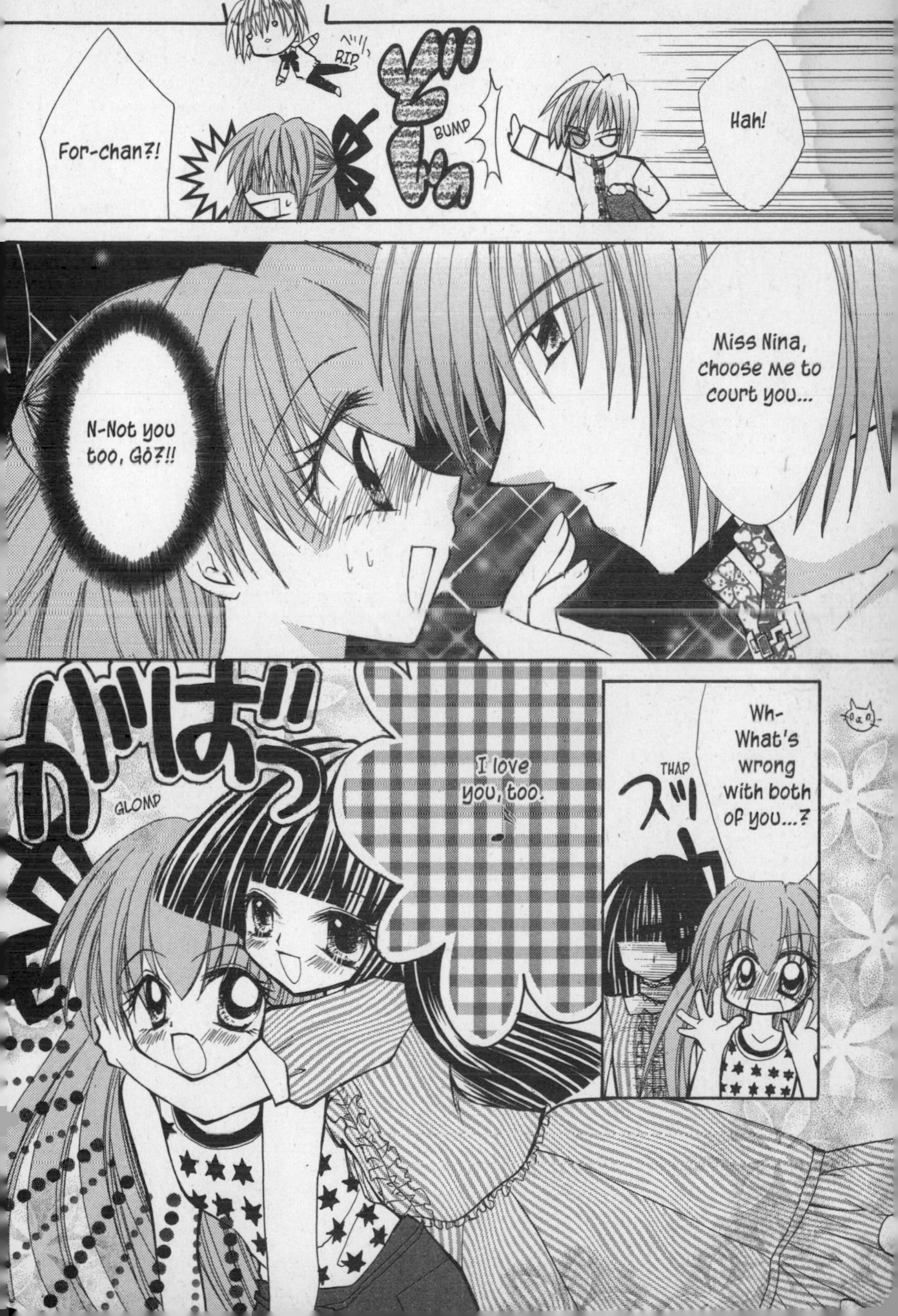
Hah!
BUMP
RIP
For-chan?!
Miss Nina, choose me to court you...
N-Not you too, Gô?!!
Wh- What's wrong with both of you...?
THAP
I love you, too.
GLOMP

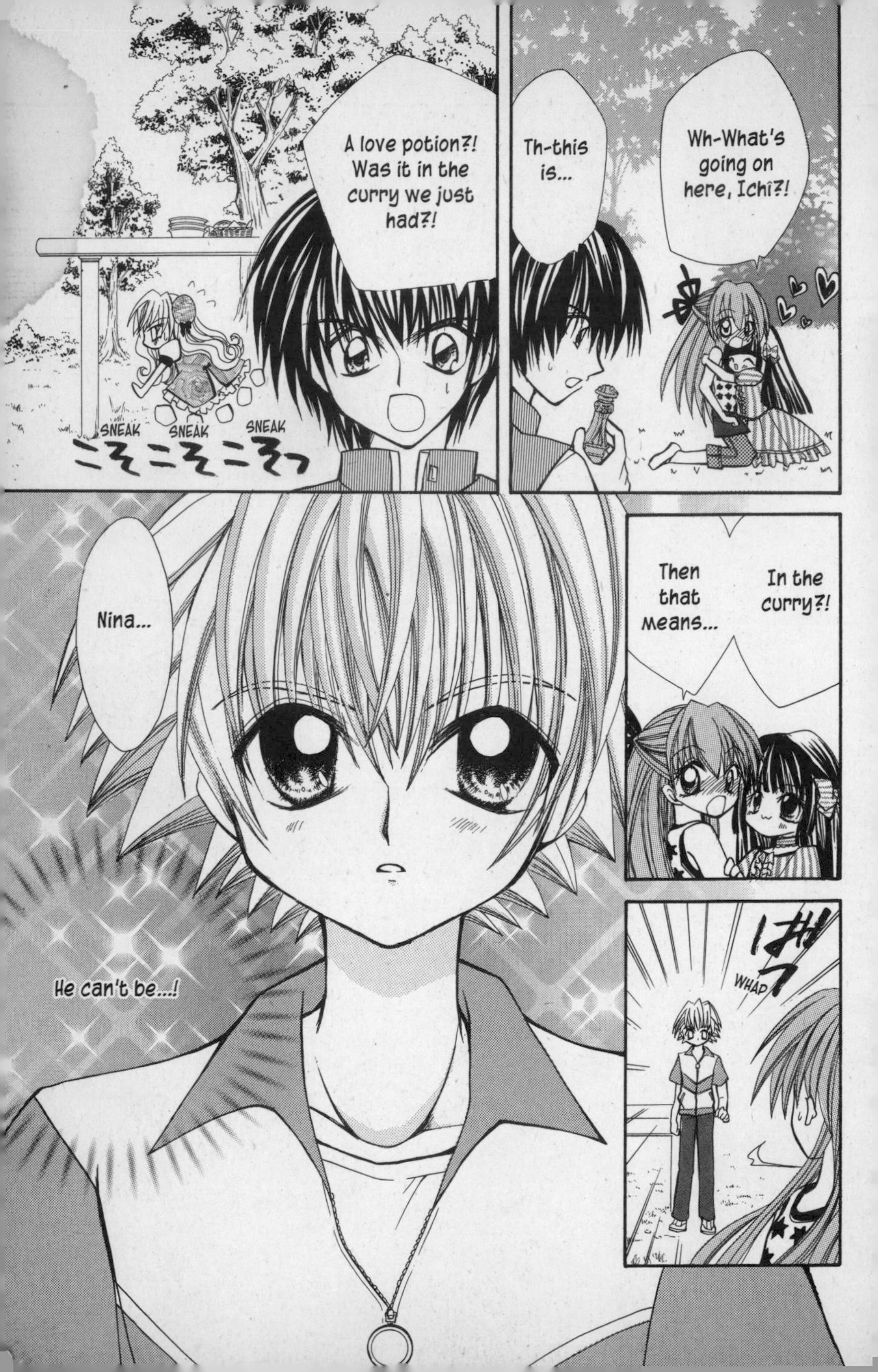

Wh-What's going on here, Ichi?!
Th-this is...
A love potion?! Was it in the curry we just had?!
SNEAK SNEAK SNEAK
こそこそこそっ
In the curry?!
Then that means...
はっ
WHAP
Nina...
He can't be...!

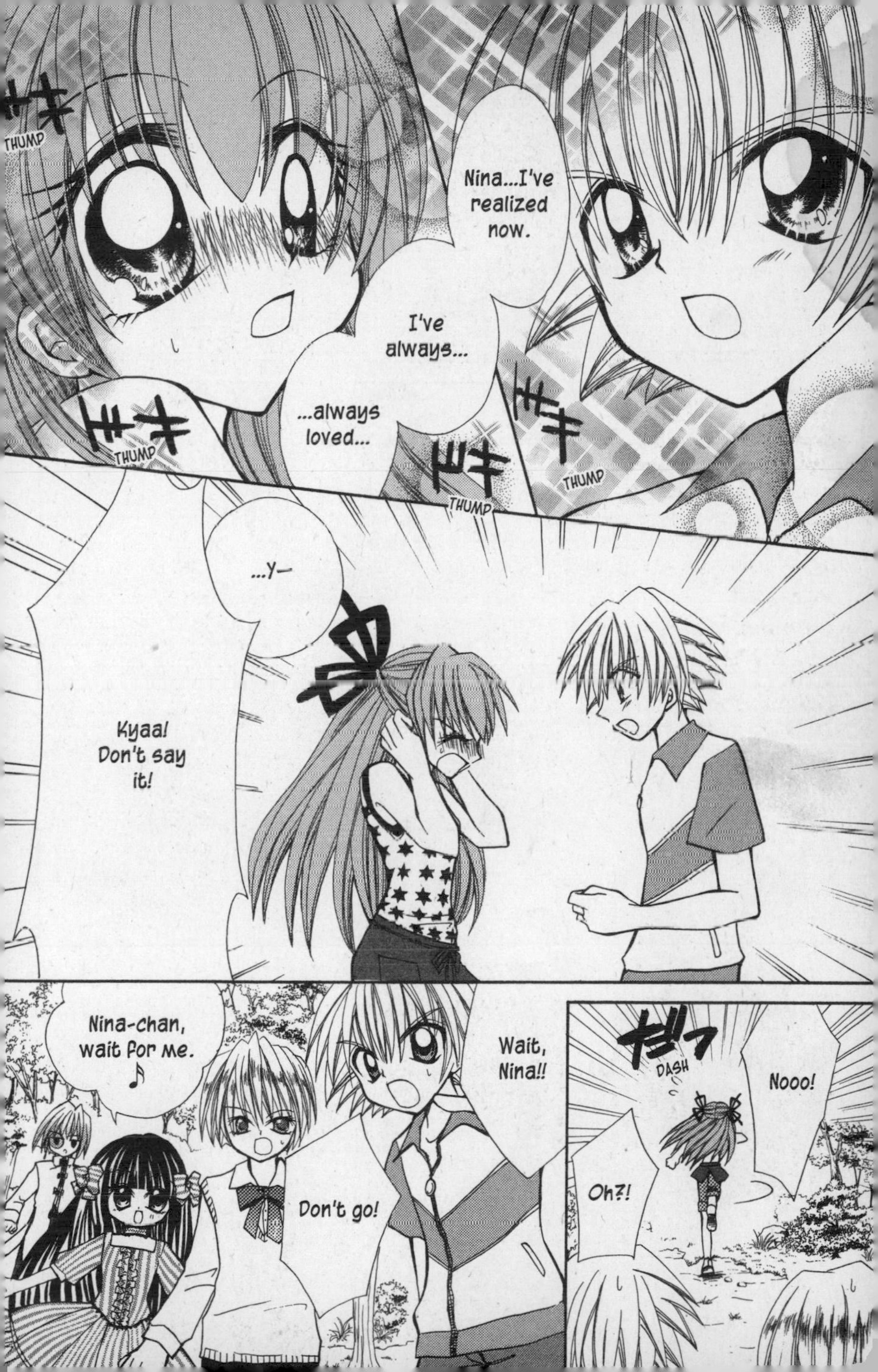
Nina...I've realized now.
I've always...
...always loved...
THUMP
THUMP
THUMP
THUMP
...y—
Kyaa! Don't say it!
DASH
Nooo!
Oh?!
Wait, Nina!!
Nina-chan, wait for me. ♪
Don't go!

Hello!

Hello to those I'm meeting for the first time and to those I'm not! This is Michiyo Kikuta.

Mamotte! Lollipop 3 is out! That was quick! I'm so happy.

I'm including my comments, Question and Answer page, character profiles and Illustration Go-Go again. We did the character popularity poll so I'll you show the results as well! I hope you'll enjoy them!!

I've been so busy lately, but I'm hanging in there. If people who follow this in the books and the magazines are both having fun reading this manga, then I'm happy. Now, I hope you'll enjoy the book.

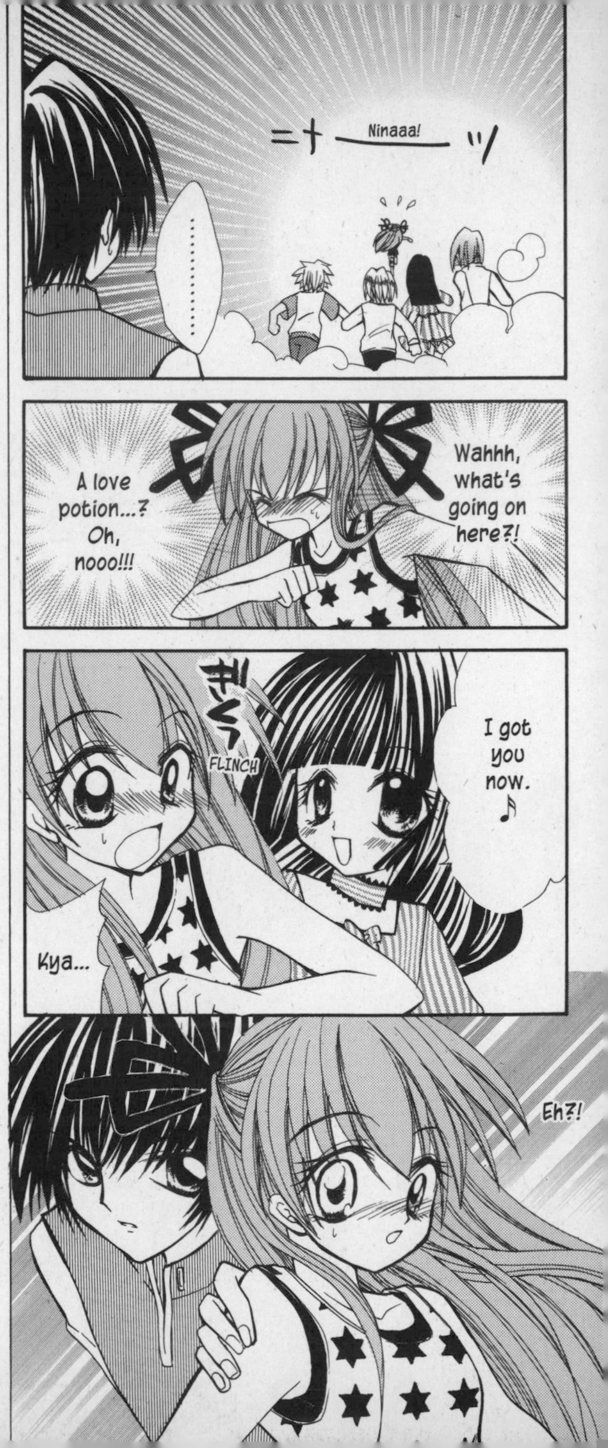
Ninaaa!
......
Wahhh, what's going on here?!
A love potion...? Oh, nooo!!!
I got you now. ♪
FLINCH
Kya...
Eh?!

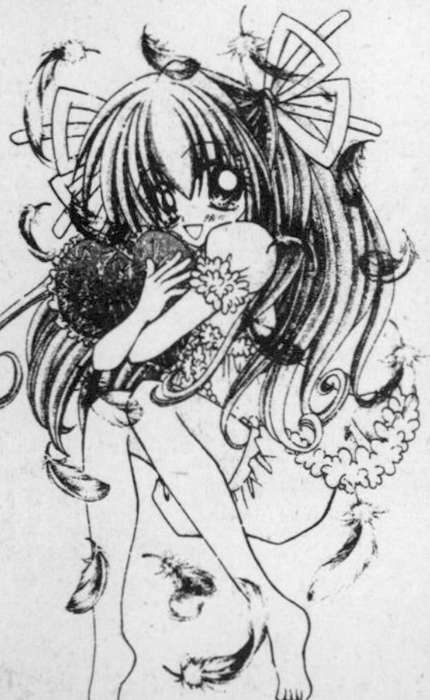

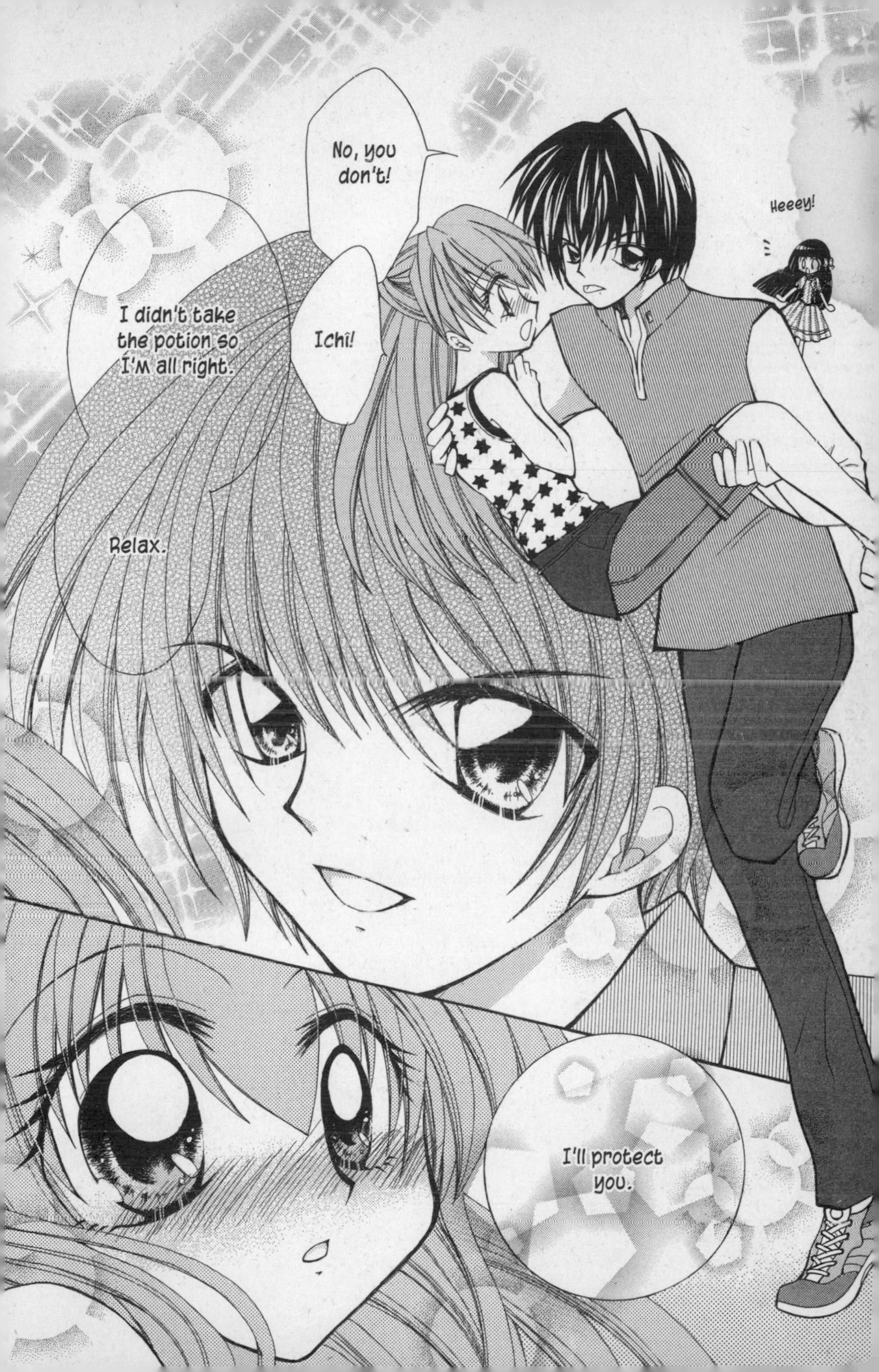
Heeey!
No, you don't!
Ichi!
I didn't take the potion so I'm all right.
Relax.
I'll protect you.

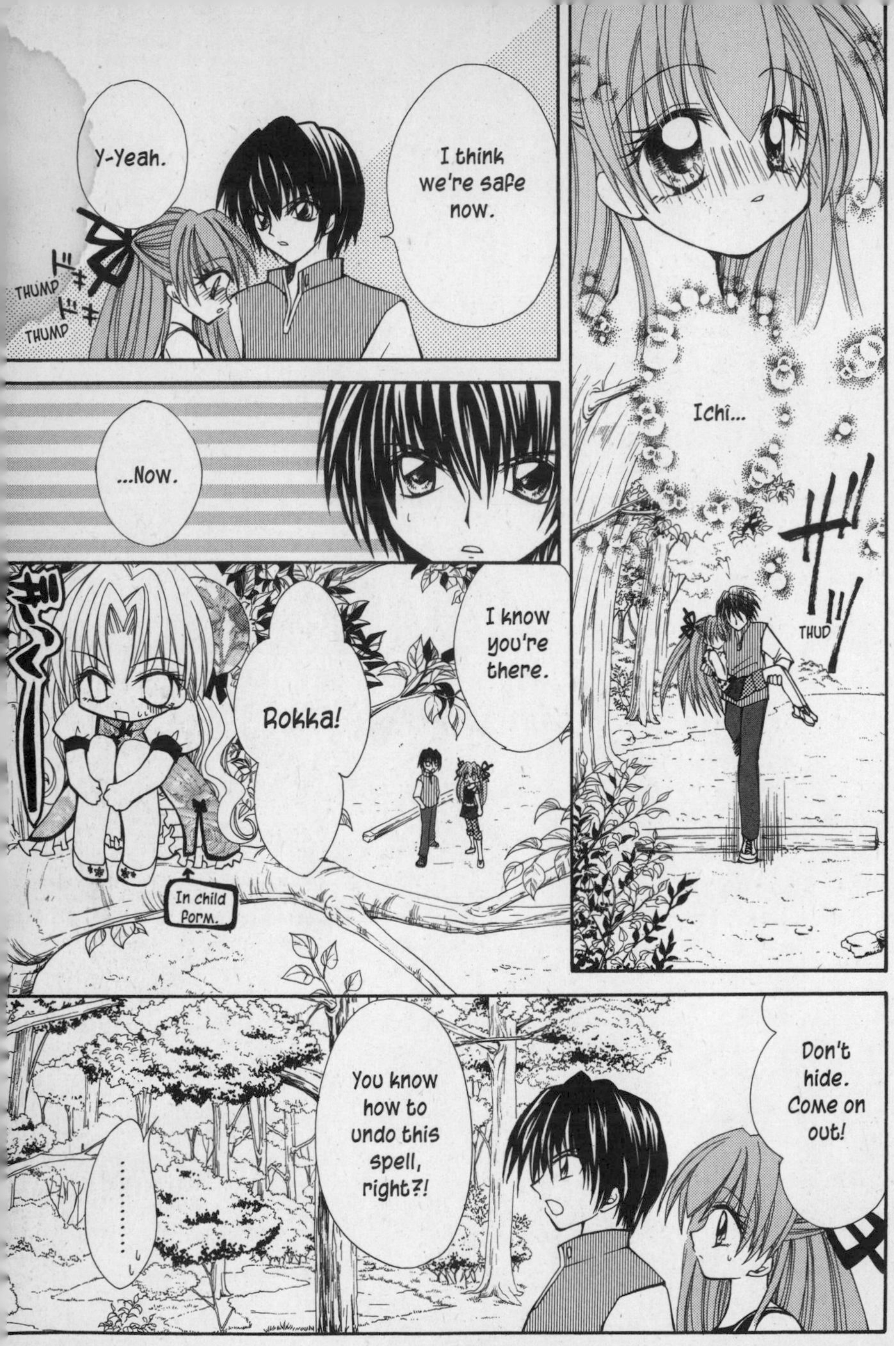
Ichi...
THUD
I think we're safe now.
Y-Yeah.
THUMP
THUMP
...Now.
I know you're there.
Rokka!
In child form.
Don't hide. Come on out!
You know how to undo this spell, right?!
......

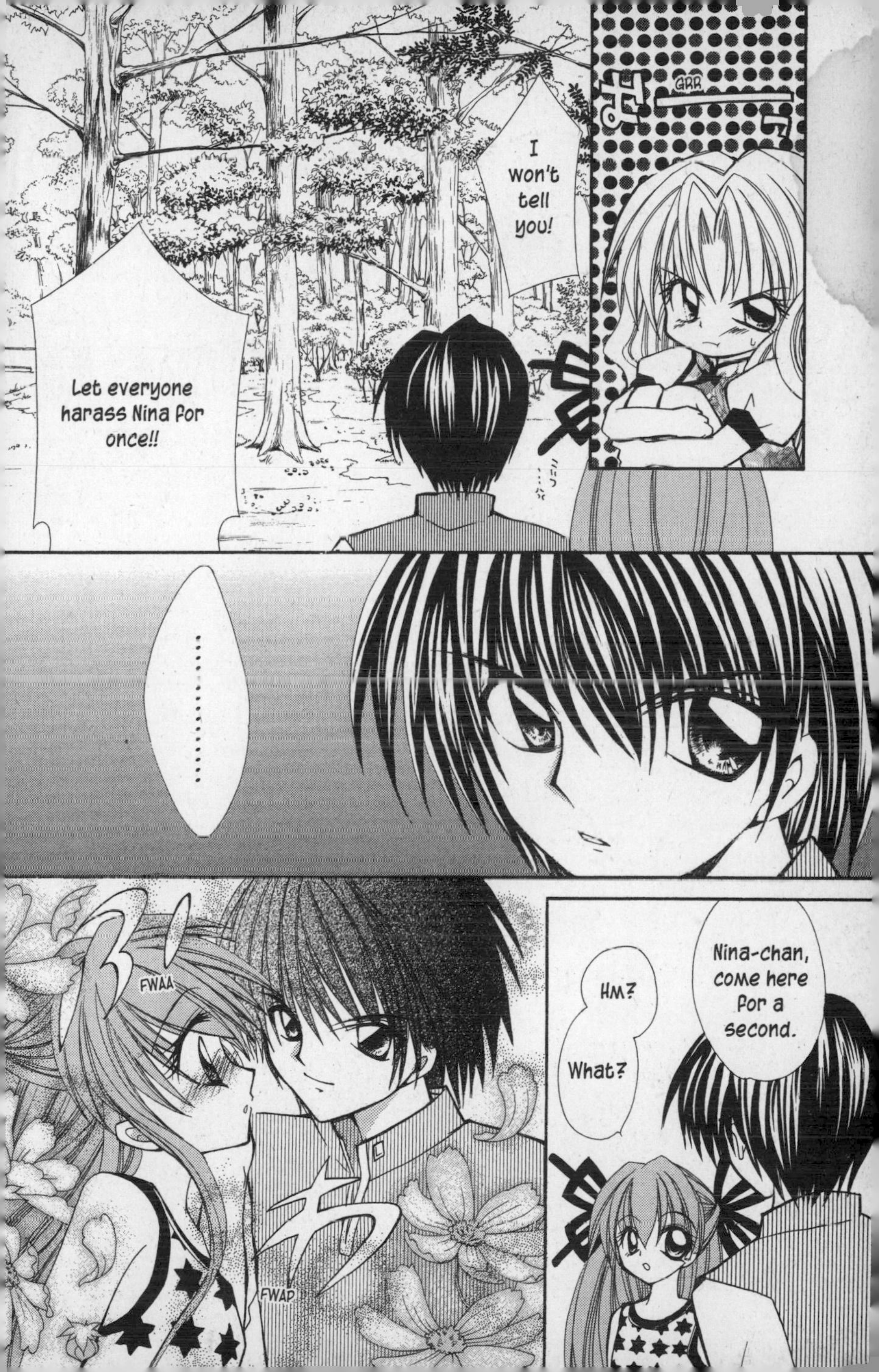
GRR
I won't tell you!
Let everyone harass Nina for once!!
......
Nina-chan, come here for a second.
Hm?
What?
FWAA
FWAP

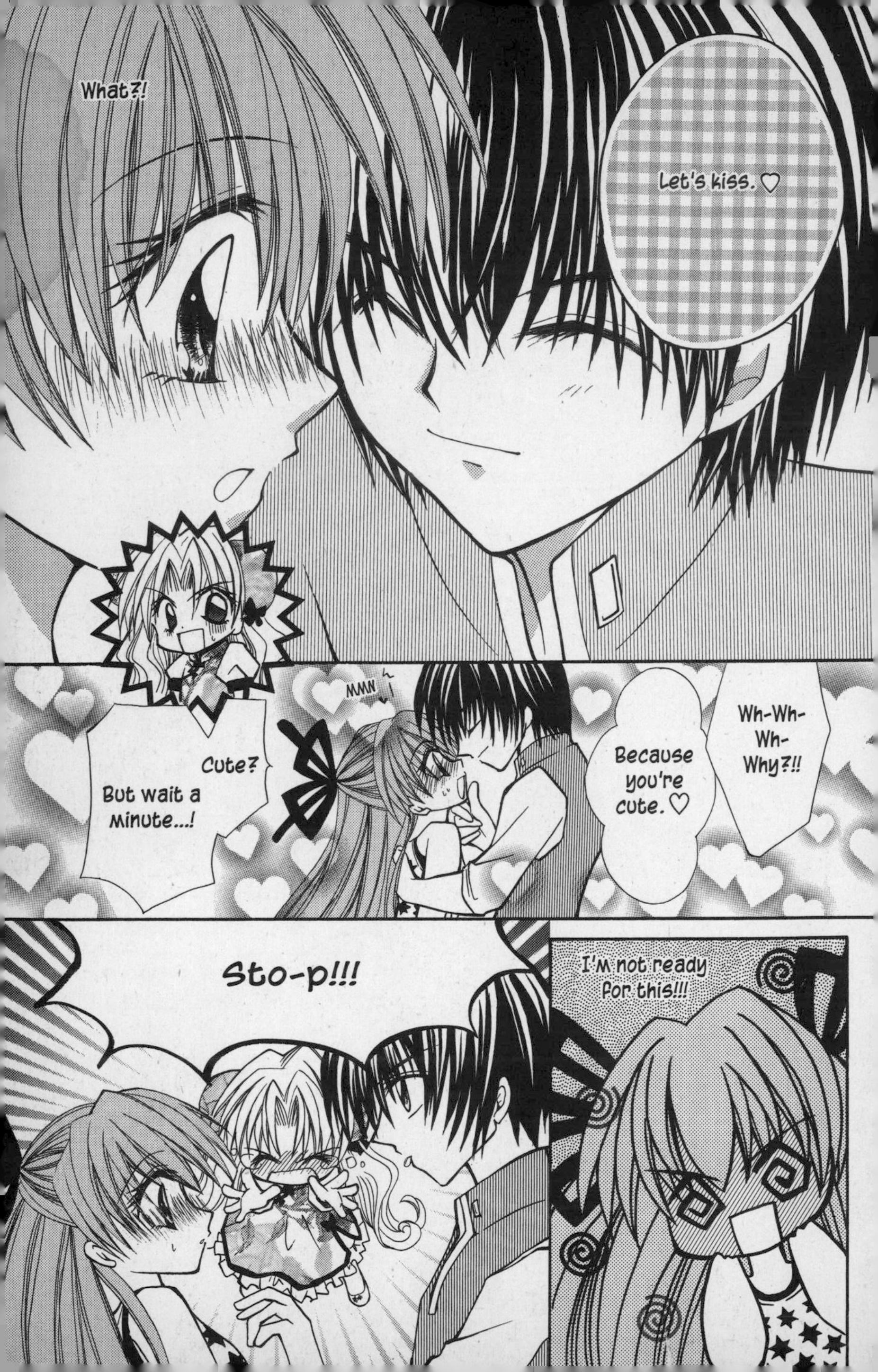
Let's kiss. ♡
What?!
Wh-Wh-Wh-Why?!!
Because you're cute. ♡
MMN
Cute? But wait a minute...!
I'M not ready for this!!!
Sto-p!!!

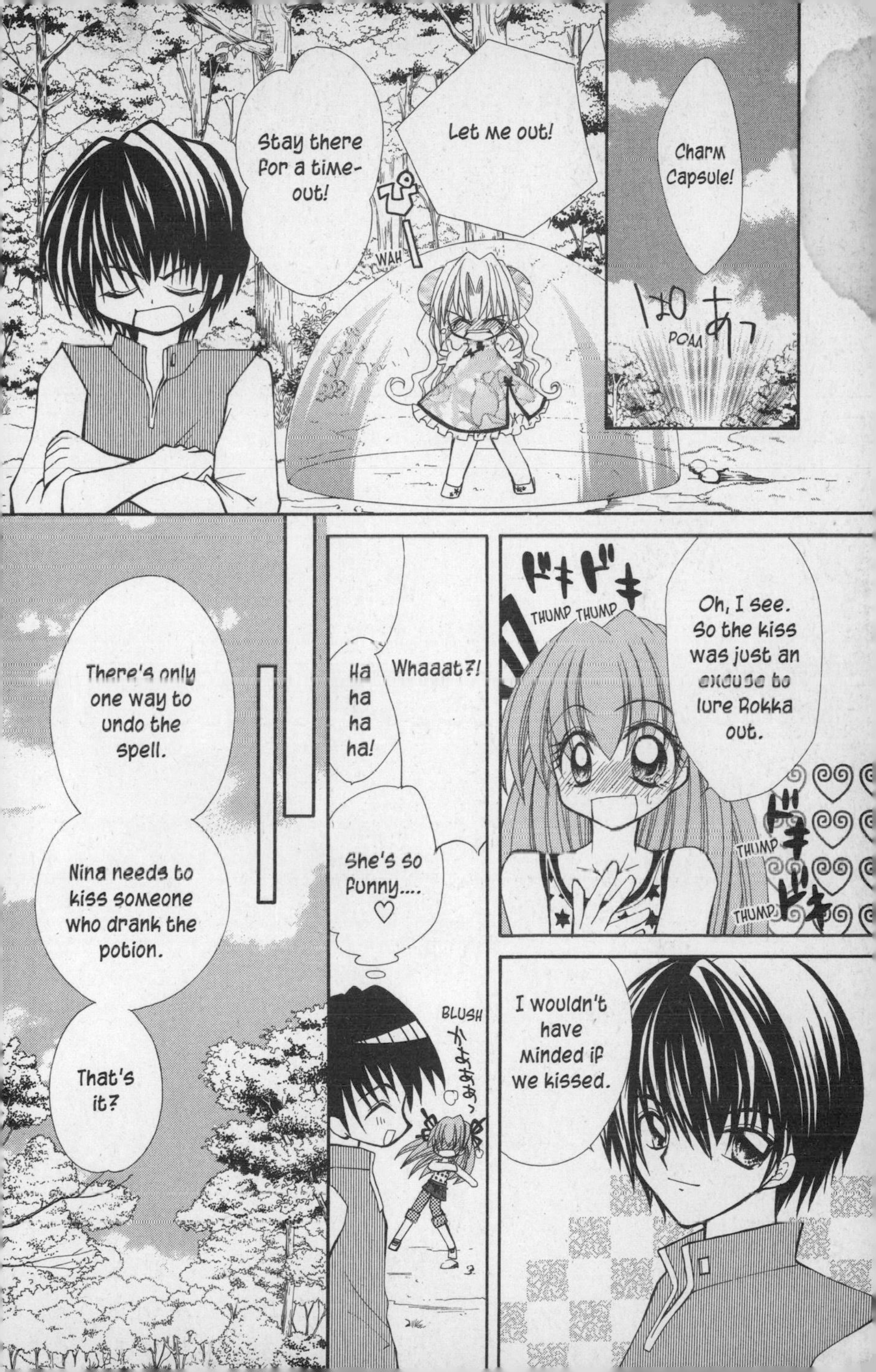
Charm Capsule!
POAA
Let me out!
Stay there for a time-out!
WAH
Oh, I see. So the kiss was just an excuse to lure Rokka out.
THUMP THUMP
THUMP
THUMP
I wouldn't have minded if we kissed.
Whaaat?!
Ha ha ha ha!
She's so funny.... ♡
BLUSH
There's only one way to undo the spell.
Nina needs to kiss someone who drank the potion.
That's it?

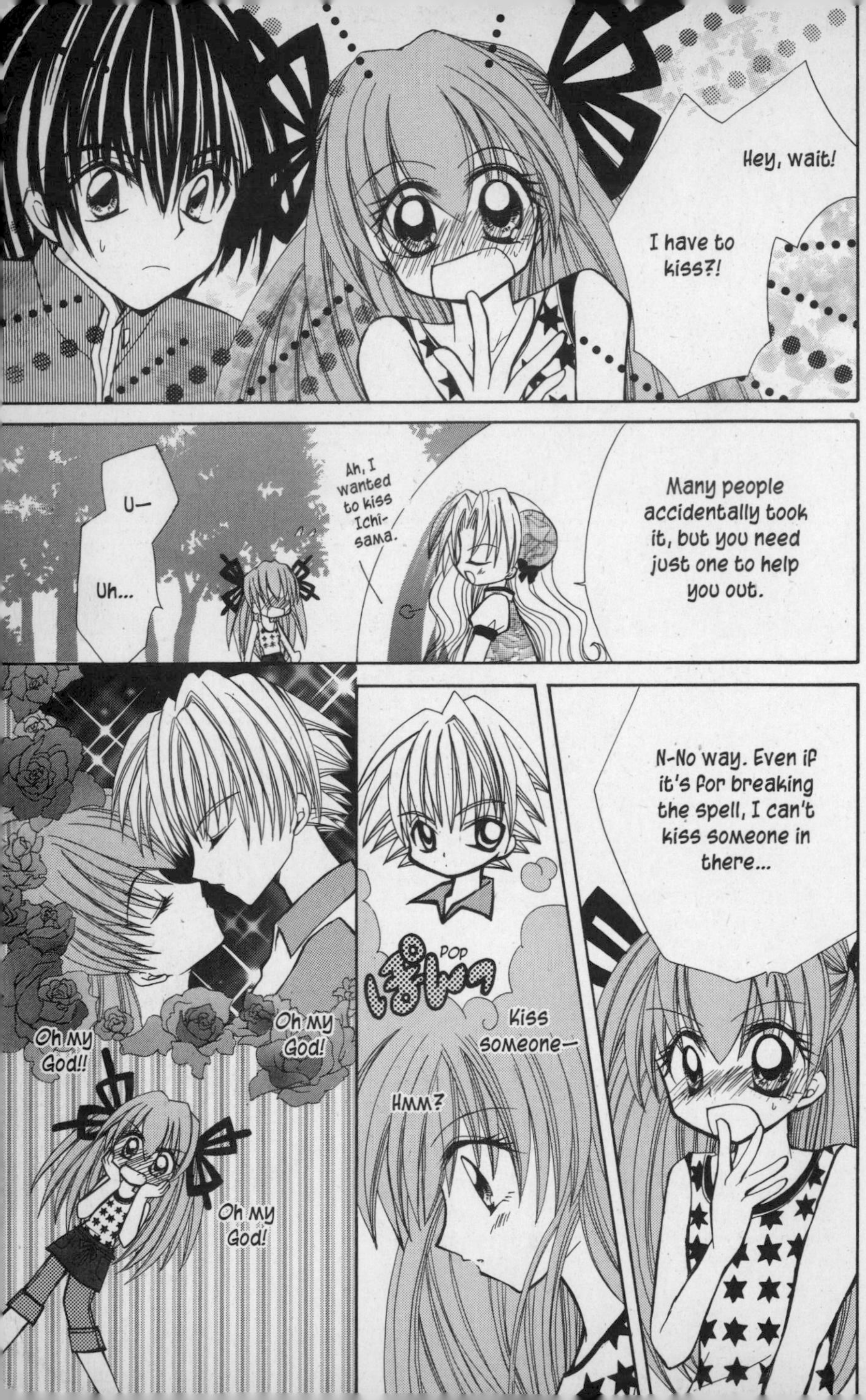
Hey, wait!
I have to kiss?!
Many people accidentally took it, but you need just one to help you out.
Ah, I wanted to kiss Ichi-sama.
U—
Uh...
N-No way. Even if it's for breaking the spell, I can't kiss someone in there...
POP
Kiss someone—
Hmm?
Oh my God!
Oh my God!!
Oh my God!

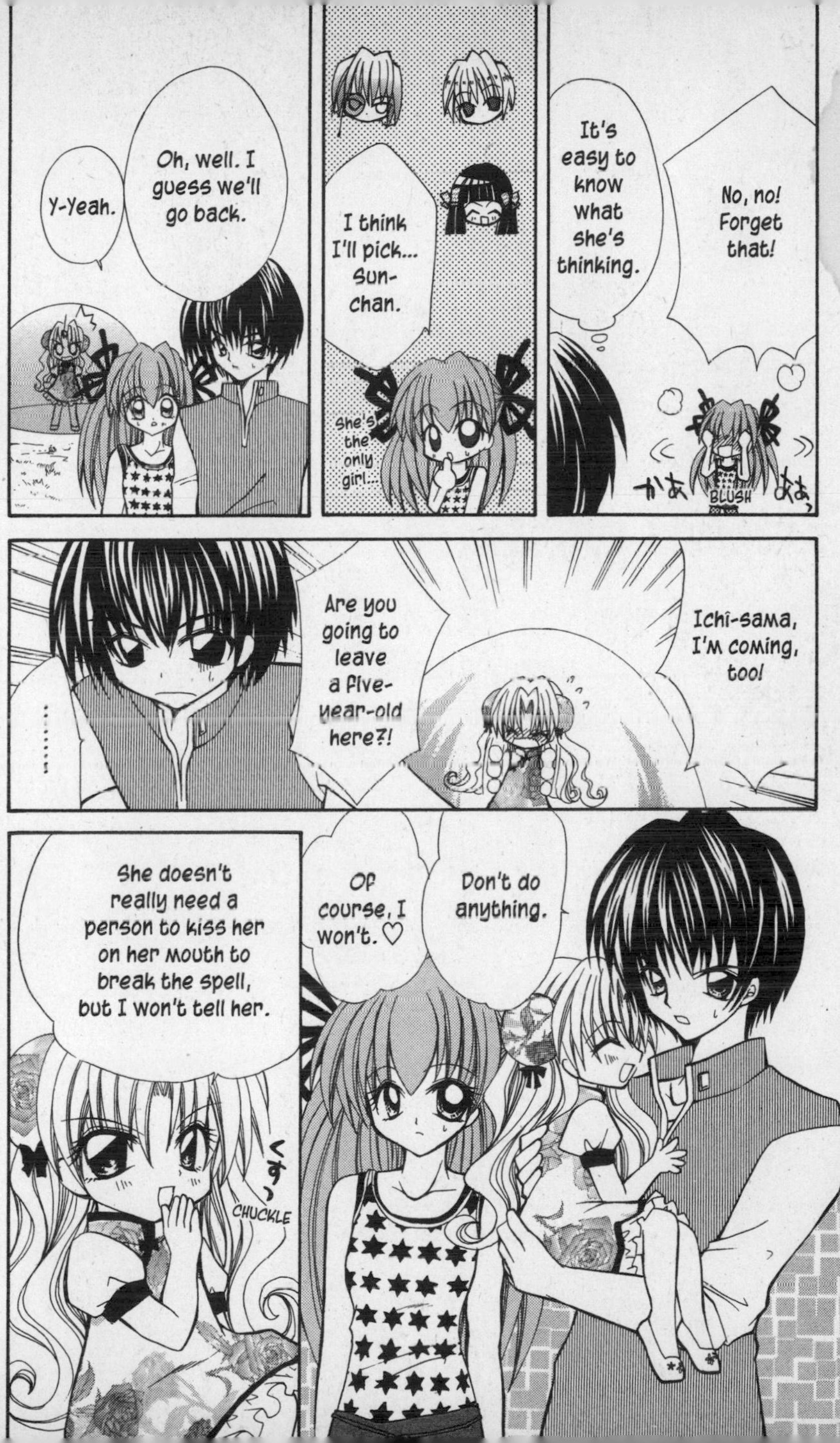
No, no! Forget that!
It's easy to know what she's thinking.
かあ
BLUSH
かあっ
I think I'll pick... Sun-chan.
She's the only girl...
Oh, well. I guess we'll go back.
Y-Yeah.
Ichî-sama, I'm coming, too!
Are you going to leave a five-year-old here?!
....
Don't do anything.
Of course, I won't. ♡
She doesn't really need a person to kiss her on her mouth to break the spell, but I won't tell her.
くすっ
CHUCKLE

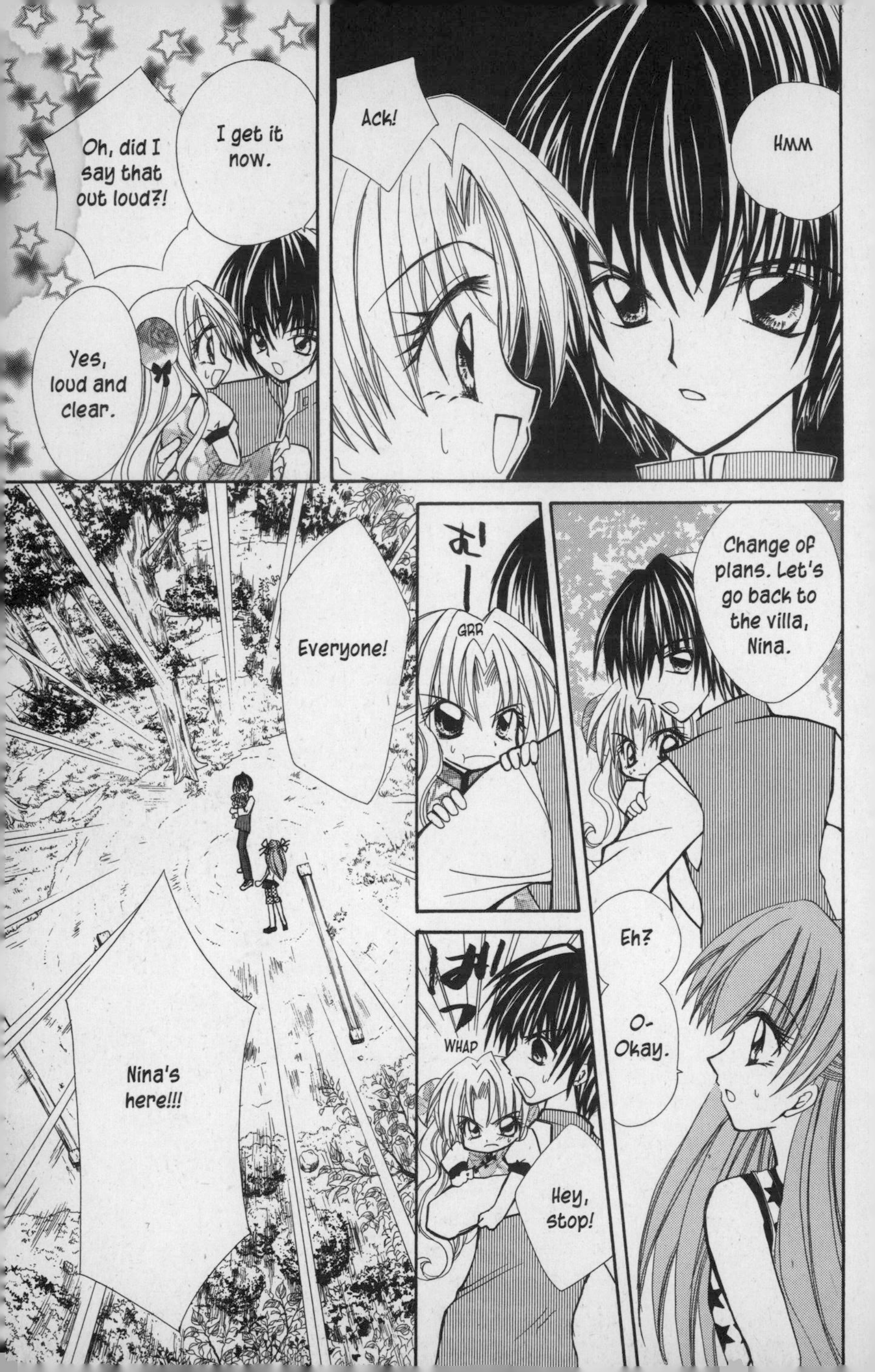
HMM
Ack!
I get it now.
Oh, did I say that out loud?!
Yes, loud and clear.
Change of plans. Let's go back to the villa, Nina.
GRR
Eh?
O-Okay.
WHAP
Hey, stop!
Everyone!
Nina's here!!!

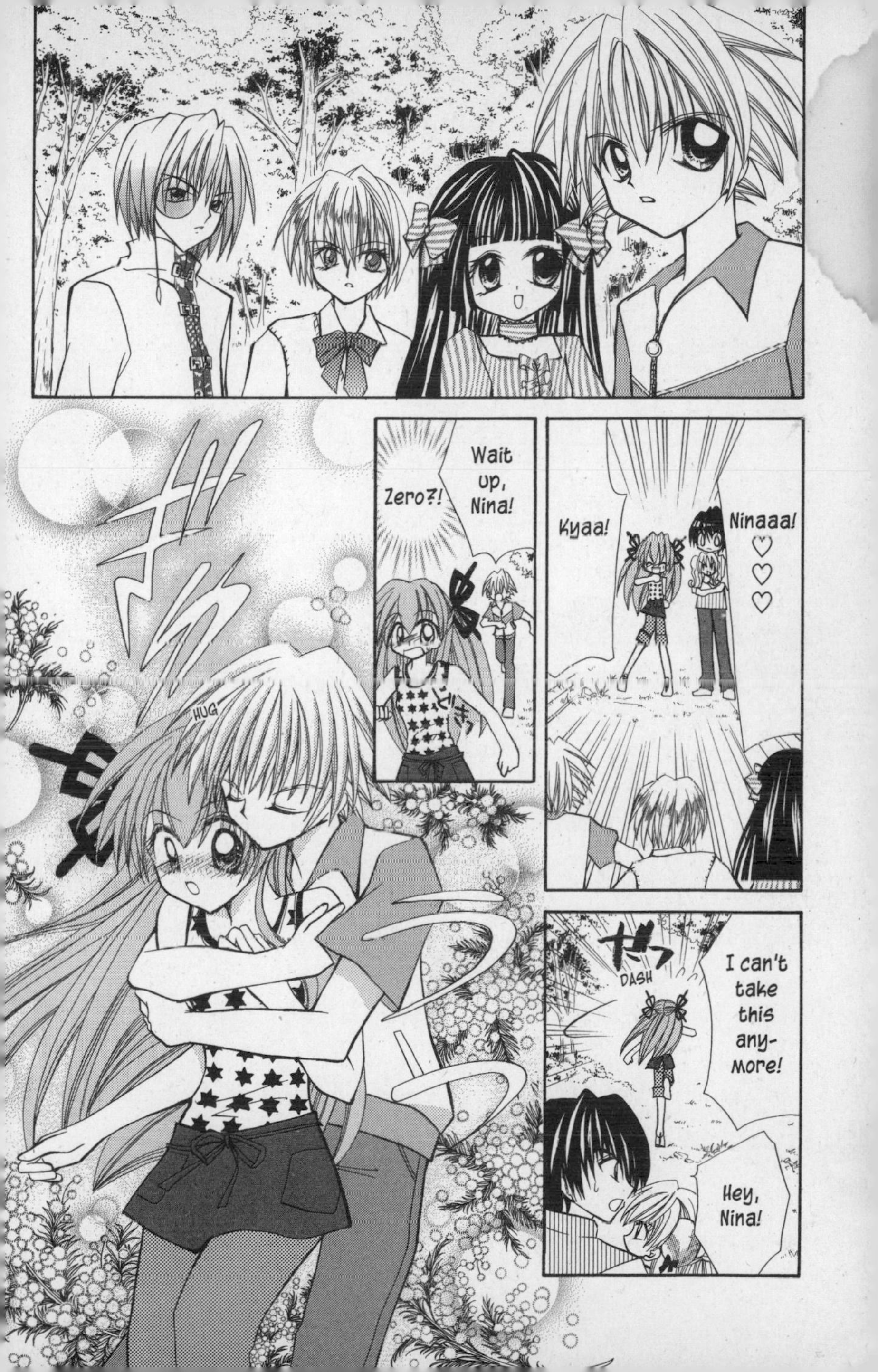
Ninaaa! ♡ ♡ ♡
Kyaa!
Wait up, Nina!
Zero?!
DASH
I can't take this anymore!
Hey, Nina!
HUG

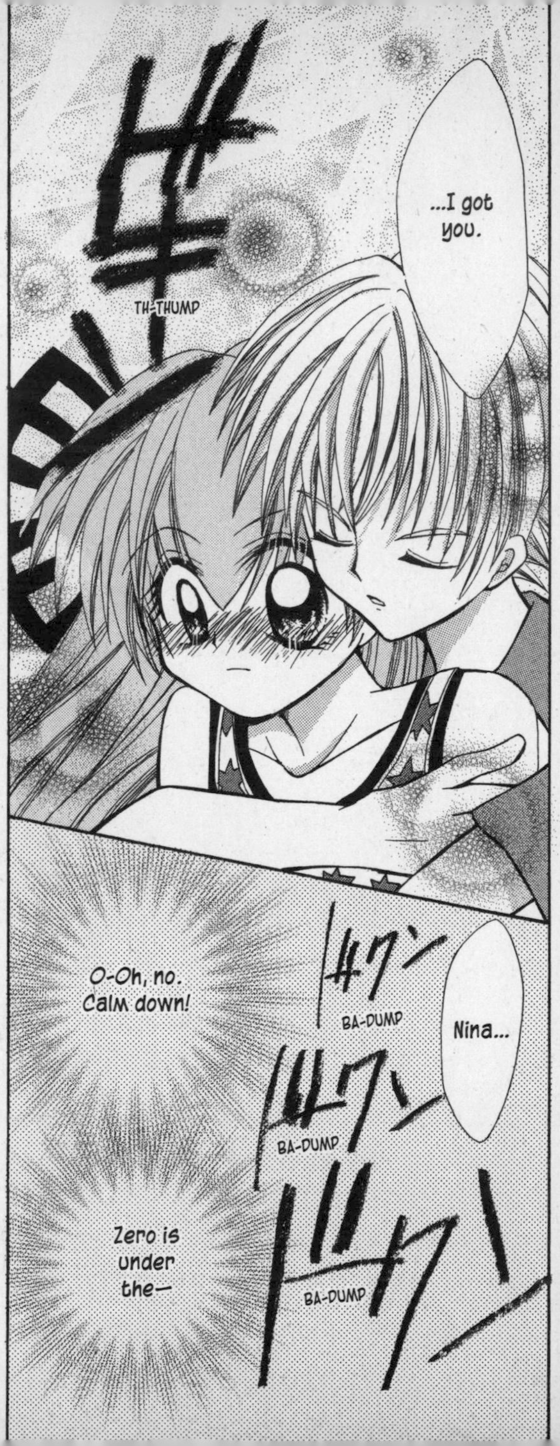
...I got you.
TH-THUMP
Nina...
BA-DUMP
BA-DUMP
O-Oh, no. Calm down!
BA-DUMP
Zero is under the—

Goddesses and Tanuki

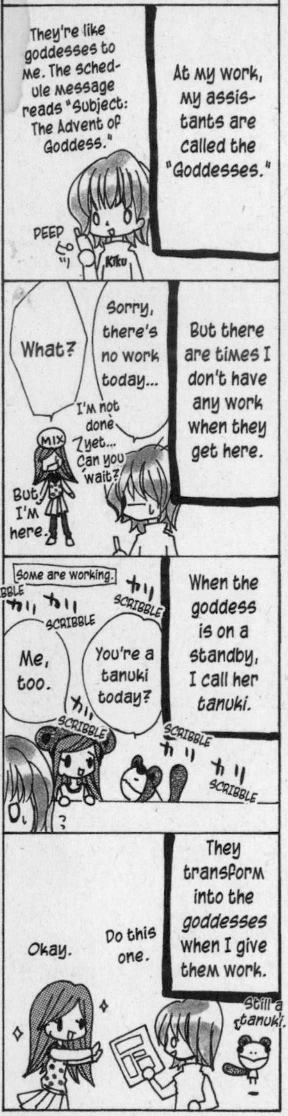
At my work, my assistants are called the "Goddesses."
They're like goddesses to me. The sched-ule message reads "Subject: The Advent of Goddess."
PEEP
Kiku
But there are times I don't have any work when they get here.
Sorry, there's no work today...
What?
I'm not done yet... Can you wait?
MIX
But I'm here.
When the goddess is on a standby, I call her tanuki.
SCRIBBLE
You're a tanuki today?
Some are working.
SCRIBBLE
SCRIBBLE
Me, too.
SCRIBBLE
SCRIBBLE
SCRIBBLE
They transform into the goddesses when I give them work.
Still a tanuki.
Do this one.
Okay.

Even when a boy comes to help, I still call him a *goddess*.

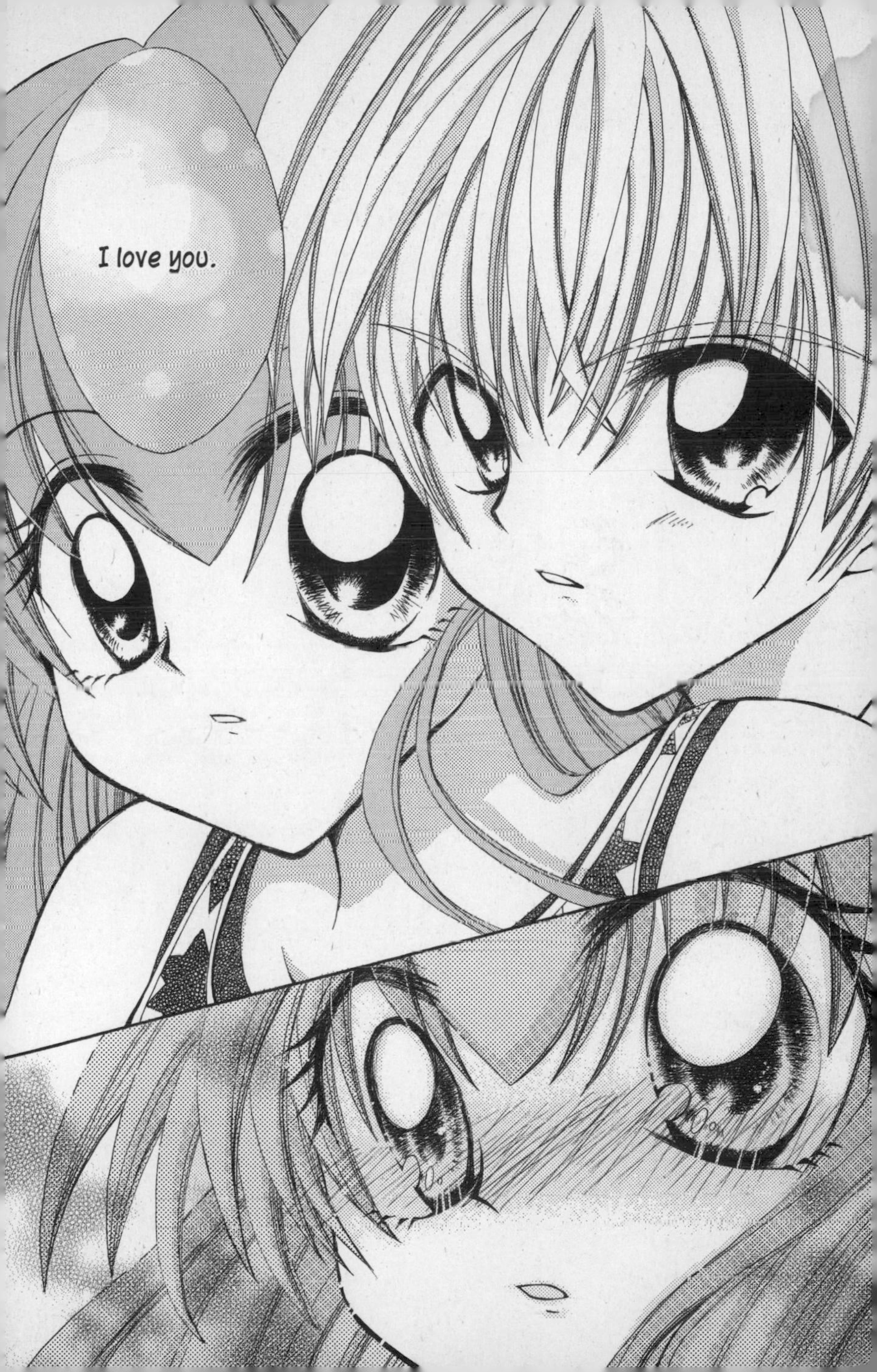
I love you.

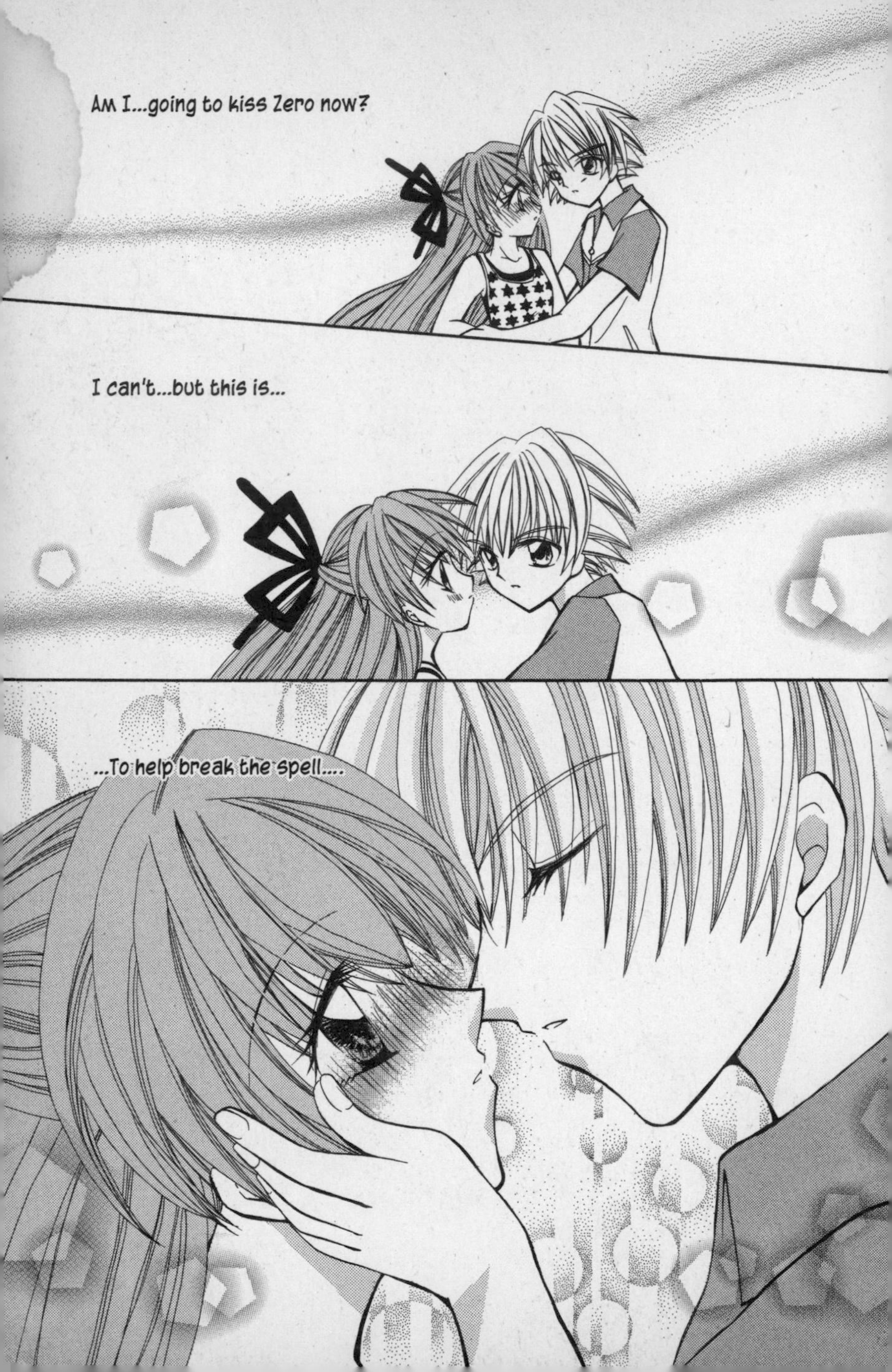
Am I...going to kiss Zero now?
I can't...but this is...
...To help break the spell....

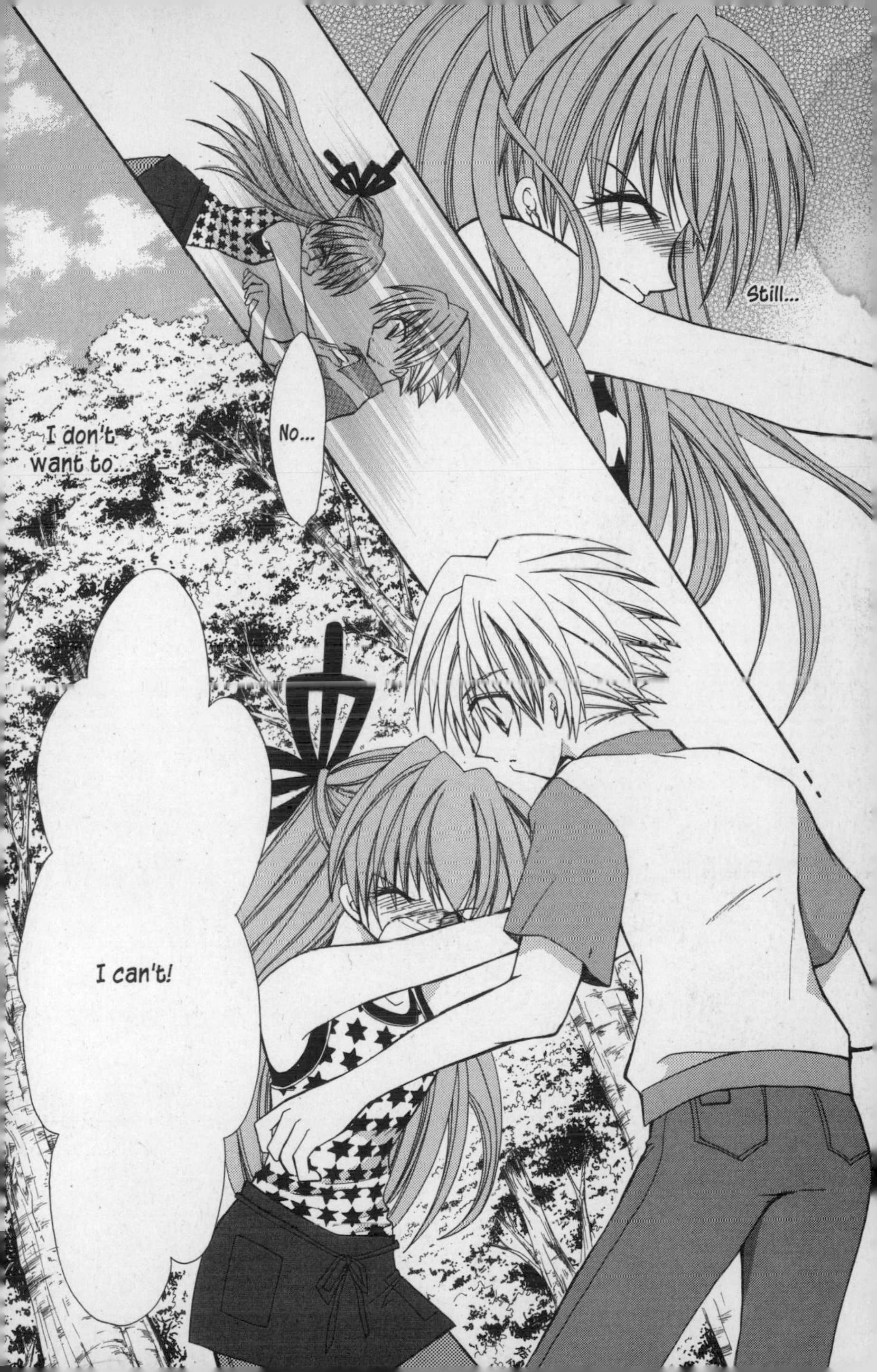
Still...
No...
I don't want to...
I can't!

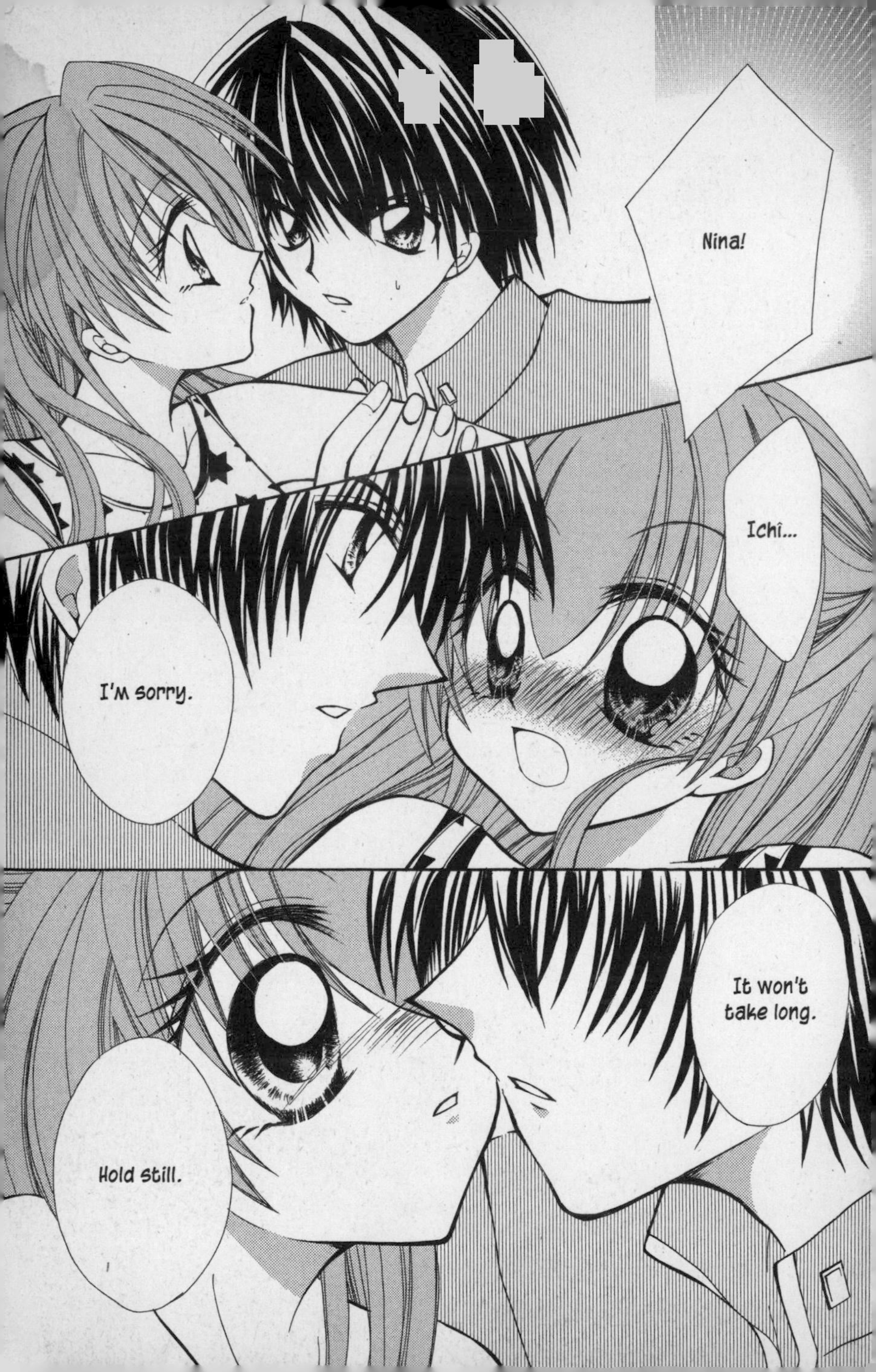
Nina!
Ichî...
I'm sorry.
It won't take long.
Hold still.

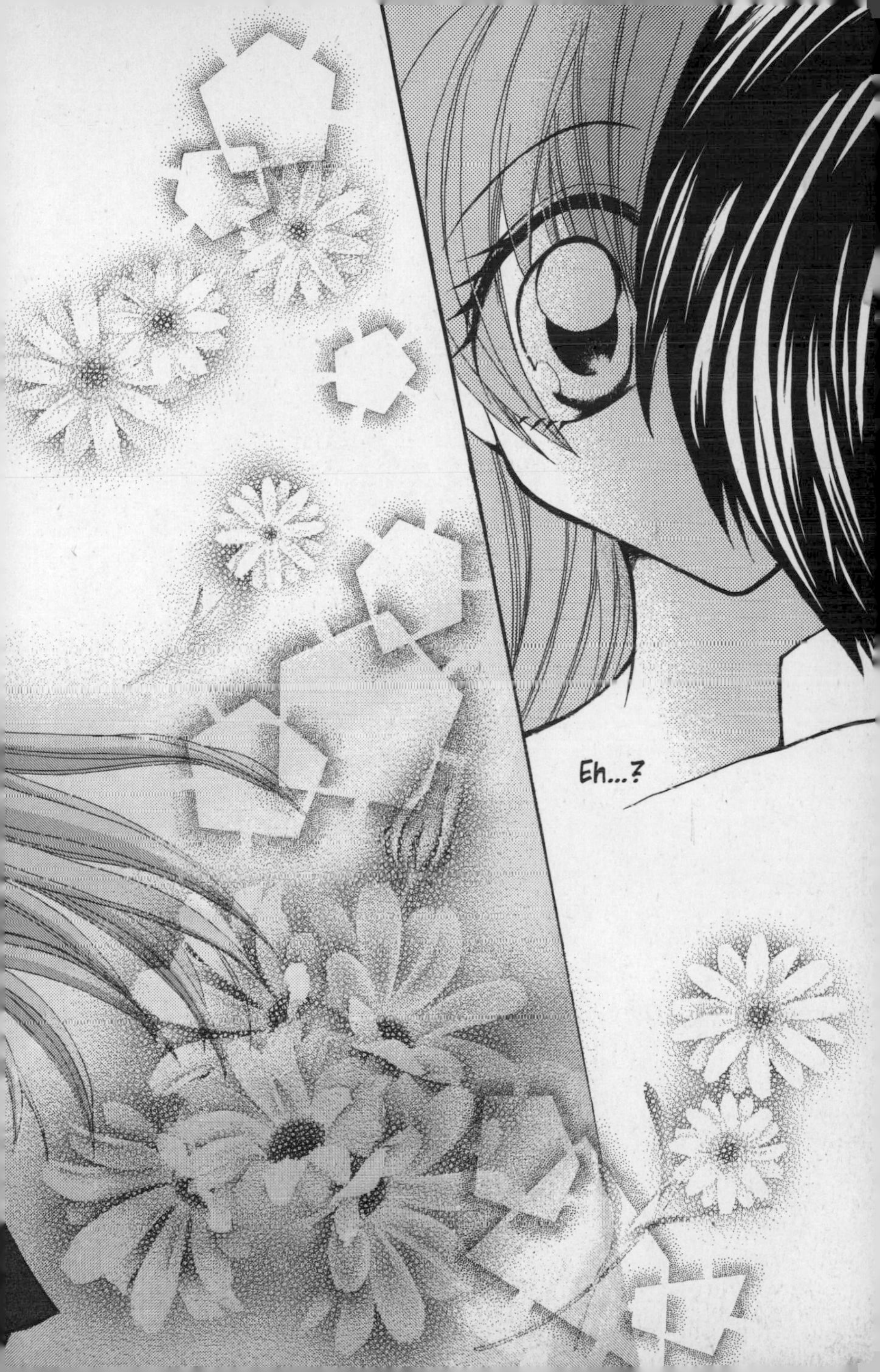
Eh...?

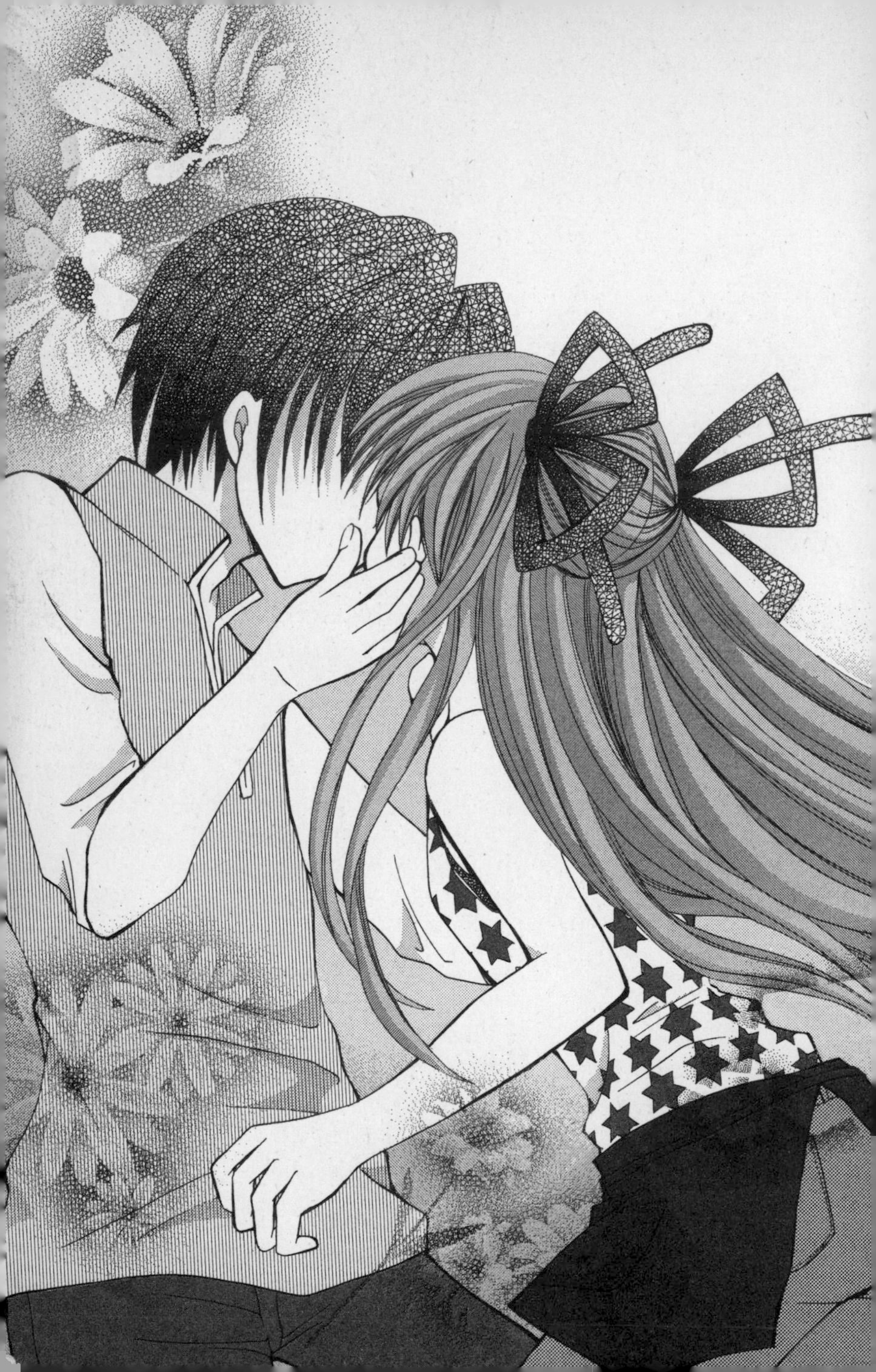

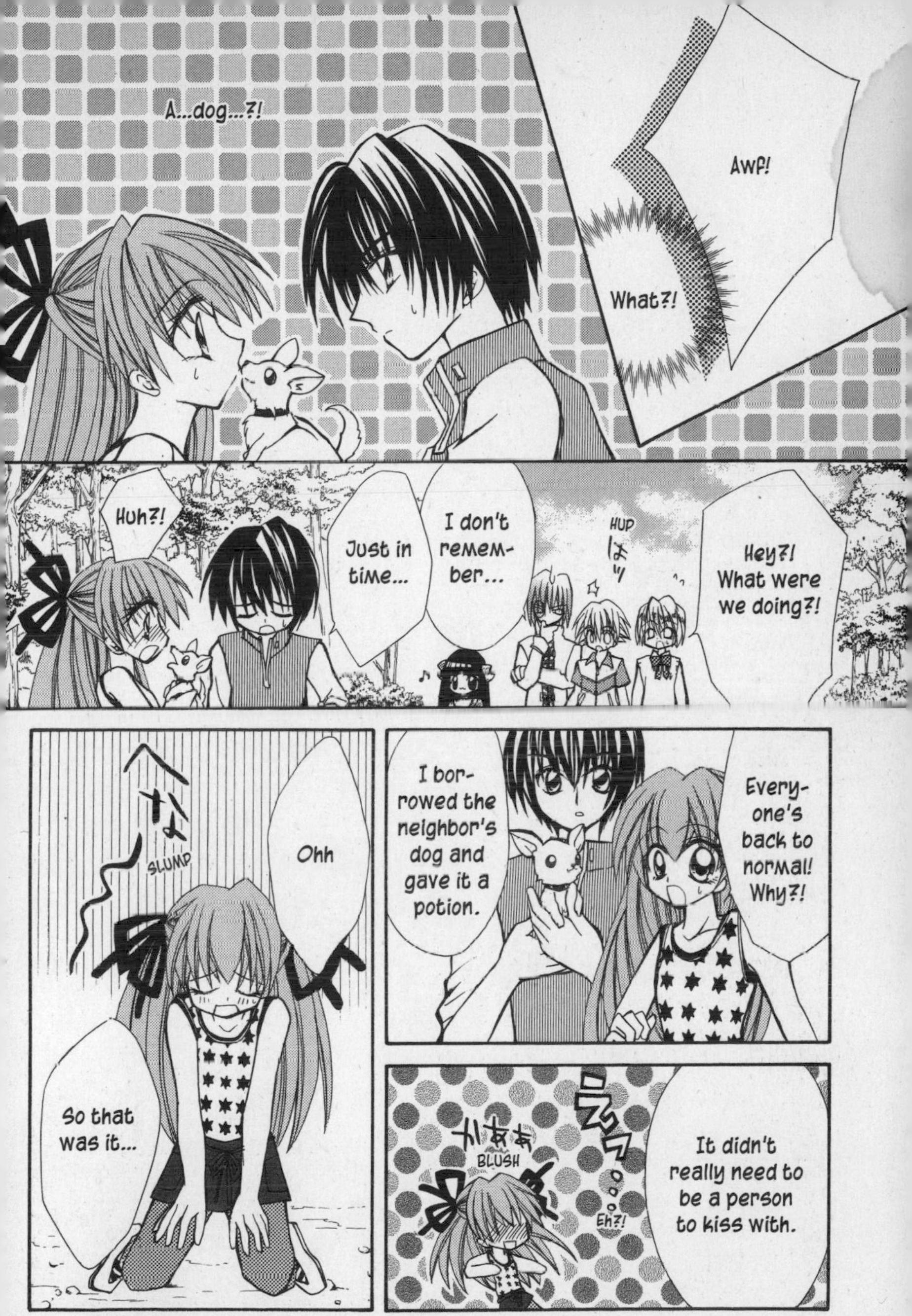
Awf!
What?!
A...dog...?!
Hey?! What were we doing?!
HUP
I don't remem-ber...
Just in time...
Huh?!
Every-one's back to normal! Why?!
I bor-rowed the neighbor's dog and gave it a potion.
It didn't really need to be a person to kiss with.
Eh?!
BLUSH
Ohh
SLUMP
So that was it...

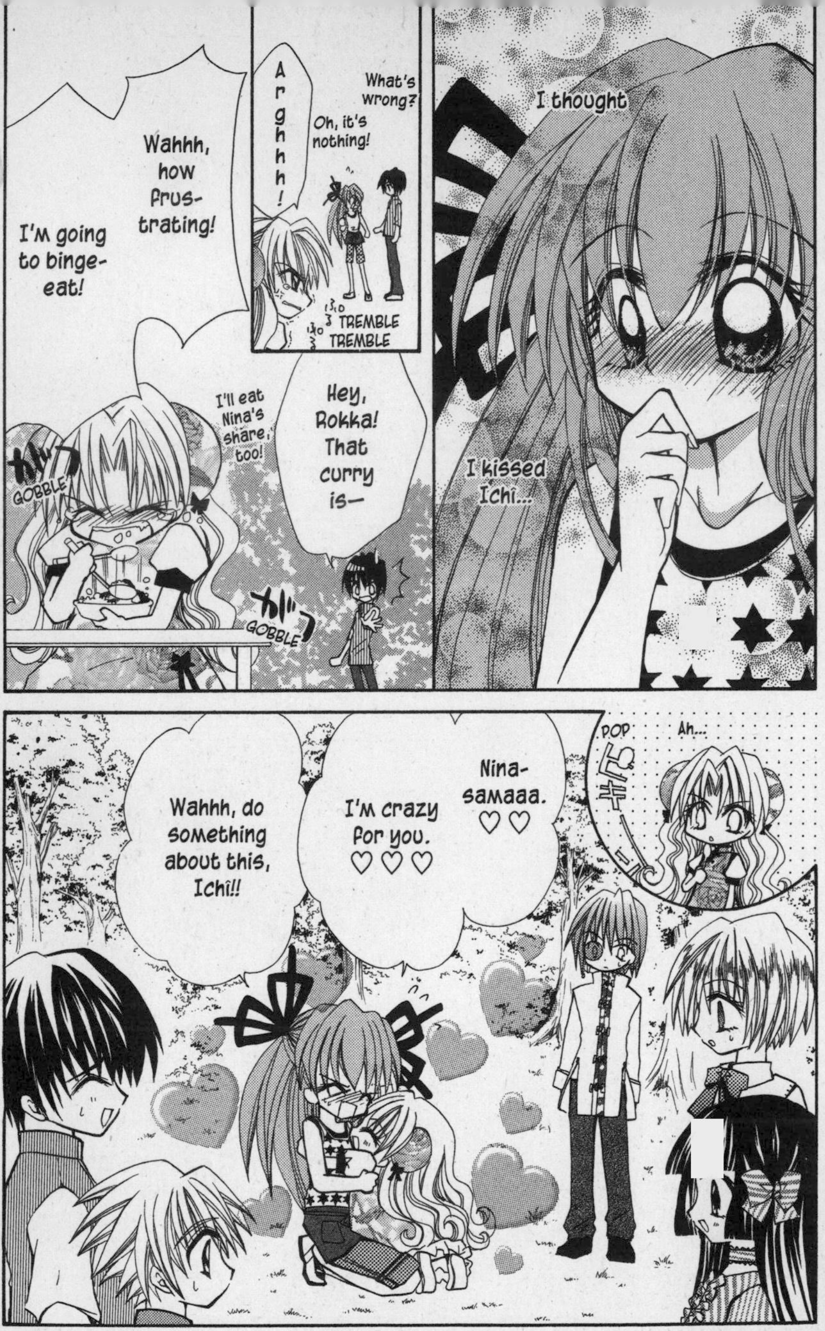
I thought
I kissed Ichi...
Arghhh!
What's wrong?
Oh, it's nothing!
TREMBLE TREMBLE
Wahhh, how frus-trating!
I'm going to binge-eat!
I'll eat Nina's share, too!
GOBBLE
Hey, Rokka! That curry is—
GOBBLE
POP
Ah...
Nina-samaaa. ♡♡
I'm crazy for you. ♡♡♡
Wahhh, do something about this, Ichi!!

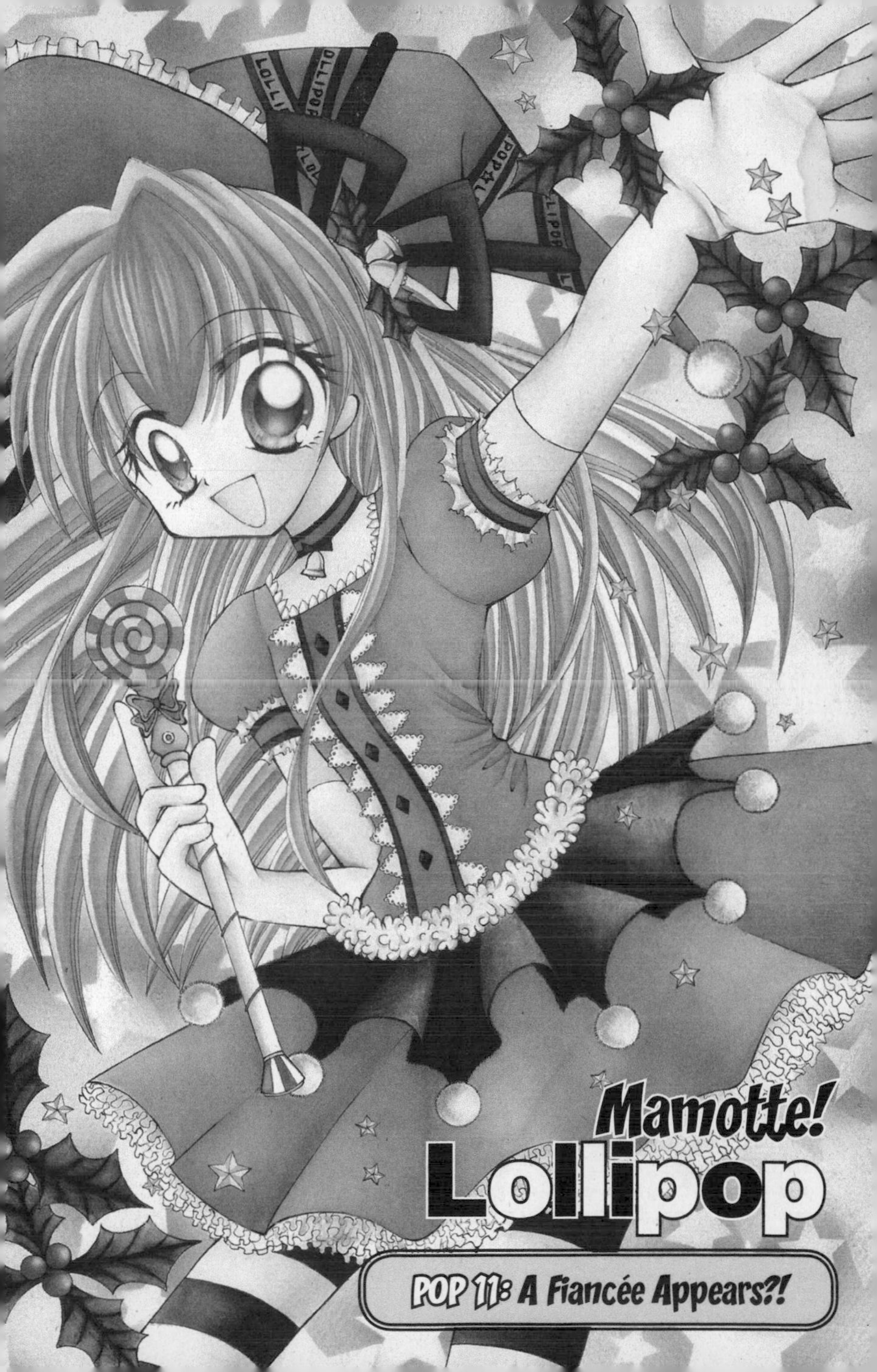
LOLLIPOP
Mamotte!
Lollipop
POP 11: A Fiancée Appears?!

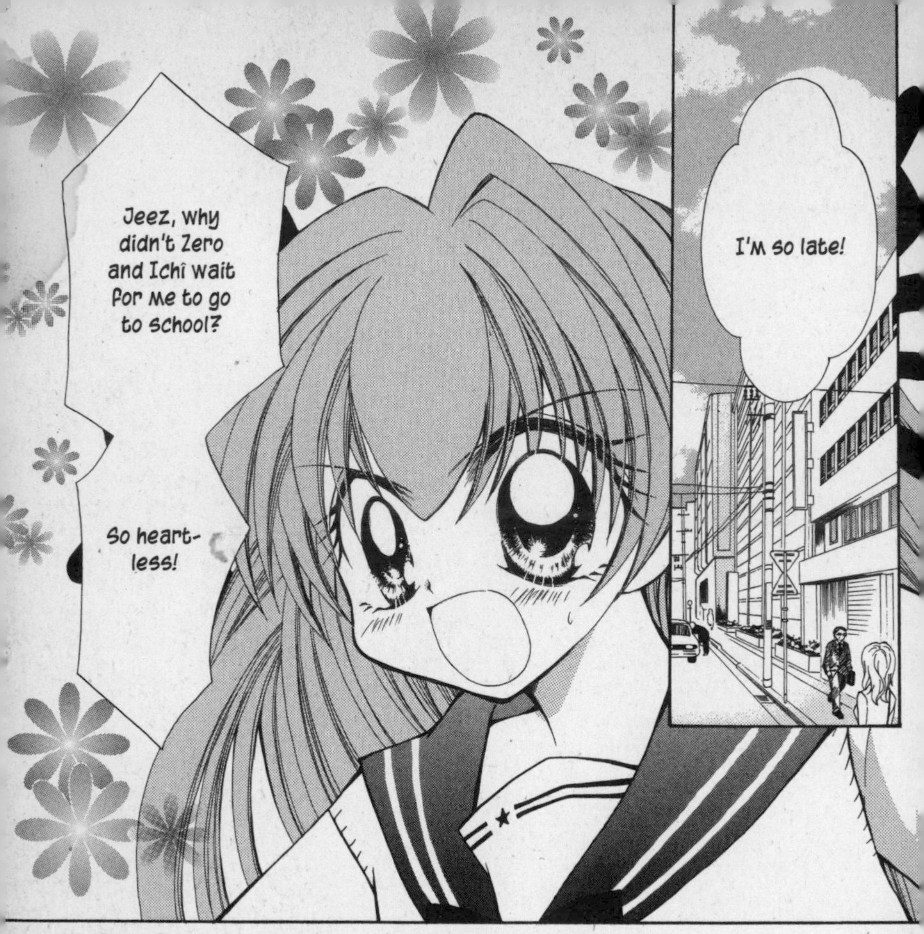
I'm so late!
Jeez, why didn't Zero and Ichi wait for me to go to school?
So heart-less!

POP 11 A Fiancée Appears?!

2

I like this cover page. You probably can't tell in black and white, but the colors came out great. It looks like it's Christmas . . .

That lollipop wand reminds me of a magical girl and I like it. It has nothing to do with the main story, though . . .. It's just something I like.

We have some new characters. It was tough creating Kuku and Toto. I think I had the hardest of all times with them . . . I stayed in the editorial department overnight and drew the storyboard. Since it was a non-business day, it was weird having no one around. But it was also fun in a way. . . .

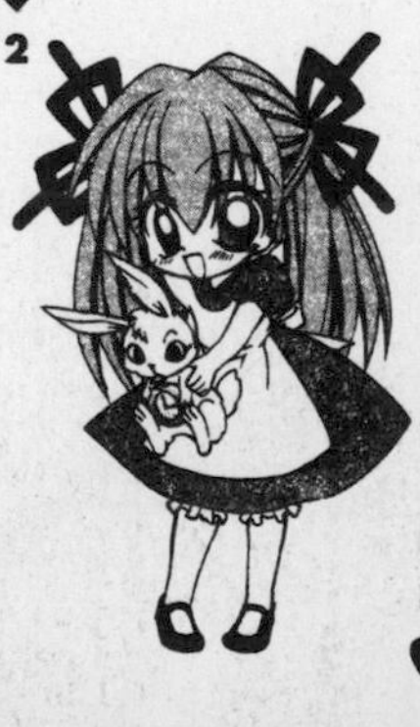

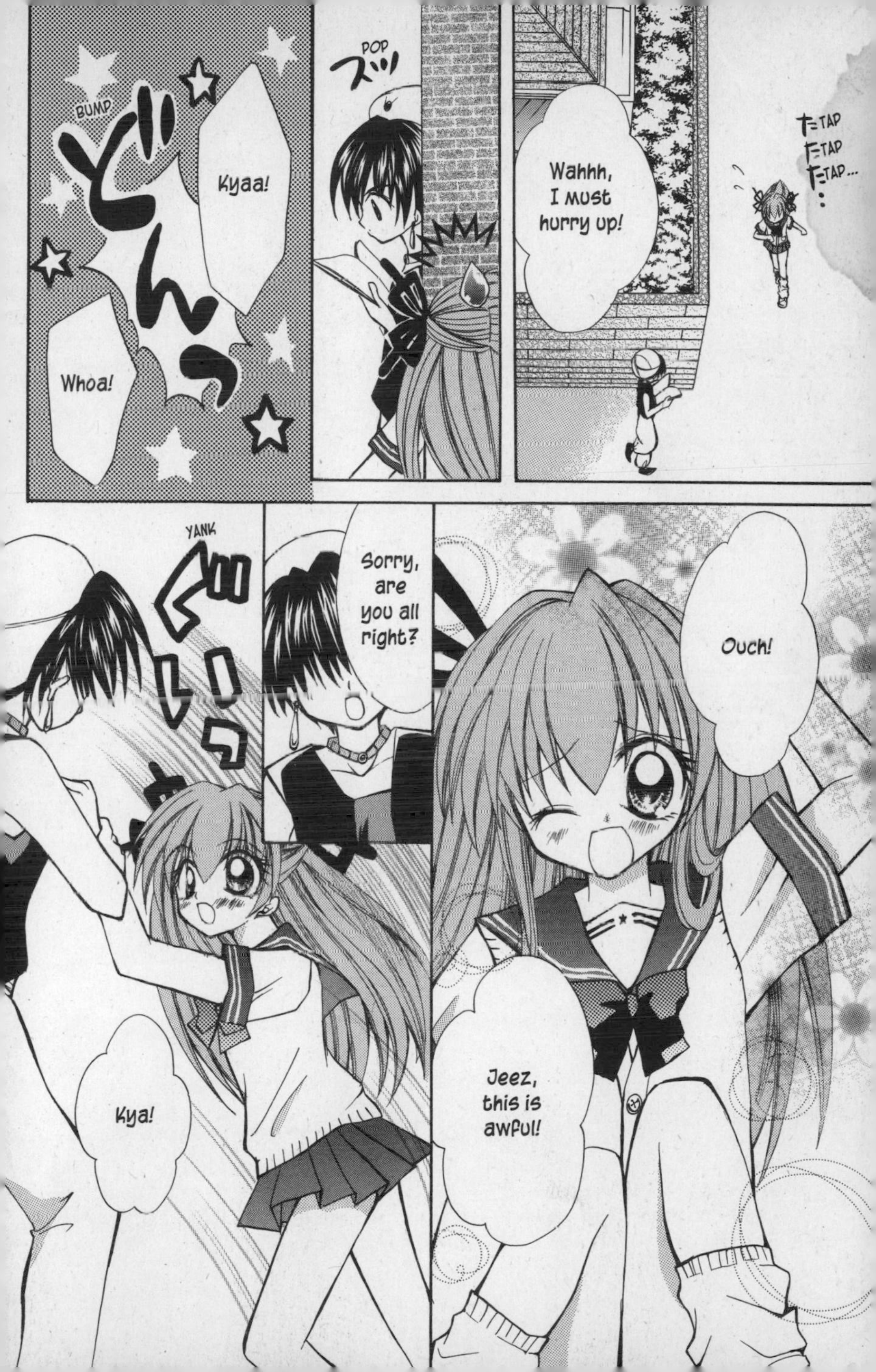

TAP
TAP
TAP...
Wahhh, I must hurry up!
POP
ズッ
BUMP
どんっ
Kyaa!
Whoa!
Ouch!
Jeez, this is awful!
Sorry, are you all right?
YANK
ぐいっ
Kya!

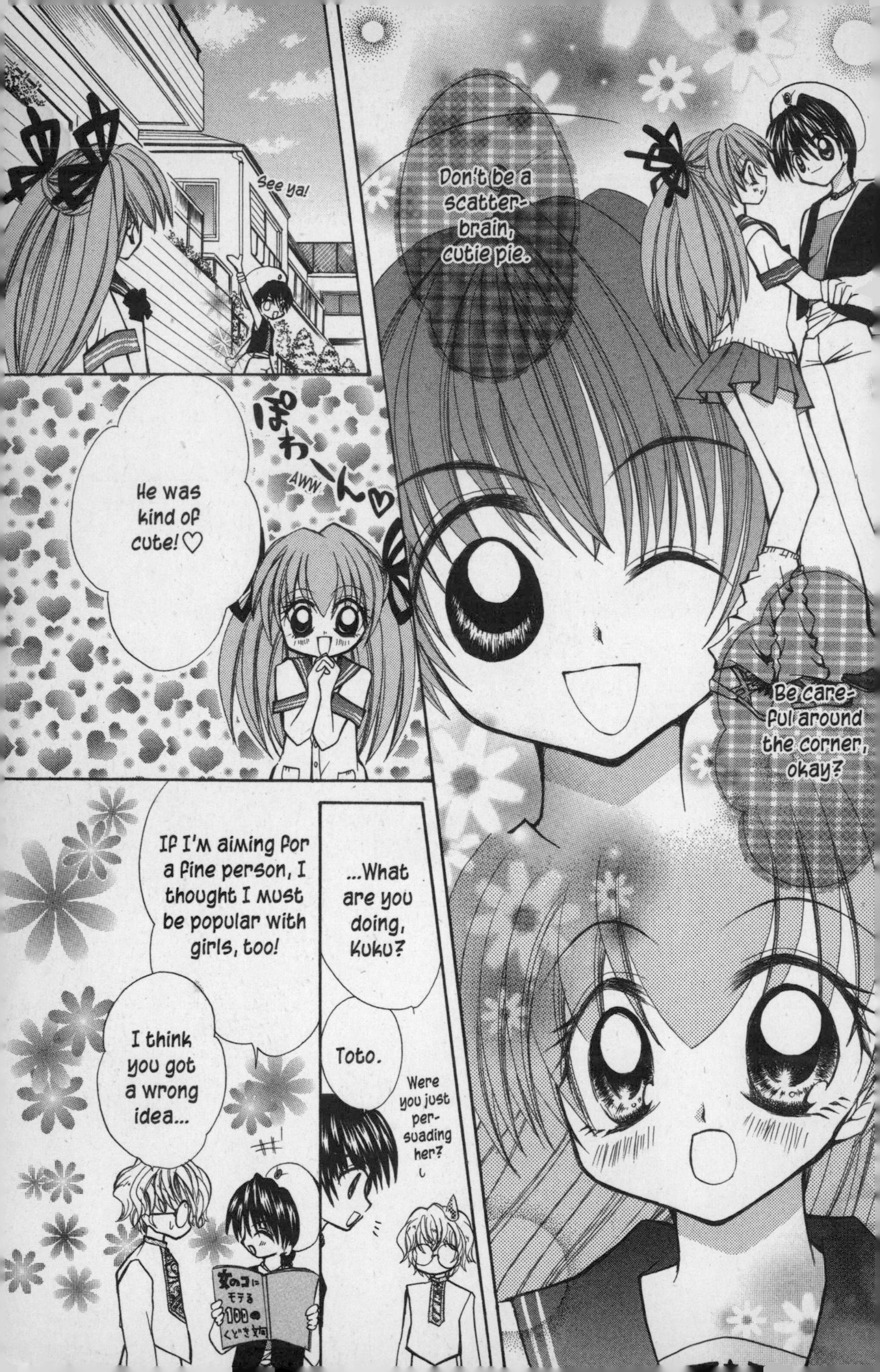

Don't be a scatter-brain, cutie pie.
Be care-ful around the corner, okay?
See ya!
ぽわ〜ん
AWW
He was kind of cute! ♡
...What are you doing, Kuku?
Toto.
Were you just per-suading her?
If I'm aiming for a fine person, I thought I must be popular with girls, too!
I think you got a wrong idea...
女のコに モテる 100の

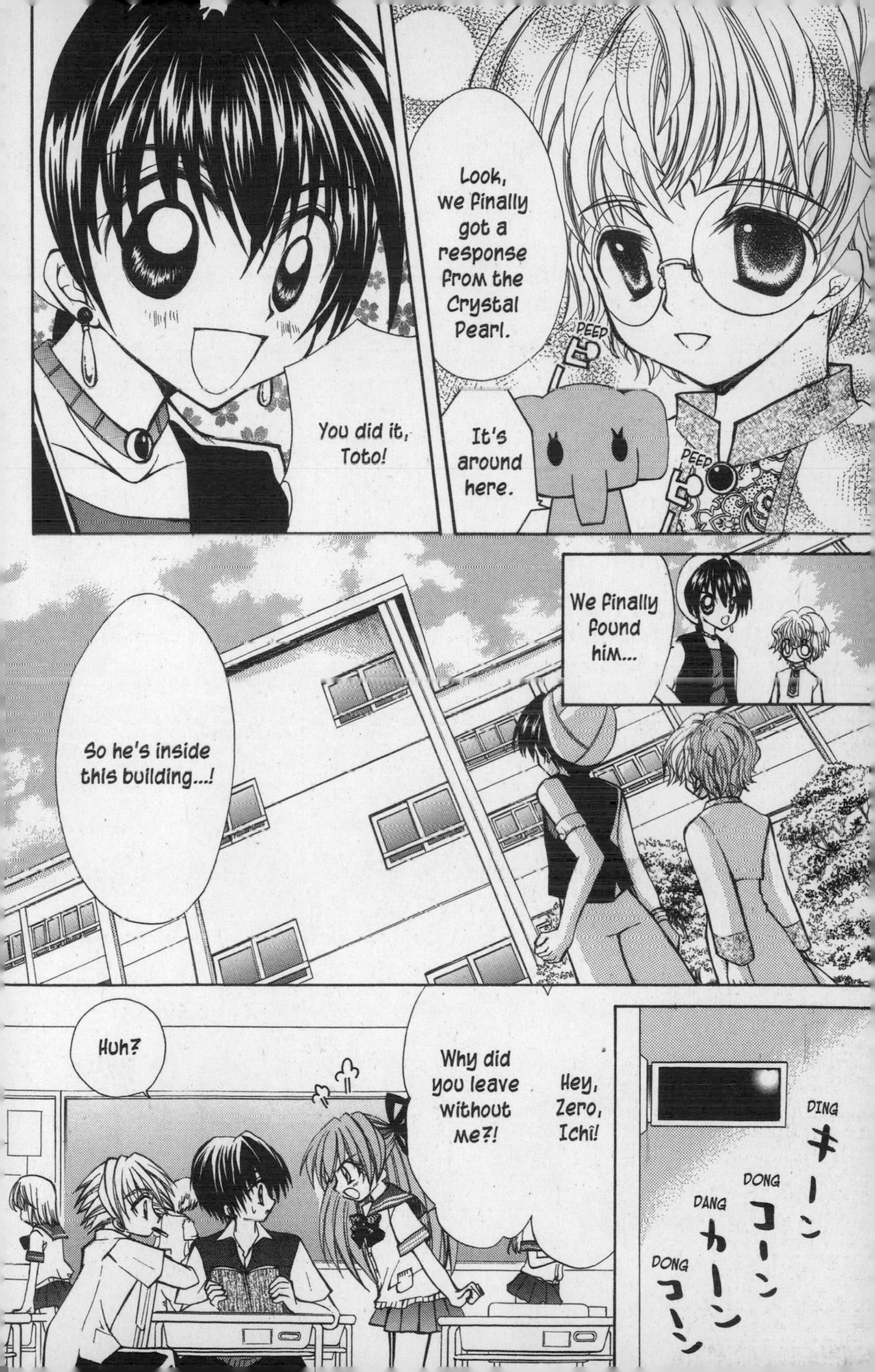
Look, we finally got a response from the Crystal Pearl.
PEEP
PEEP
It's around here.
You did it, Toto!
We finally found him...
So he's inside this building...!
DING
キーン
DONG
コーン
DANG
カーン
DONG
コーン
Hey, Zero, Ichi!
Why did you leave without me?!
Huh?

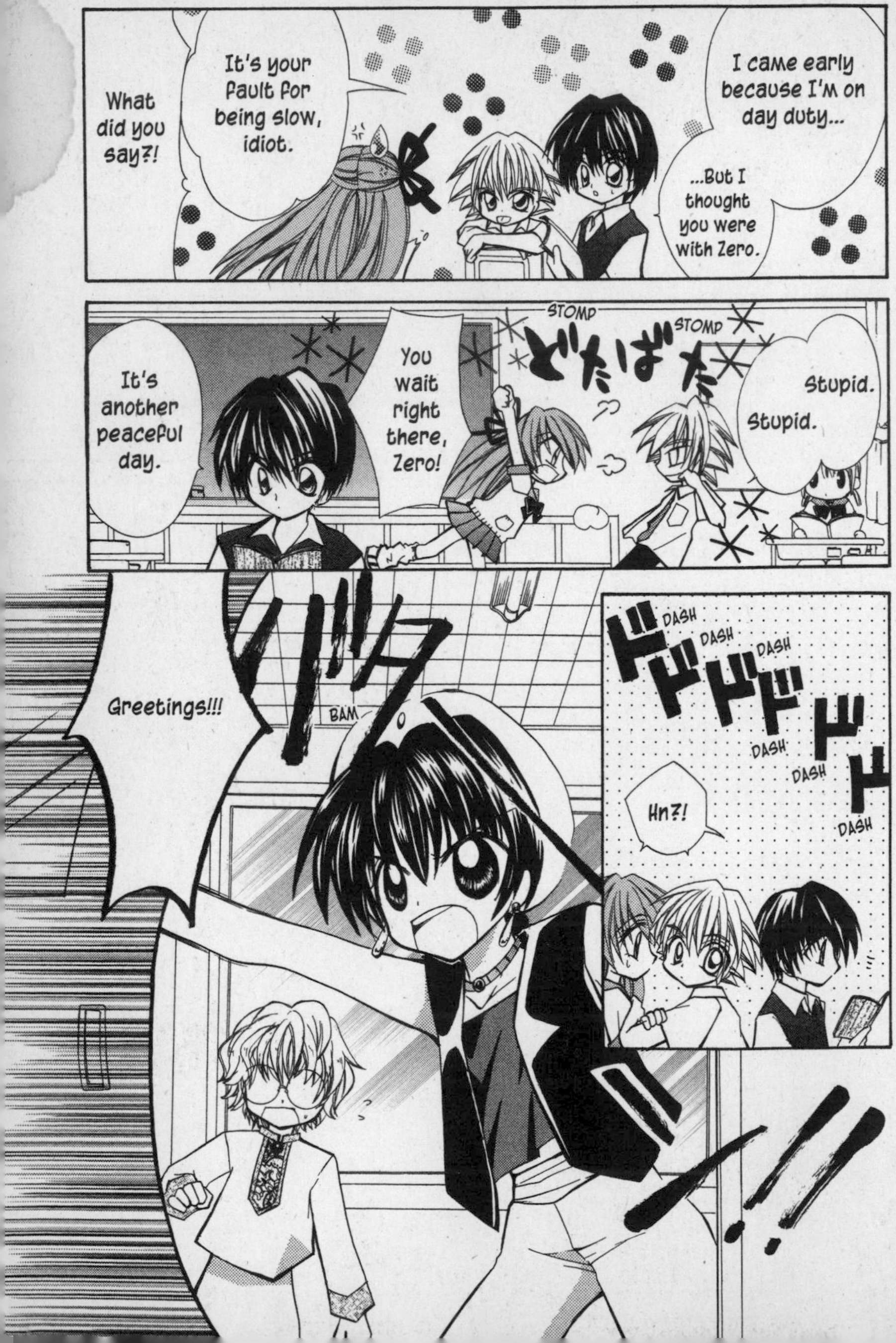

I came early because I'm on day duty...
...But I thought you were with Zero.
It's your fault for being slow, idiot.
What did you say?!
Stupid.
Stupid.
STOMP
STOMP
どたばた
You wait right there, Zero!
It's another peaceful day.
DASH
DASH
DASH
DASH
DASH
DASH
Hn?!
BAM
Greetings!!!

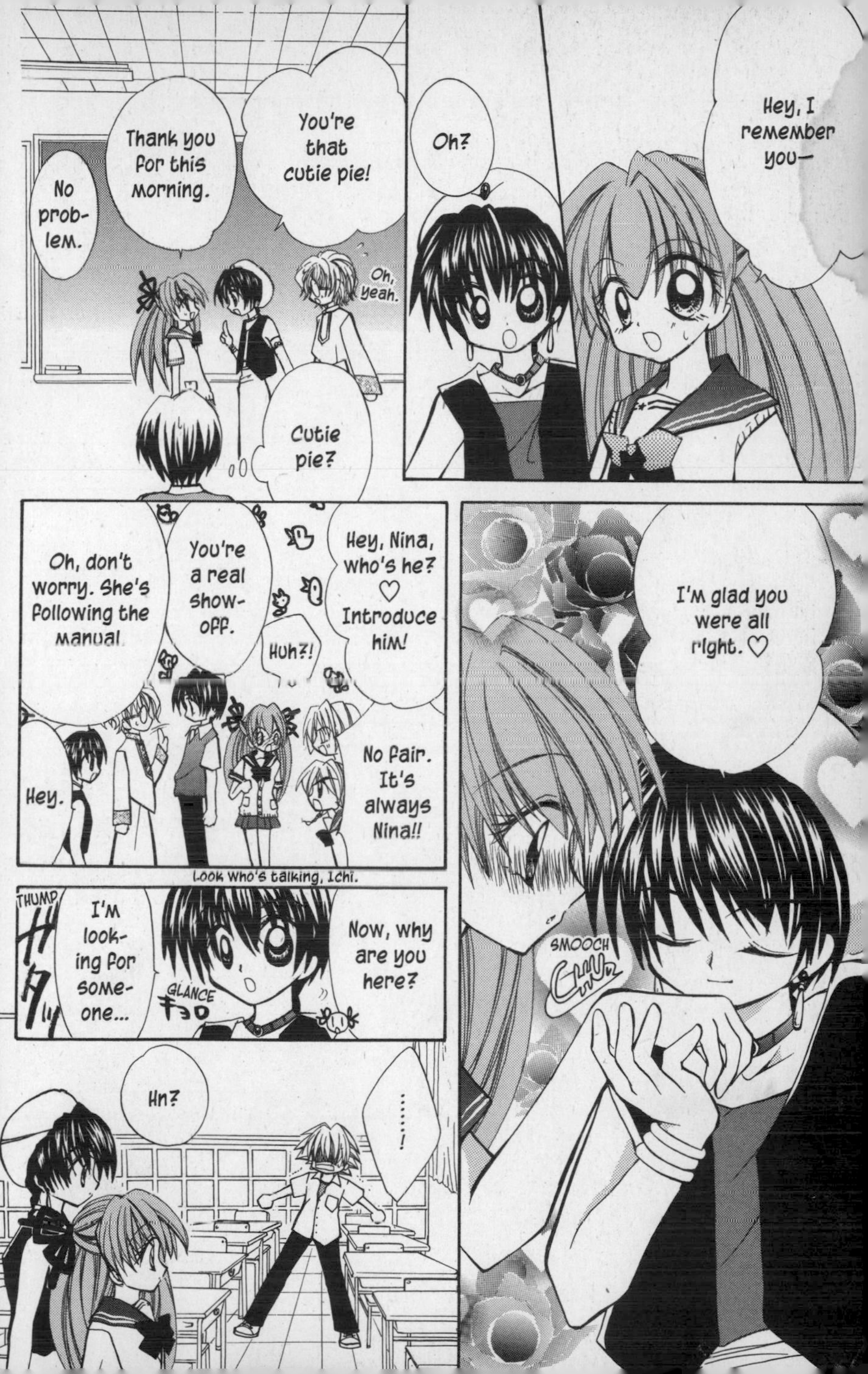
Hey, I remember you—
Oh?
You're that cutie pie!
Thank you for this morning.
No problem.
Oh, yeah.
Cutie pie?
I'm glad you were all right. ♡
SMOOCH
Hey, Nina, who's he? ♡ Introduce him!
You're a real show-off.
Oh, don't worry. She's following the manual.
Huh?!
No fair. It's always Nina!!
Hey.
Look who's talking, Ichi.
Now, why are you here?
I'm looking for someone...
GLANCE
THUMP
......!
Hn?

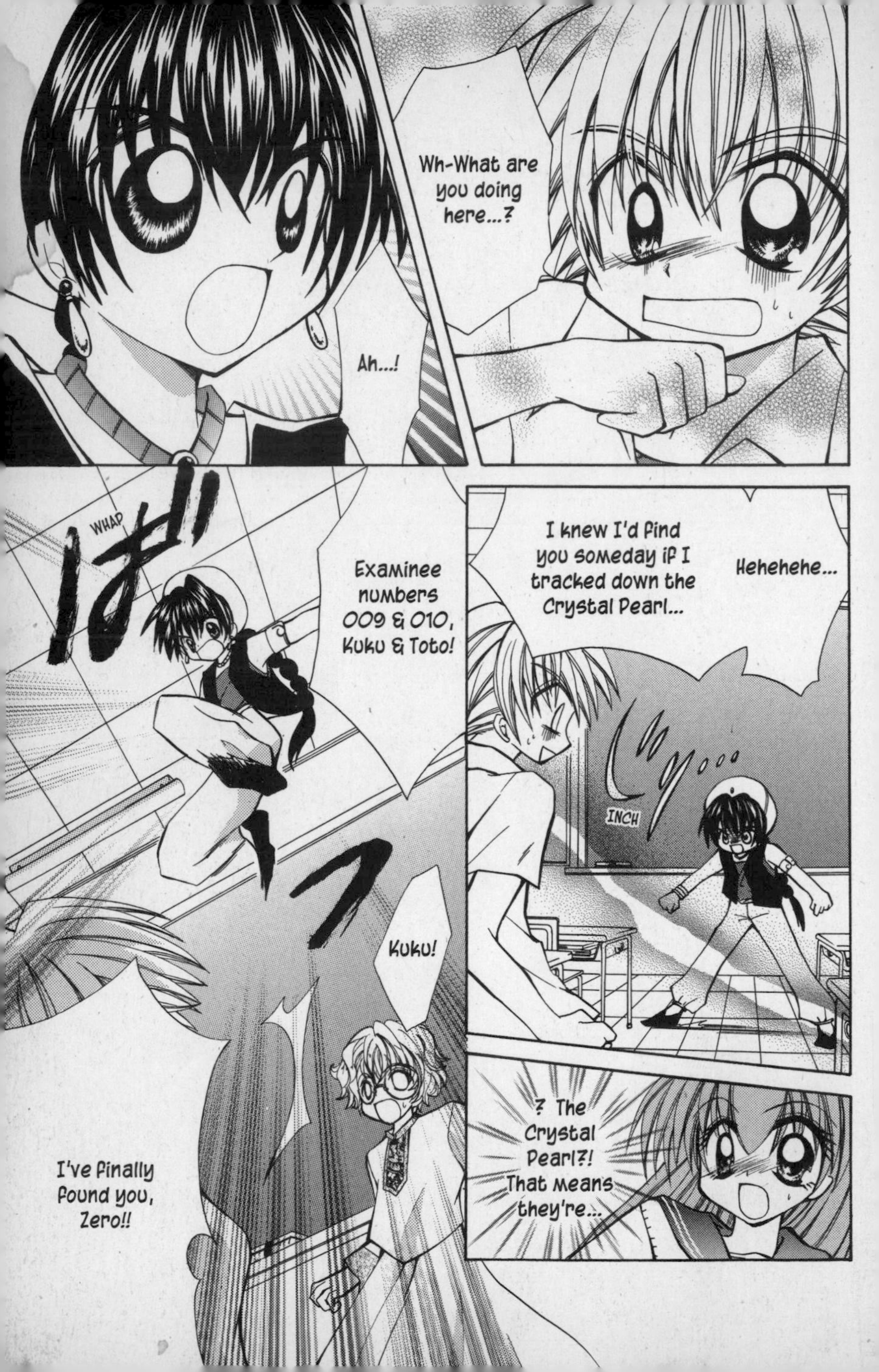
Wh-What are you doing here...?
Ah...!
Hehehehe...
I knew I'd find you someday if I tracked down the Crystal Pearl...
INCH
? The Crystal Pearl?! That means they're...
WHAP
Examinee numbers 009 & 010, Kuku & Toto!
Kuku!
I've finally found you, Zero!!

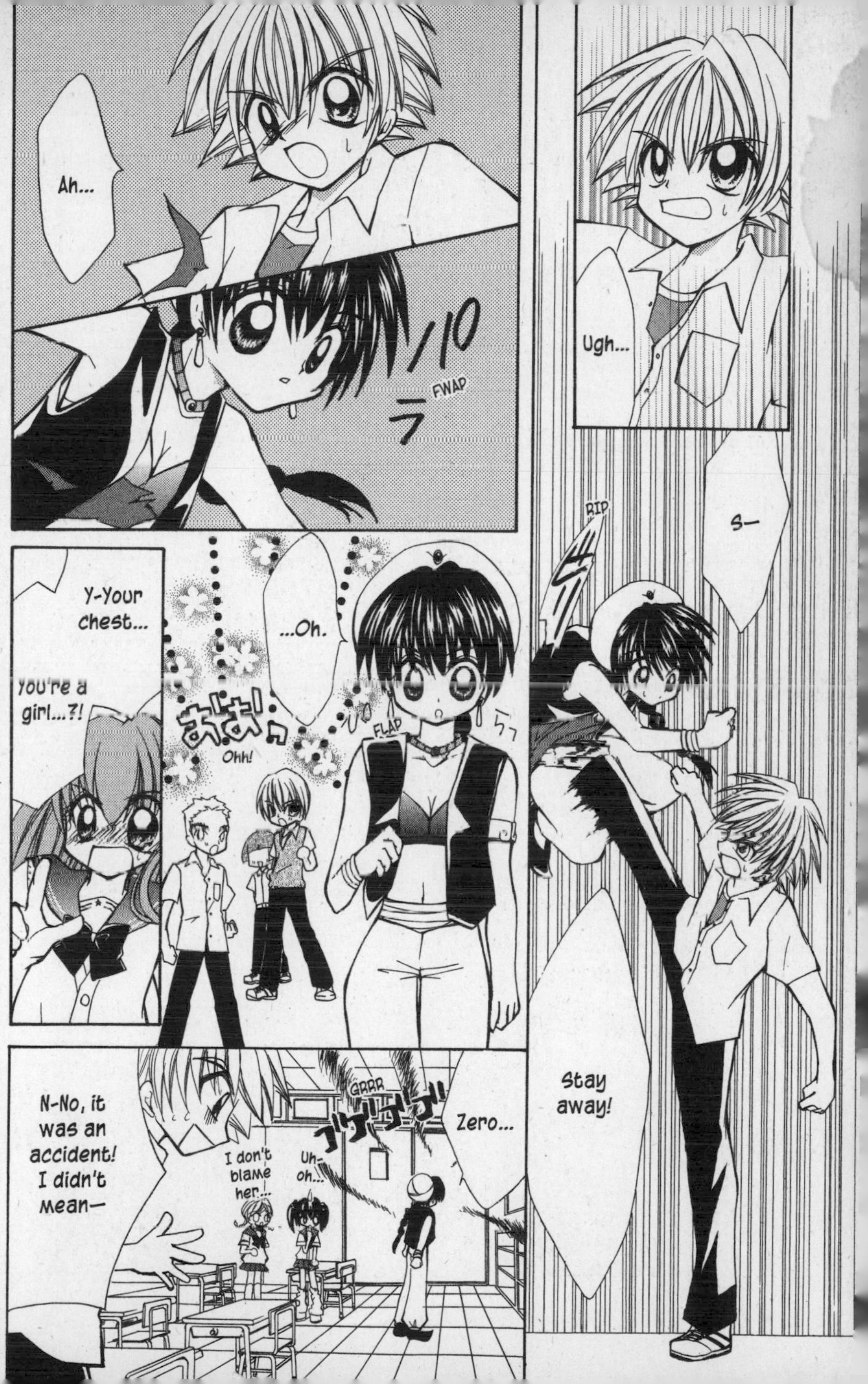
Ugh...
S—
RIP
Stay away!
Ah...
FWAP
...Oh.
FLAP
Ohh!
Y-Your chest...
You're a girl...?!
Zero...
GRRR
Uh-oh...
I don't blame her...
N-No, it was an accident! I didn't mean—

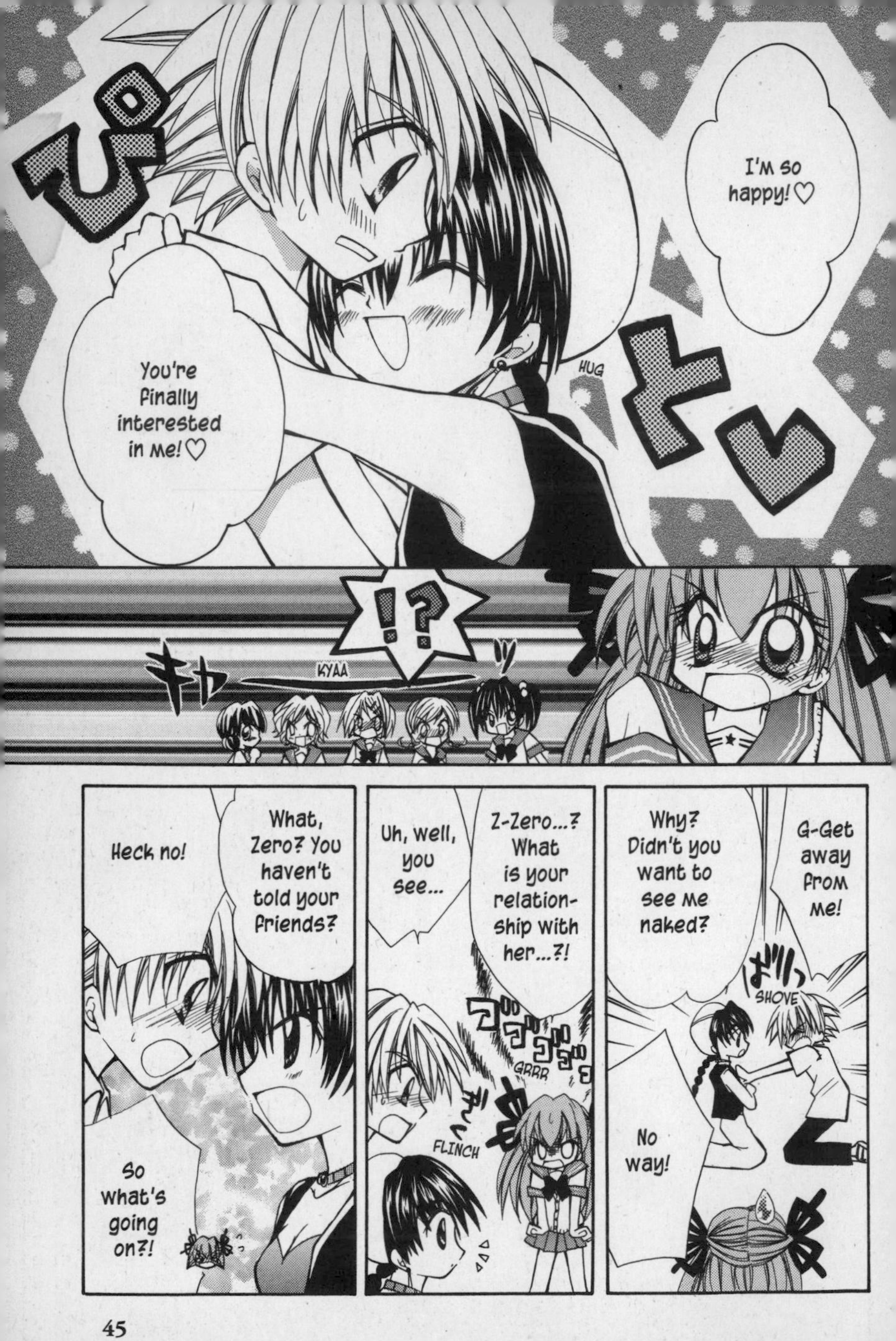
I'm so happy!♡
You're finally interested in me!♡
HUG
!?
KYAA
G-Get away from me!
Why? Didn't you want to see me naked?
SHOVE
No way!
Z-Zero...? What is your relationship with her...?!
Uh, well, you see...
GRRR
FLINCH
What, Zero? You haven't told your friends?
Heck no!
So what's going on?!

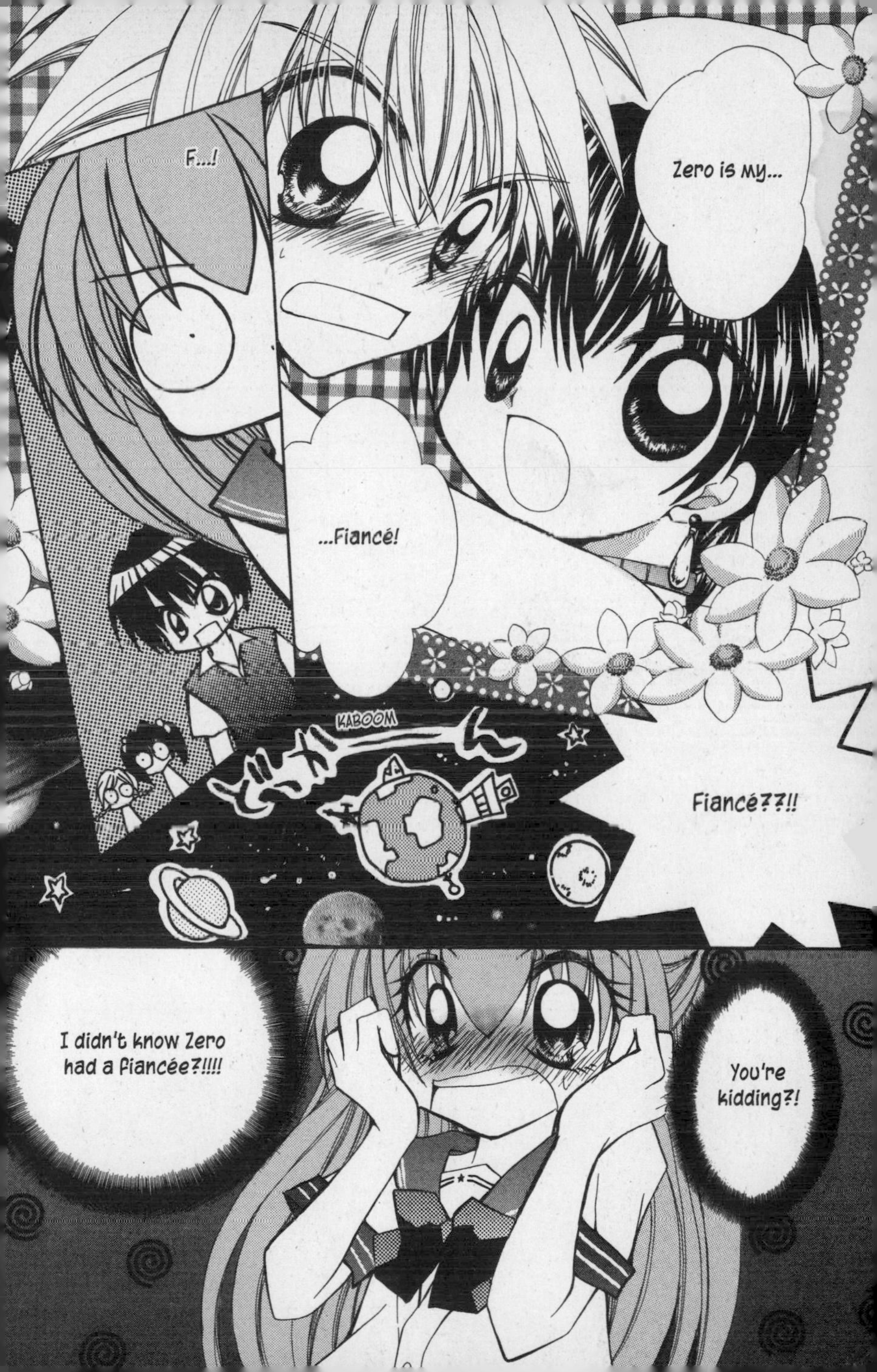
Zero is my...
...Fiancé!
F...!
Fiancé??!!
KABOOM
You're kidding?!
I didn't know Zero had a fiancée?!!!!

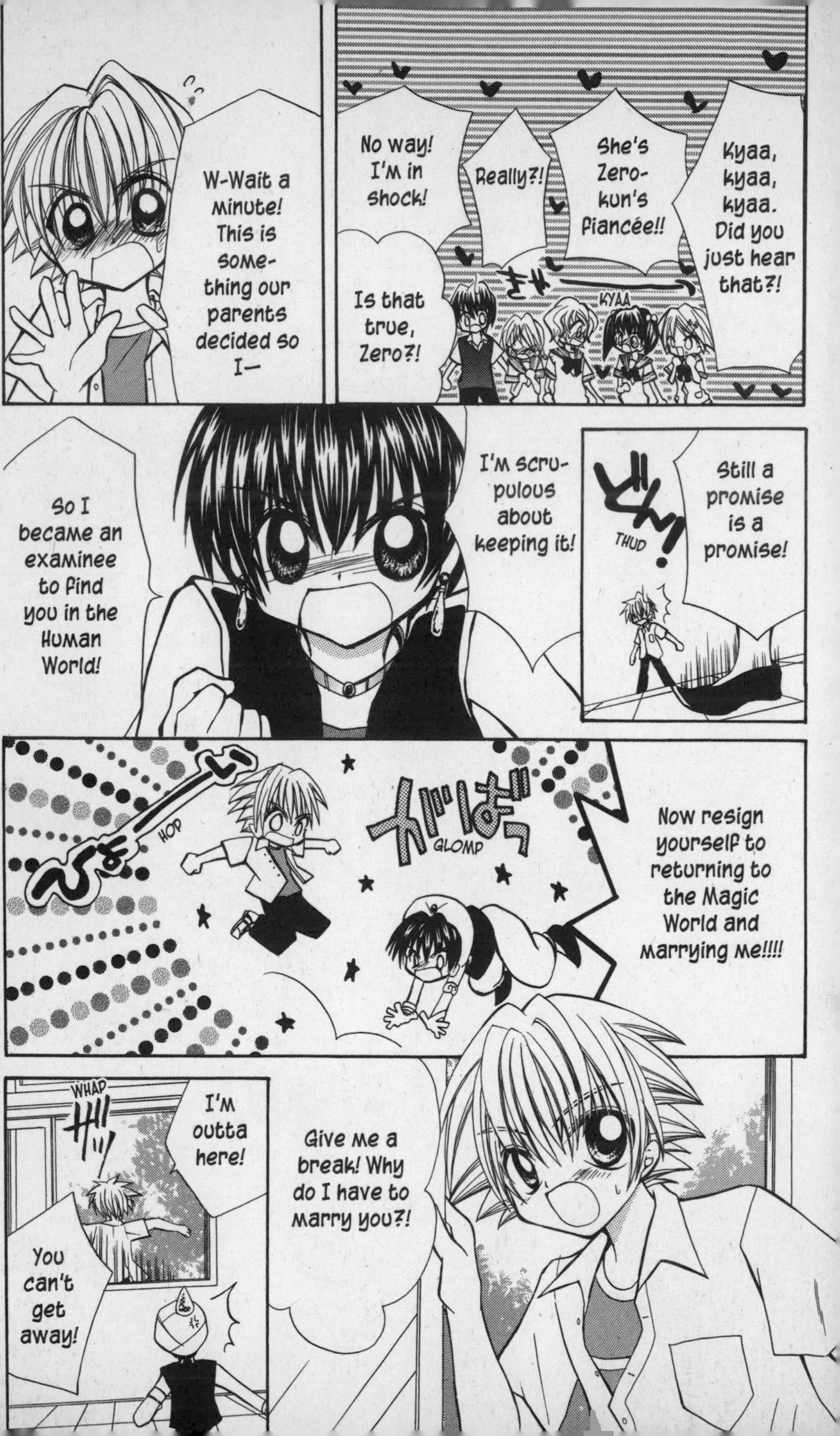

Kyaa, kyaa, kyaa. Did you just hear that?!
She's Zero-kun's fiancée!!
Really?!
No way! I'm in shock!
KYAA
Is that true, Zero?!
W-Wait a minute! This is some-thing our parents decided so I—
Still a promise is a promise!
THUD
I'm scru-pulous about keeping it!
So I became an examinee to find you in the Human World!
Now resign yourself to returning to the Magic World and marrying me!!!!
GLOMP
HOP
Give me a break! Why do I have to marry you?!
I'm outta here!
WHAP
You can't get away!

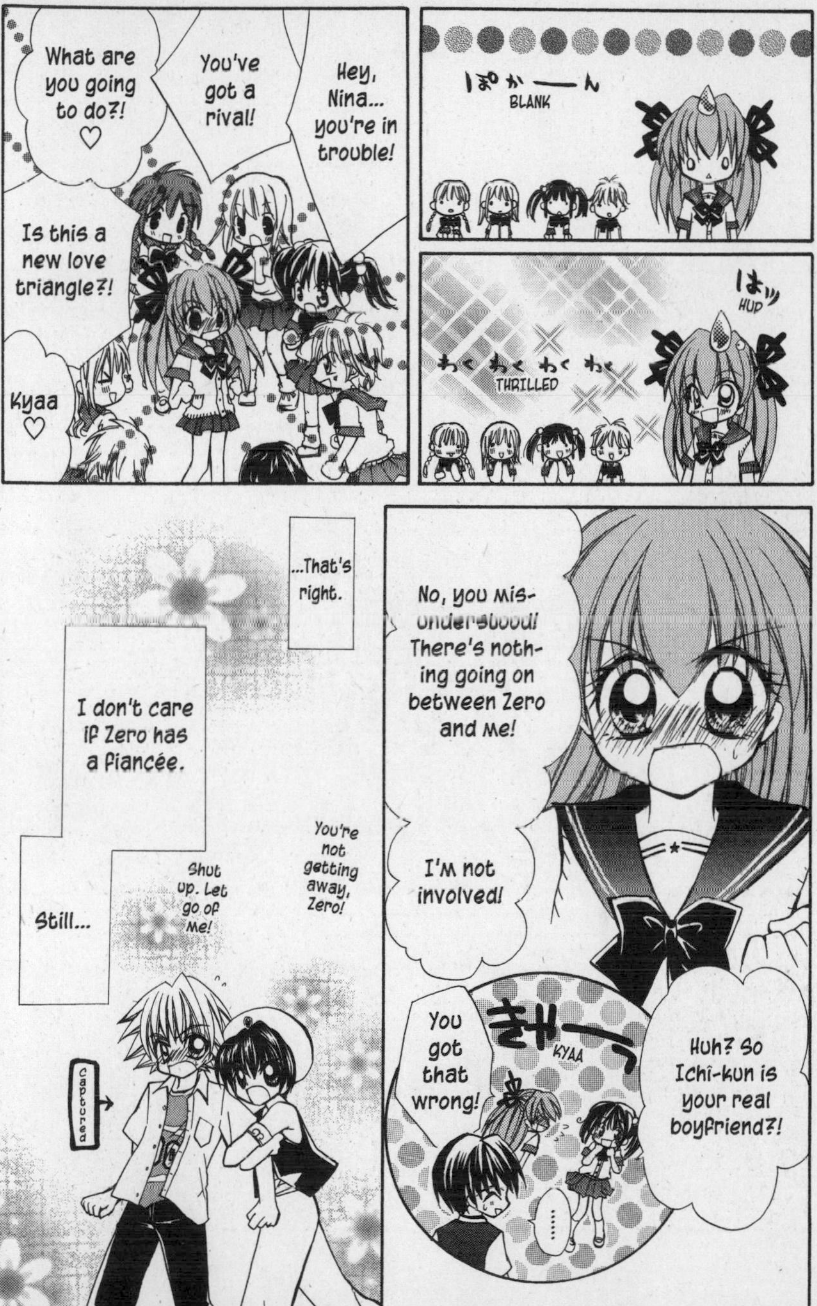
ぽかーん
BLANK
はッ
HUD
わくわくわくわく
THRILLED
Hey, Nina... you're in trouble!
You've got a rival!
What are you going to do?! ♡
Is this a new love triangle?!
Kyaa ♡
No, you mis-understood! There's noth-ing going on between Zero and me!
I'm not involved!
Huh? So Ichi-kun is your real boyfriend?!
きゃー
KYAA
You got that wrong!
......
...That's right.
I don't care if Zero has a fiancée.
Still...
You're not getting away, Zero!
Shut up. Let go of me!
Captured

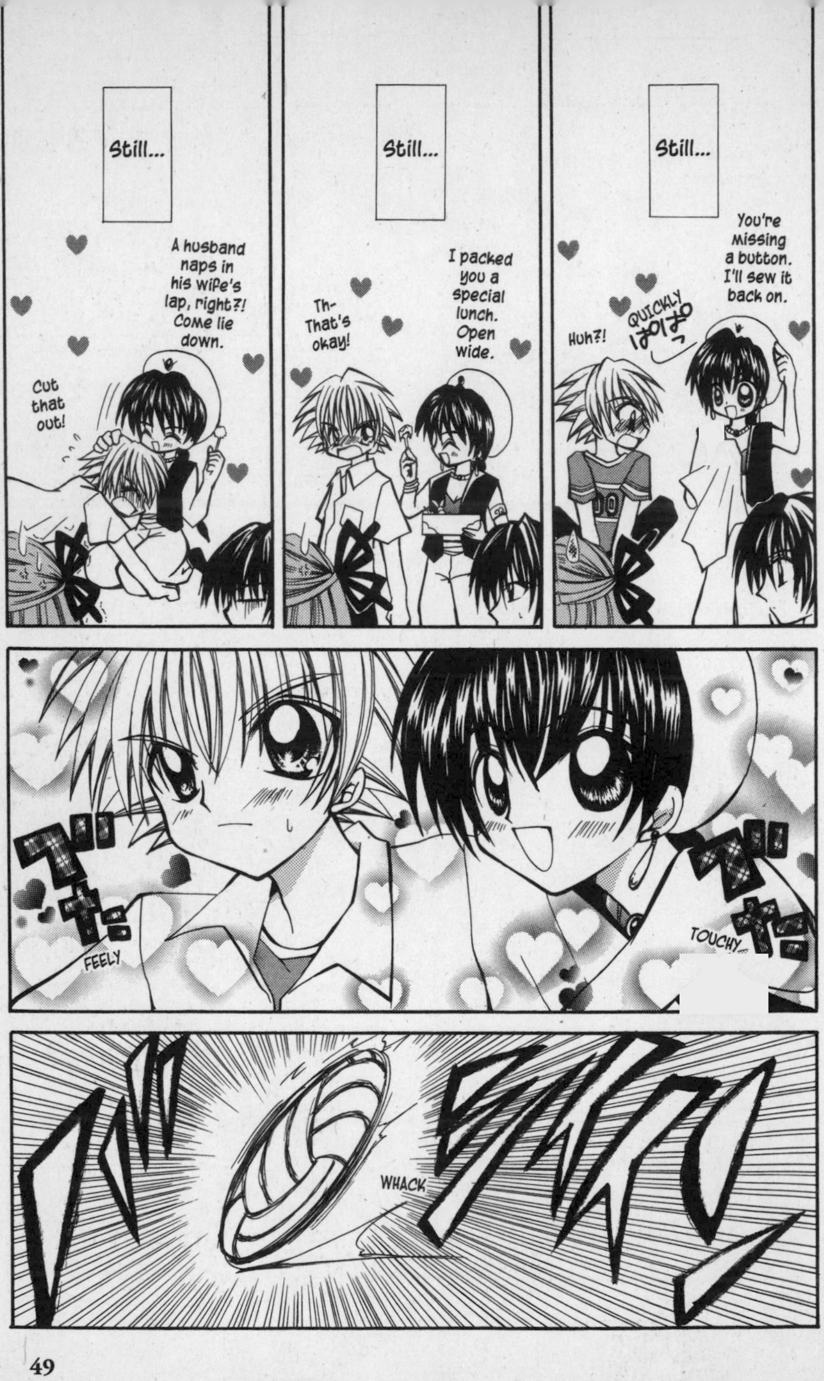
Still...
You're missing a button. I'll sew it back on.
QUICKLY
ぱぱっ
Huh?!
Still...
I packed you a special lunch. Open wide.
Th-That's okay!
Still...
A husband naps in his wife's lap, right?! Come lie down.
Cut that out!
TOUCHY
FEELY
WHACK

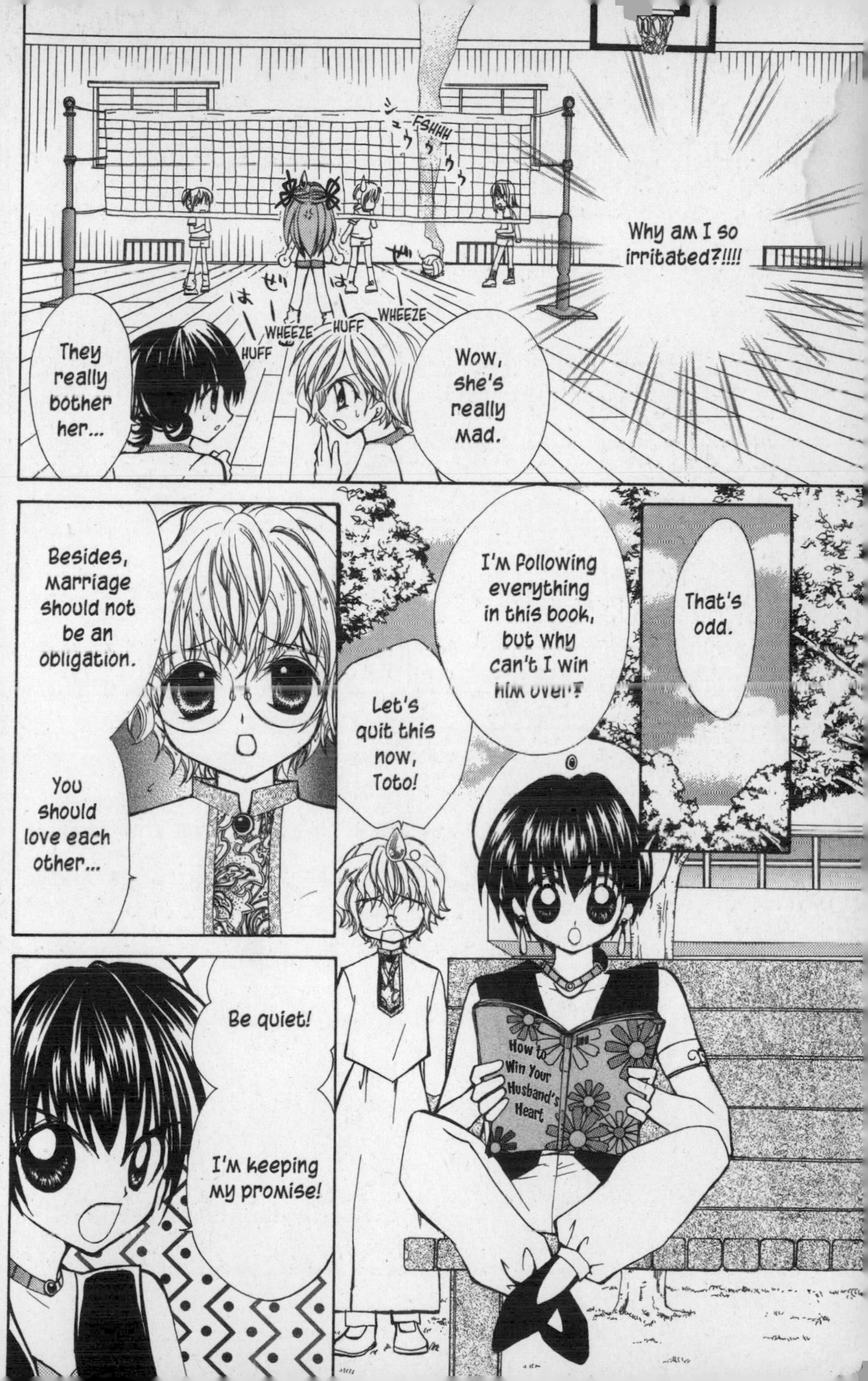

Why am I so irritated?!!!!
シュウウウ
FSHHH
ゼ
は
ゼ
は
HUFF
WHEEZE
HUFF
WHEEZE
Wow, she's really mad.
They really bother her...
That's odd.
I'm following everything in this book, but why can't I win him over?
Let's quit this now, Toto!
How to Win Your Husband's Heart
Besides, marriage should not be an obligation.
You should love each other...
Be quiet!
I'm keeping my promise!

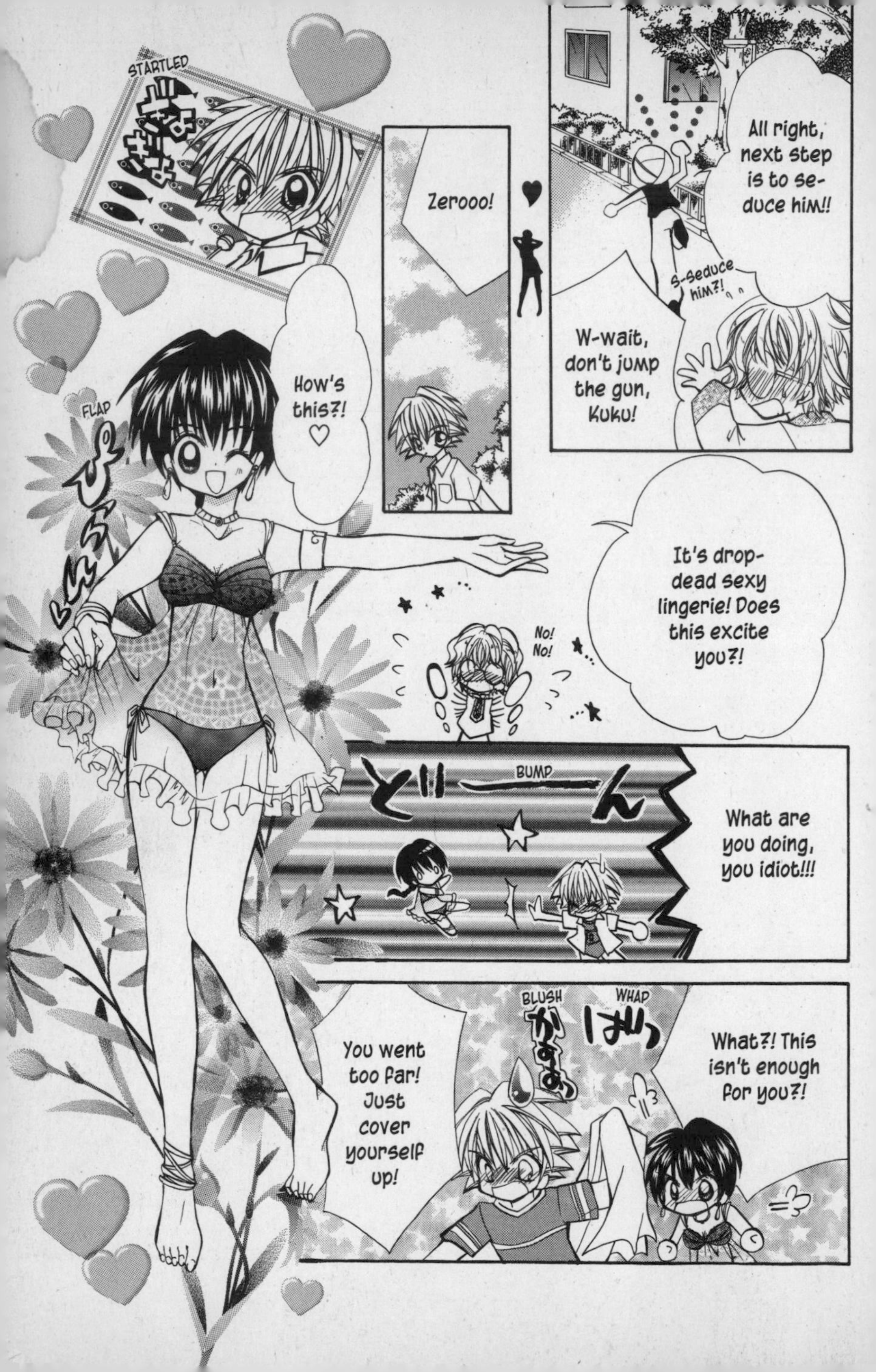
All right, next step is to se-duce him!!
S-seduce him?!
W-wait, don't jump the gun, Kuku!
Zerooo!
STARTLED
FLAP
How's this?! ♡
It's drop-dead sexy lingerie! Does this excite you?!
No! No!
BUMP
What are you doing, you idiot!!!
WHAP
BLUSH
What?! This isn't enough for you?!
You went too far! Just cover yourself up!

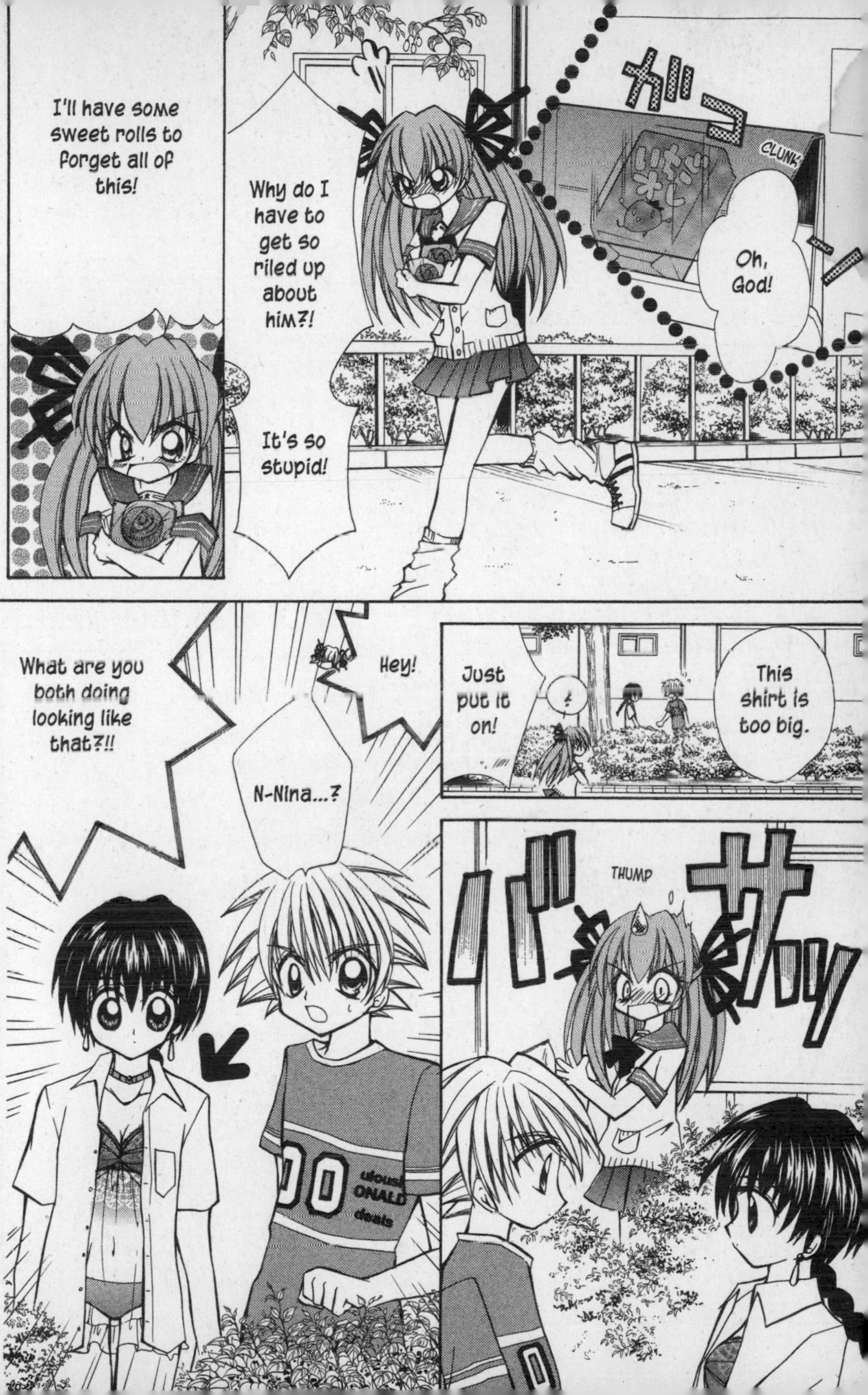
CLUNK
Oh, God!
Why do I have to get so riled up about him?!
It's so stupid!
I'll have some sweet rolls to forget all of this!
This shirt is too big.
Just put it on!
バサッ
THUMP
Hey!
N-Nina...?
What are you both doing looking like that?!!

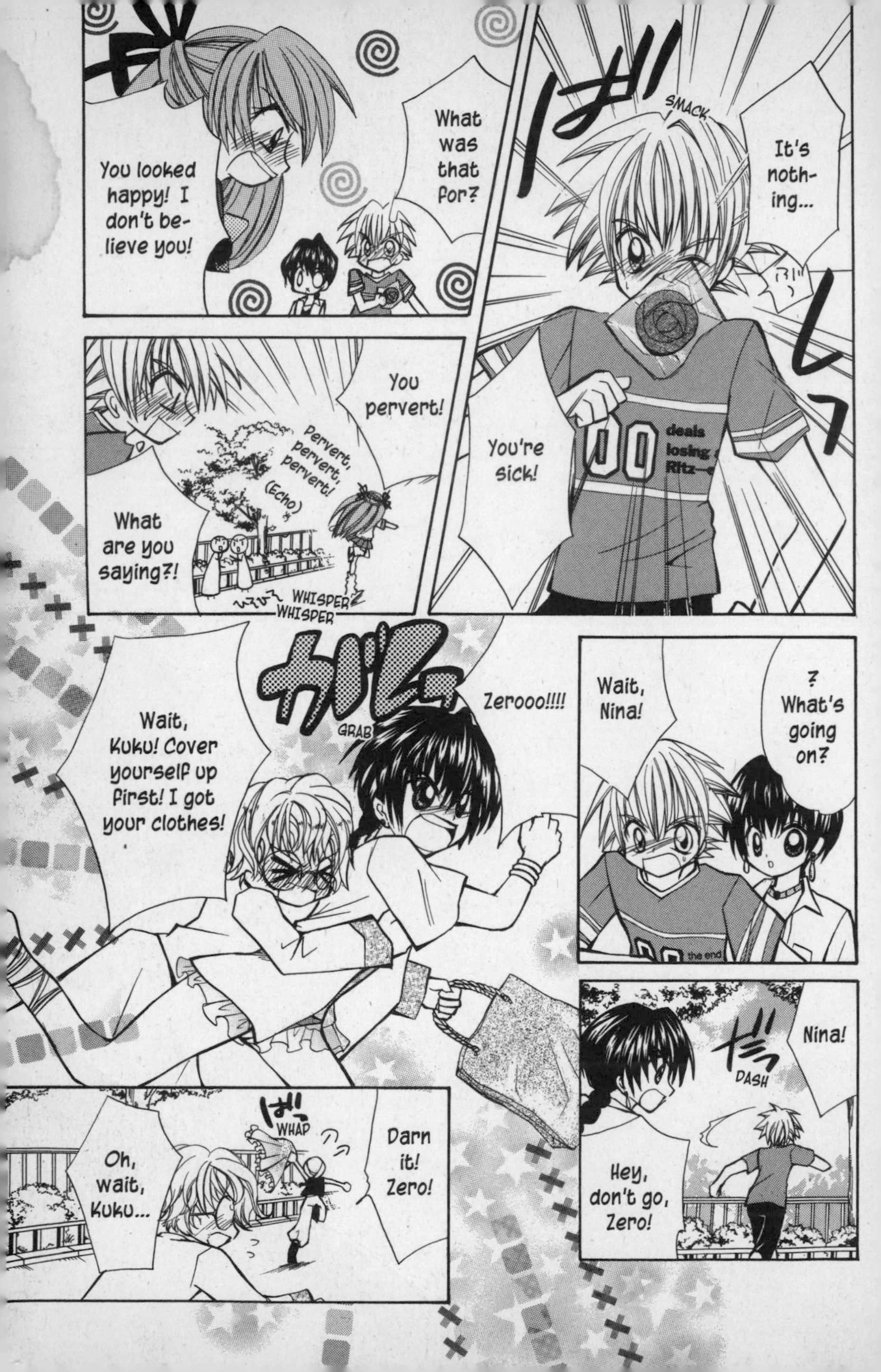

It's nothing...
SMACK
You're sick!
What was that for?
You looked happy! I don't believe you!
You pervert!
Pervert, pervert, pervert! (Echo)
What are you saying?!
WHISPER WHISPER
? What's going on?
Wait, Nina!
Nina!
DASH
Hey, don't go, Zero!
Zerooo!!!!
GRAB
Wait, Kuku! Cover yourself up first! I got your clothes!
Darn it! Zero!
WHAP
Oh, wait, Kuku...

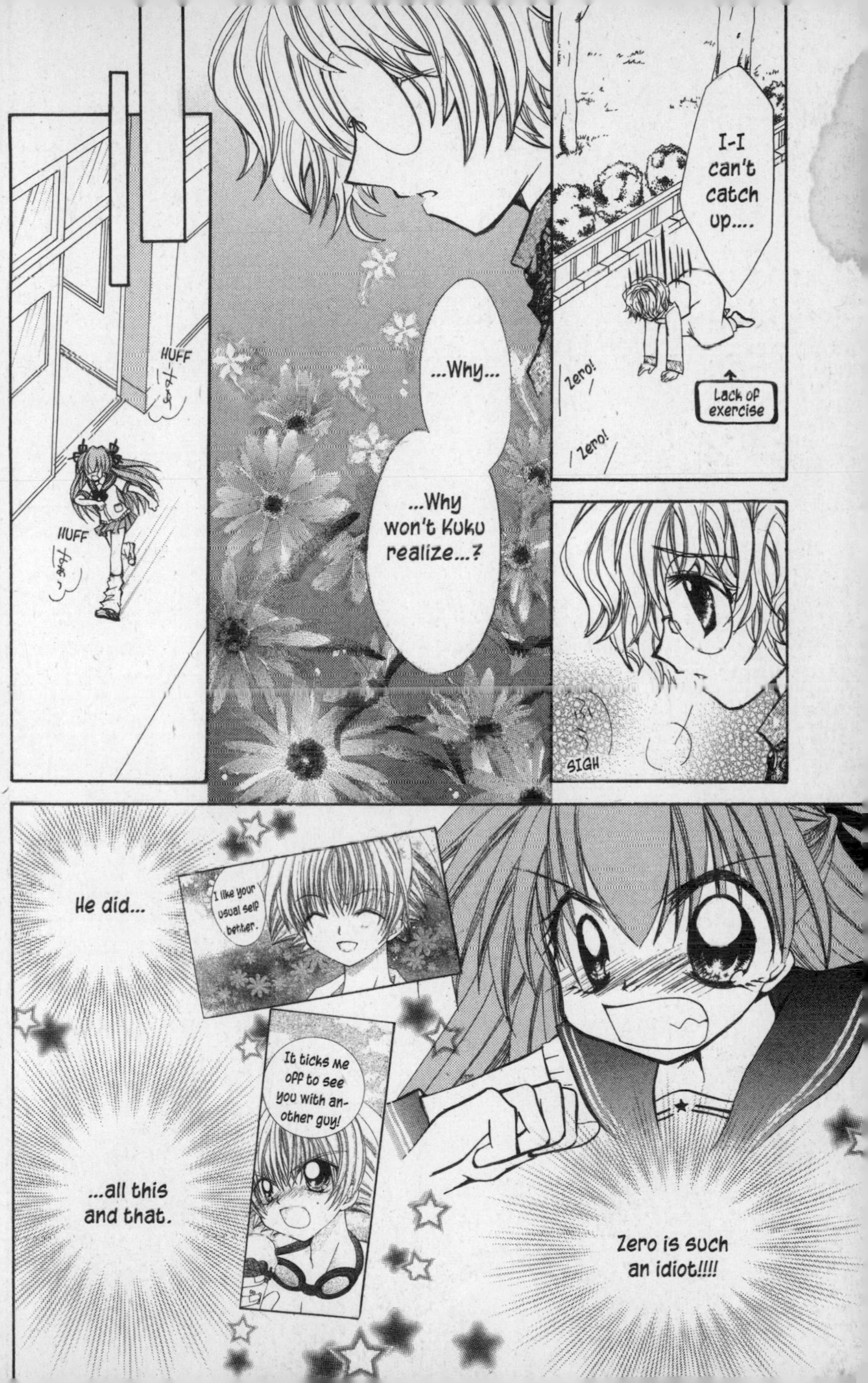
I-I can't catch up....
Lack of exercise
Zero!
Zero!
SIGH
...Why...
...Why won't Kuku realize...?
HUFF
HUFF
He did...
I like your usual self better.
It ticks me off to see you with an-other guy!
...all this and that.
Zero is such an idiot!!!!

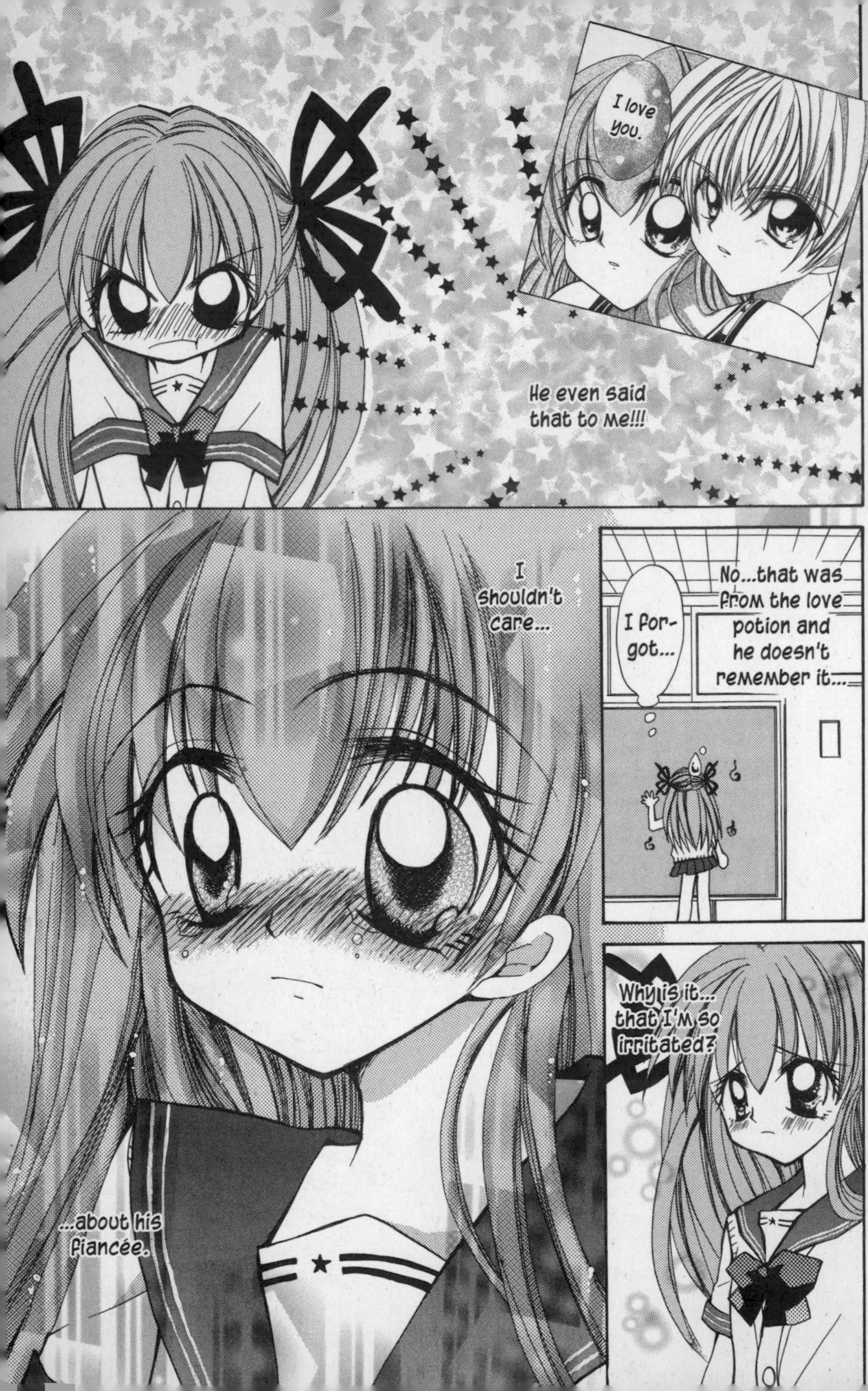
I love you.
He even said that to me!!!
No...that was from the love potion and he doesn't remember it...
I for-got...
Why is it... that I'm so irritated?
I shouldn't care...
...about his fiancée.

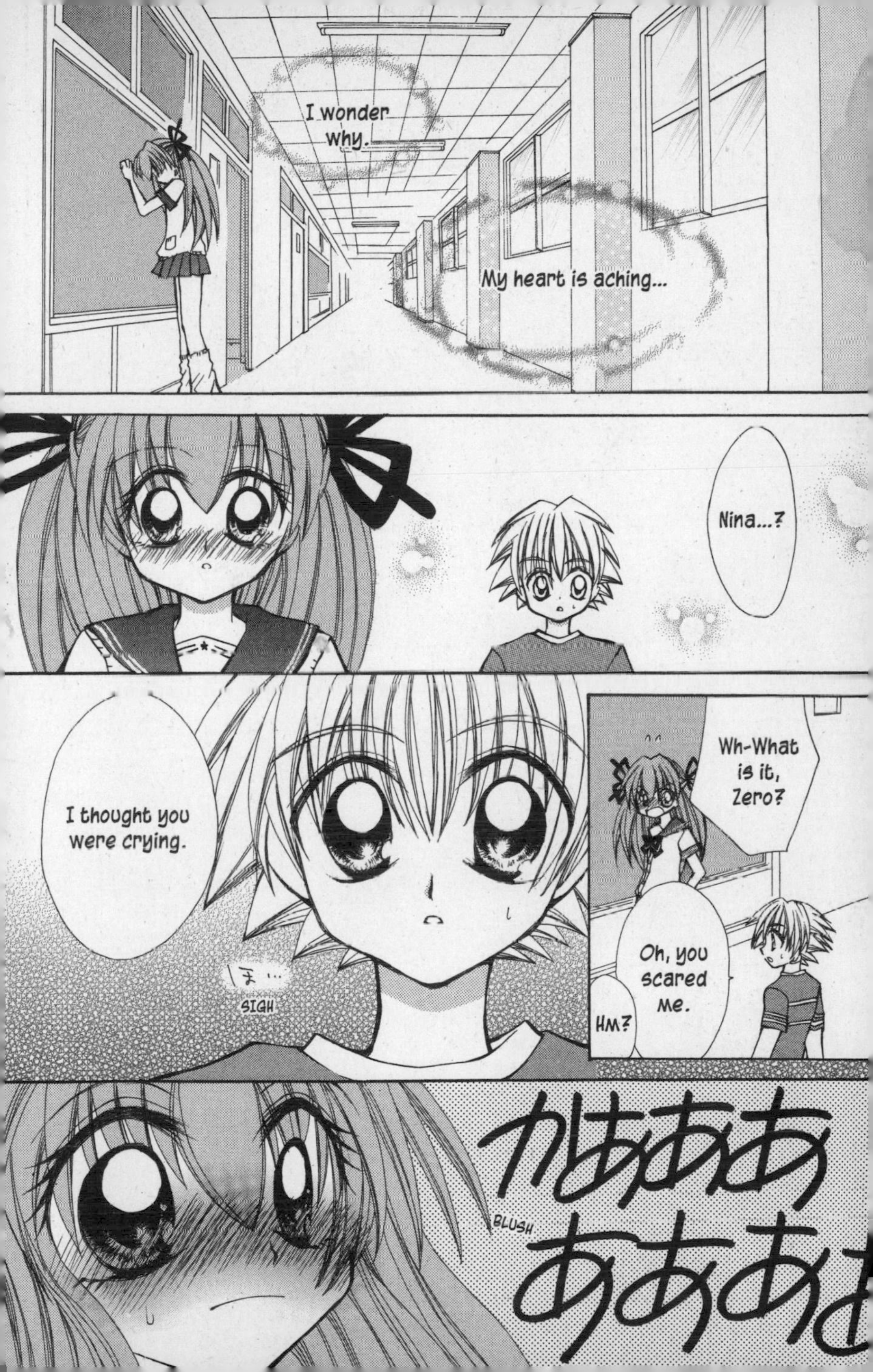
I wonder why.
My heart is aching...
Nina...?
Wh-What is it, Zero?
Oh, you scared me.
Hm?
I thought you were crying.
ほ…
SIGH
かあああ
ああああ
BLUSH

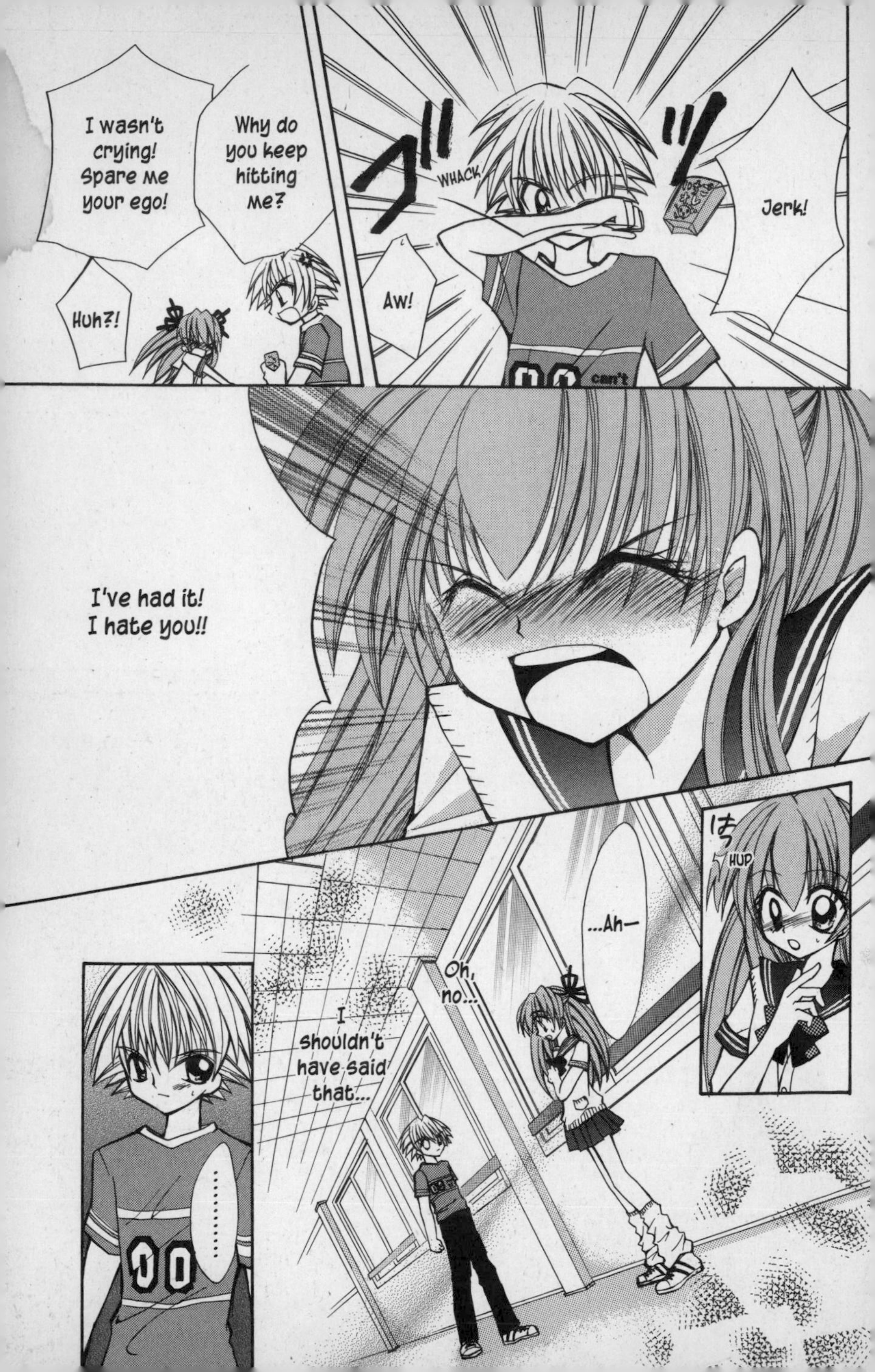
Jerk!
WHACK
Aw!
Why do you keep hitting me?
I wasn't crying! Spare me your ego!
Huh?!
I've had it! I hate you!!
HUP
...Ah—
Oh, no...
I shouldn't have said that...
....

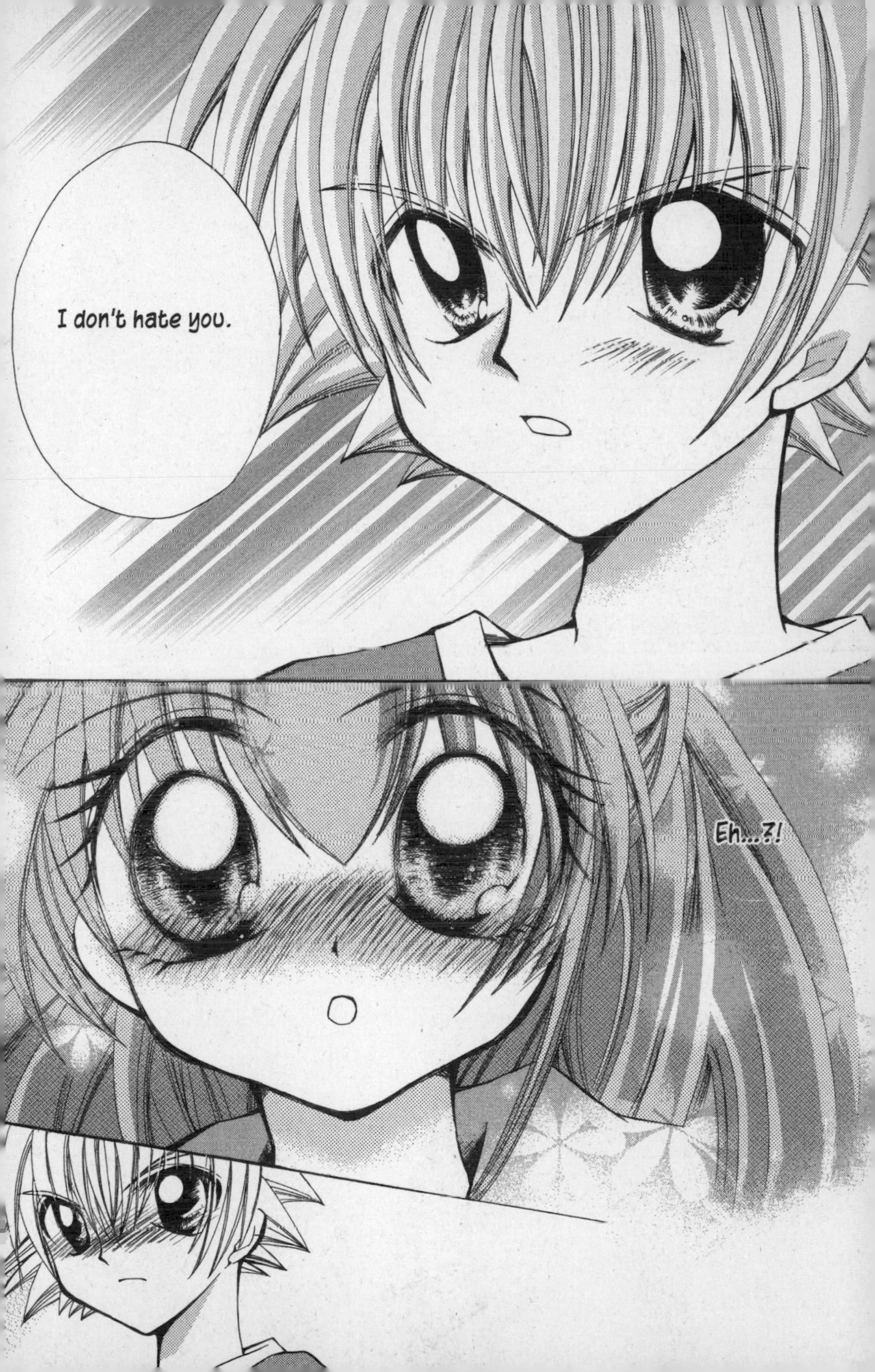
I don't hate you.
Eh...?!

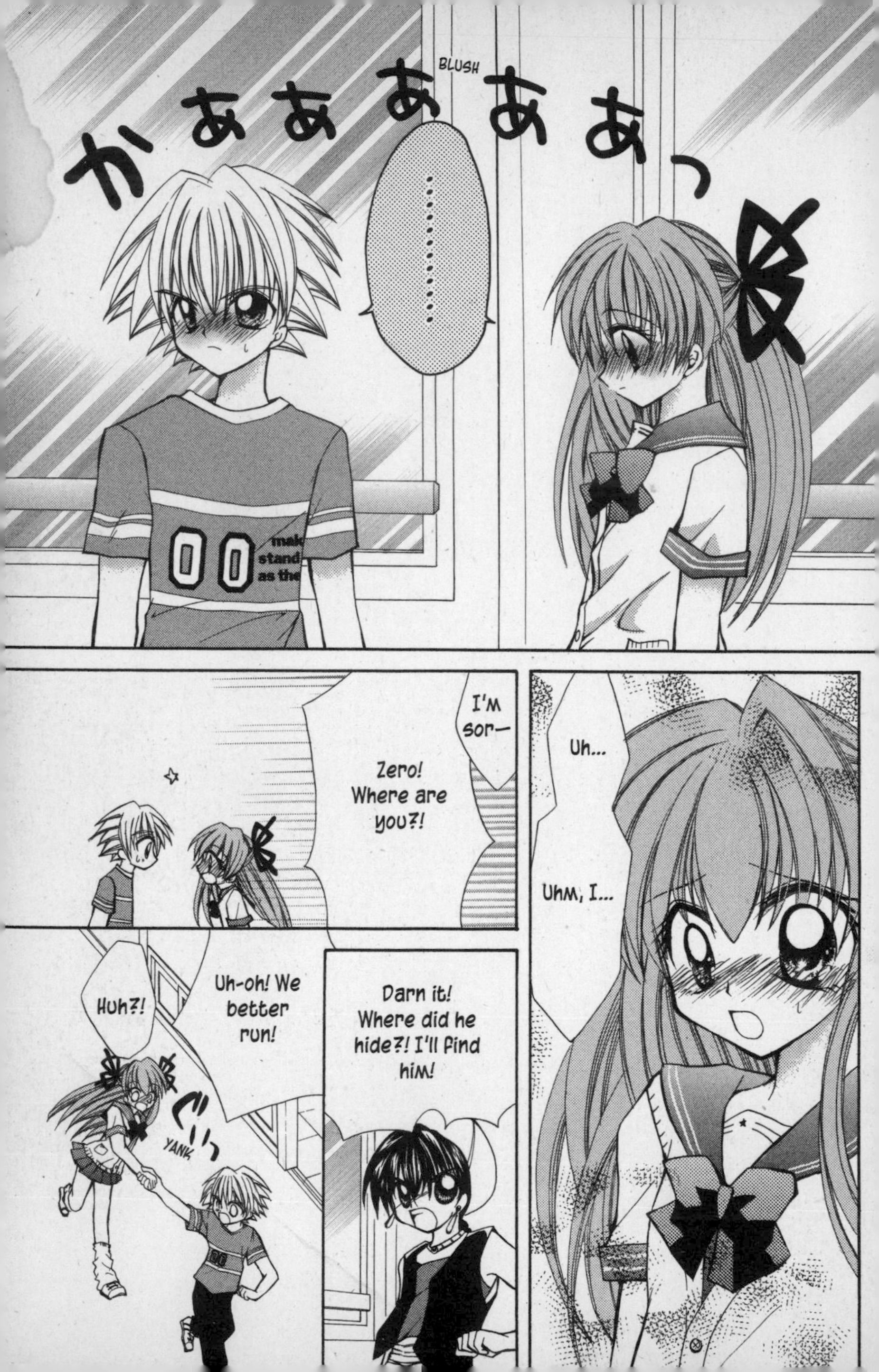
かぁぁぁぁぁぁっ
BLUSH
......
Uh...
Uhm, I...
I'm sor—
Zero! Where are you?!
Darn it! Where did he hide?! I'll find him!
Huh?!
Uh-oh! We better run!
YANK

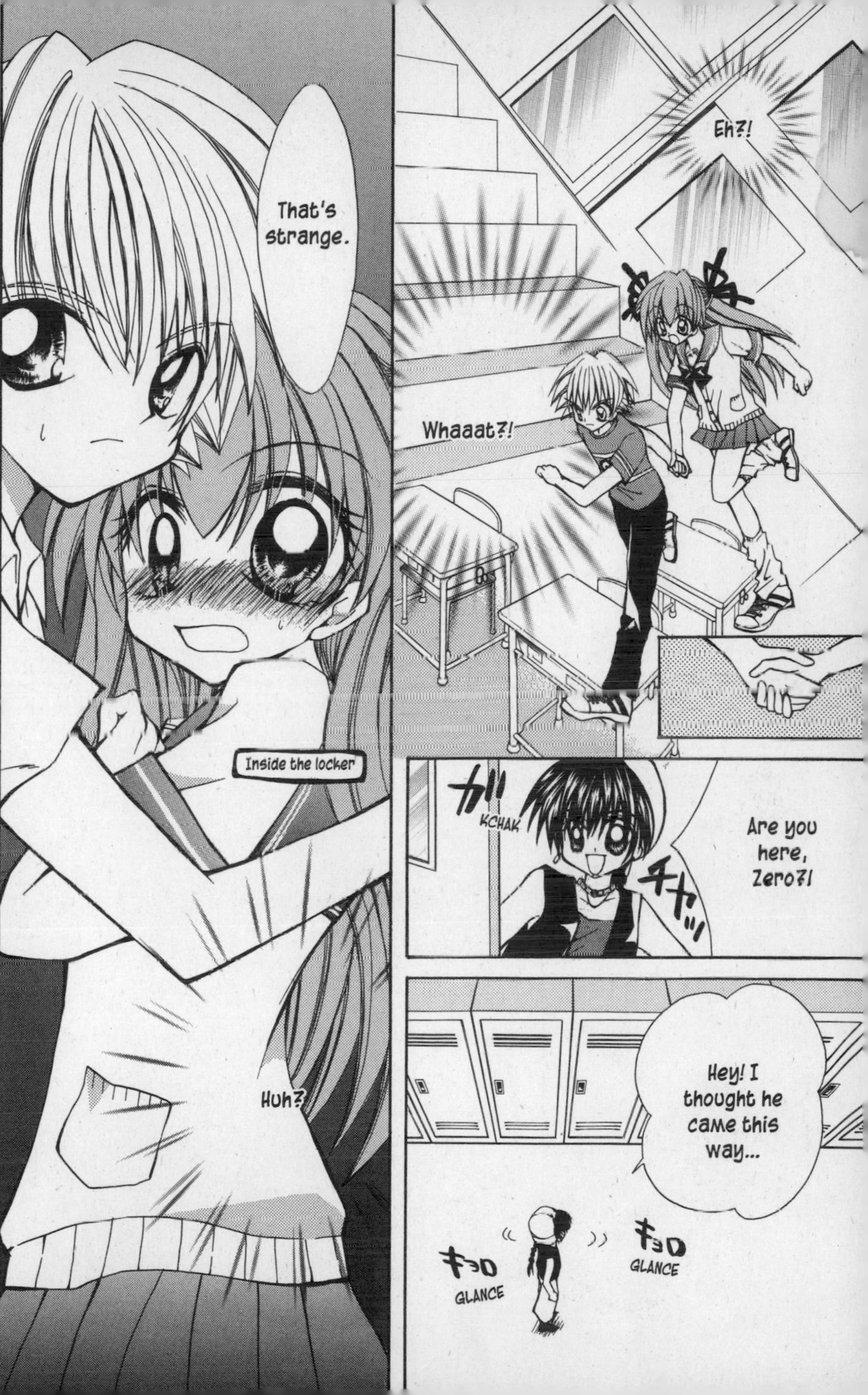
Eh?!
Whaaat?!
KCHAK
Are you here, Zero?!
Hey! I thought he came this way...
GLANCE
GLANCE
That's strange.
Inside the locker
Huh?

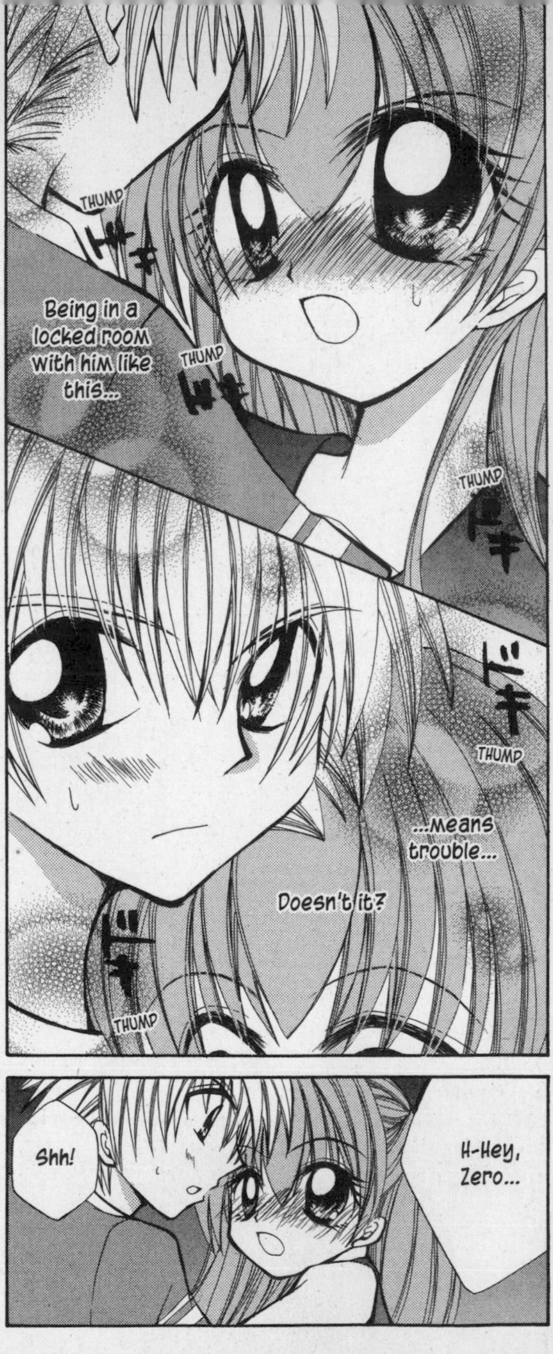
THUMP
Being in a locked room with him like this...
THUMP
THUMP
THUMP
...means trouble...
Doesn't it?
THUMP
H-Hey, Zero...
Shh!

The Secret of Her Braid

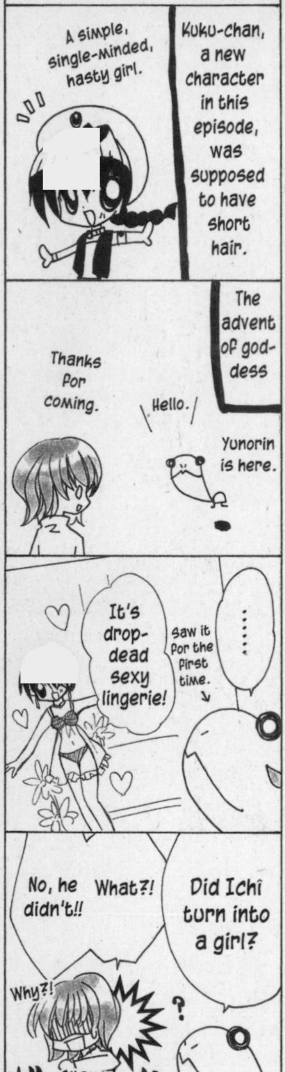
Kuku-chan, a new character in this episode, was supposed to have short hair.
A simple, single-minded, hasty girl.
The advent of god-dess
Yunorin is here.
Hello.
Thanks for coming.
......
Saw it for the first time.
It's drop-dead sexy lingerie!
Did Ichi turn into a girl?
What?!
No, he didn't!!
?
Why?!
SHOCK

So I added a braid on her later.

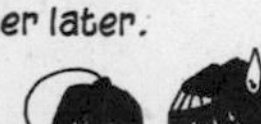
Identical?

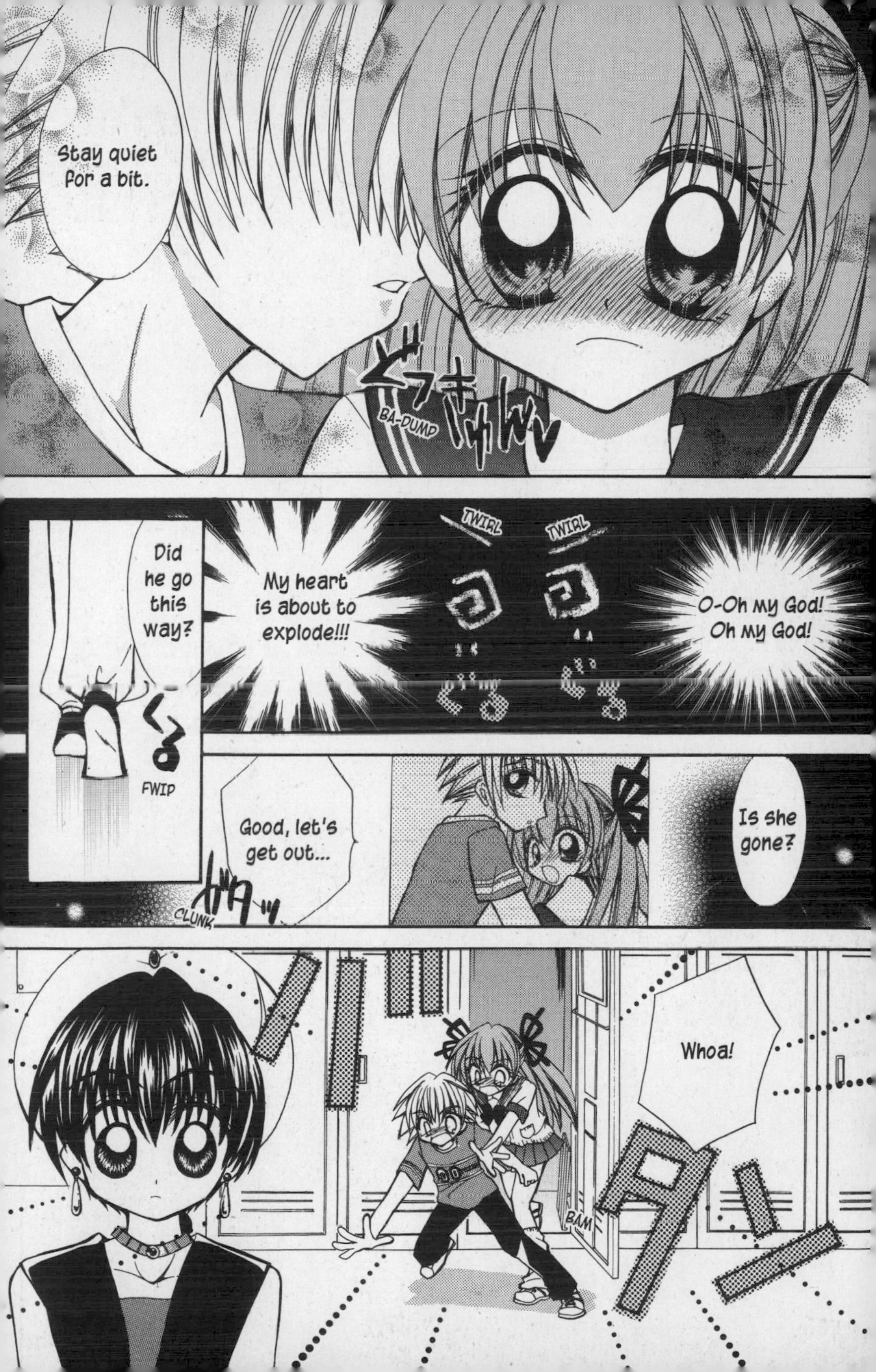
Stay quiet for a bit.
BA-DUMP
O-Oh my God! Oh my God!
TWIRL
TWIRL
My heart is about to explode!!!
Is she gone?
Good, let's get out...
CLUNK
Did he go this way?
FWIP
Whoa!
BAM

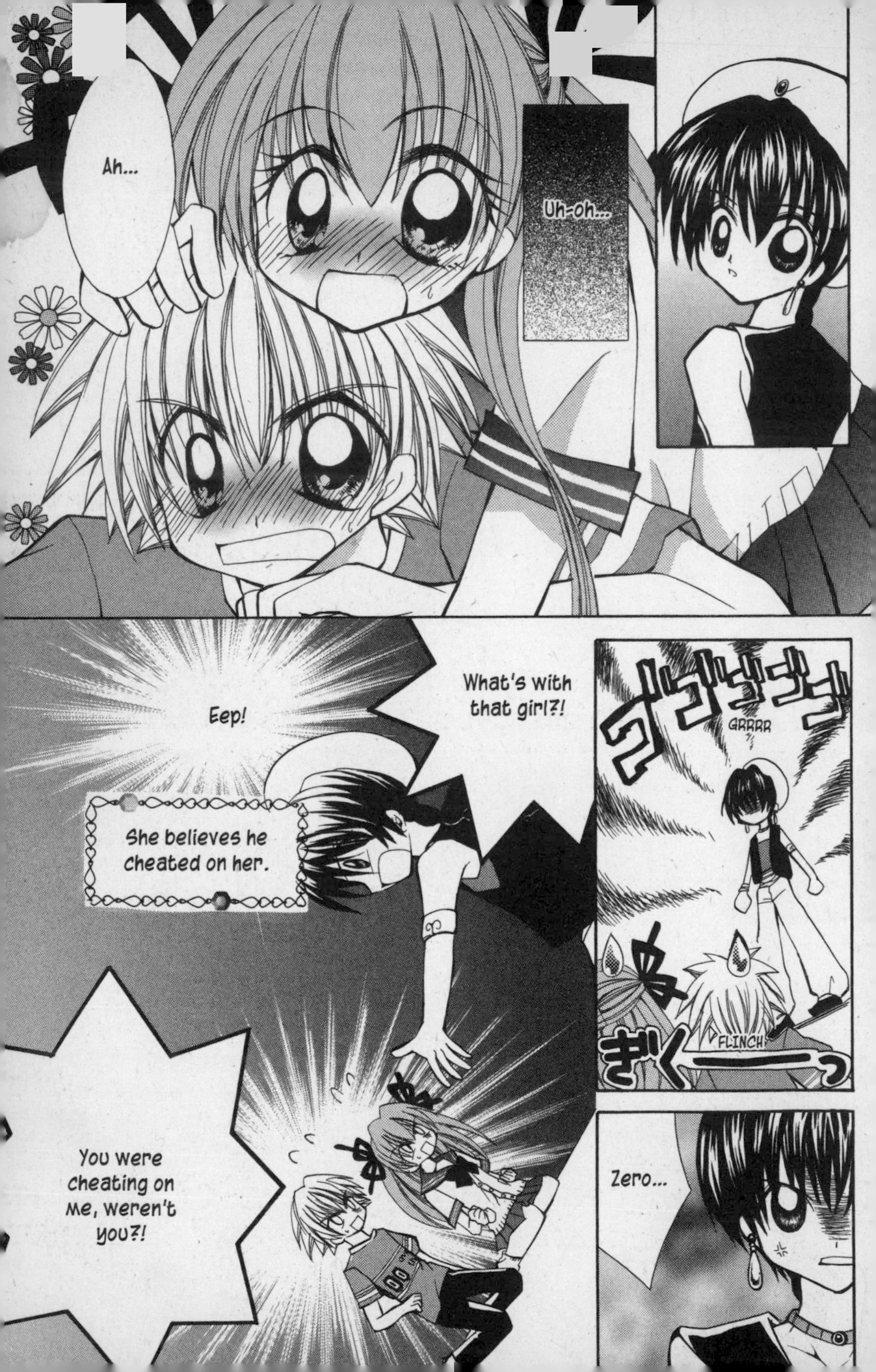
Uh-oh...
Ah...
GRRRR
ぎくーーっ
FLINCH
Zero...
What's with that girl?!
Eep!
She believes he cheated on her.
You were cheating on me, weren't you?!

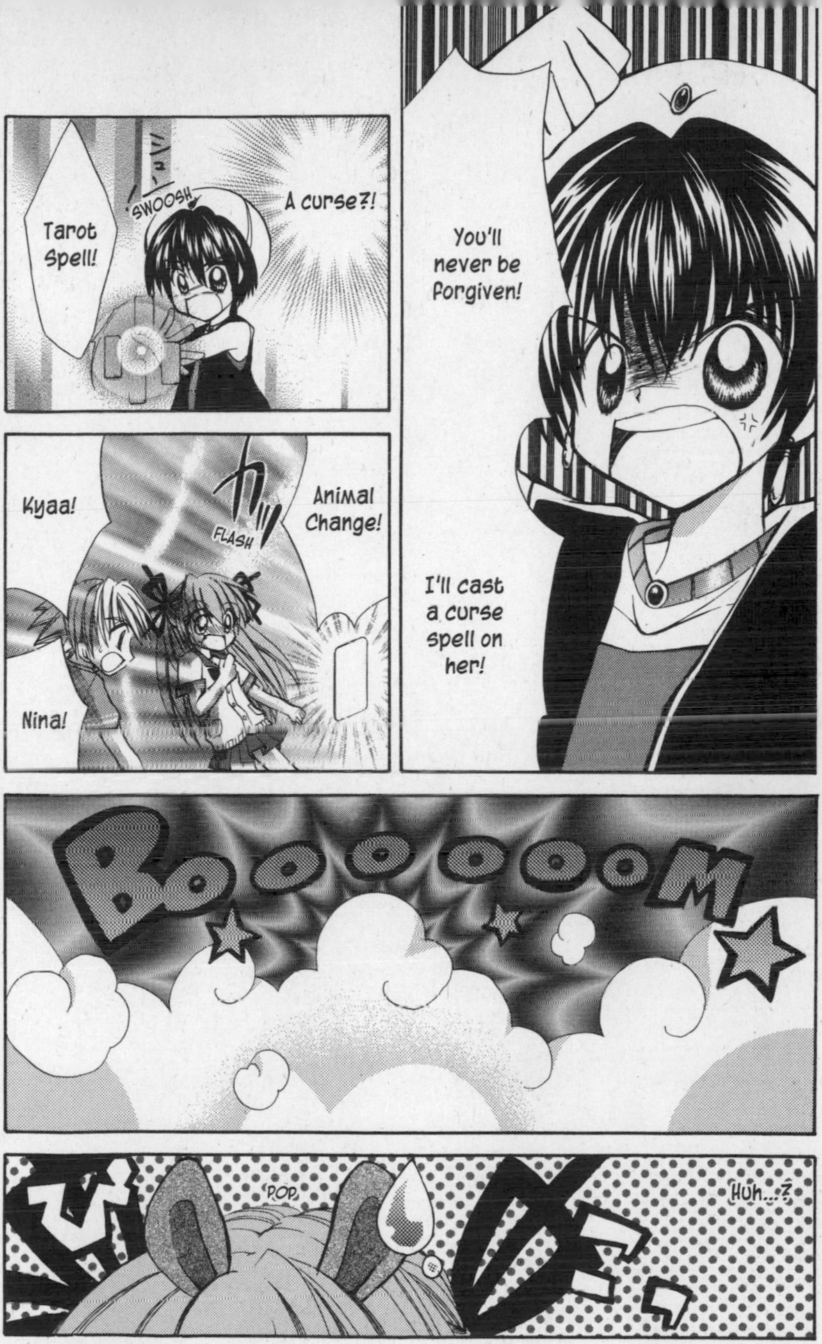
You'll never be forgiven!
I'll cast a curse spell on her!
A curse?!
SWOOSH
Tarot Spell!
Animal Change!
FLASH
Kyaa!
Nina!
BOOOOOOM
Huh...?
POP

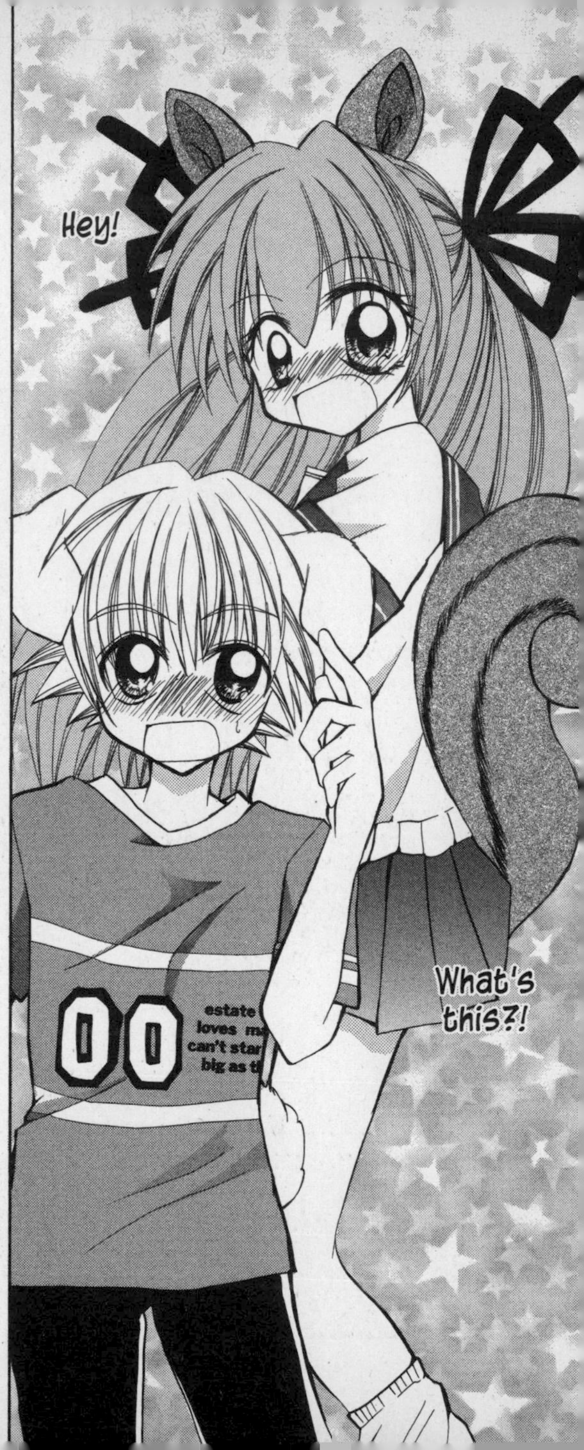
What's this?!
Hey!

Data 4
* Sun *

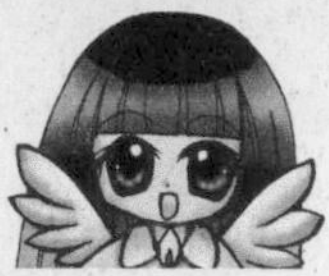

Name:	Sun
Birthday:	February 29th
Blood Type:	B
Height:	148 cm*
Favorite Food:	For-chan's cookies/cakes
Least Favorite Food:	None
Weak Point:	Grandfather
Treasure:	For-chan
Hobbies:	Making For-chan cross-dress
Special Talent:	Summoning spell
Favorite Type of Boy:	For-chan
Remarks:	Has a huge appetite.

*4'10"

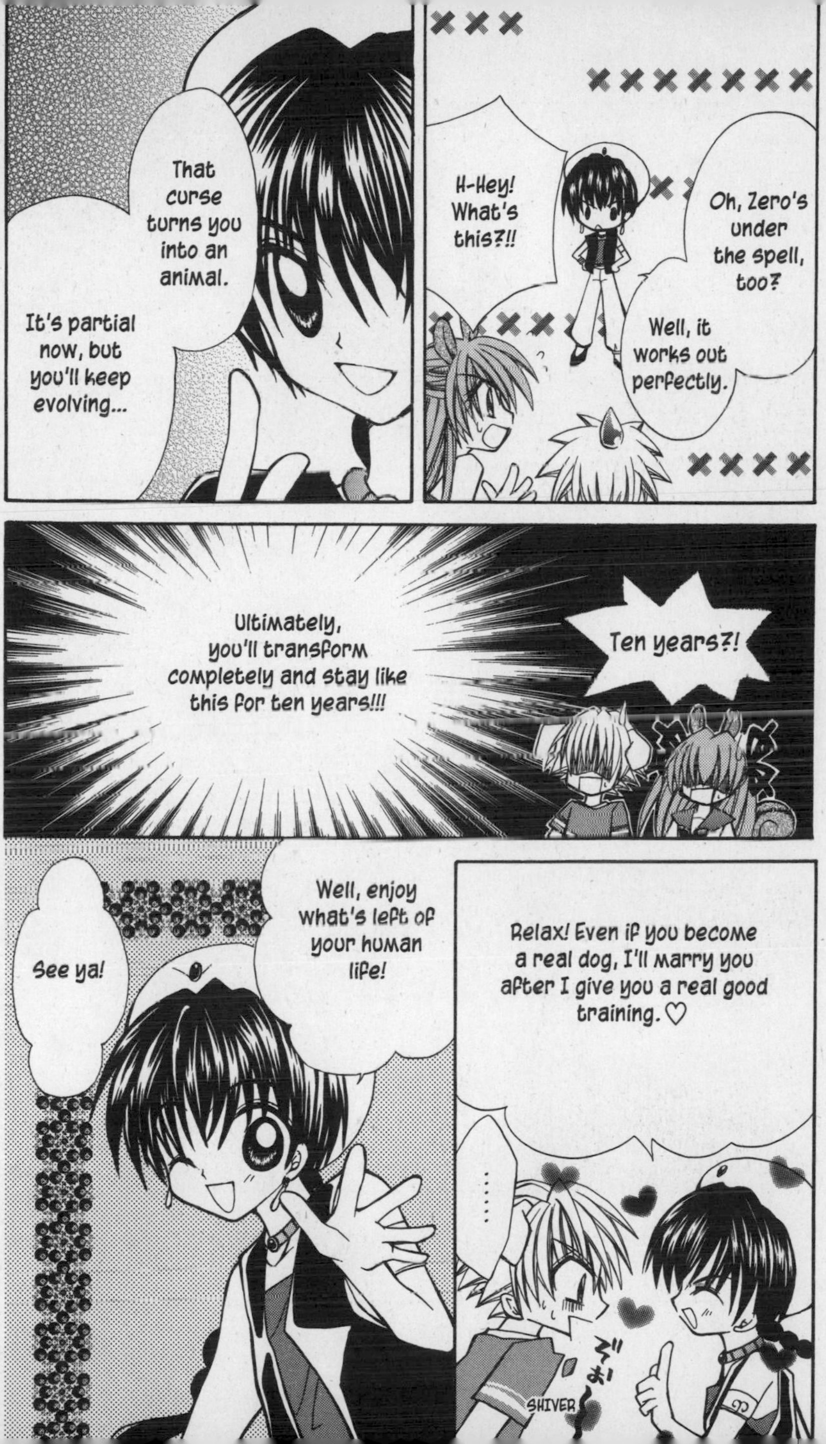
Oh, Zero's under the spell, too?
H-Hey! What's this?!!
Well, it works out perfectly.
That curse turns you into an animal.
It's partial now, but you'll keep evolving...
Ultimately, you'll transform completely and stay like this for ten years!!!
Ten years?!
Relax! Even if you become a real dog, I'll marry you after I give you a real good training. ♡
......
SHIVER
Well, enjoy what's left of your human life!
See ya!

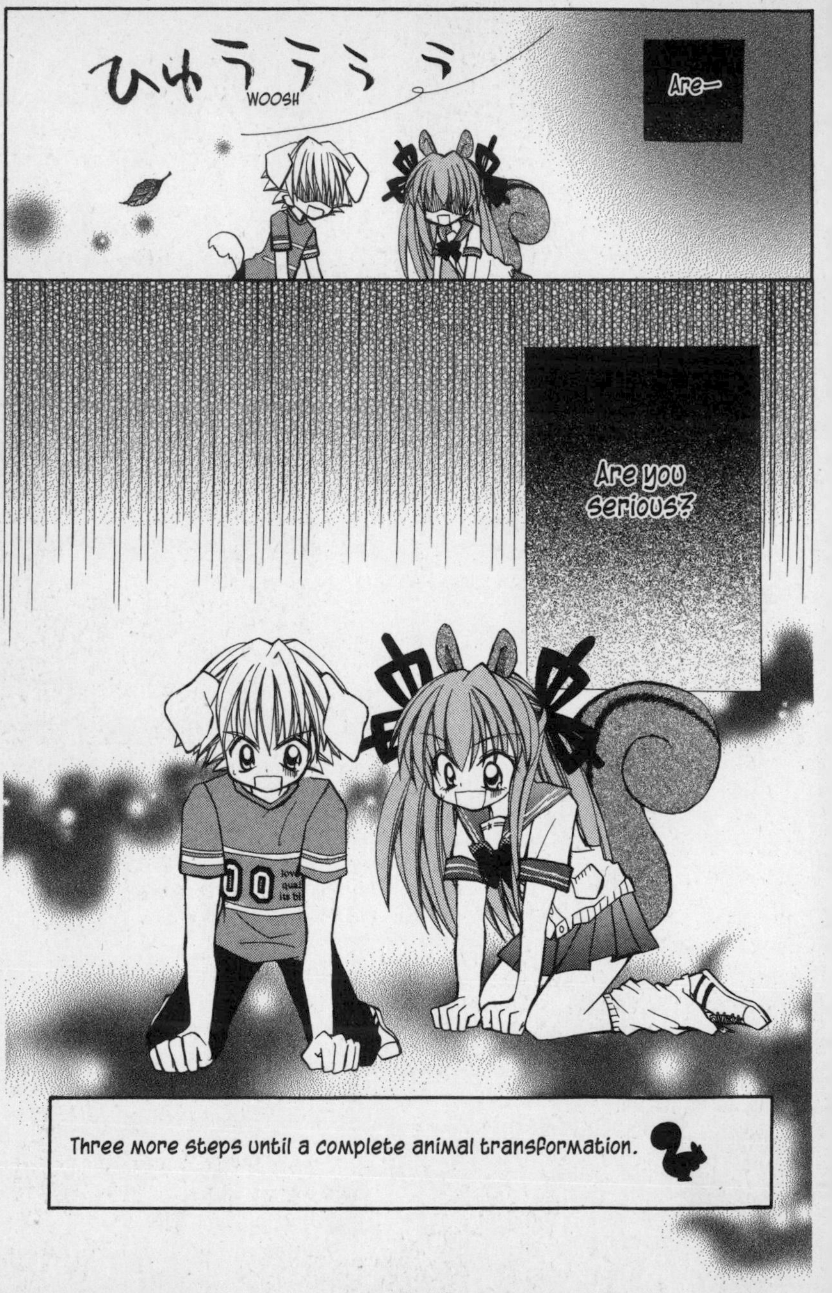
Are—
ひゅラララ
WOOSH
Are you serious?
Three more steps until a complete animal transformation.

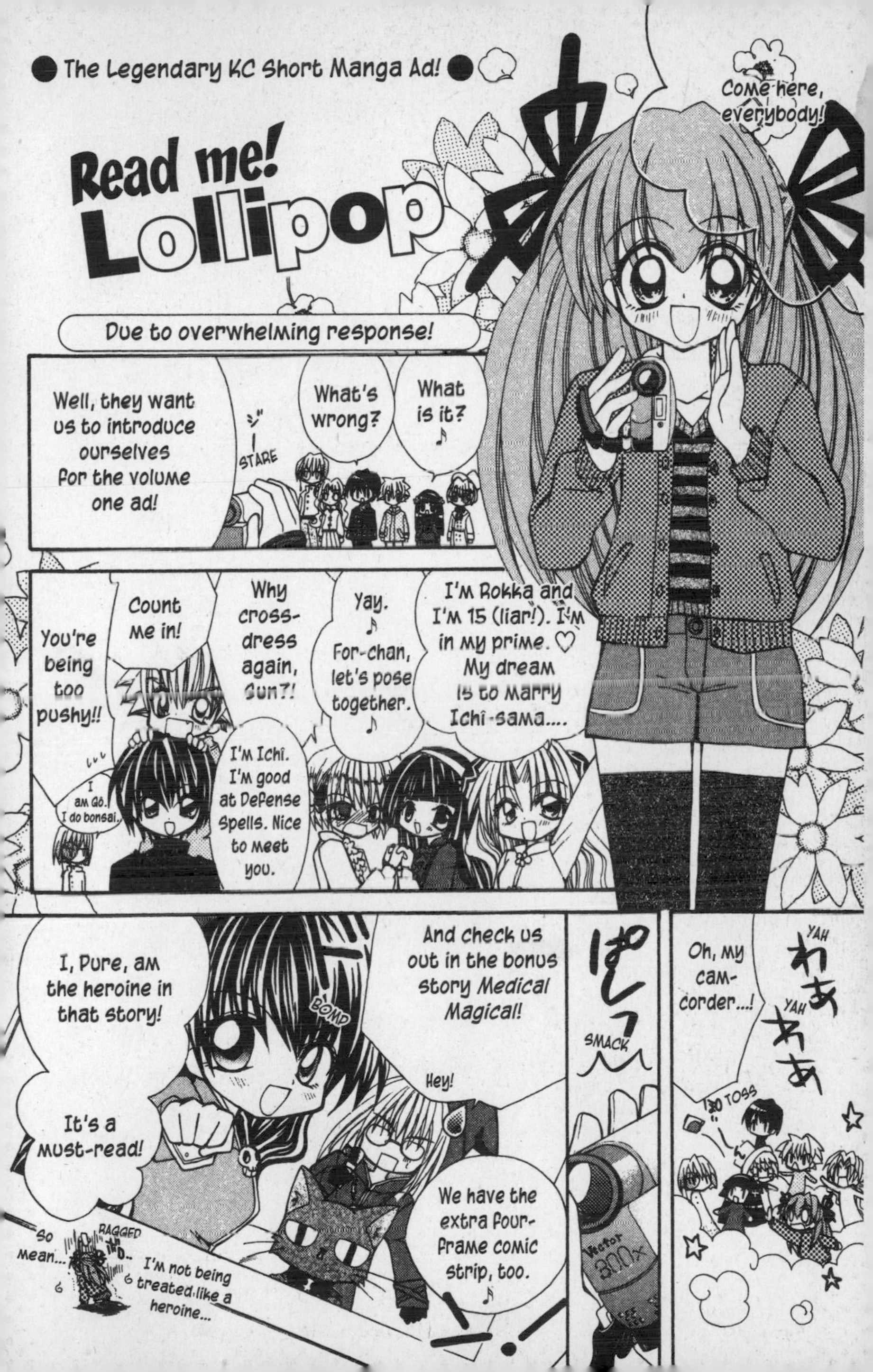
The Legendary KC Short Manga Ad!
Come here, everybody!
Read me! Lollipop
Due to overwhelming response!
What is it? ♪
What's wrong?
STARE
Well, they want us to introduce ourselves for the volume one ad!
I'm Rokka and I'm 15 (liar!). I'm in my prime. ♡ My dream is to marry Ichi-sama....
Yay. ♪ For-chan, let's pose together. ♪
Why cross-dress again, Sun?!
Count me in!
I'm Ichi. I'm good at Defense Spells. Nice to meet you.
You're being too pushy!!
I am Gô. I do bonsai.
Oh, my camcorder...!
わあ YAH
わあ YAH
TOSS
ぱしっ
SMACK
And check us out in the bonus story Medical Magical!
I, Pure, am the heroine in that story!
BOMP
Hey!
It's a must-read!
We have the extra four-frame comic strip, too. ♪
So mean...
RAGGED
I'm not being treated like a heroine...

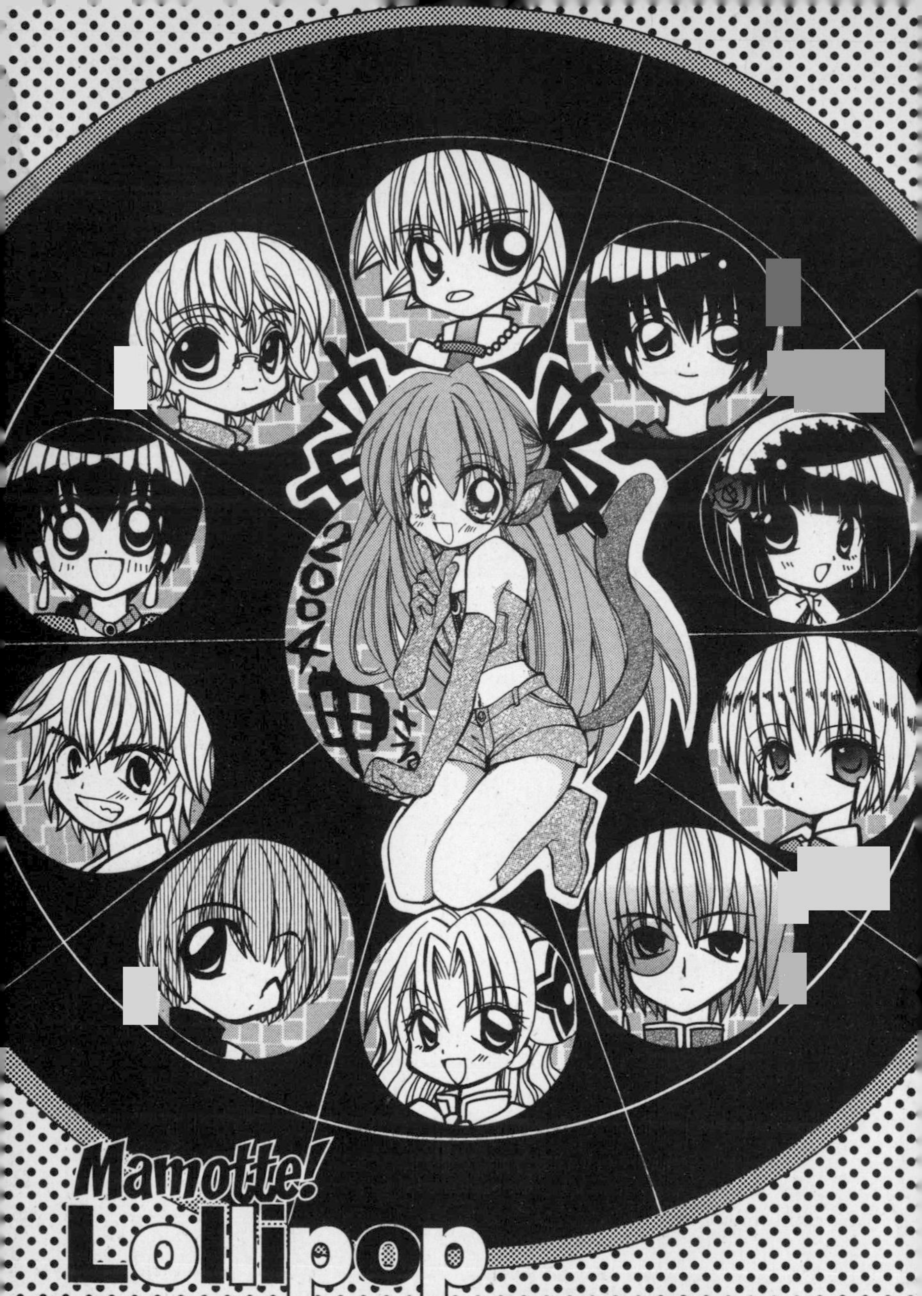

Mamotte! Lollipop

POP 12: Feeling Like An Animal Is Awesome?!

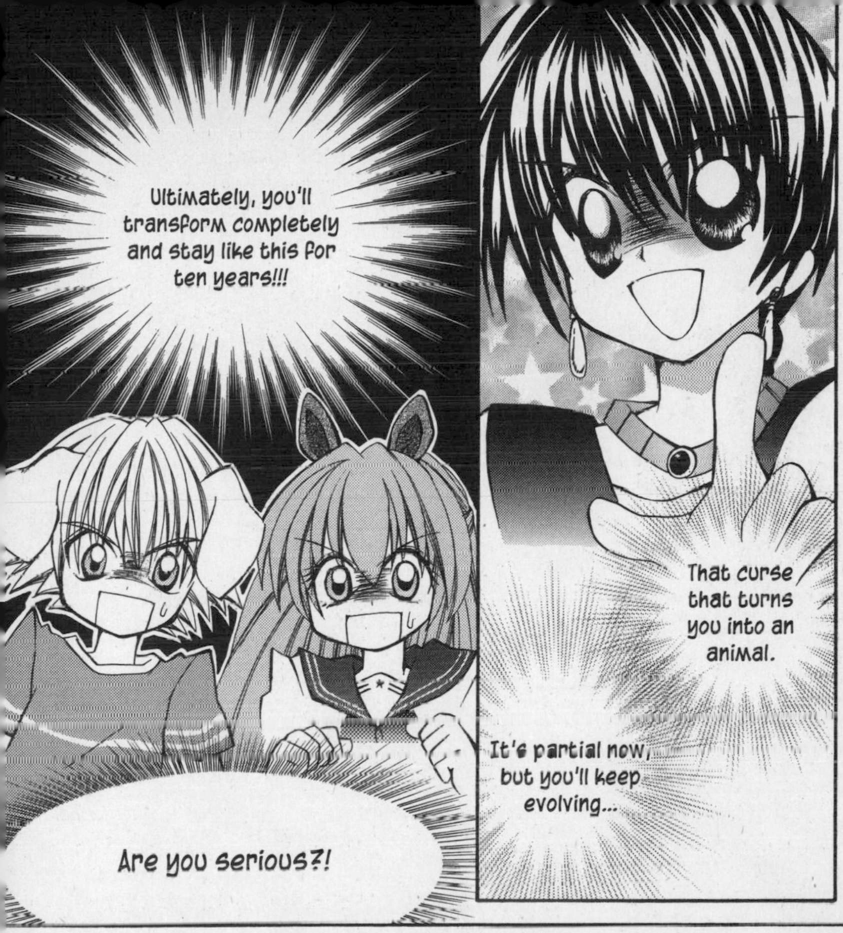
That curse that turns you into an animal.
It's partial now, but you'll keep evolving...
Ultimately, you'll transform completely and stay like this for ten years!!!
Are you serious?!

POP12 Feeling Like An Animal Is Awesome?!

I tried to make this cover page look like a New Year's greeting card, since it was the New Year. If I had another examinee, I could have dressed everyone up as the twelve zodiac signs. So close! I like Nina and Zero as a squirrel and a dog. I heard Zero resembles my assistant's dog and everyone often calls him by that name, Sora. I guess he is like a dog. Actually, Nina and Zero embarrass me in this episode . . . (Laughs) When will Nina be able to kiss someone?? Kuku becoming a maidenly girl was unexpected.

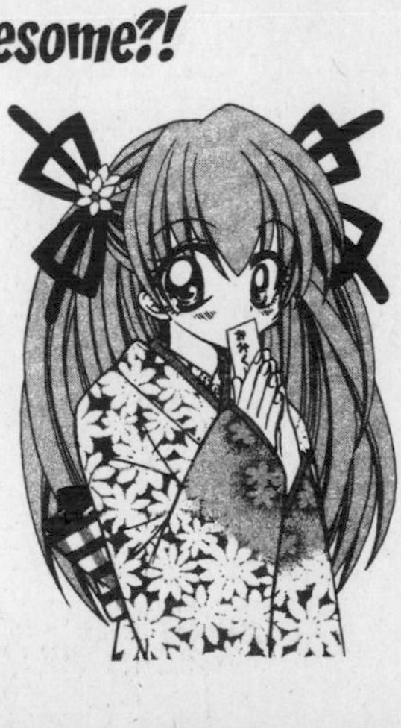

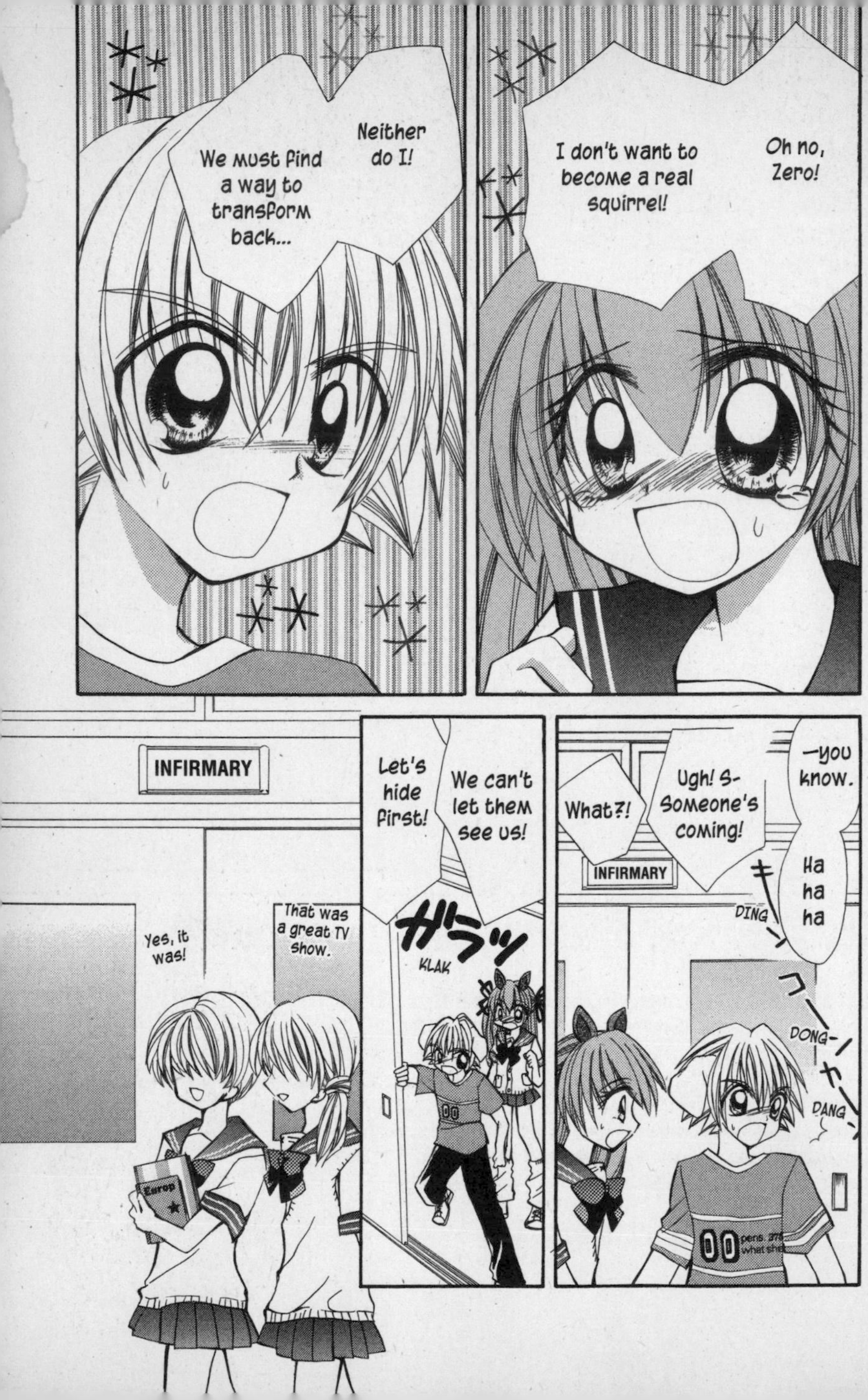
Oh no, Zero!
I don't want to become a real squirrel!
Neither do I!
We must find a way to transform back...
—you know.
Ha ha ha
DING
DONG
DANG
Ugh! S-Someone's coming!
What?!
INFIRMARY
We can't let them see us!
Let's hide first!
KLAK
INFIRMARY
That was a great TV show.
Yes, it was!
Europ

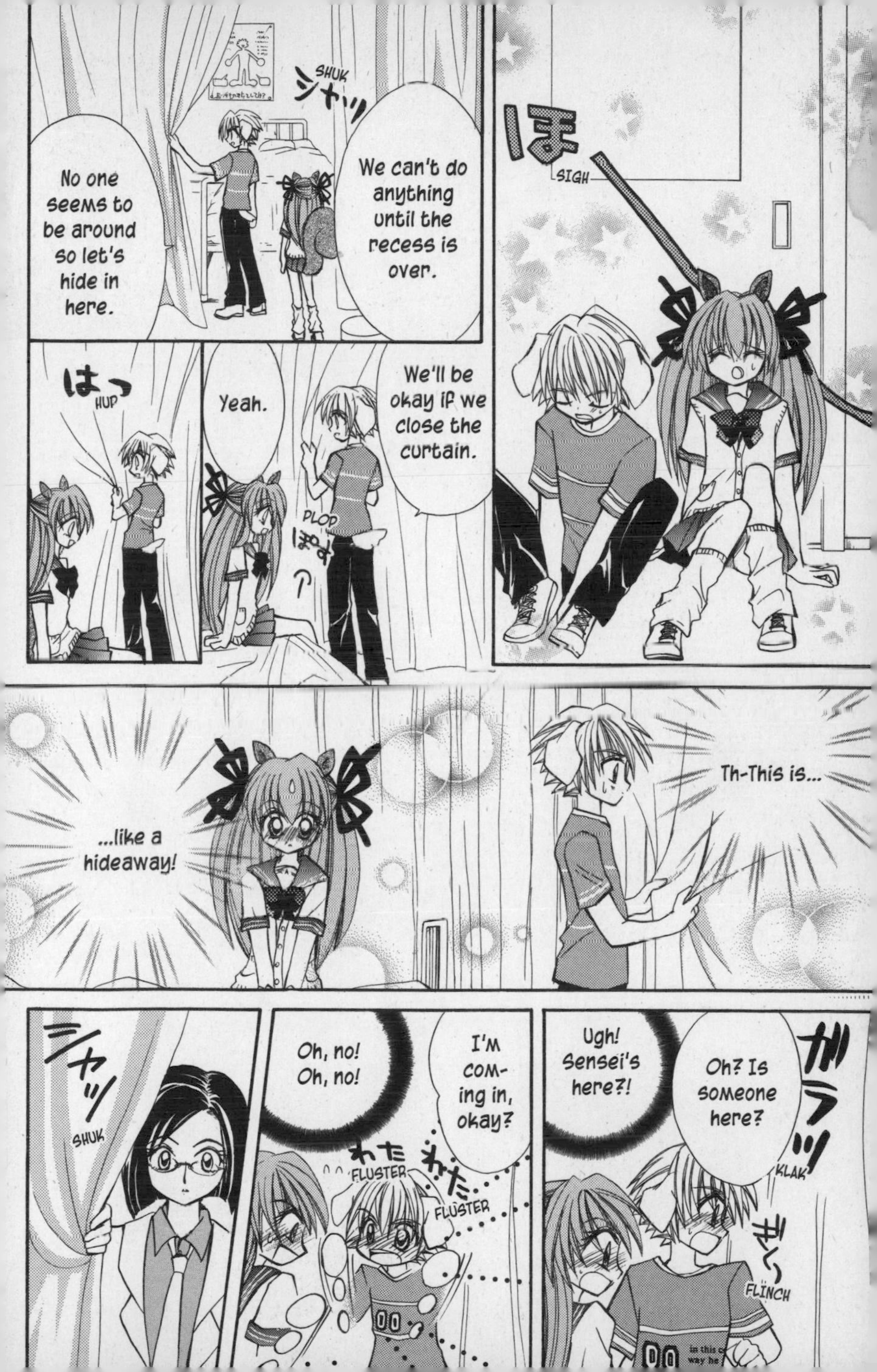
ほ
SIGH
シャッ
SHUK
We can't do anything until the recess is over.
No one seems to be around so let's hide in here.
We'll be okay if we close the curtain.
Yeah.
ぽす
PLOP
はっ
HUP
Th-This is...
...like a hideaway!
ガラッ
KLAK
Oh? Is someone here?
Ugh! Sensei's here?!
ぎくっ
FLINCH
I'M COMING in, okay?
Oh, no! Oh, no!
わた
FLUSTER
わた
FLUSTER
シャッ
SHUK

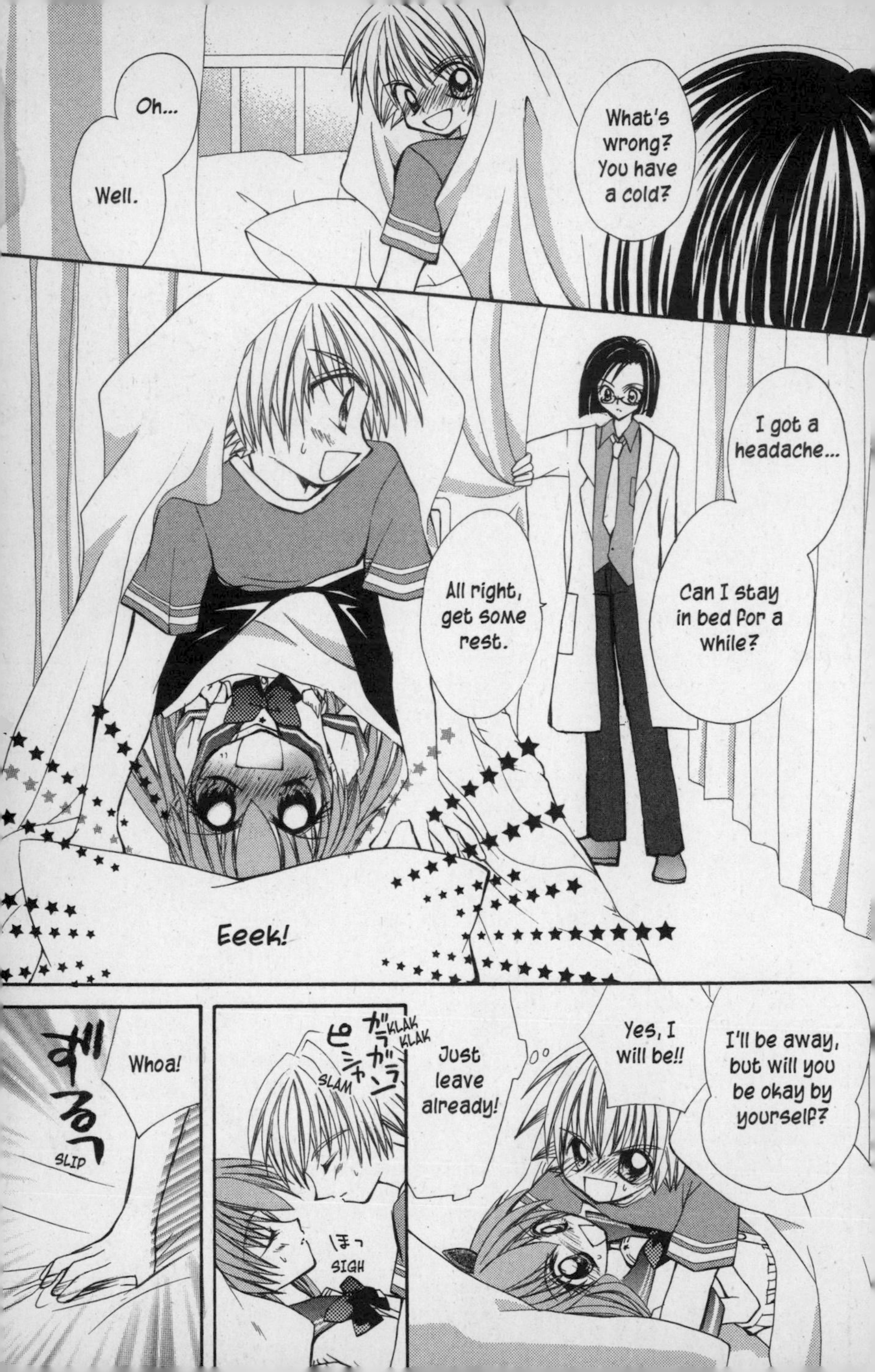
What's wrong? You have a cold?
Oh...
Well.
I got a headache...
Can I stay in bed for a while?
All right, get some rest.
Eeek!
I'll be away, but will you be okay by yourself?
Yes, I will be!!
Just leave already!
ガラガラ
KLAK KLAK
ピシャン
SLAM
ほっ
SIGH
Whoa!
ずるっ
SLIP

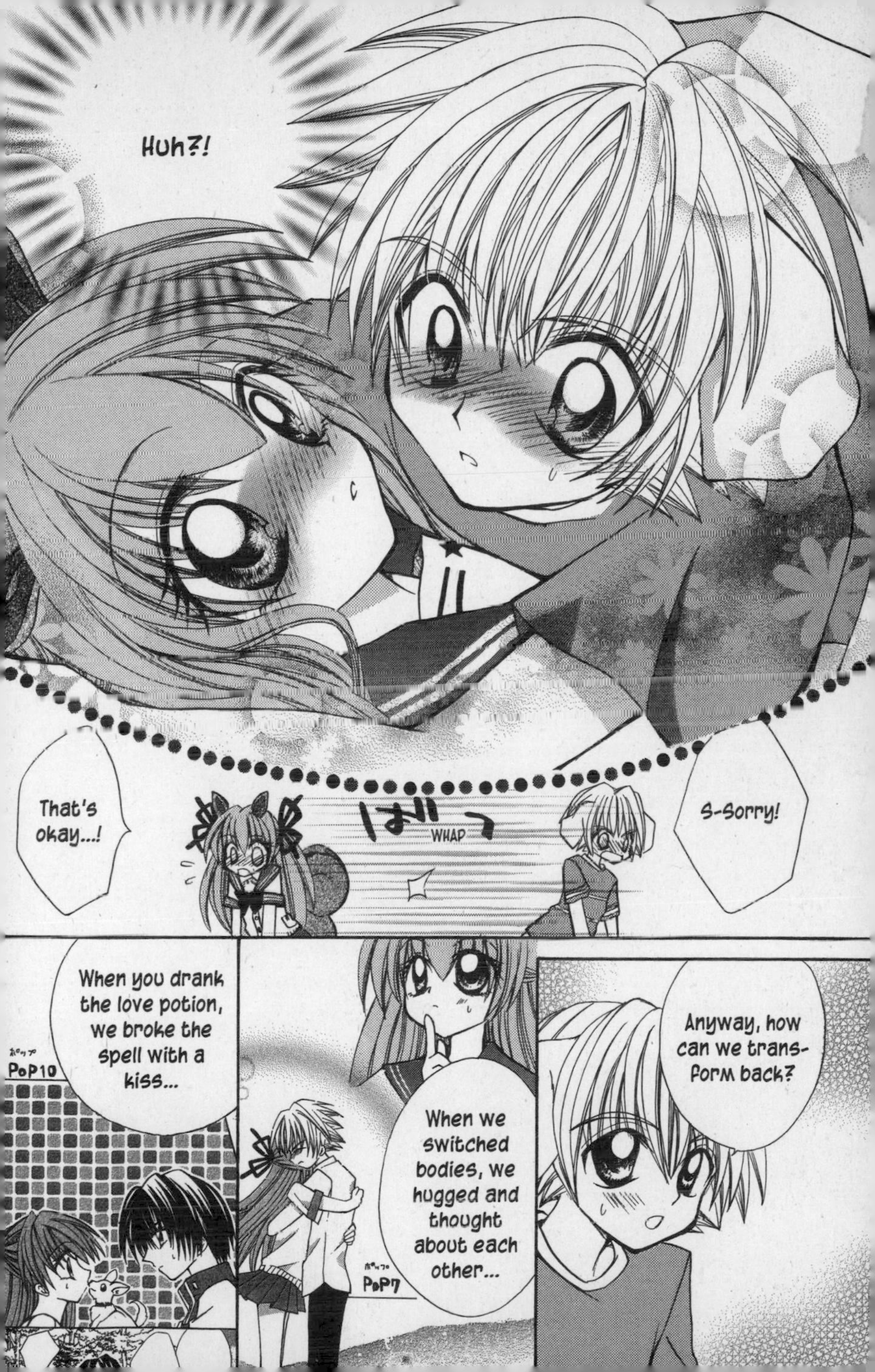
HUH?!
S-Sorry!
ばっ
WHAP
That's okay...!
Anyway, how can we transform back?
When we switched bodies, we hugged and thought about each other...
POP7
When you drank the love potion, we broke the spell with a kiss...
POP10

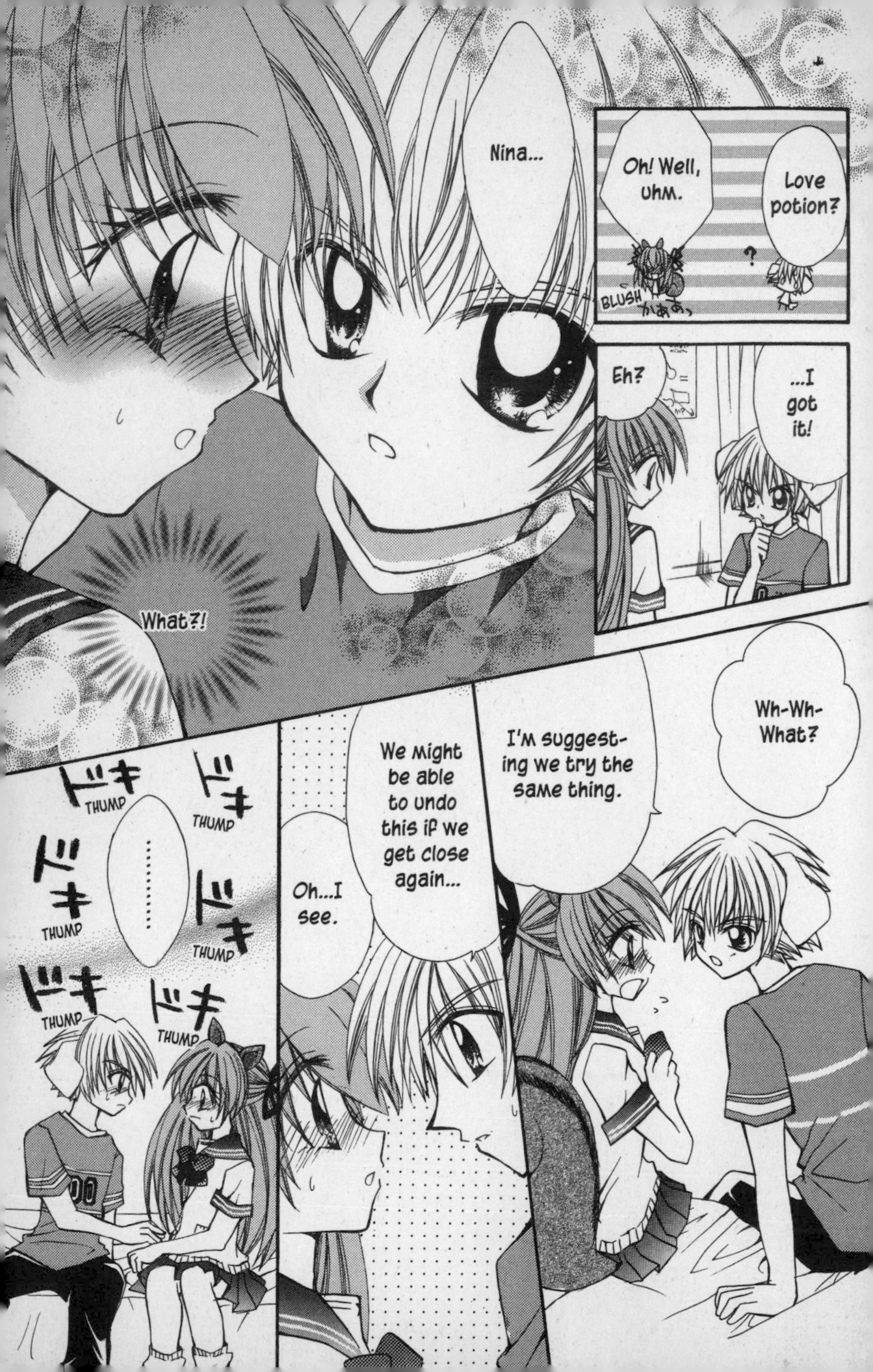
Love potion?
Oh! Well, uhm.
BLUSH
...I got it!
Eh?
Nina...
What?!
Wh-Wh-What?
I'm suggest-ing we try the same thing.
We might be able to undo this if we get close again...
Oh...I see.
ドキ THUMP
ドキ THUMP
......
ドキ THUMP
ドキ THUMP
ドキ THUMP
ドキ THUMP

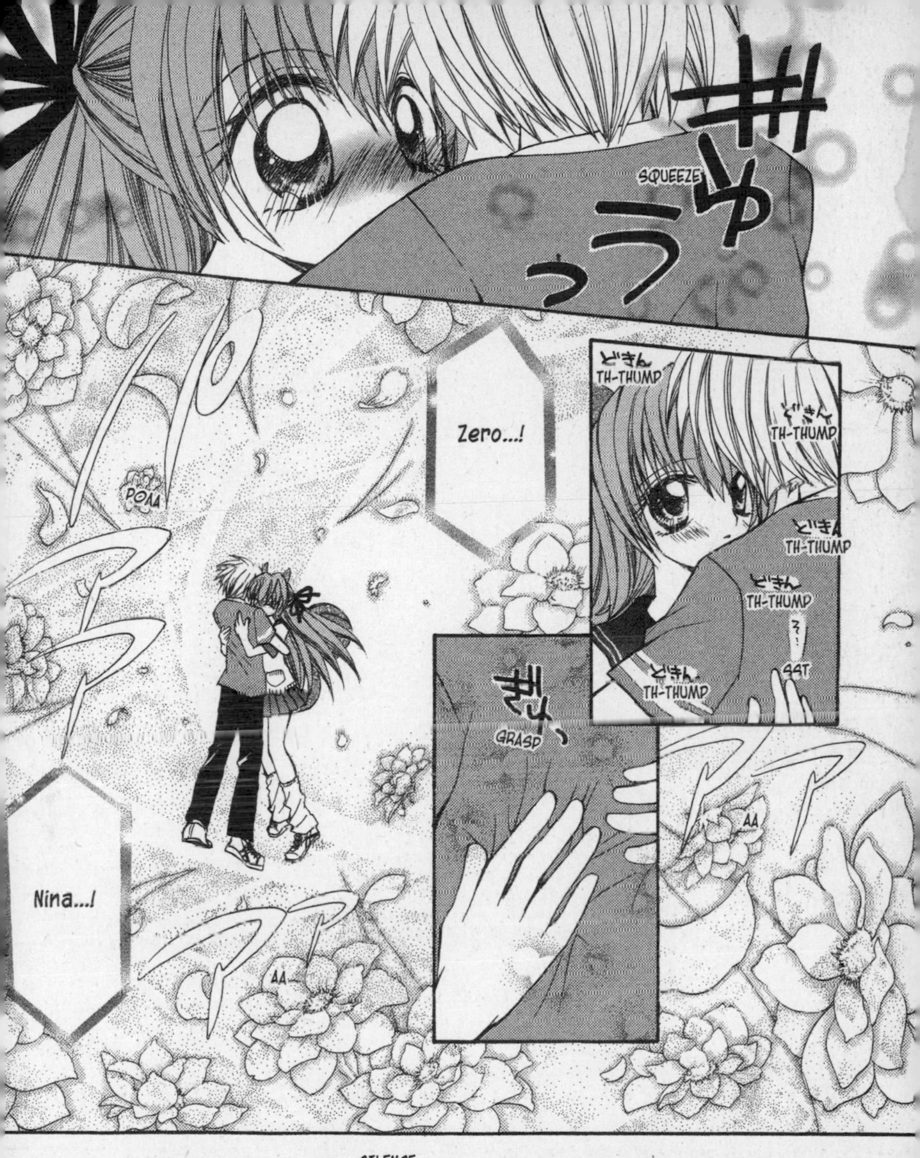
ぎゅうっ
SQUEEZE
どきん
TH-THUMP
どきん
TH-THUMP
どきん
TH-THUMP
どきん
TH-THUMP
どきん
TH-THUMP
そ…
SST
ぎゅ
GRASP
Zero...!
POAA
AA
AA
Nina...!
SILENCE
しーん

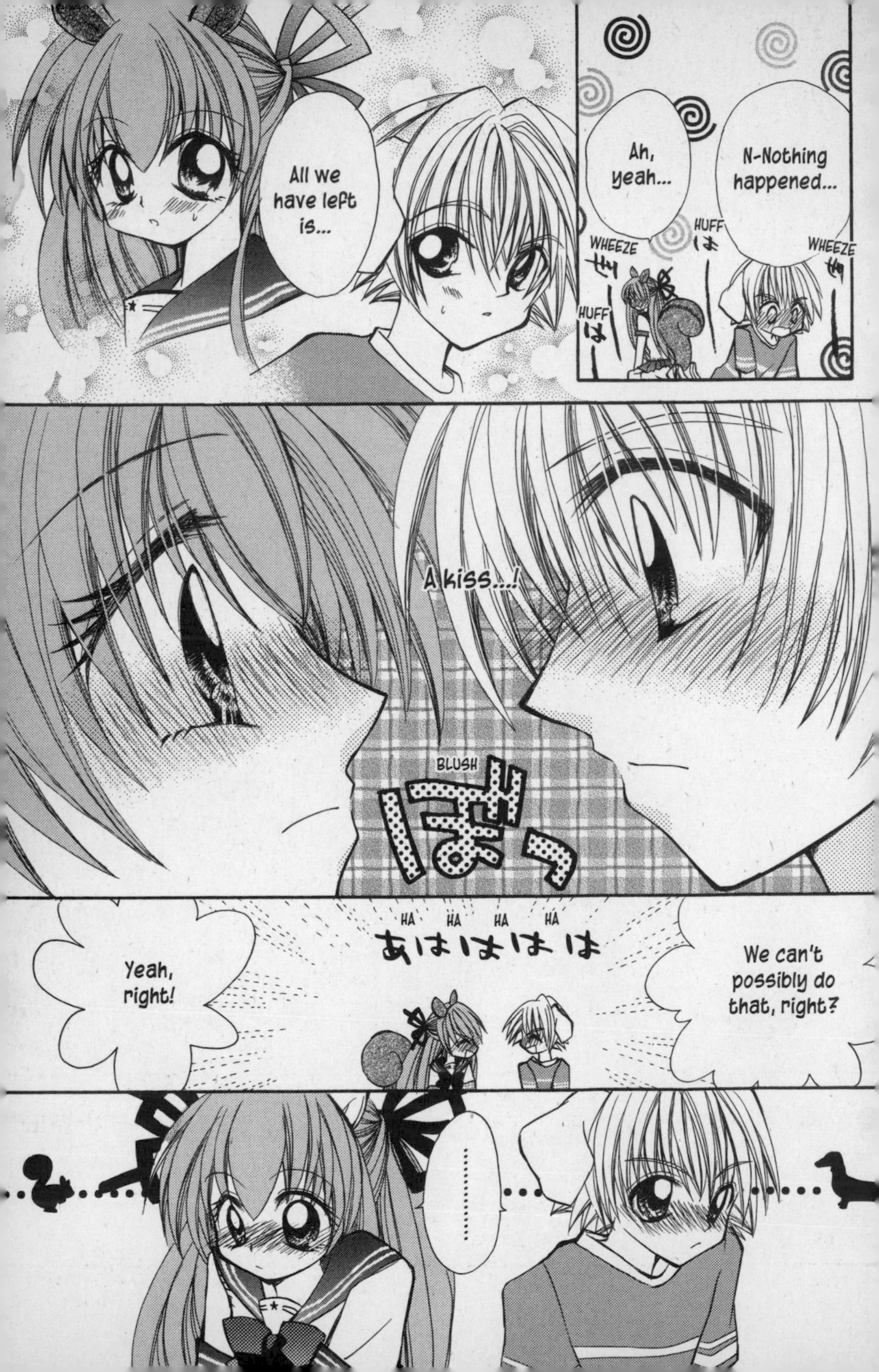
N-Nothing happened...
WHEEZE
HUFF
は
Ah, yeah...
WHEEZE
HUFF
は
All we have left is...
A kiss...!
BLUSH
ぼっ
We can't possibly do that, right?
HA HA HA HA
あははははは
Yeah, right!
....

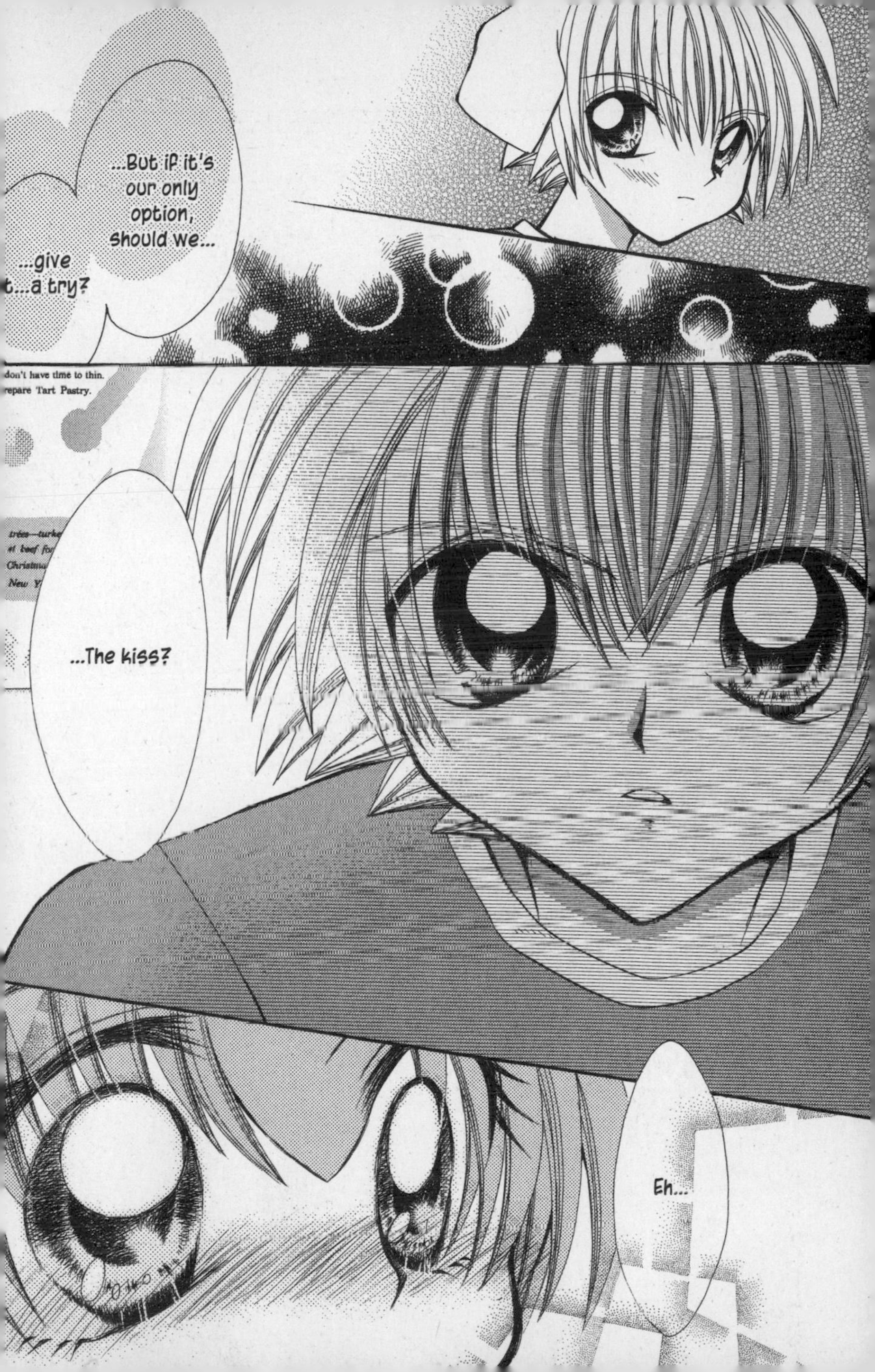
...But if it's our only option, should we...
...give it...a try?
...The kiss?
Eh...

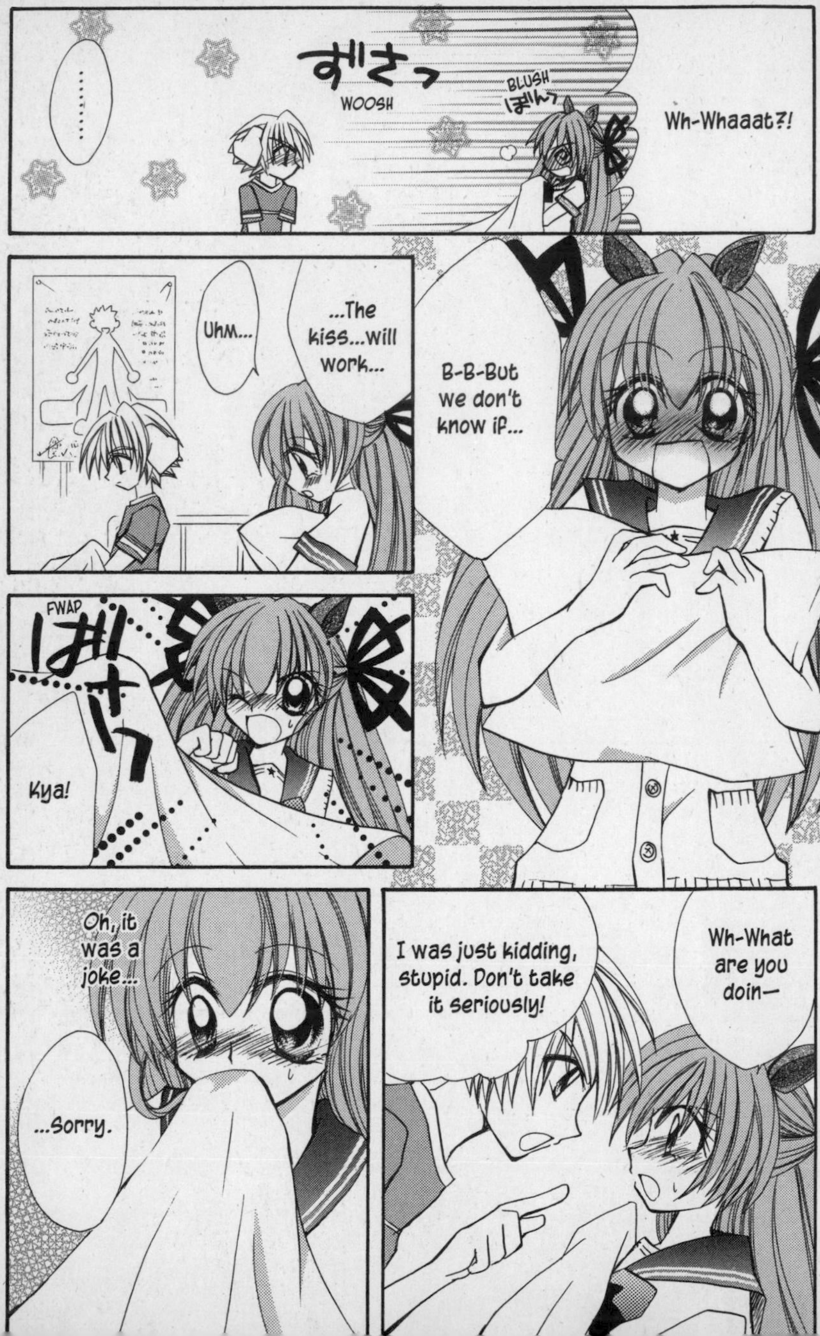

Wh-Whaaat?!
BLUSH
ぼんっ
ずさっ
WOOSH
......
B-B-But we don't know if...
...The kiss...will work...
Uhm...
FWAP
ばさっ
Kya!
Wh-What are you doin—
I was just kidding, stupid. Don't take it seriously!
Oh, it was a joke...
...Sorry.

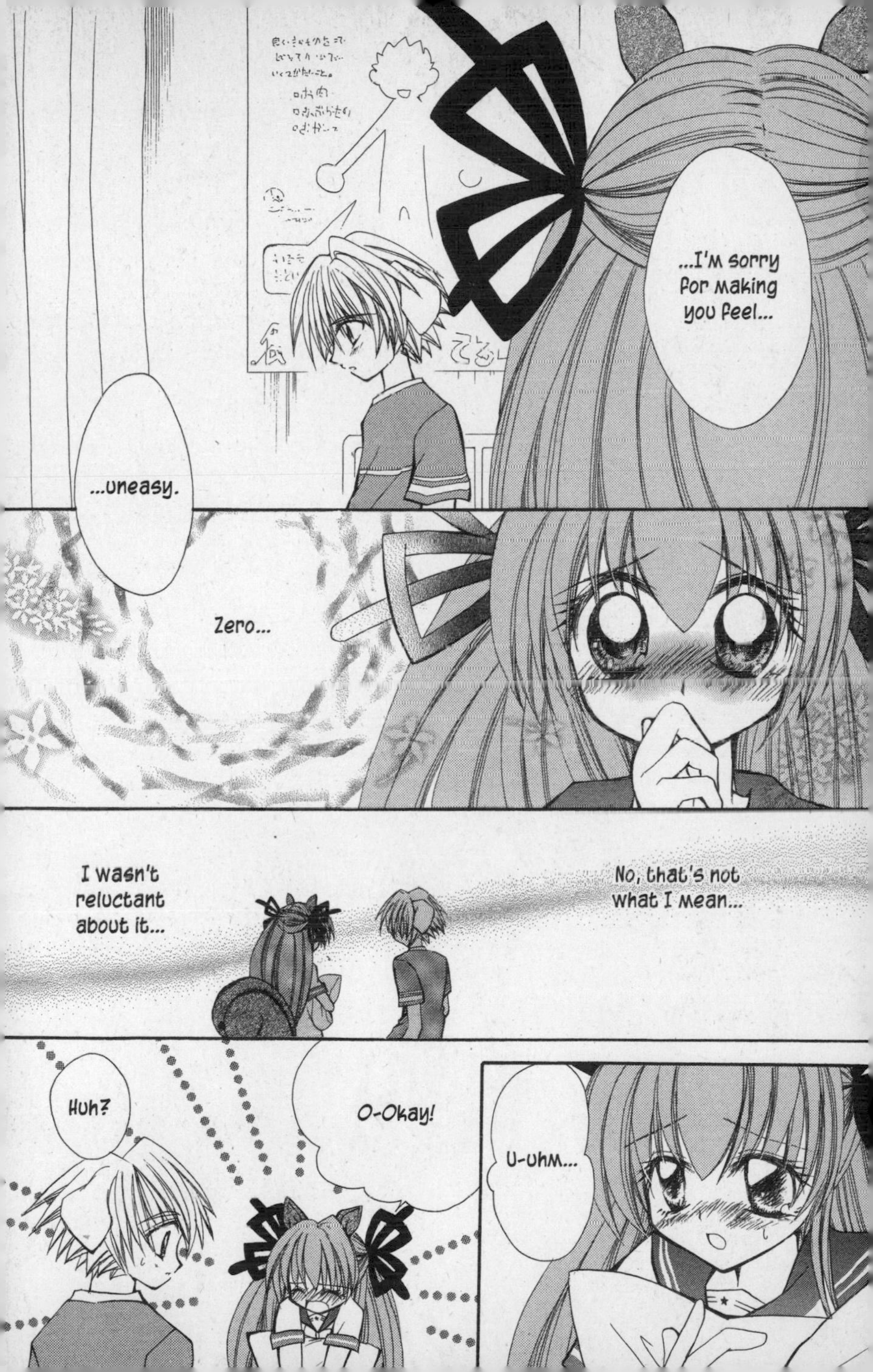
...I'm sorry for making you feel...
...uneasy.
Zero...
No, that's not what I mean...
I wasn't reluctant about it...
U-uhm...
O-Okay!
Huh?

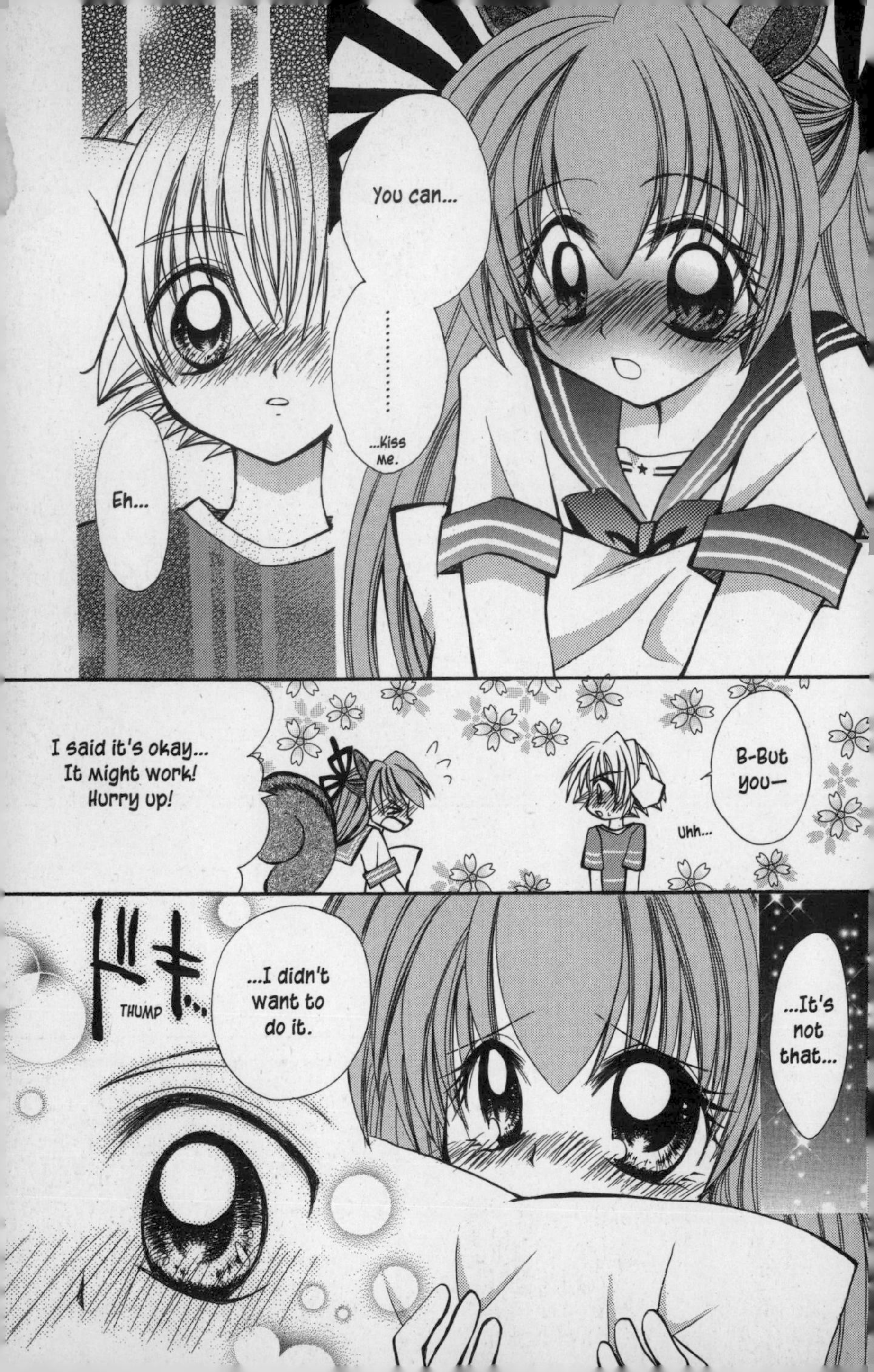
You can...
....
...Kiss me.
Eh...
B-But you—
Uhh...
I said it's okay... It might work! Hurry up!
...It's not that...
...I didn't want to do it.
ドキ
THUMP

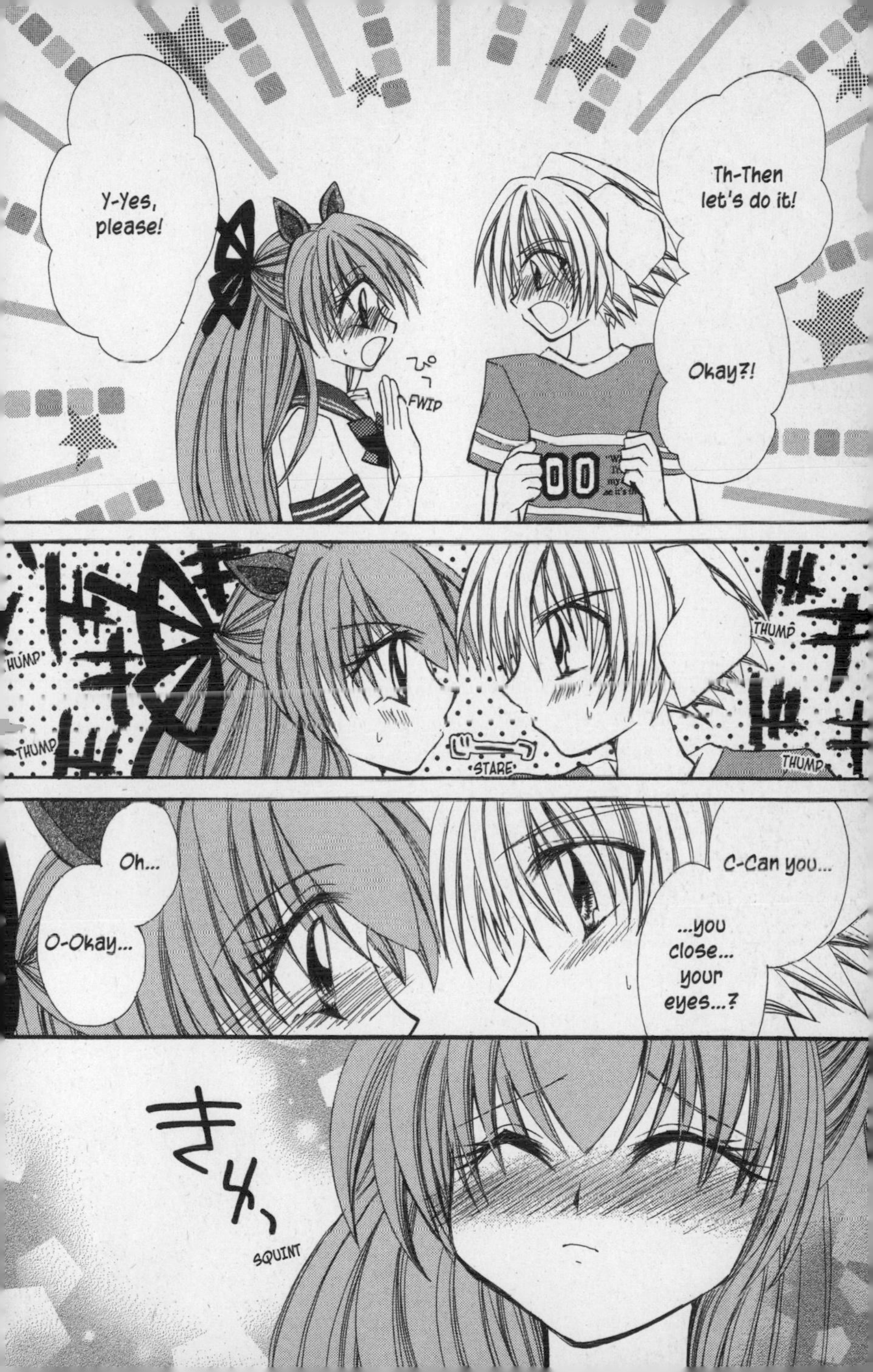
Th-Then let's do it!
Okay?!
Y-Yes, please!
FWIP
THUMP
THUMP
STARE
HUMP
THUMP
C-Can you...
...you close... your eyes...?
Oh...
O-Okay...
SQUINT

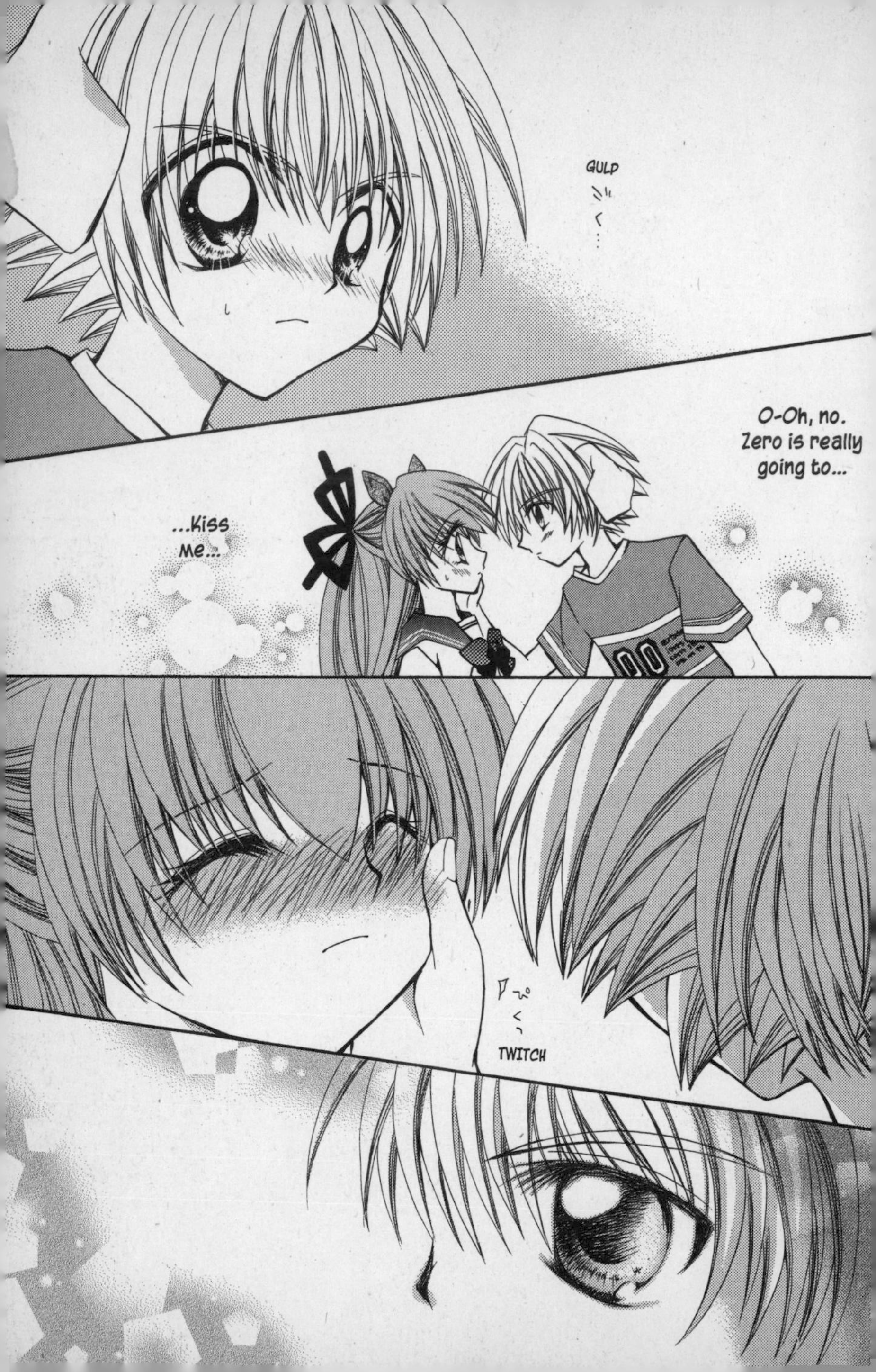
GULP
O-Oh, no. Zero is really going to...
...Kiss me...
TWITCH

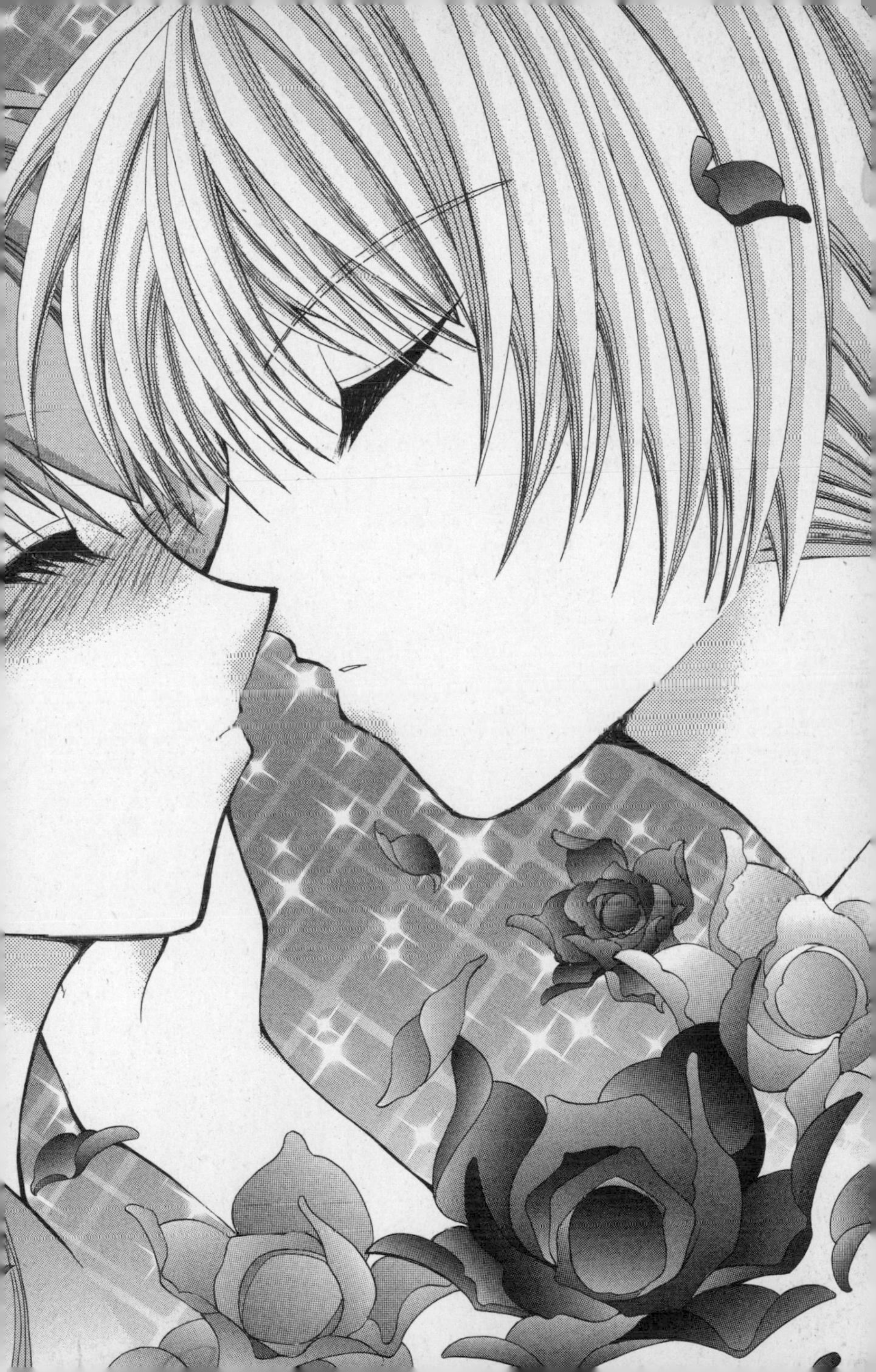

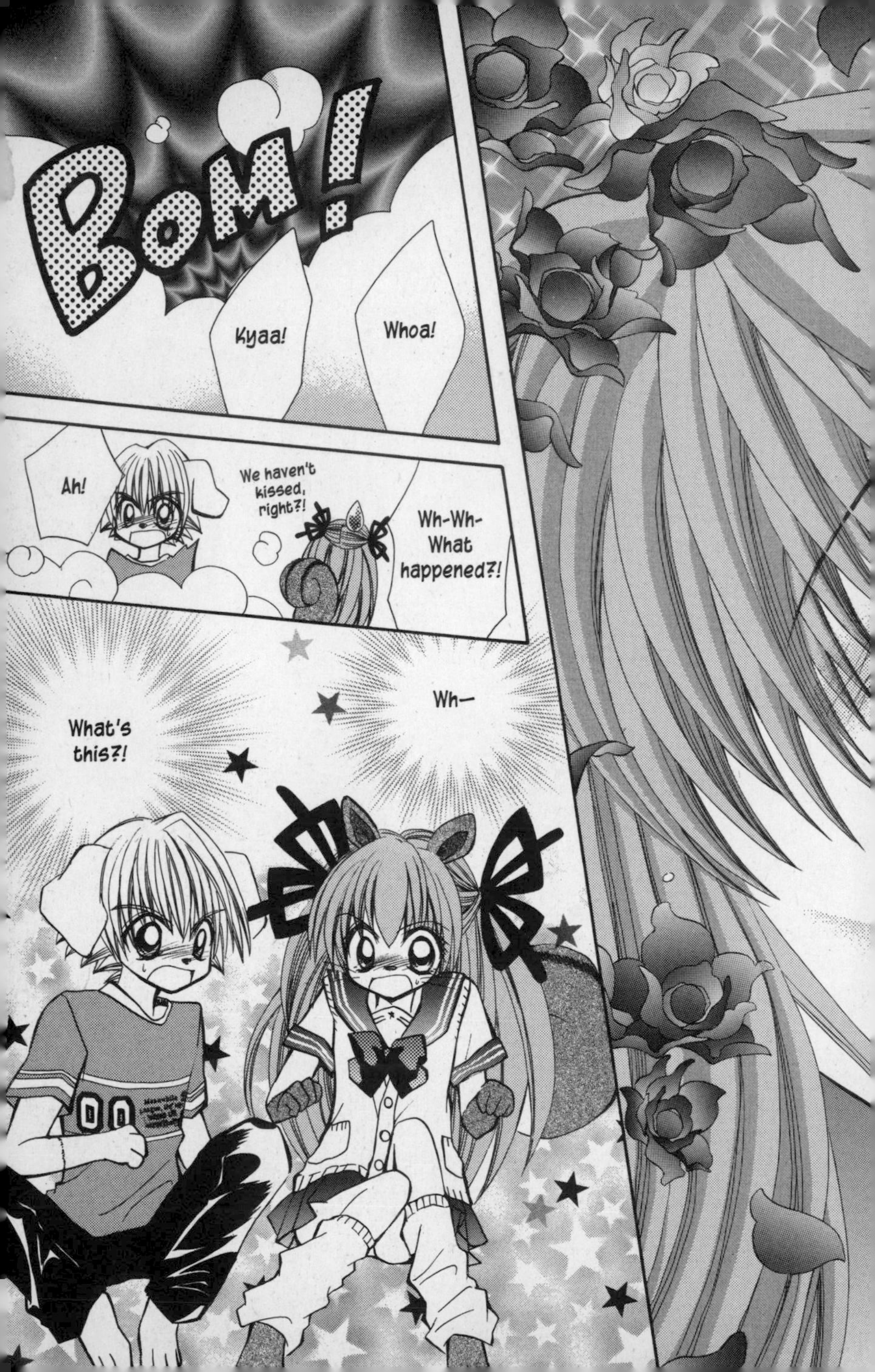
BOM!
Whoa!
Kyaa!
Wh-Wh-What happened?!
We haven't kissed, right?!
Ah!
Wh—
What's this?!

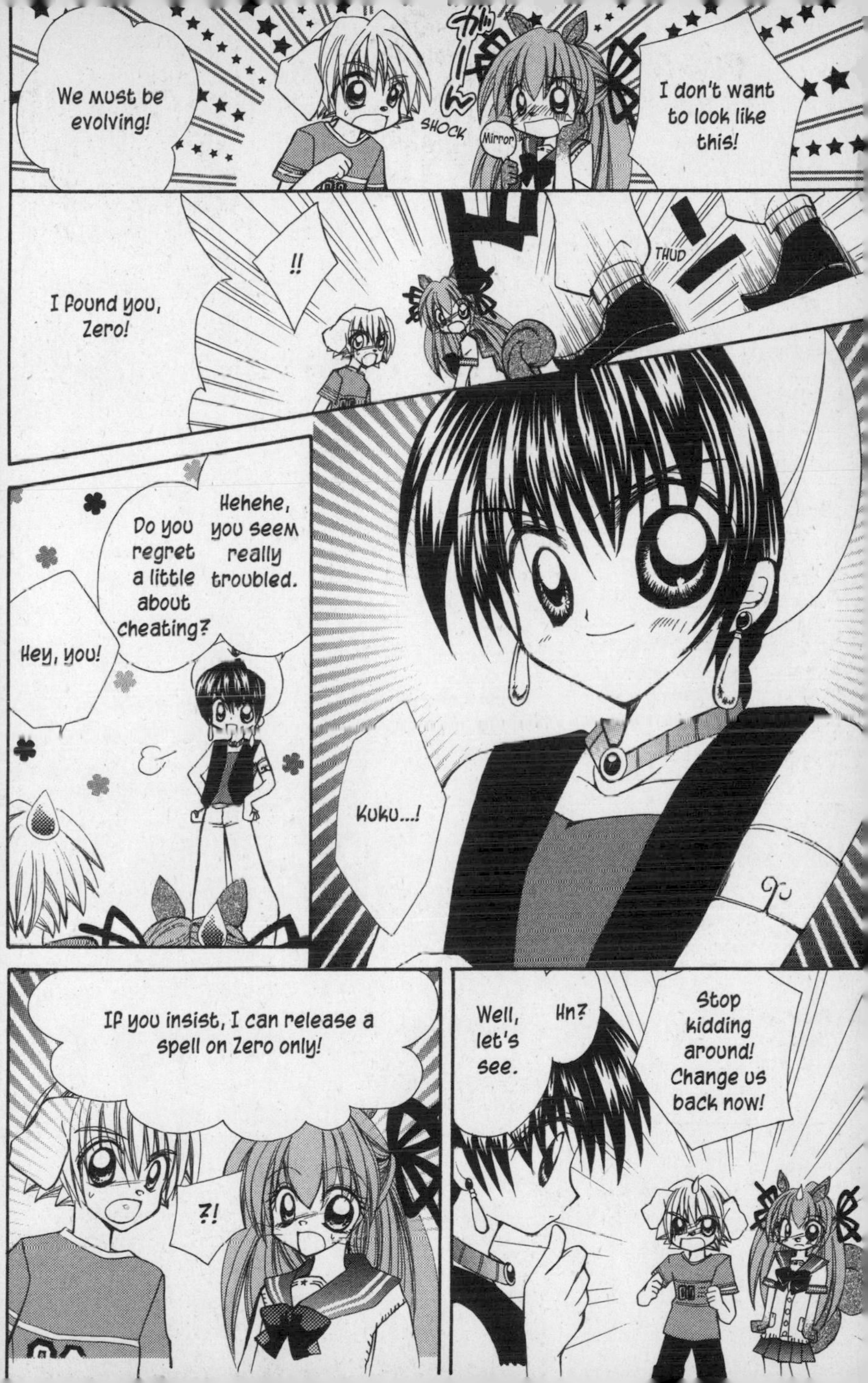
I don't want to look like this!
SHOCK
Mirror
We must be evolving!
THUD
!!
I found you, Zero!
Kuku...!
Hehehe, you seem really troubled.
Do you regret a little about cheating?
Hey, you!
Stop kidding around! Change us back now!
Hn?
Well, let's see.
If you insist, I can release a spell on Zero only!
?!

Data 5
* Forte *

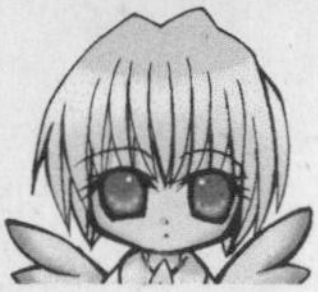

Name:	Forte
Birthday:	December 24th
Blood Type:	A
Height:	163 cm*
Favorite Food:	Tea/Cookies
Least Favorite Food:	Anything spicy
Weak Point:	Sun cross-dressing him.
Treasure:	Flute/Ribbons
Hobbies:	Music listening
Special Talent:	Hypnosis Spell
Favorite Type of Girl:	Someone kind
Remarks:	Has the thickest lashes in *Lollipop*.

*5'4"

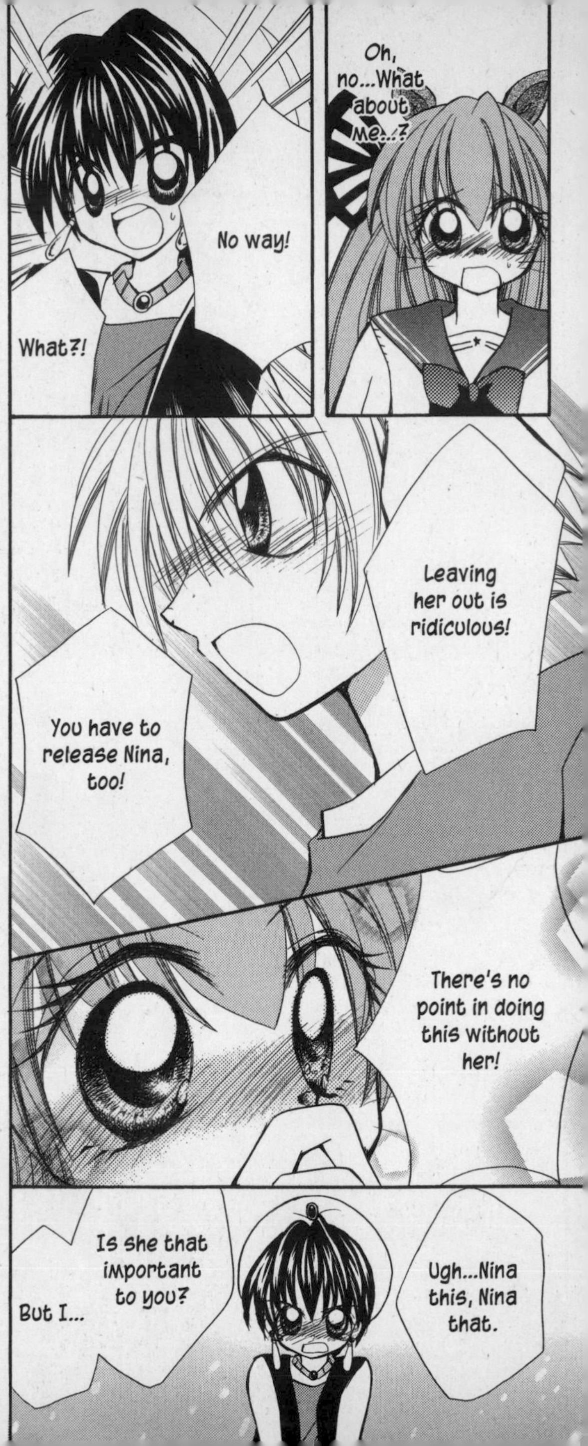
Oh, no...What about me...?
No way!
What?!
Leaving her out is ridiculous!
You have to release Nina, too!
There's no point in doing this without her!
Ugh...Nina this, Nina that.
Is she that important to you?
But I...

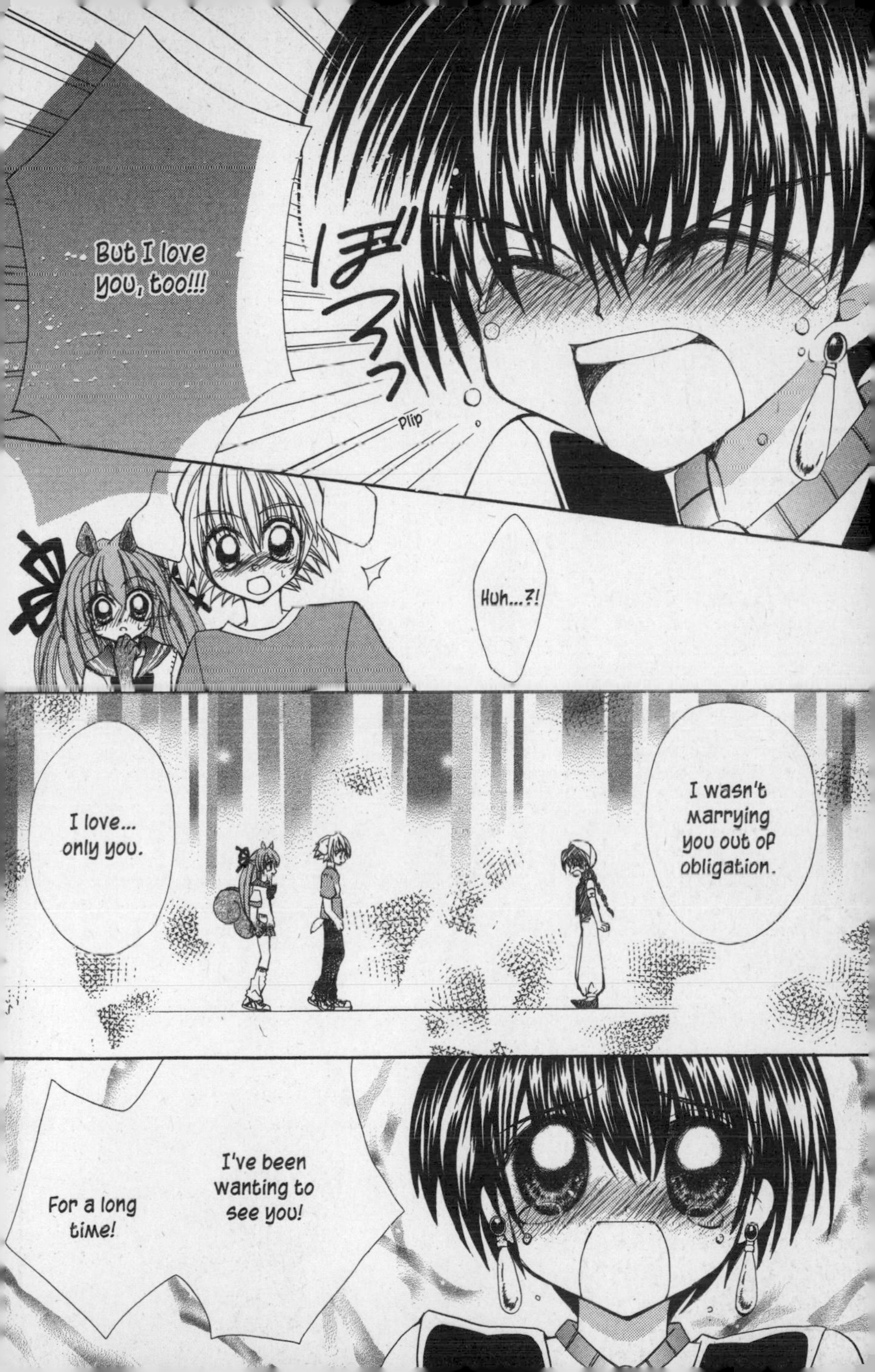
ぼろっ
Plip
But I love you, too!!!
Huh...?!
I wasn't marrying you out of obligation.
I love... only you.
I've been wanting to see you!
For a long time!

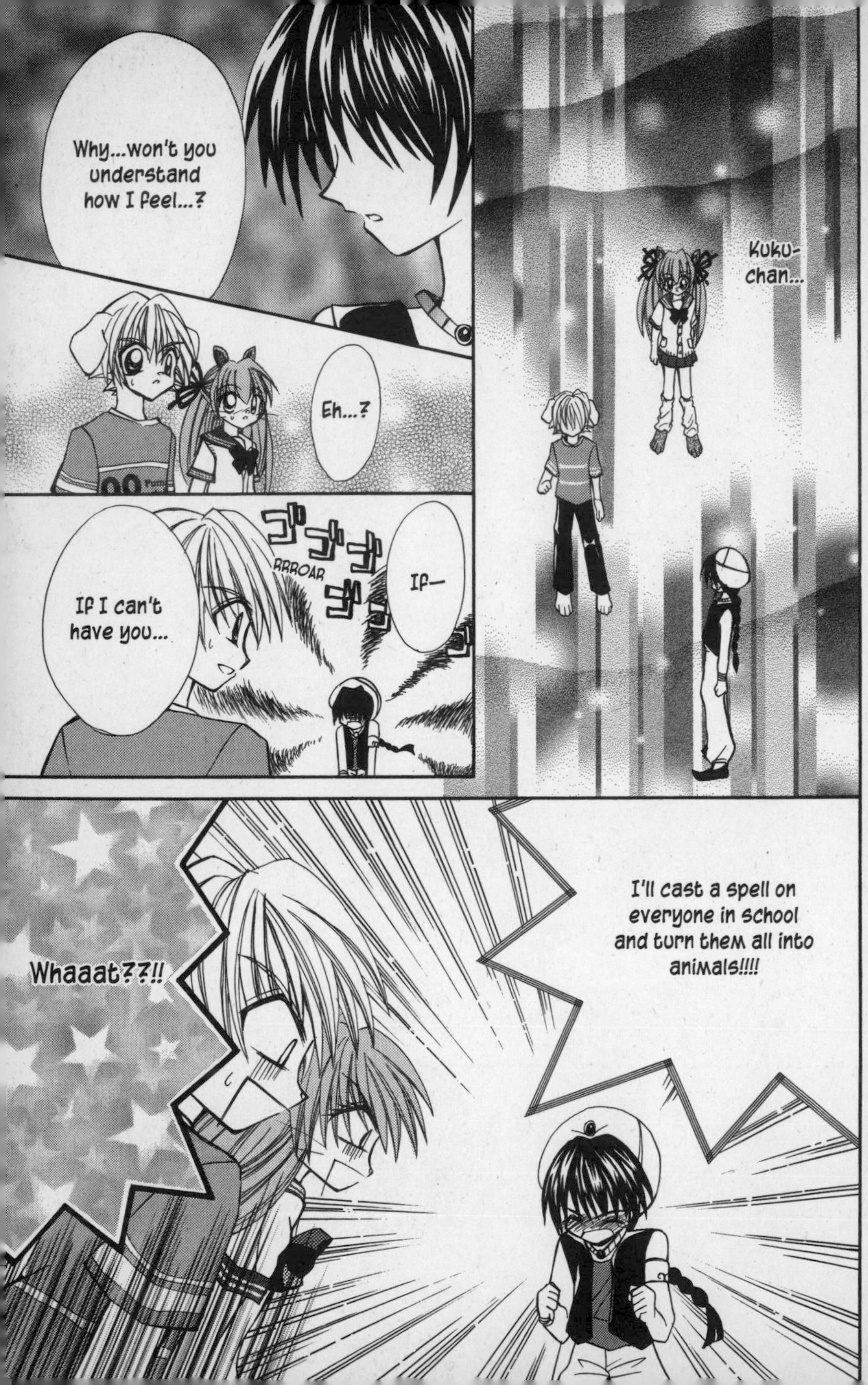
Kuku-chan...
Why...won't you understand how I feel...?
Eh...?
If—
RRROAR
If I can't have you...
I'll cast a spell on everyone in school and turn them all into animals!!!!
Whaaat??!!

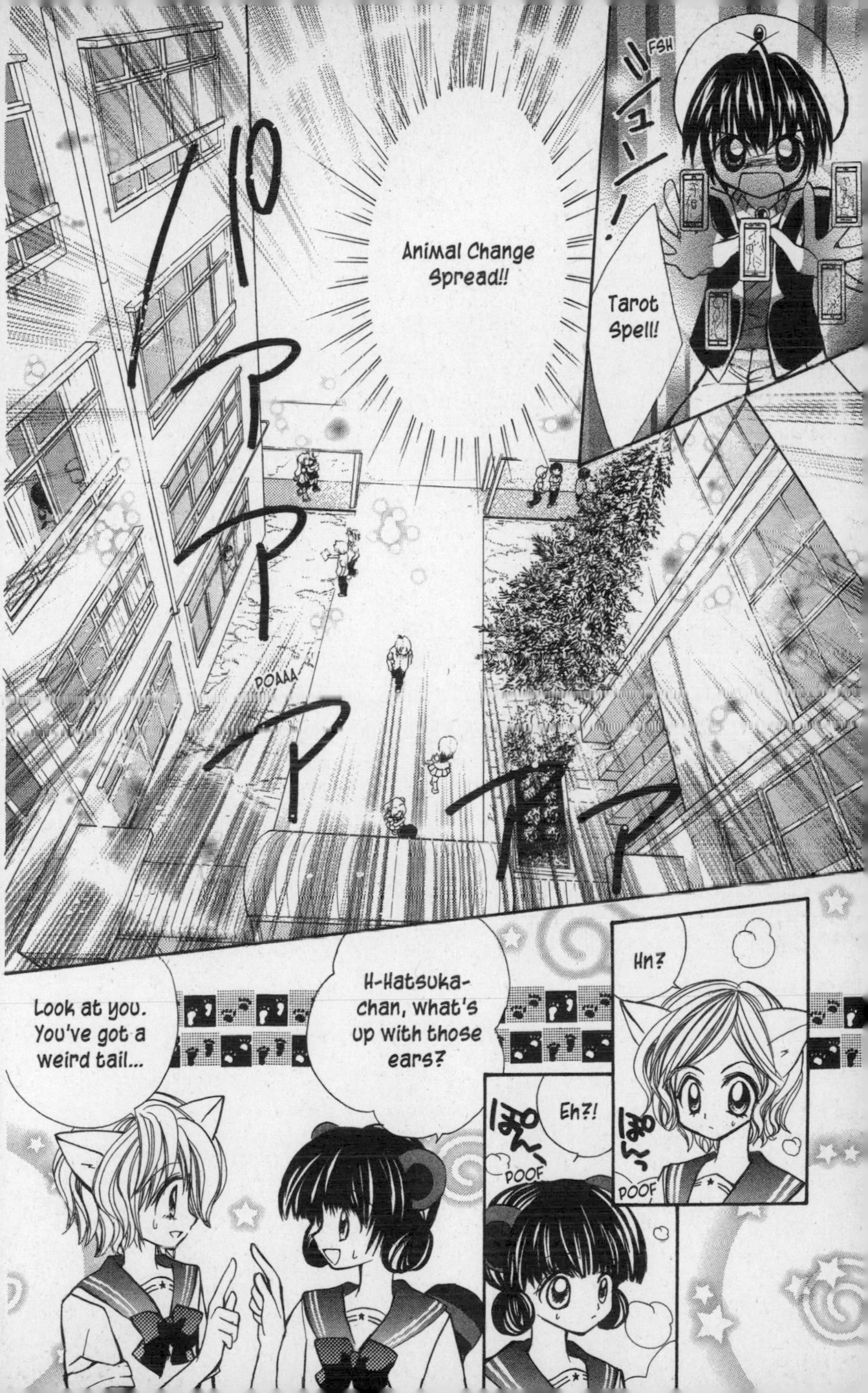
FSH
Tarot Spell!
Animal Change Spread!!
POAAA
Hn?
POOF
Eh?!
POOF
H-Hatsuka-chan, what's up with those ears?
Look at you. You've got a weird tail...

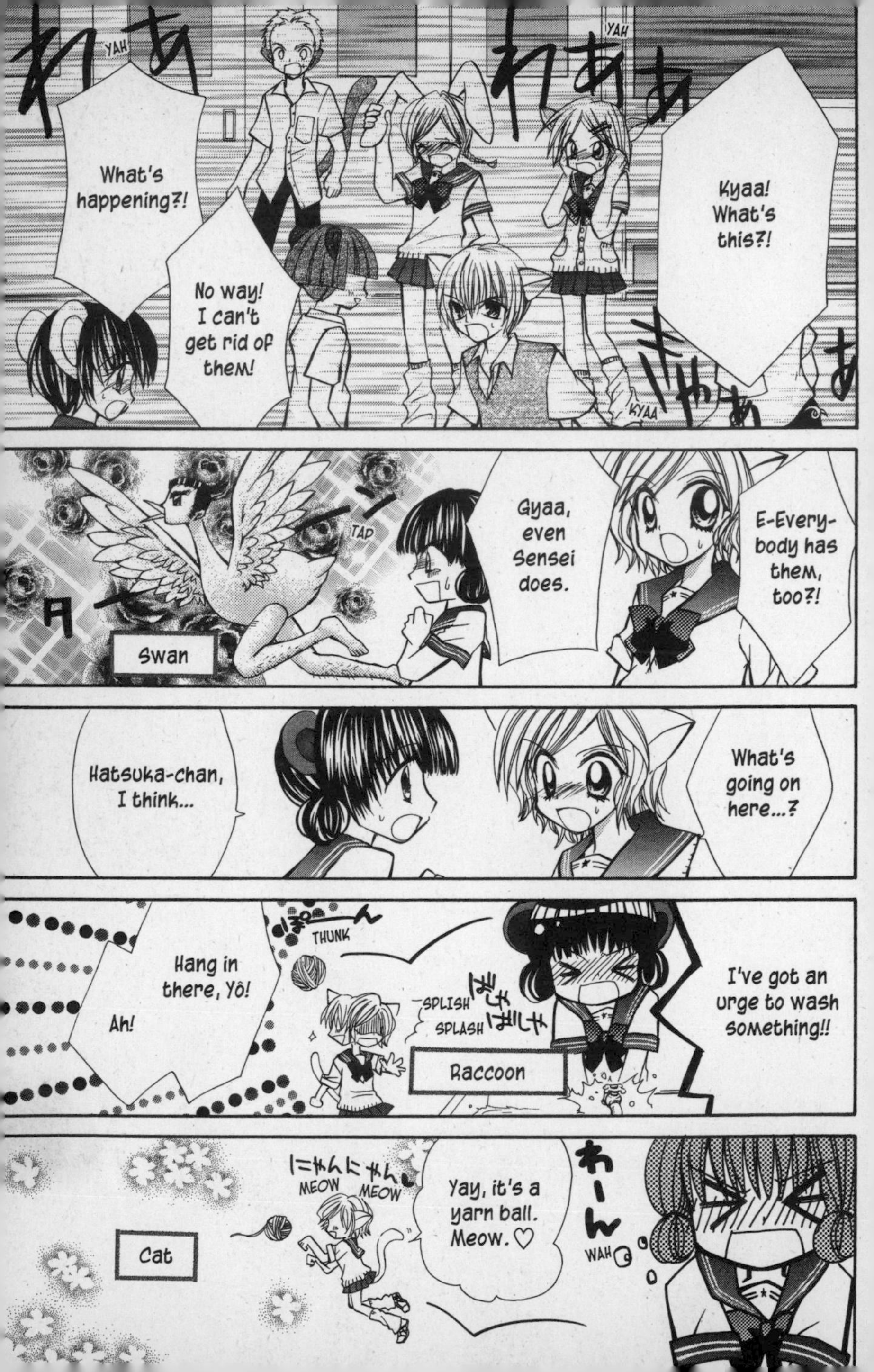
YAH
Kyaa! What's this?!
YAH
What's happening?!
No way! I can't get rid of them!
KYAA
E-Every-body has them, too?!
Gyaa, even Sensei does.
TAP
Swan
What's going on here...?
Hatsuka-chan, I think...
I've got an urge to wash something!!
Raccoon
SPLISH
SPLASH
THUNK
Hang in there, Yô!
Ah!
WAH
Yay, it's a yarn ball. Meow. ♡
MEOW
MEOW
Cat

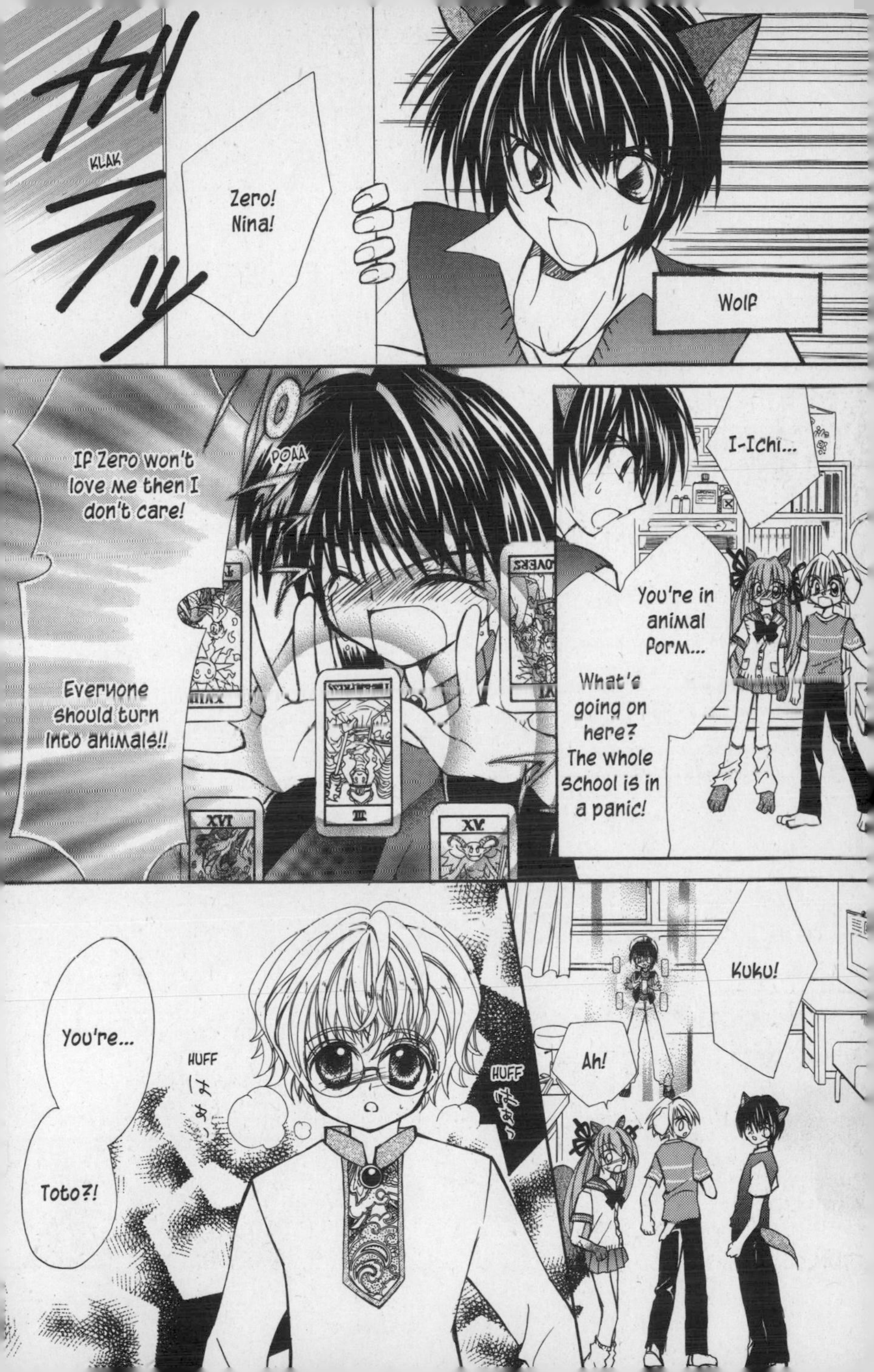
Wolf
Zero! Nina!
KLAK
I-Ichi...
You're in animal form...
What's going on here? The whole school is in a panic!
POAA
If Zero won't love me then I don't care!
Everyone should turn into animals!!
Kuku!
Ah!
HUFF
HUFF
You're...
Toto?!

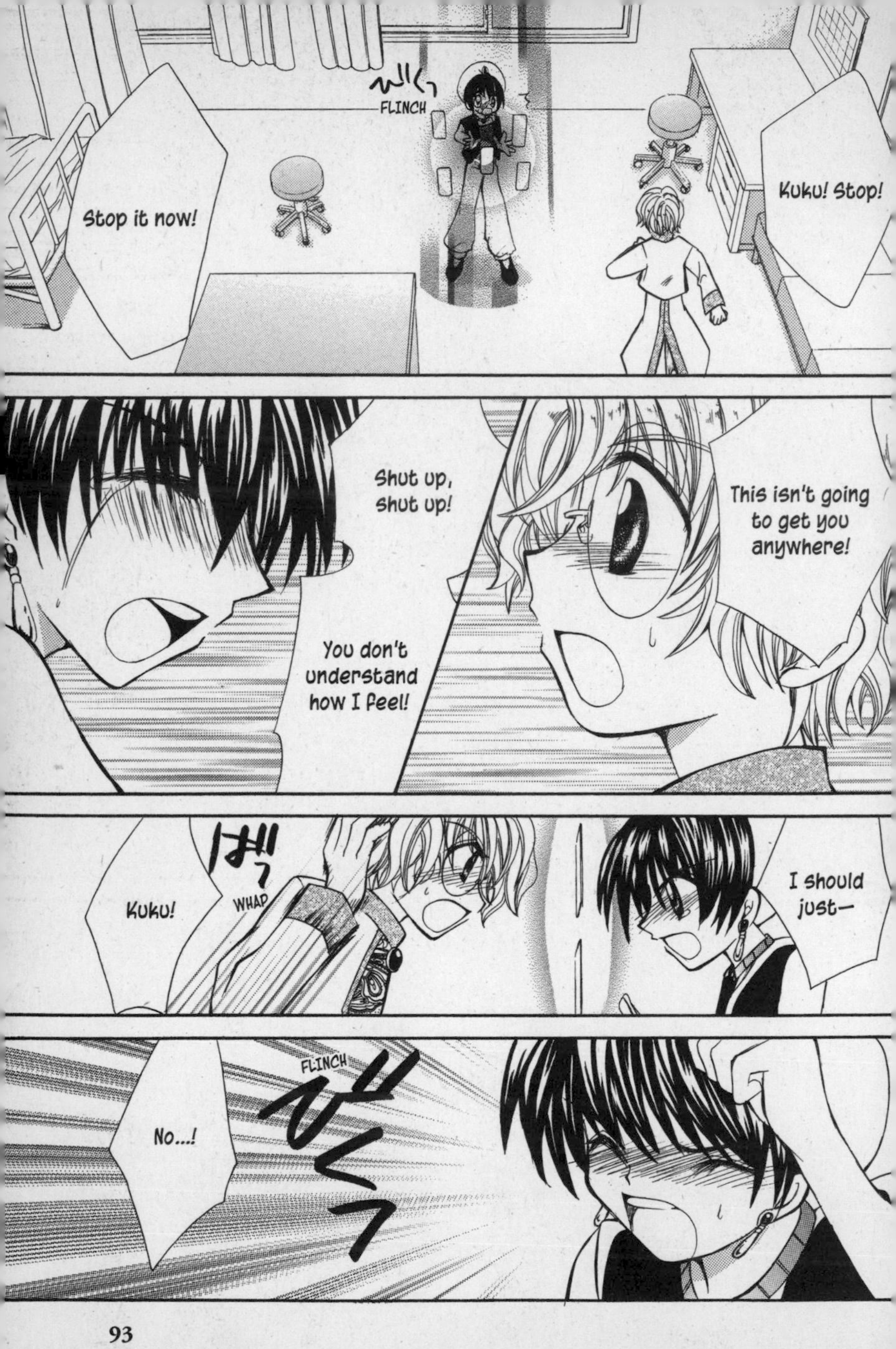
Kuku! Stop!
FLINCH
Stop it now!
This isn't going to get you anywhere!
Shut up, shut up!
You don't understand how I feel!
I should just—
WHAP
Kuku!
FLINCH
No...!

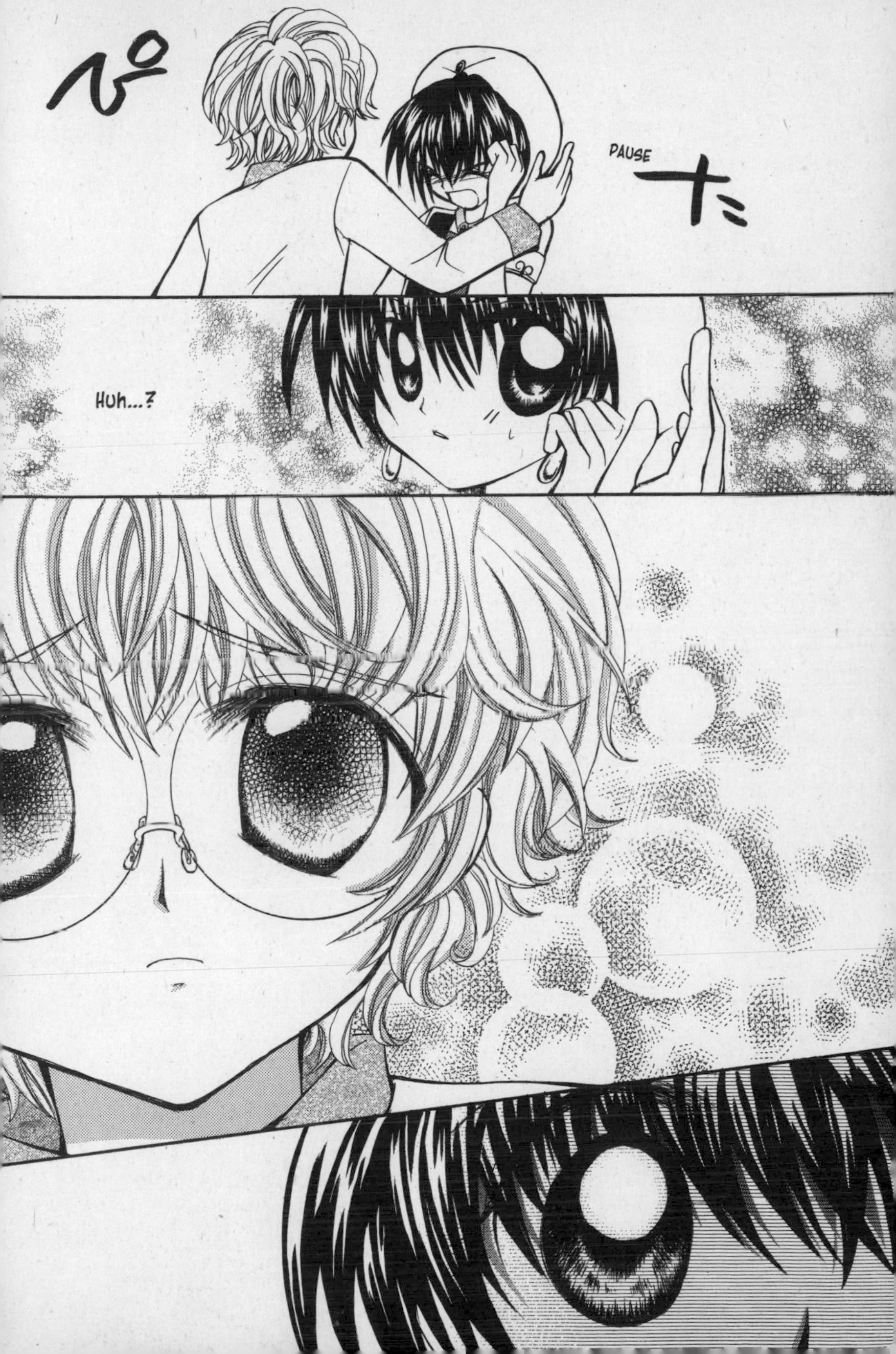
PAUSE
た
ぴ
Huh...?

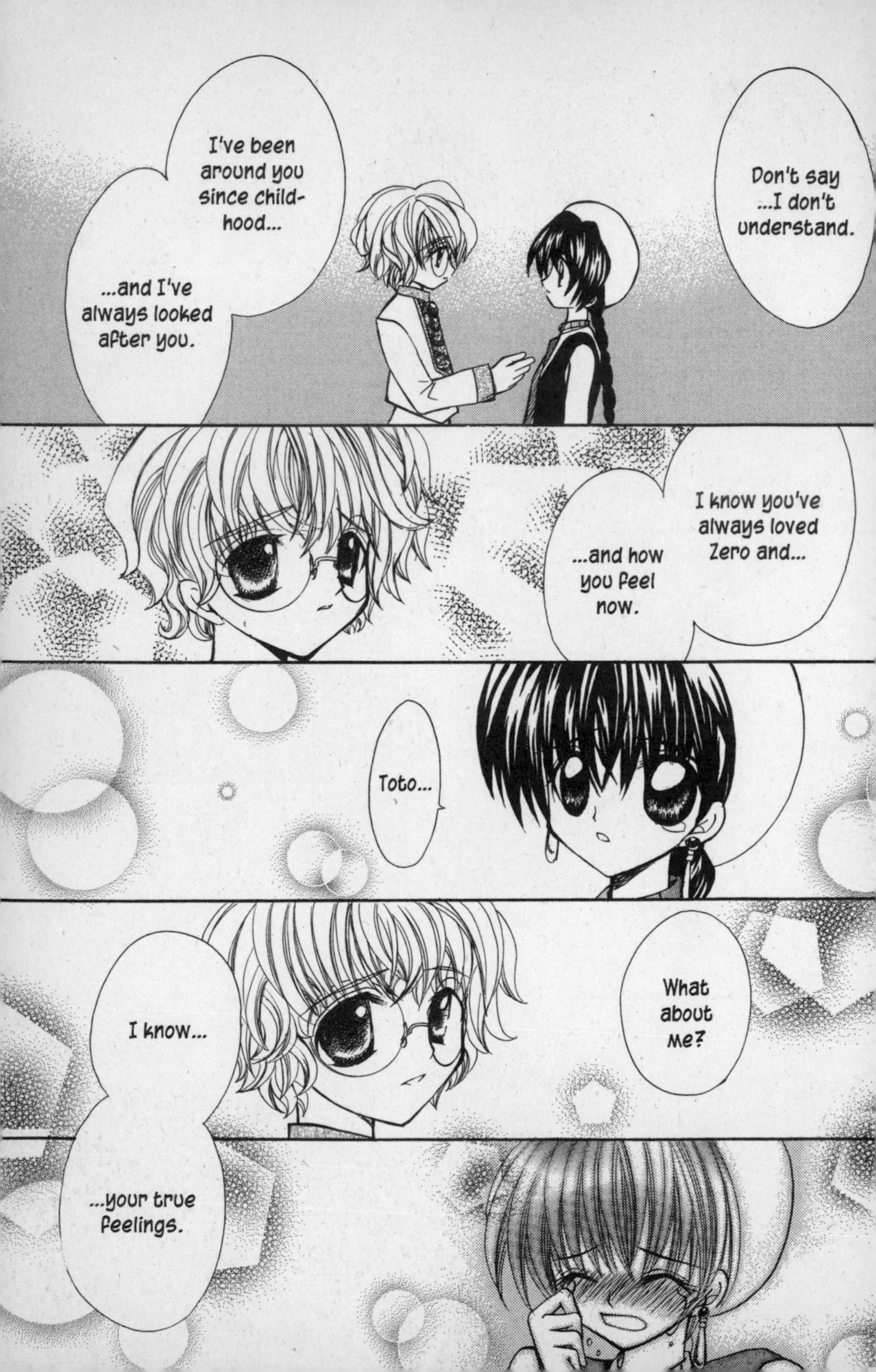
Don't say ...I don't understand.
I've been around you since child-hood...
...and I've always looked after you.
I know you've always loved Zero and...
...and how you feel now.
Toto...
What about me?
I know...
...your true feelings.

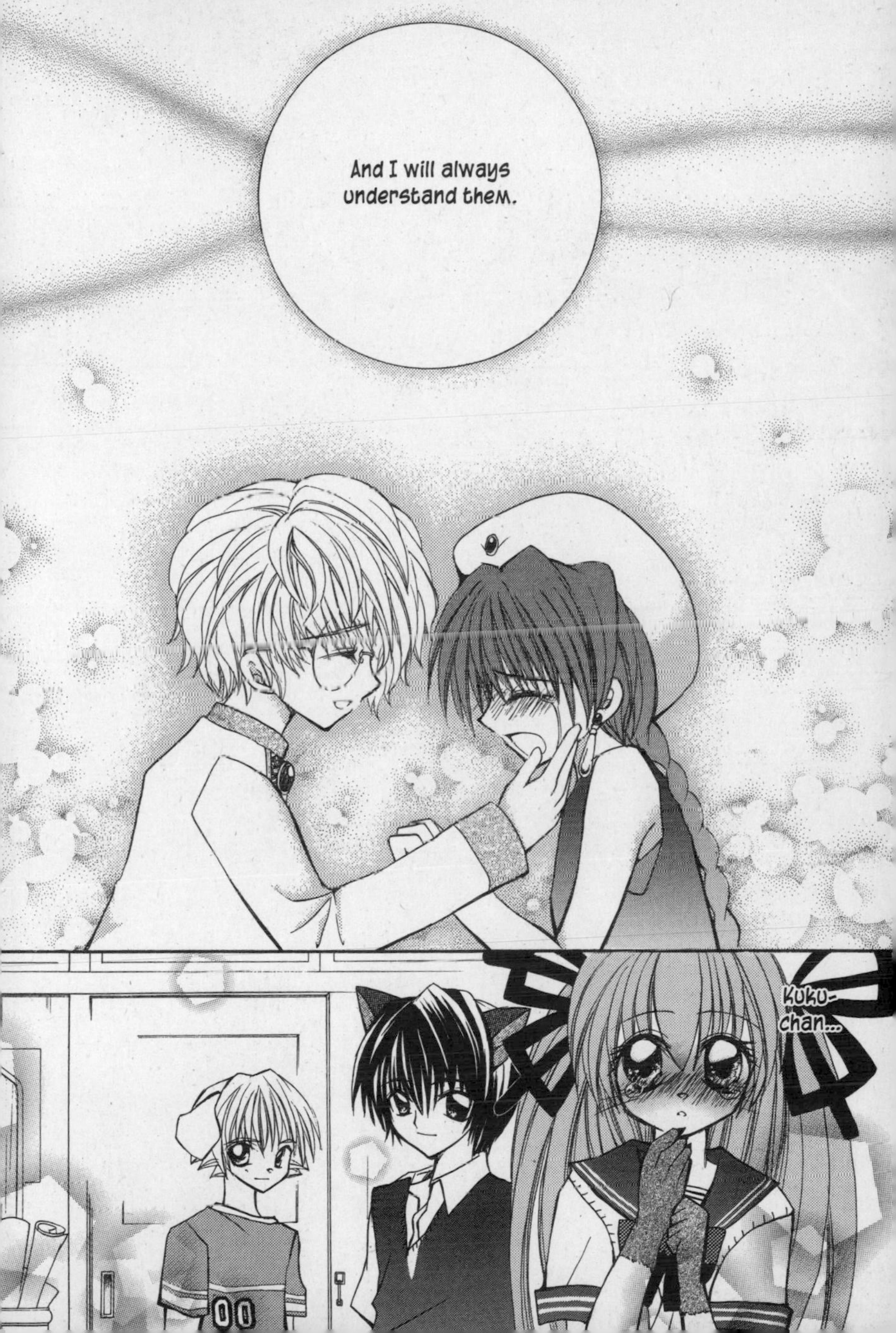
And I will always understand them.
Kuku-chan...

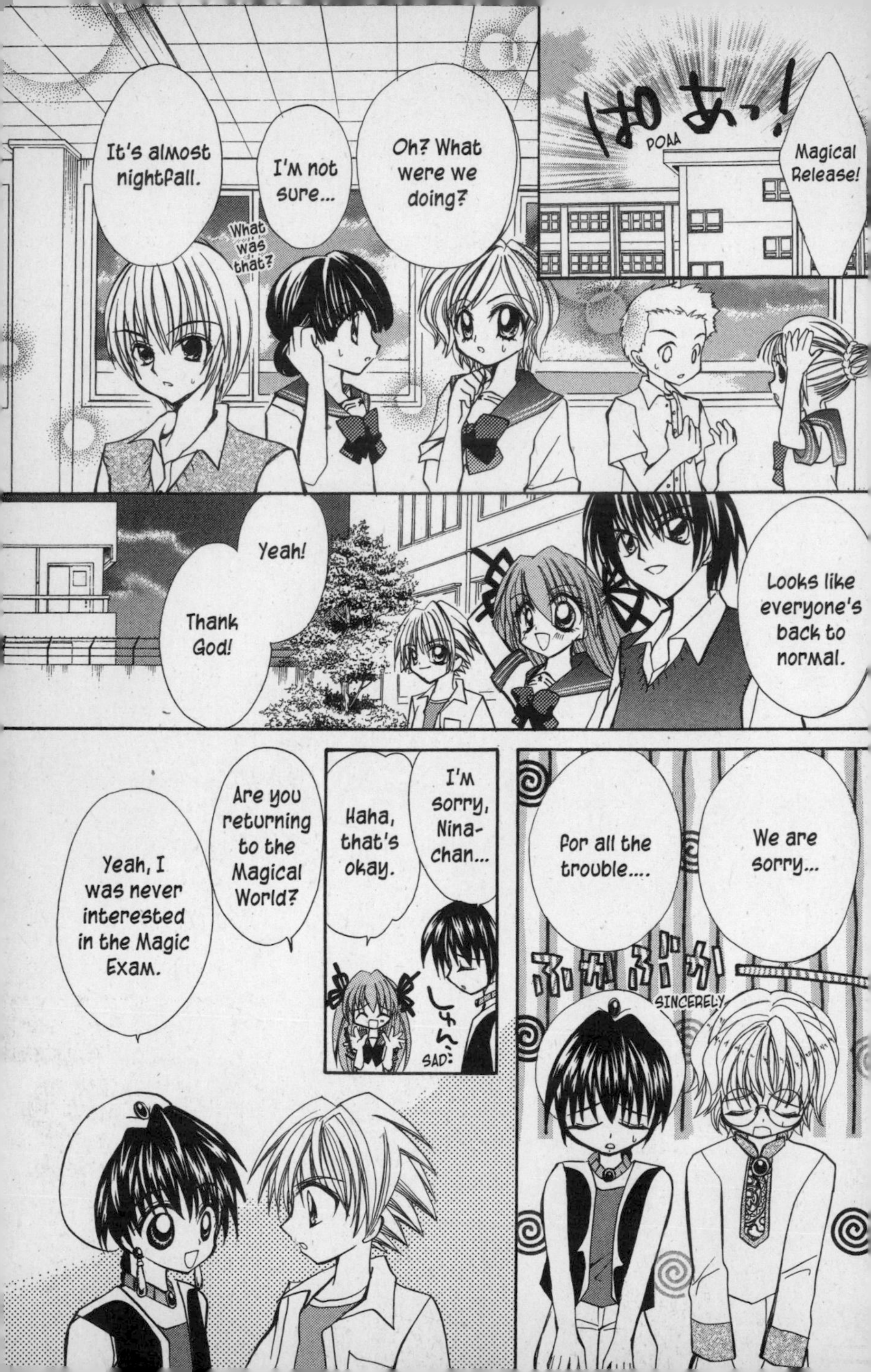
ぱあっ!
POAA
Magical Release!
Oh? What were we doing?
I'm not sure...
What was that?
It's almost nightfall.
Looks like everyone's back to normal.
Yeah!
Thank God!
We are sorry...
for all the trouble....
ふかぶか
SINCERELY
I'm sorry, Nina-chan...
Haha, that's okay.
しゅん
SAD
Are you returning to the Magical World?
Yeah, I was never interested in the Magic Exam.

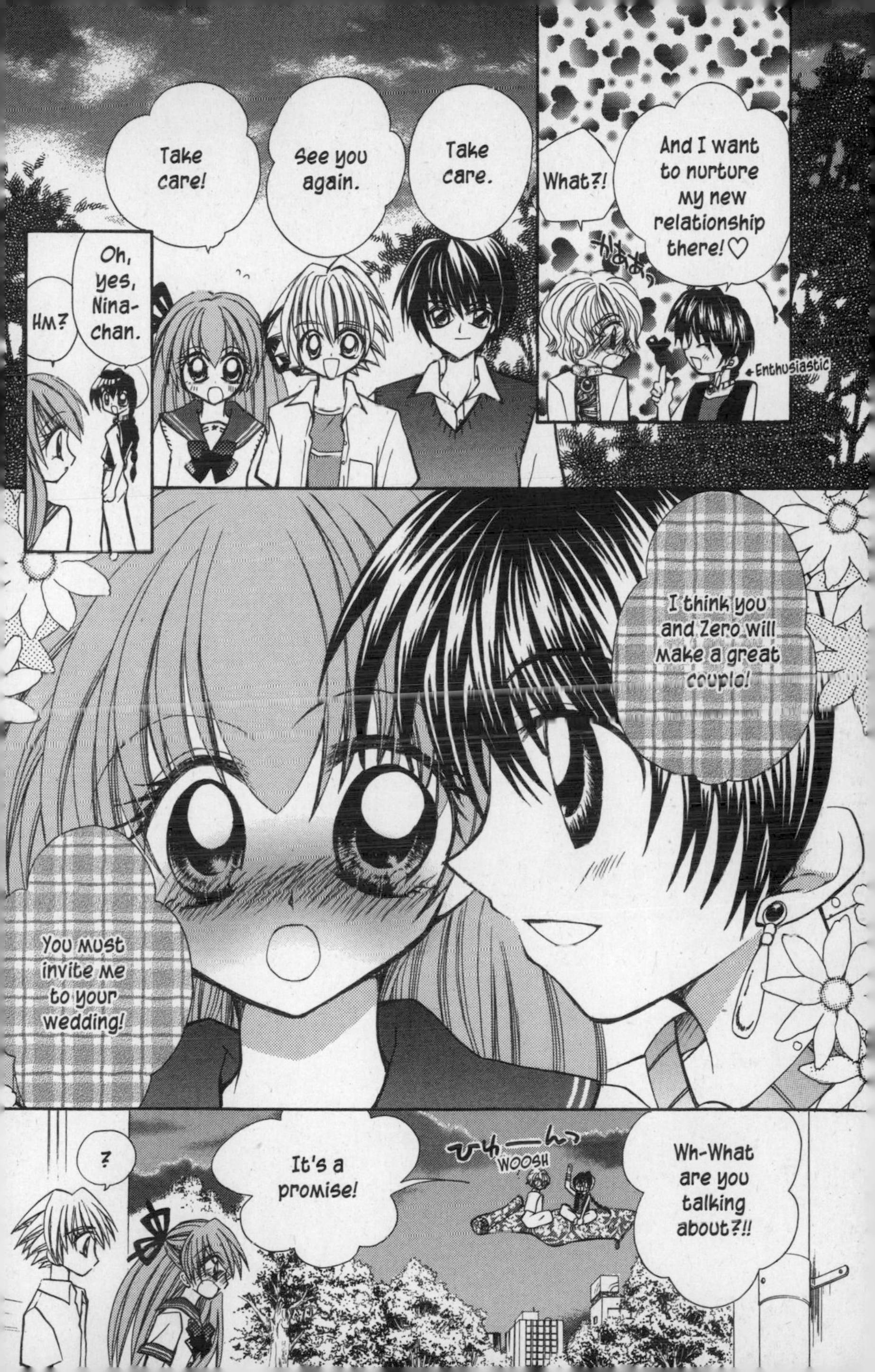
And I want to nurture my new relationship there! ♡
What?!
Enthusiastic
Take care.
See you again.
Take care!
Oh, yes, Nina-chan.
Hm?
I think you and Zero will make a great couple!
You must invite me to your wedding!
Wh-What are you talking about?!!
WOOSH
It's a promise!
?

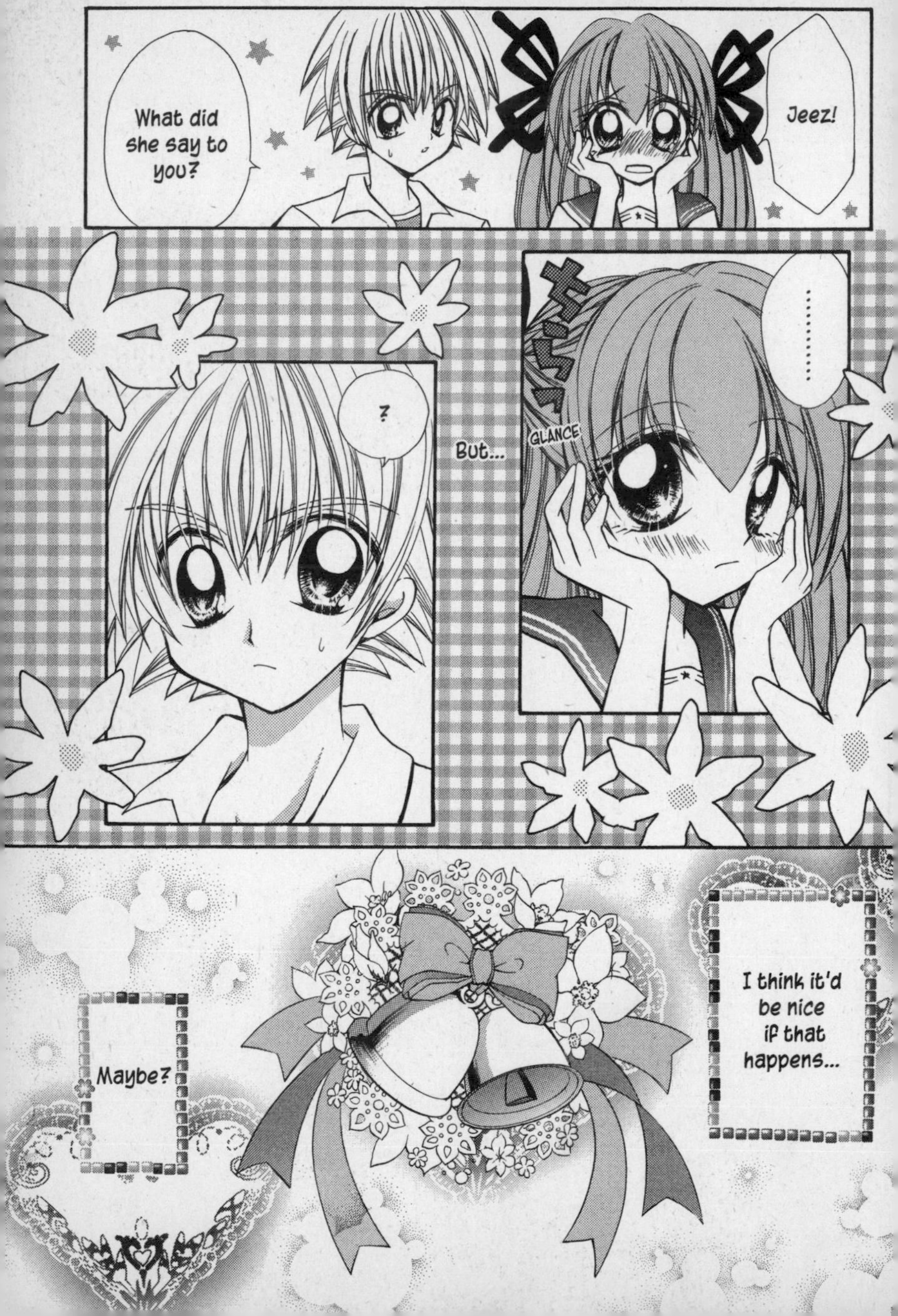
Jeez!
What did she say to you?
......
GLANCE
But...
?
I think it'd be nice if that happens...
Maybe?

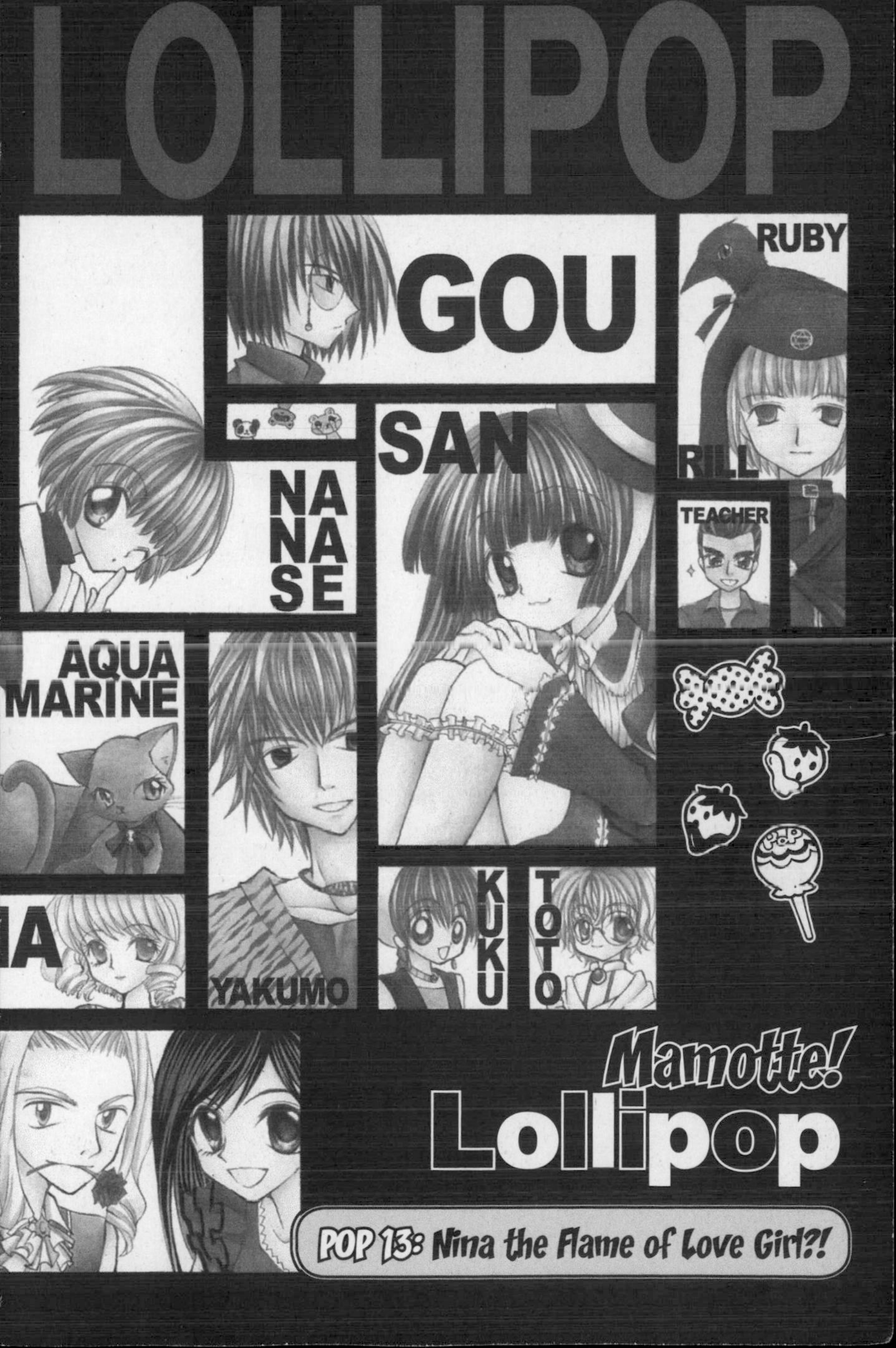
LOLLIPOP
RUBY
GOU
SAN
RILL
TEACHER
NANASE
AQUA MARINE
YAKUMO
KUKU
TOTO
Mamotte!
Lollipop
POP 13: Nina the Flame of Love Girl?!

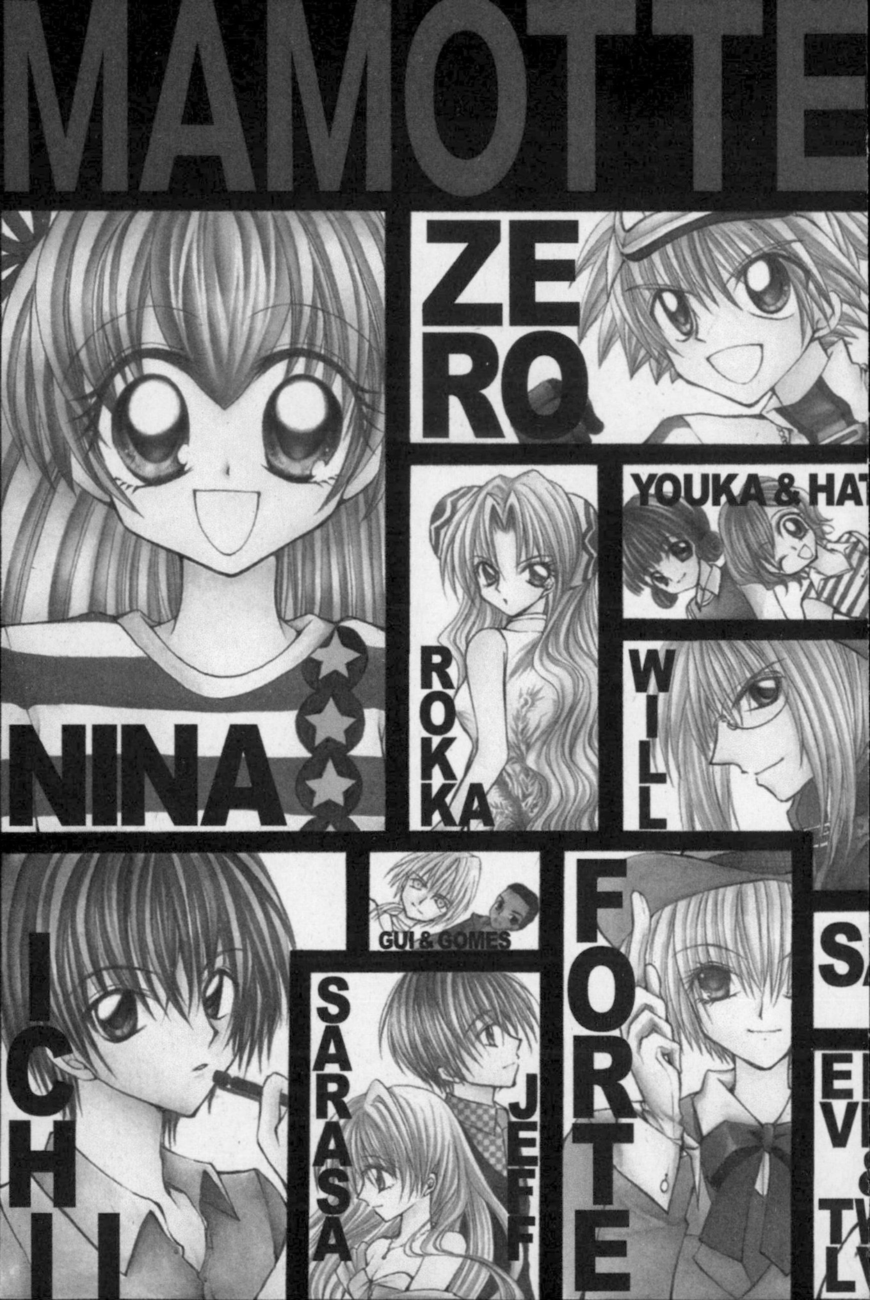
MAMOTTE
ZERO
YOUKA
ROKKA
WILL
NINA
FORTE
GUI & GOMES
JEFF
SARASA

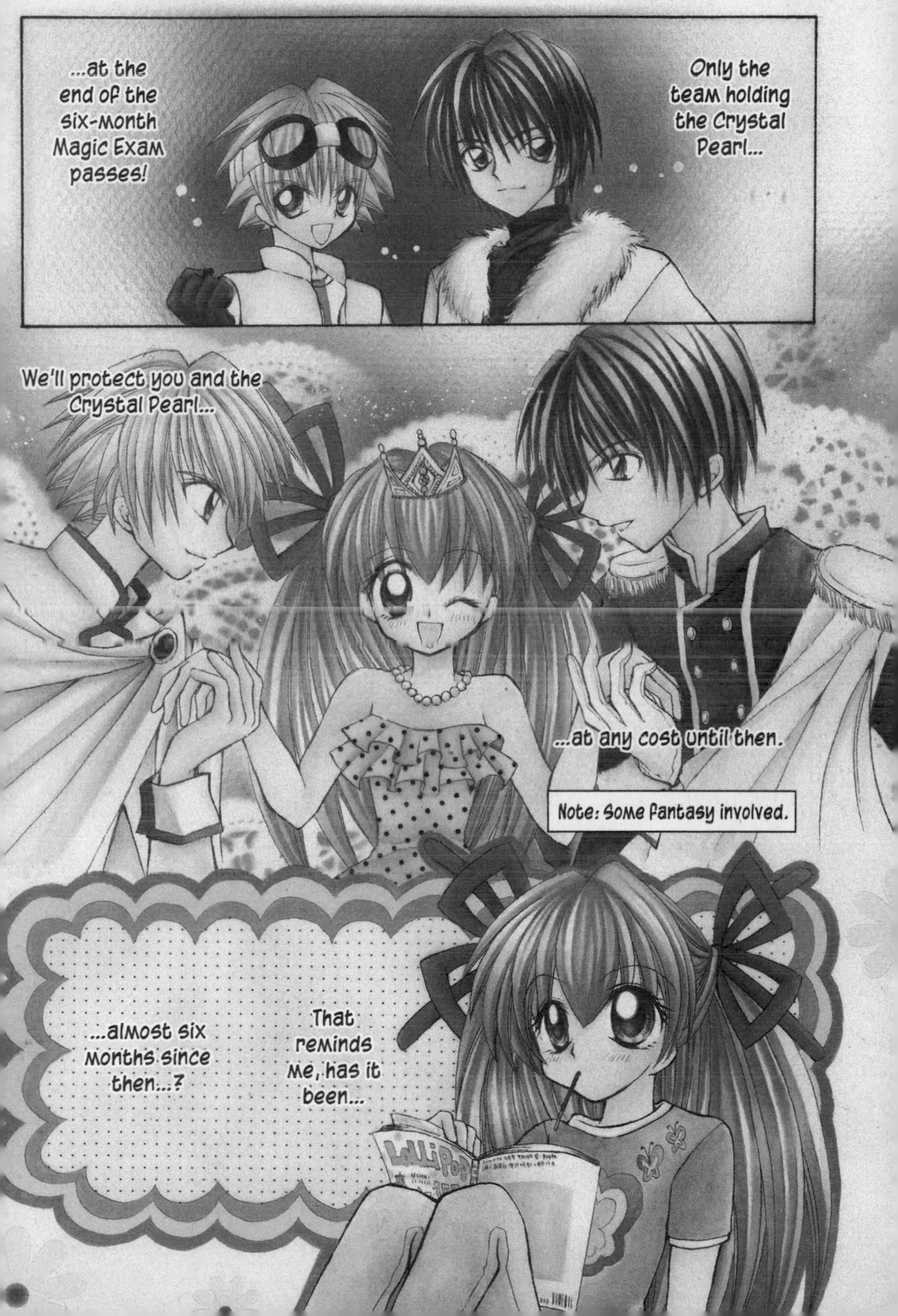
Only the team holding the Crystal Pearl...
...at the end of the six-month Magic Exam passes!
We'll protect you and the Crystal Pearl...
...at any cost until then.
Note: Some fantasy involved.
That reminds me, has it been...
...almost six months since then...?

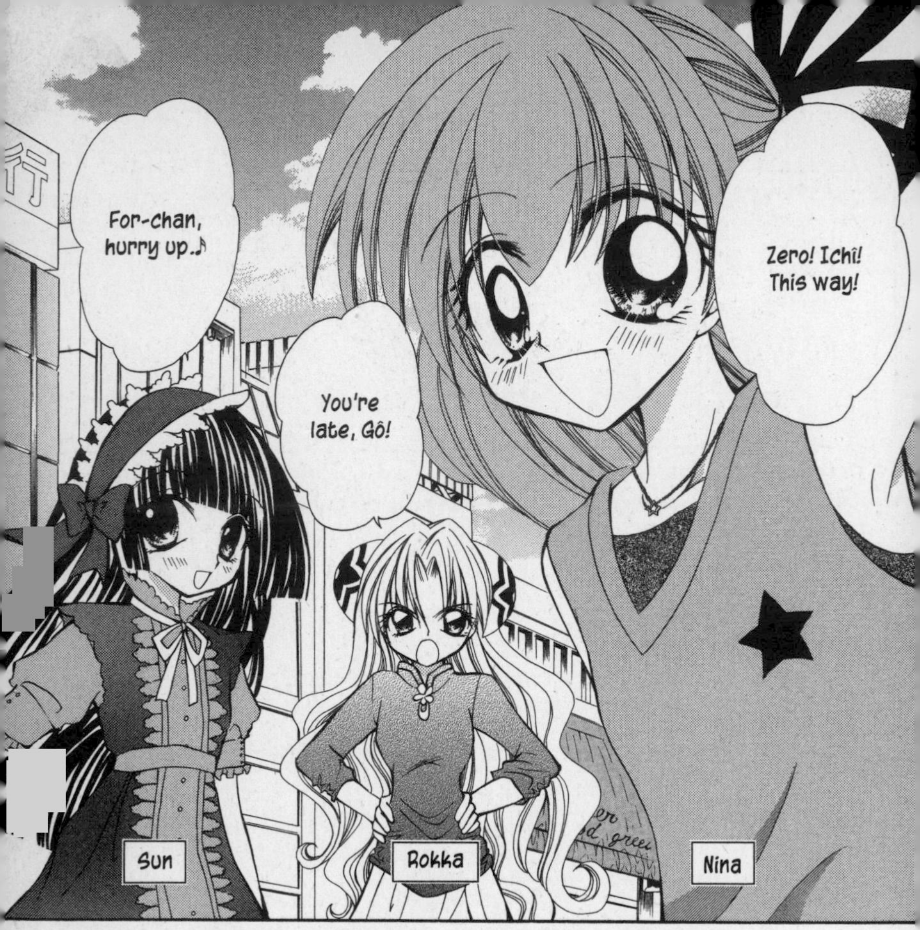
Zero! Ichî! This way!
You're late, Gô!
For-chan, hurry up.♪
行
Nina
Rokka
Sun

POP13 Nina the Flame of Love Girl?!

Yay!! It's the opening page in color! The first one ever! I'm so excited. Since I've never worked on such a huge illustration before, I was drawing it so slowly and carefully that it ended up taking me forever to finish it . . . It was also for the character popularity poll we were conducting so I had to include so many characters. But I like this illustration!

We got some new characters again. There are so many of them in this episode . . . Rill is my favorite. (He's a boy.) I like Eleven and Twelve's assertiveness, too. (Laughs) The psych test works so give it try. I heard it's pretty accurate. . . . And I'm so glad that I got a chance to draw Nina with a ponytail. I like her outfit, too.

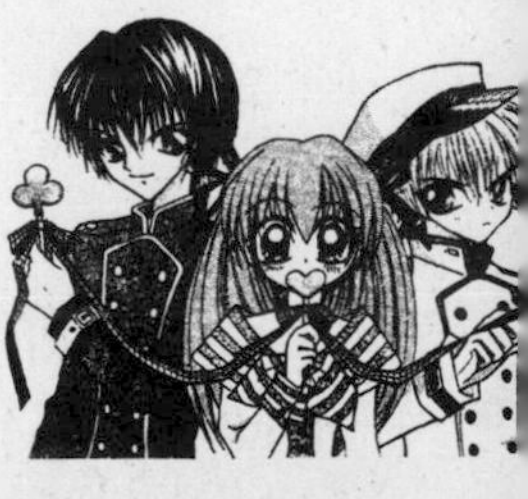

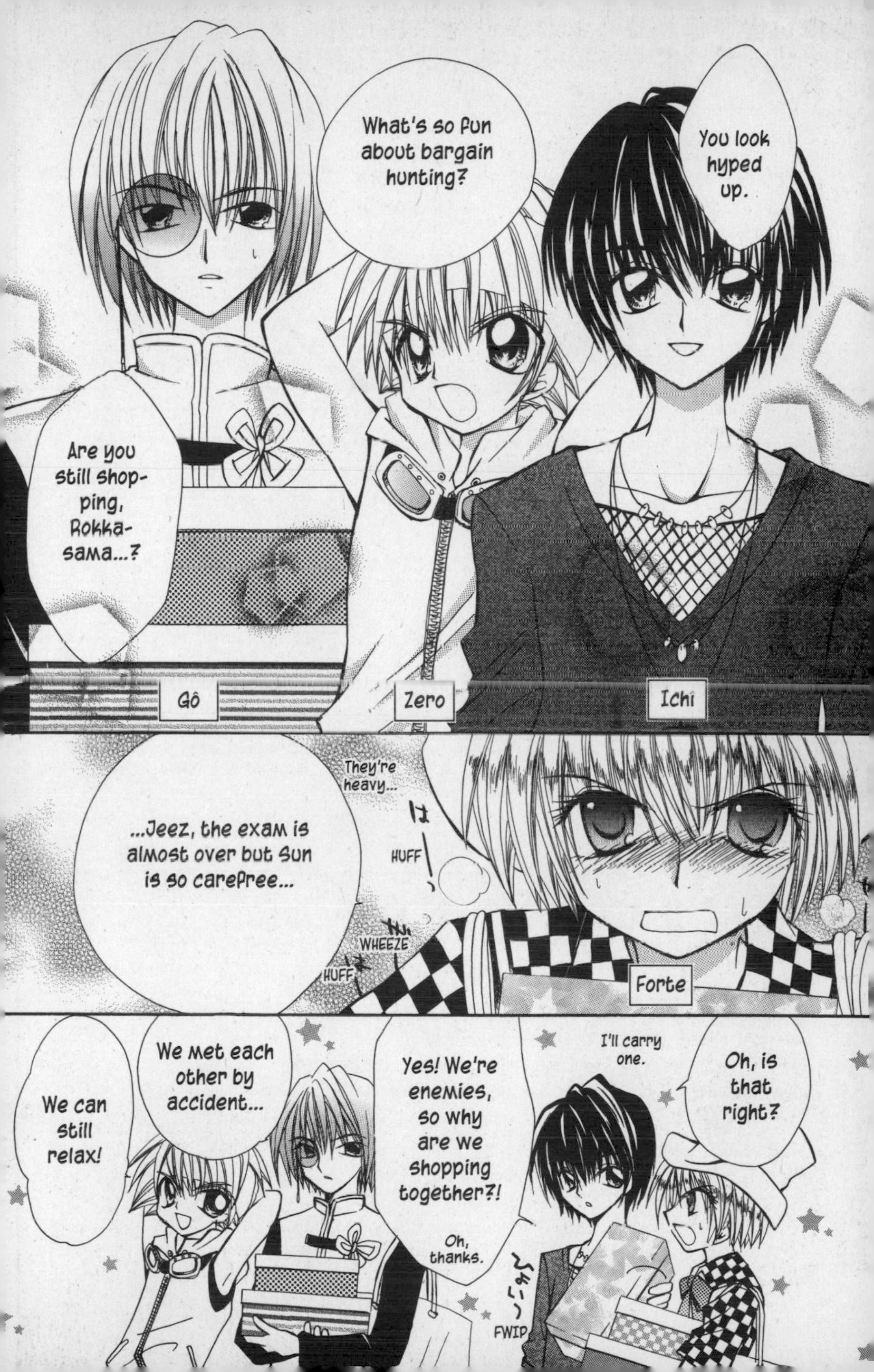
You look hyped up.
What's so fun about bargain hunting?
Are you still shopping, Rokka-sama...?
Ichi
Zero
Gô
They're heavy...
HUFF
WHEEZE
HUFF
...Jeez, the exam is almost over but Sun is so carefree...
Forte
Oh, is that right?
I'll carry one.
FWIP
Oh, thanks.
Yes! We're enemies, so why are we shopping together?!
We met each other by accident...
We can still relax!

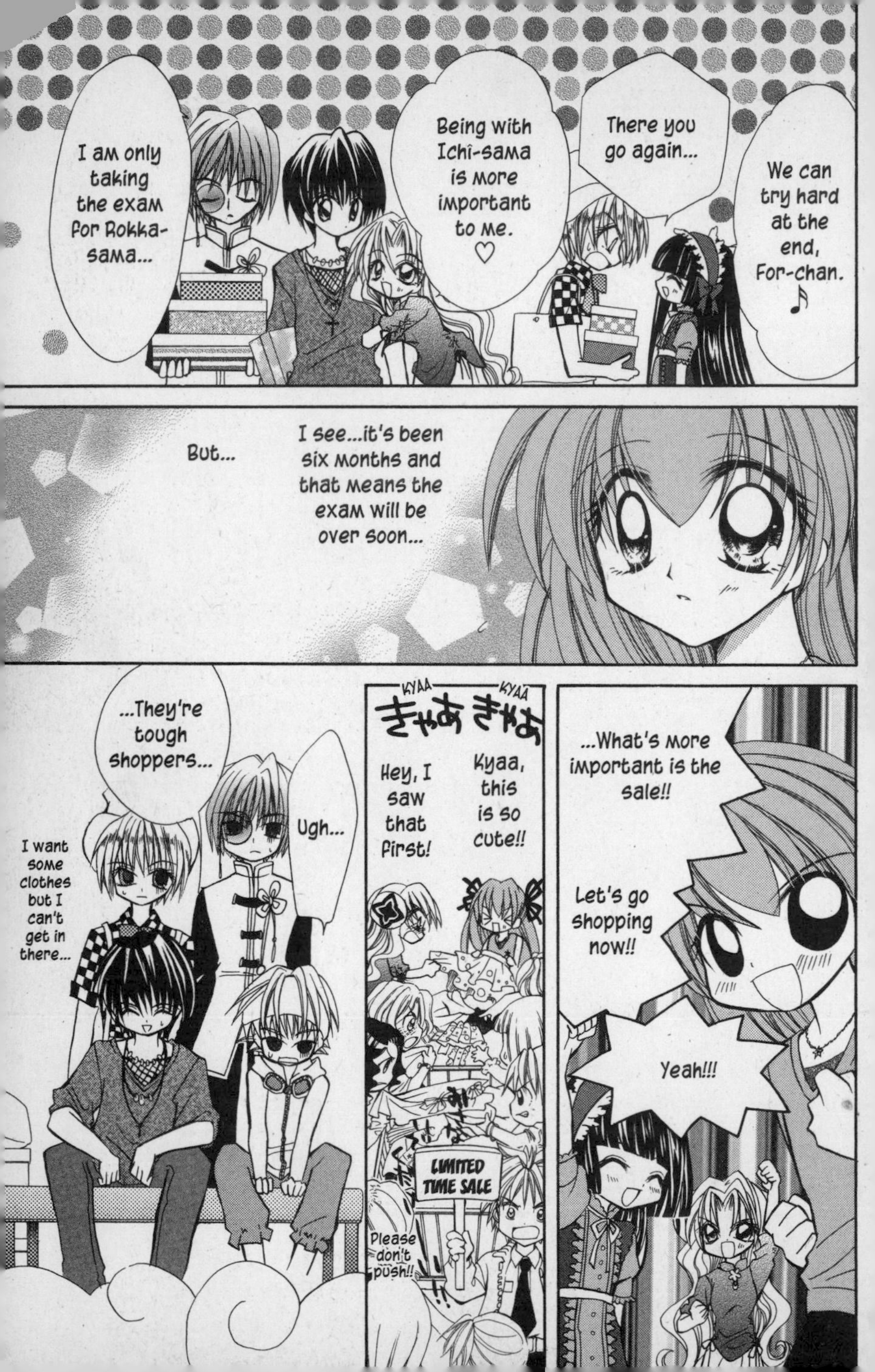

We can try hard at the end, For-chan. ♪
There you go again...
Being with Ichi-sama is more important to me. ♡
I am only taking the exam for Rokka-sama...
I see...it's been six months and that means the exam will be over soon...
But...
...What's more important is the sale!!
Let's go shopping now!!
Yeah!!!
KYAA KYAA
きゃあ きゃあ
Kyaa, this is so cute!!
Hey, I saw that first!
LIMITED TIME SALE
Please don't push!!
...They're tough shoppers...
Ugh...
I want some clothes but I can't get in there...

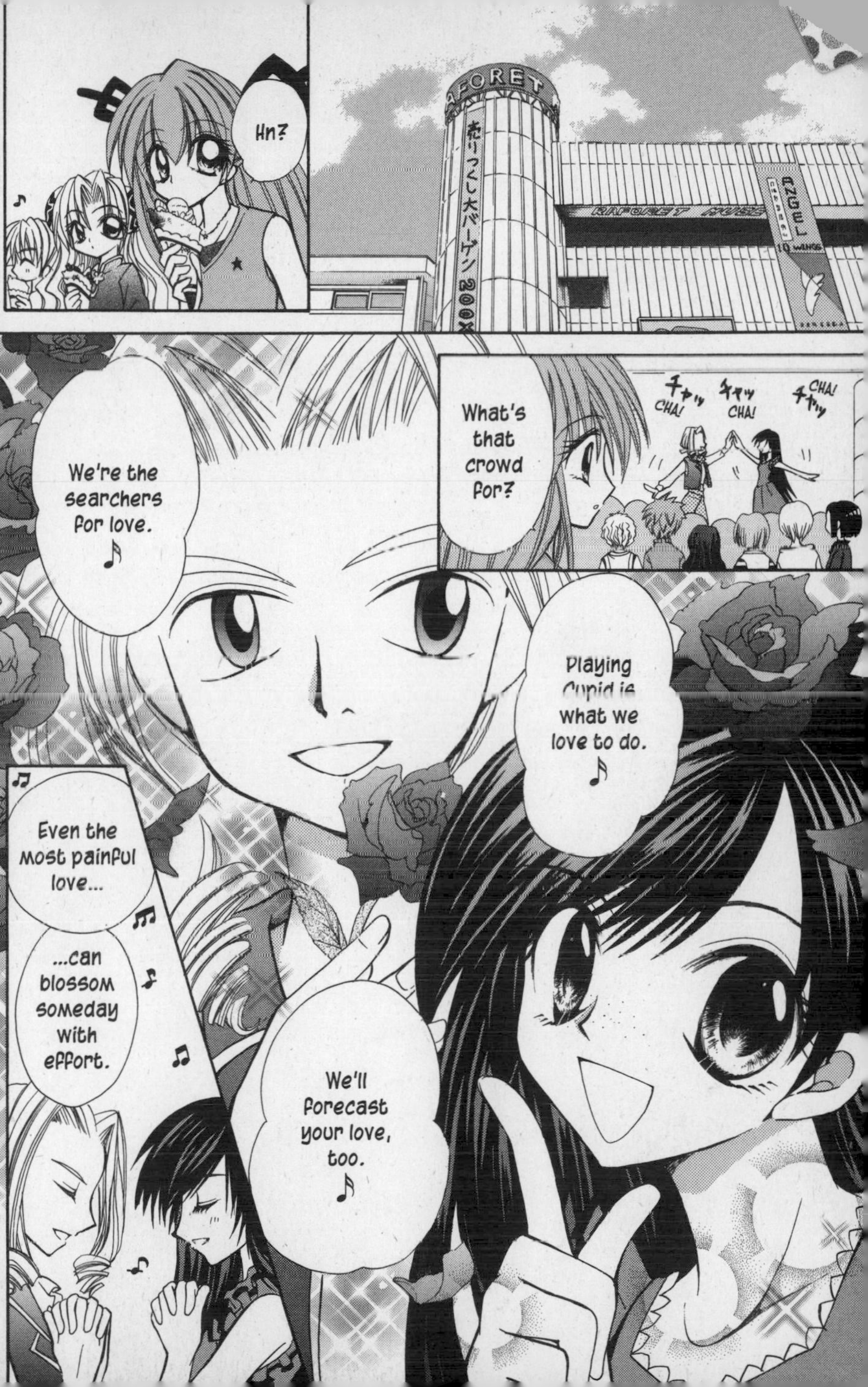
RAFORET
売りつくし大バーゲン 200X
ANGEL
10 WINGS
Hn?
What's that crowd for?
チャッ CHA!
チャッ CHA!
CHA! チャッ
We're the searchers for love. ♪
Playing Cupid is what we love to do. ♪
Even the most painful love...
...can blossom someday with effort.
We'll forecast your love, too. ♪

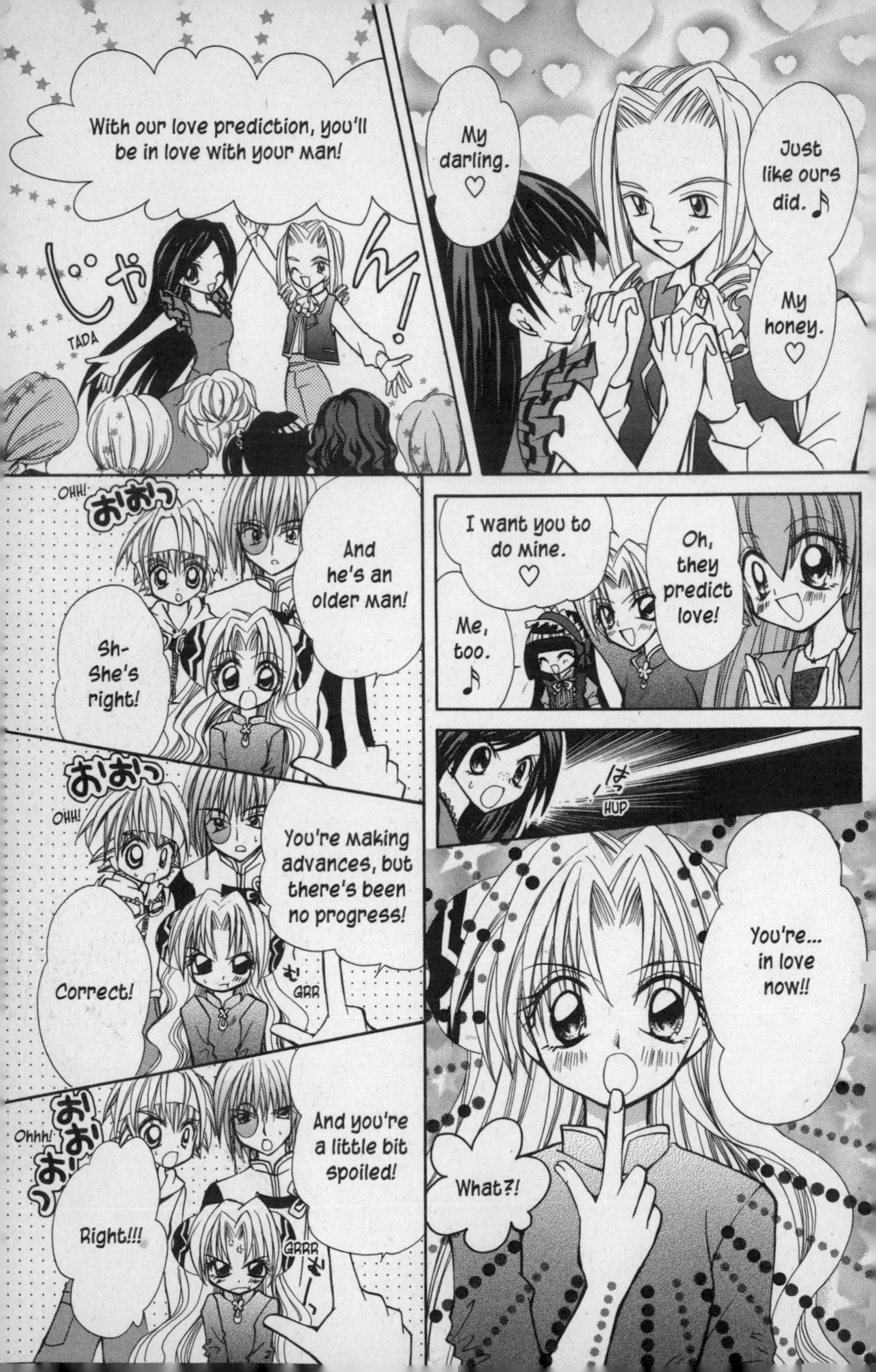
Just like ours did. ♪
My darling. ♡
My honey. ♡
With our love prediction, you'll be in love with your man!
じゃん!
TADA
Oh, they predict love!
I want you to do mine. ♡
Me, too. ♪
はっ
HUP
You're... in love now!!
What?!
おおっ
OHH!
And he's an older man!
Sh-She's right!
おおっ
OHH!
You're making advances, but there's been no progress!
Correct!
GRR
おおおっ
Ohhh!
And you're a little bit spoiled!
Right!!!
GRRR

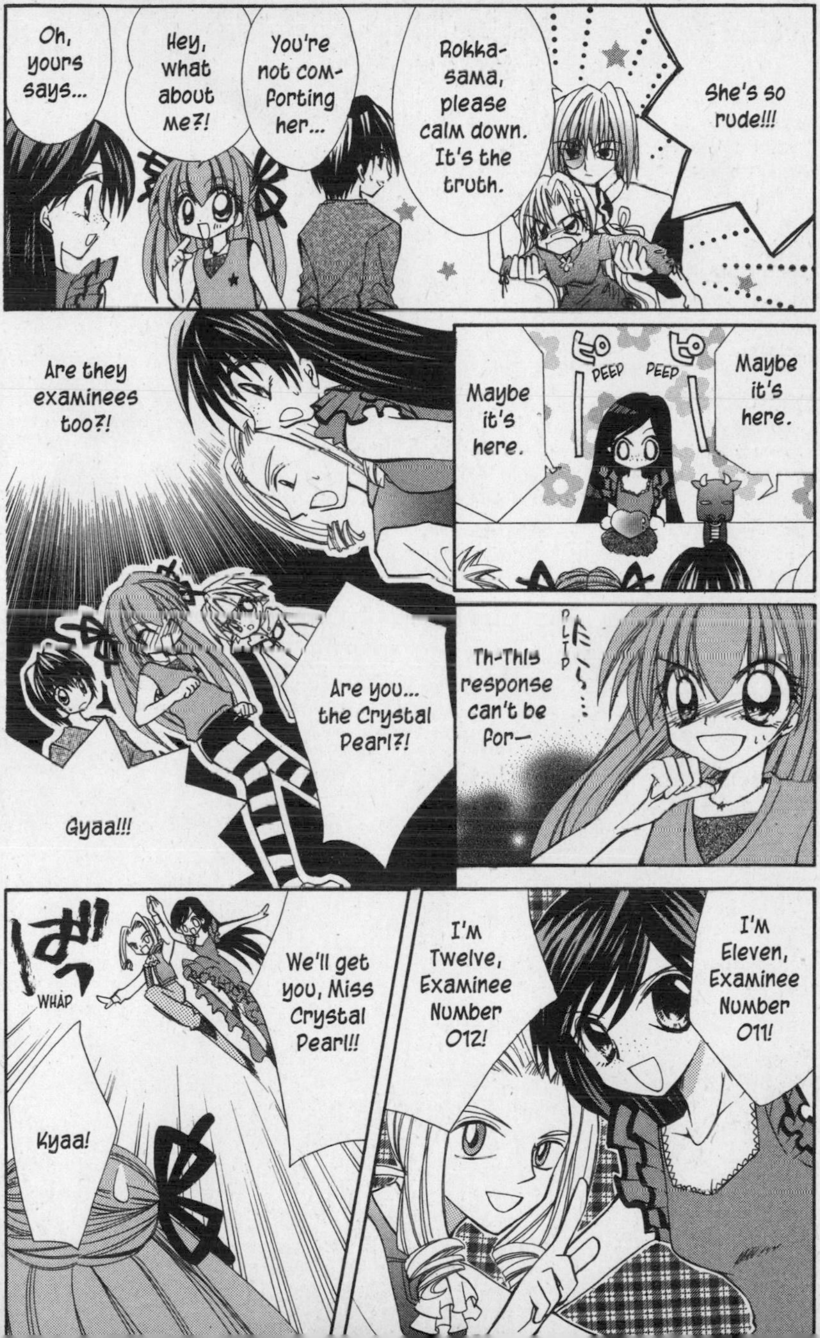
She's so rude!!!
Rokka-sama, please calm down. It's the truth.
You're not comforting her...
Hey, what about me?!
Oh, yours says...
PEEP
PEEP
Maybe it's here.
Maybe it's here.
PLIP
Th-Thly response can't be for—
Are they examinees too?!
Are you... the Crystal Pearl?!
Gyaa!!!
I'm Eleven, Examinee Number 011!
I'm Twelve, Examinee Number 012!
We'll get you, Miss Crystal Pearl!!
WHAP
Kyaa!

Q&A

Q1. Don't Zero or Ichî (people in the Magical World) have last names?

A1. Well, I think they do. I just haven't thought of any. Someone please give me some ideas! I might announce them once I've decided. . . .

Q2. What would you do if someone like Zero or Ichî really existed and confessed his love to you?!

A2. What?! Oh, no! My answer will be "yes"! That's so obvious! (← A fool.)

Q3. When do you come up your story ideas?

A3. Hmm . . . I usually think about it while I'm doodling. And when I'm wandering around or fantasizing, too.

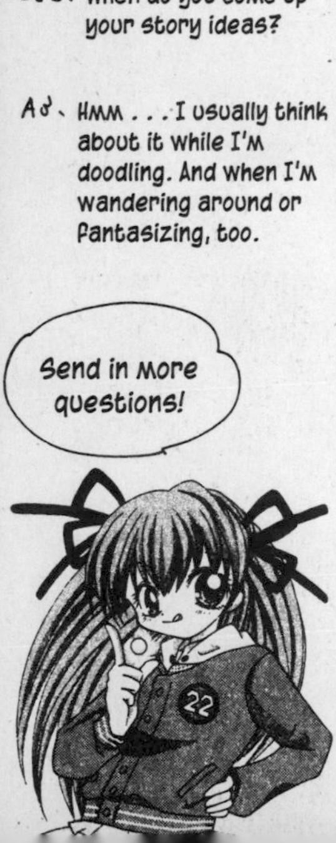
Send in more questions!

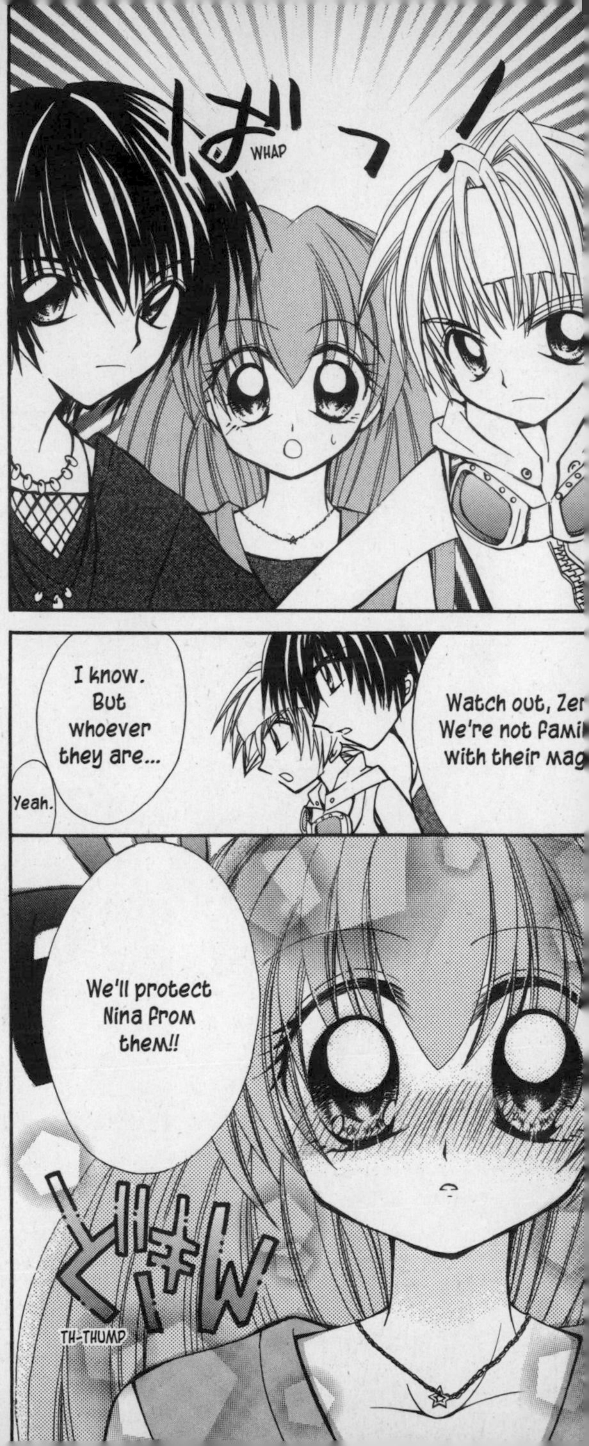
WHAP
Watch out, Zer
We're not fami
with their mag
I know. But whoever they are...
Yeah.
We'll protect Nina from them!!
TH-THUMP

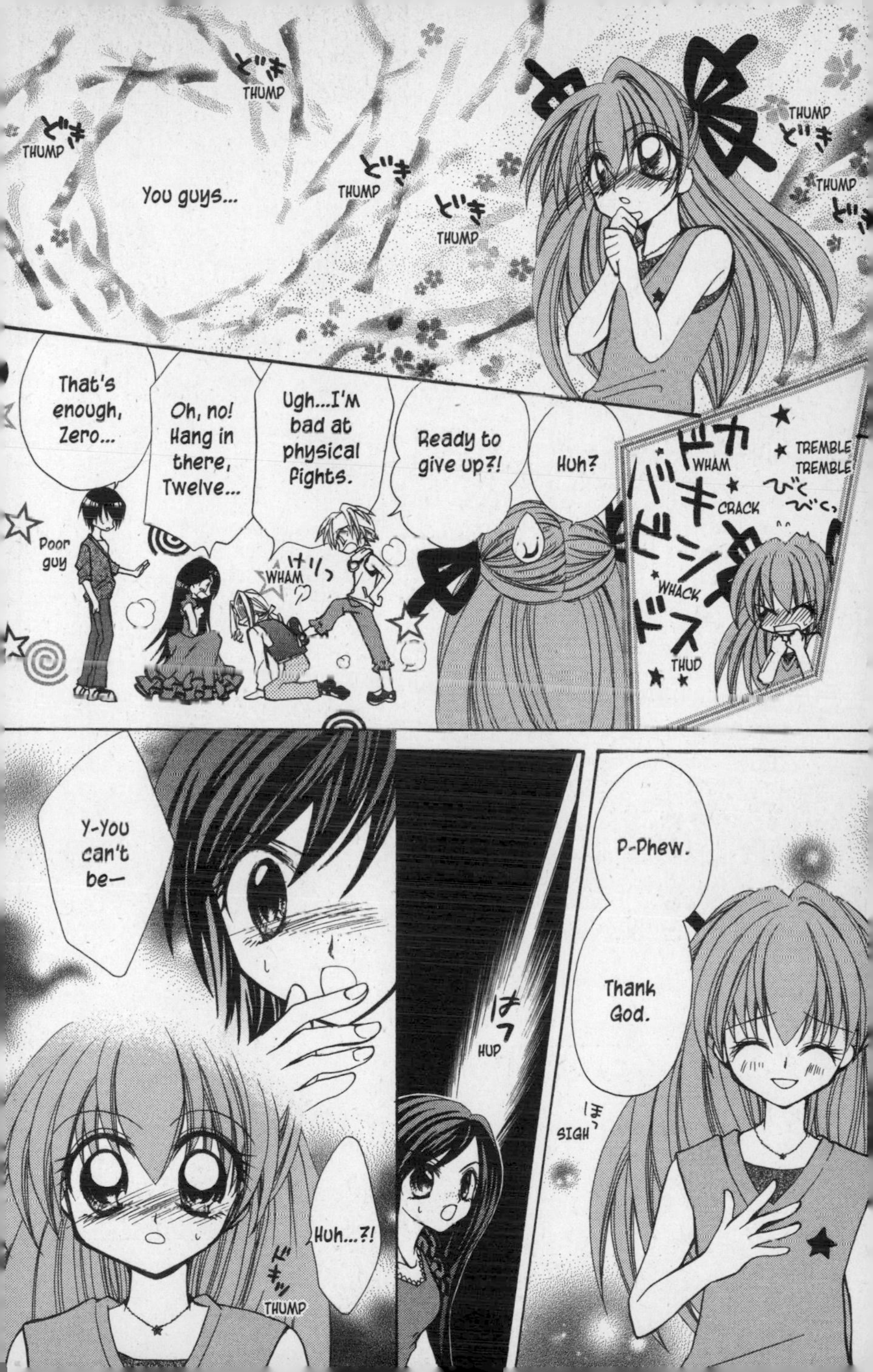
どき
THUMP
どき
THUMP
どき
THUMP
どき
THUMP
どき
THUMP
どき
THUMP
You guys...
ドカ
WHAM
バキ
CRACK
ビシ
WHACK
ドス
THUD
びくびくっ
TREMBLE TREMBLE
Huh?
Ready to give up?!
Ugh...I'm bad at physical fights.
ケリっ
WHAM
Oh, no! Hang in there, Twelve...
That's enough, Zero...
Poor guy
P-Phew.
Thank God.
ほっ
SIGH
はっ
HUP
Y-You can't be—
Huh...?!
ドキッ
THUMP

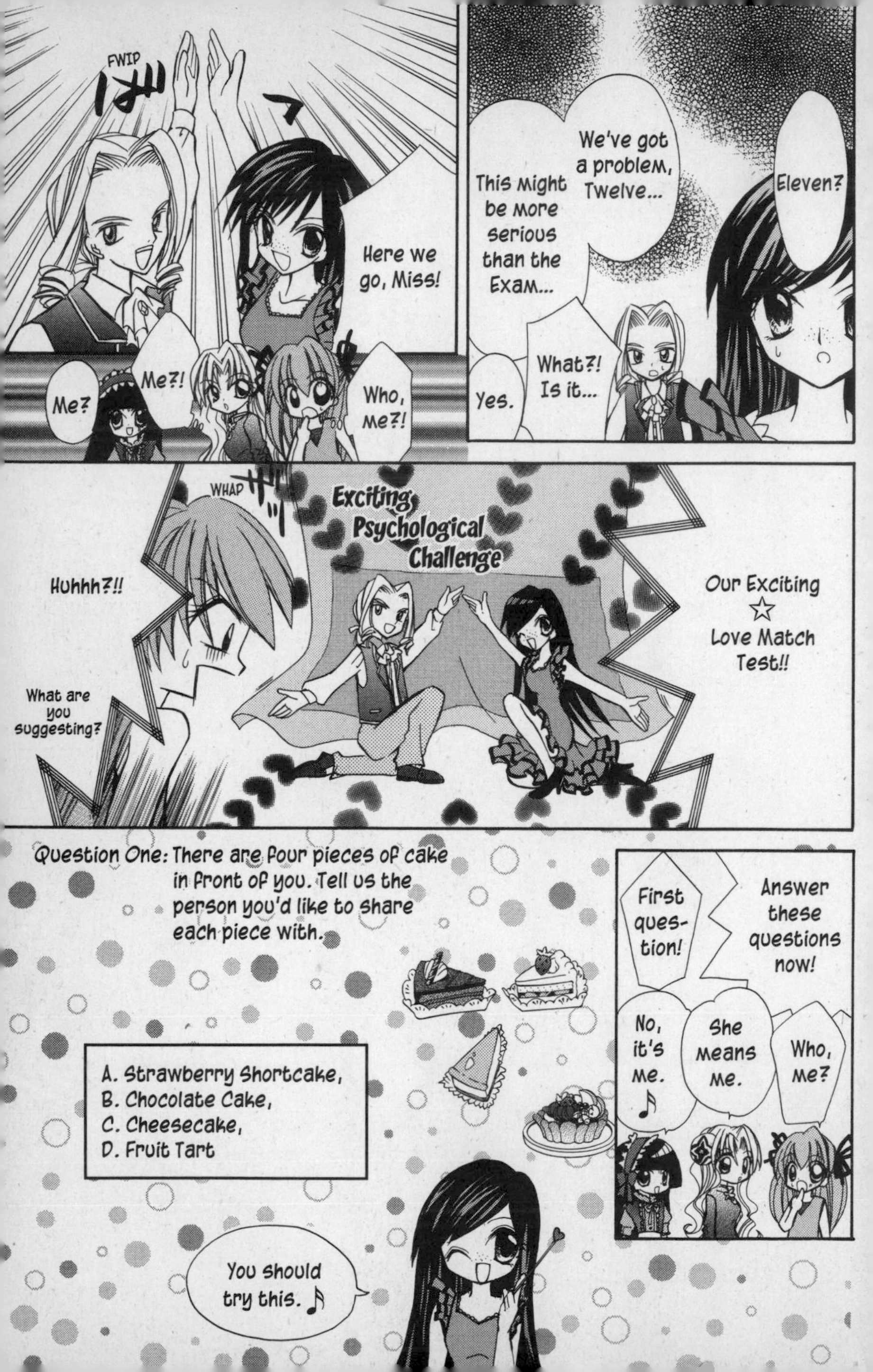
Eleven?
We've got a problem, Twelve...
This might be more serious than the Exam...
What?! Is it...
Yes.
FWIP
Here we go, Miss!
Who, me?!
Me?!
Me?
Exciting Psychological Challenge
WHAP
Our Exciting ☆ Love Match Test!!
Huhhh?!!
What are you suggesting?
Answer these questions now!
First question!
Who, me?
She means me.
No, it's me. ♪
Question One: There are four pieces of cake in front of you. Tell us the person you'd like to share each piece with.
A. Strawberry Shortcake,
B. Chocolate Cake,
C. Cheesecake,
D. Fruit Tart
You should try this. ♪

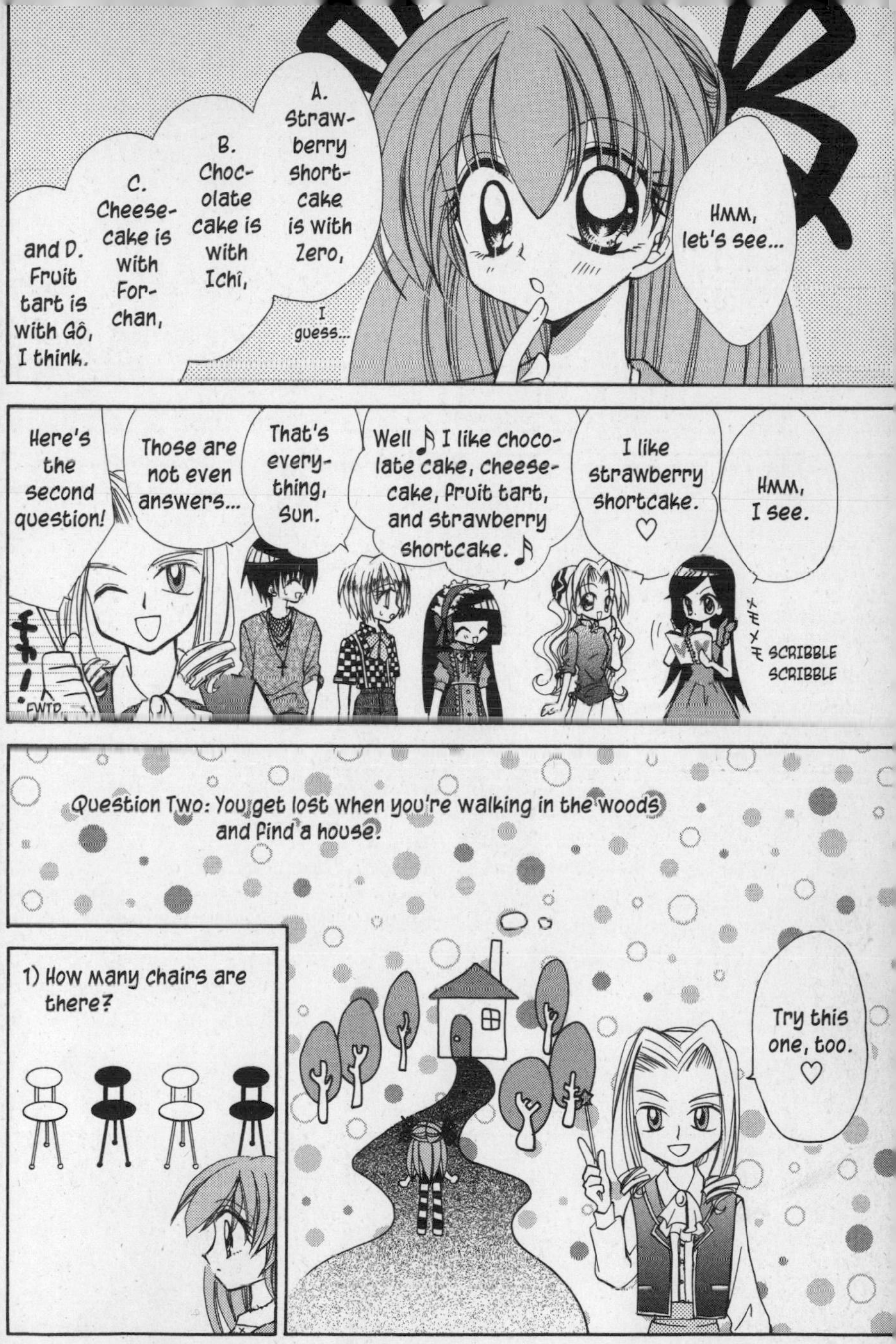
HMM, let's see...
A. Straw-berry short-cake is with Zero,
I guess...
B. Choc-olate cake is with Ichi,
C. Cheese-cake is with For-chan,
and D. Fruit tart is with Gô, I think.
HMM, I see.
SCRIBBLE SCRIBBLE
I like strawberry shortcake. ♡
Well ♪ I like choco-late cake, cheese-cake, fruit tart, and strawberry shortcake. ♪
That's every-thing, Sun.
Those are not even answers...
Here's the second question!
Question Two: You get lost when you're walking in the woods and find a house.
Try this one, too. ♡
1) How many chairs are there?

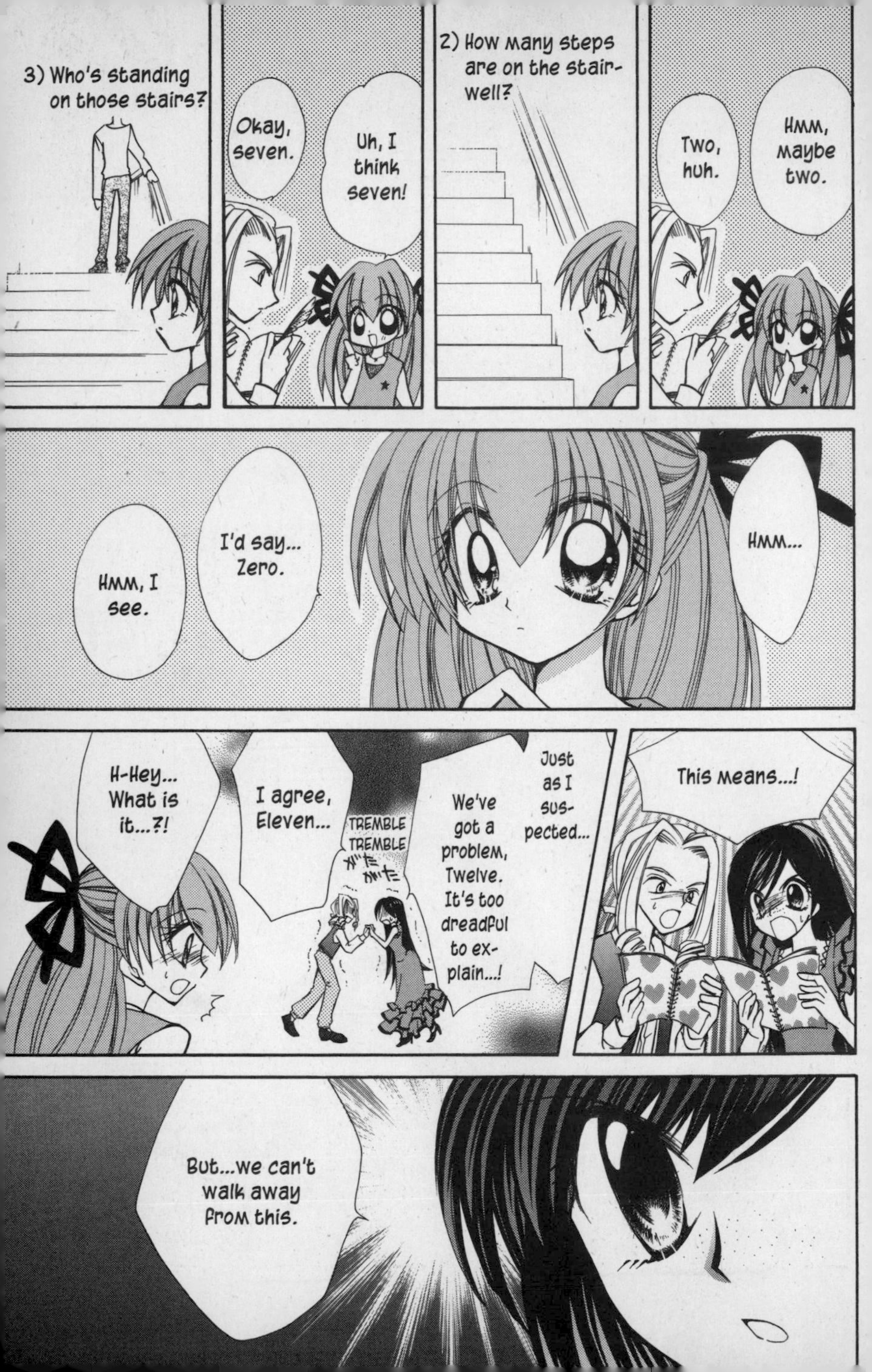
Hmm, maybe two.
Two, huh.
2) How many steps are on the stair-well?
Uh, I think seven!
Okay, seven.
3) Who's standing on those stairs?
Hmm...
I'd say... Zero.
Hmm, I see.
This means...!
Just as I sus-pected...
We've got a problem, Twelve. It's too dreadful to ex-plain...!
TREMBLE TREMBLE
I agree, Eleven...
H-Hey... What is it...?!
But...we can't walk away from this.

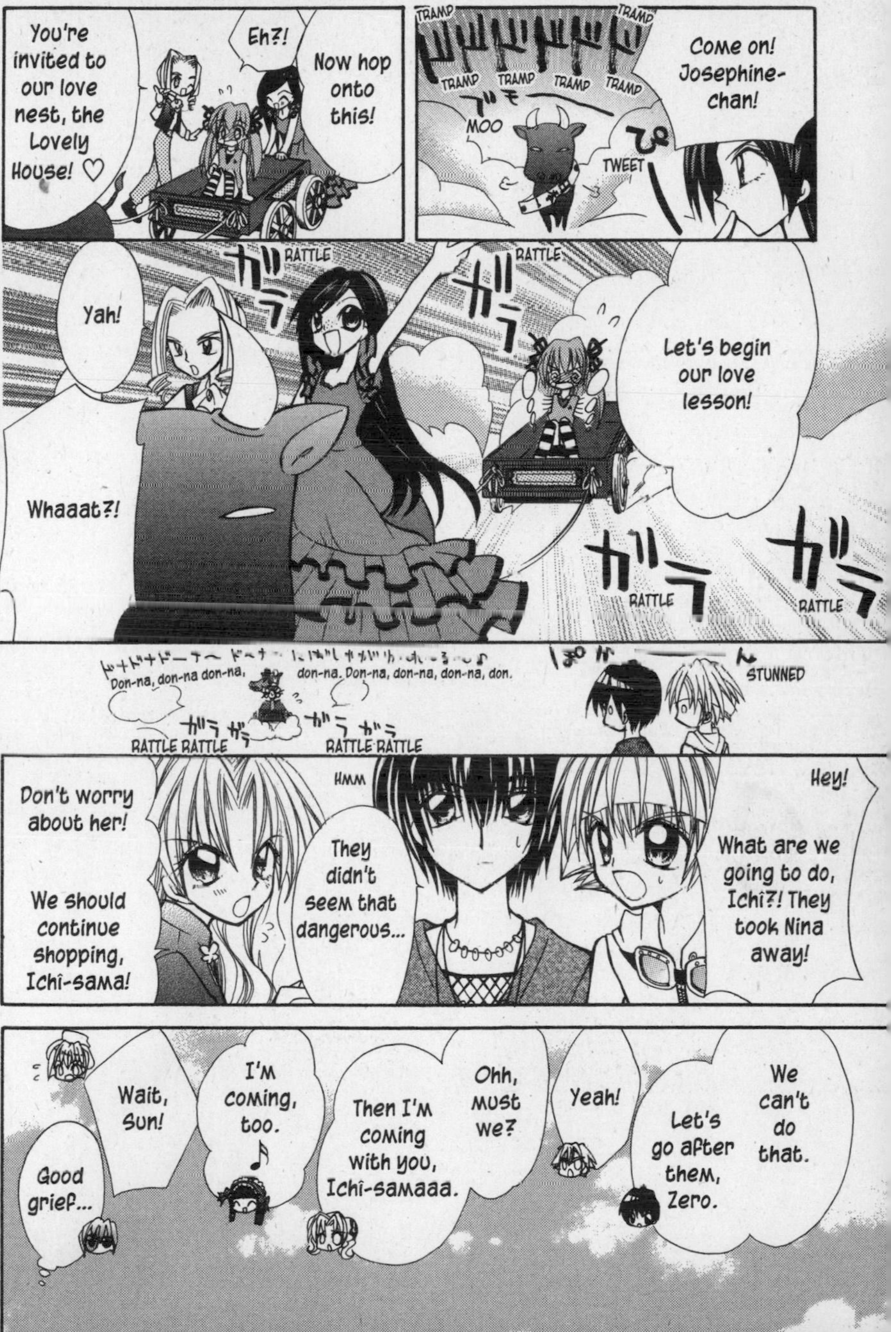
TRAMP TRAMP TRAMP TRAMP TRAMP TRAMP
Come on! Josephine-chan!
MOO
TWEET
Now hop onto this!
Eh?!
You're invited to our love nest, the Lovely House! ♡
RATTLE RATTLE
Let's begin our love lesson!
RATTLE RATTLE
Yah!
Whaaat?!
STUNNED
Don-na, don-na don-na, don-na. Don-na, don-na, don-na, don.
RATTLE RATTLE RATTLE RATTLE
Hey!
What are we going to do, Ichî?! They took Nina away!
HMM
They didn't seem that dangerous...
Don't worry about her!
We should continue shopping, Ichî-sama!
We can't do that.
Let's go after them, Zero.
Yeah!
Ohh, must we?
Then I'm coming with you, Ichî-samaaa.
I'm coming, too. ♪
Wait, Sun!
Good grief...

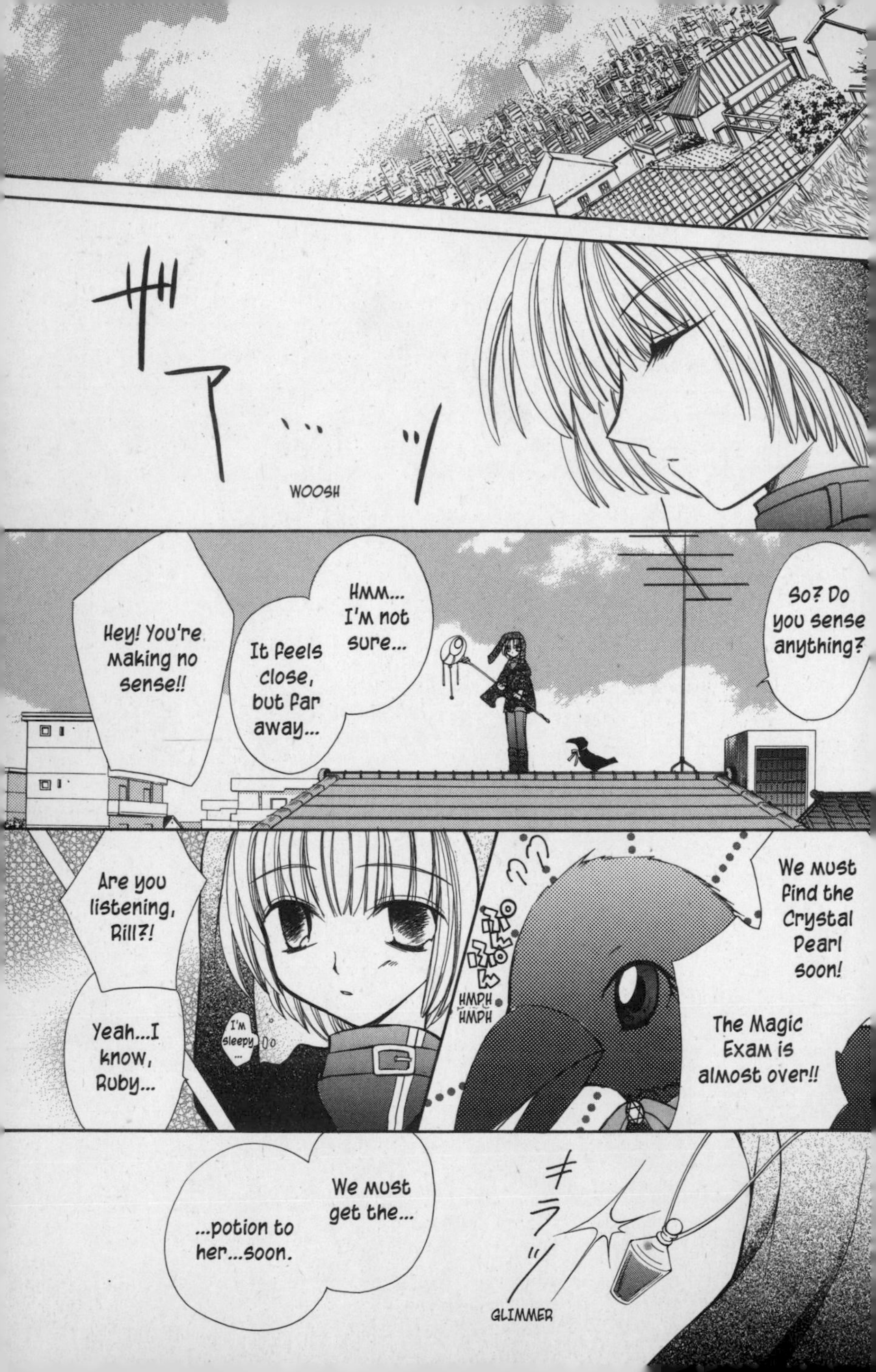
ザア…ッ
WOOSH
So? Do you sense anything?
Hmm... I'm not sure...
It feels close, but far away...
Hey! You're making no sense!!
We must find the Crystal Pearl soon!
The Magic Exam is almost over!!
ぷんぷん
HMPH HMPH
Are you listening, Rill?!
I'm sleepy...
Yeah...I know, Ruby...
キラッ
GLIMMER
We must get the...
...potion to her...soon.

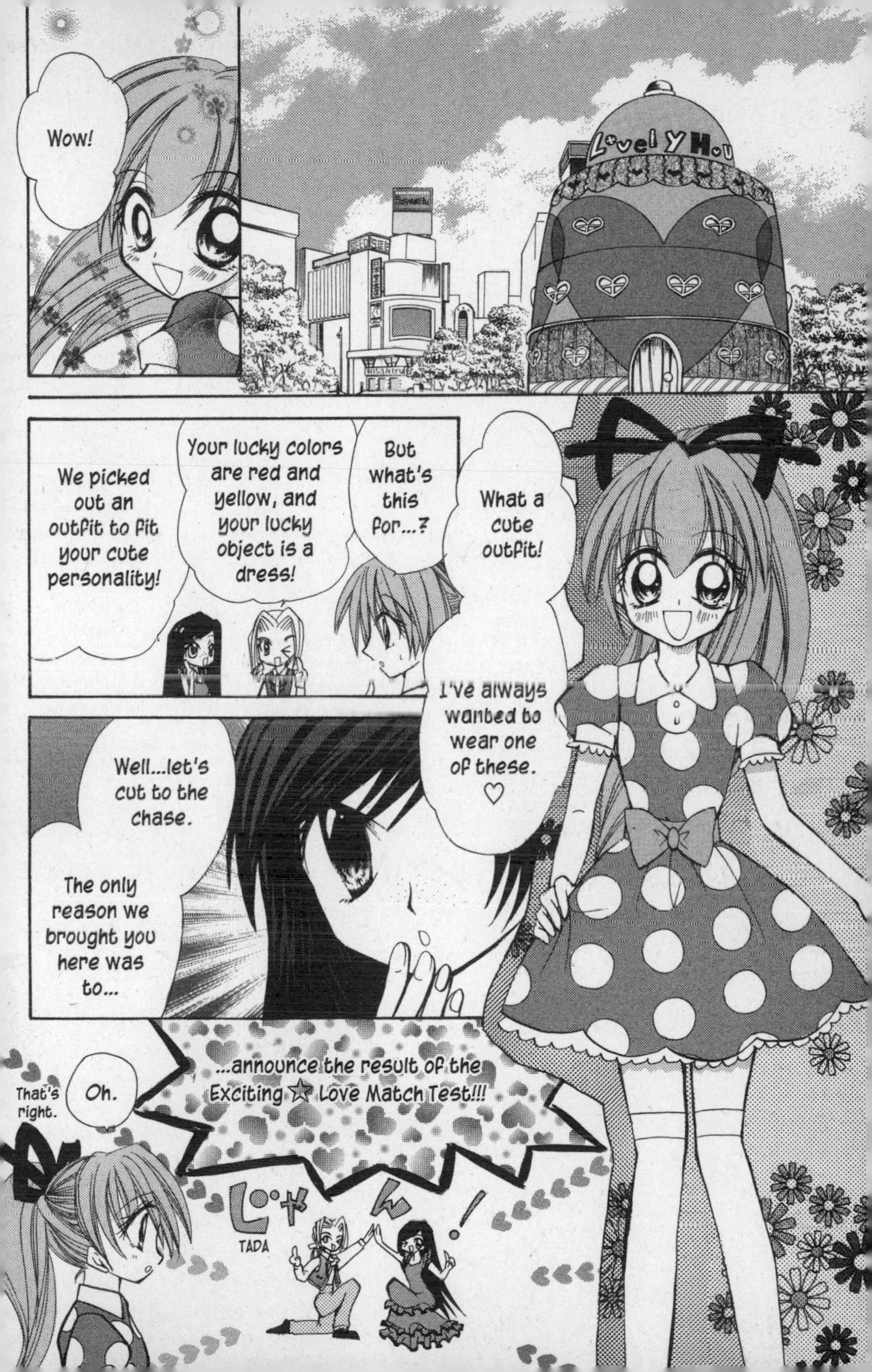
Wow!
What a cute outfit!
I've always wanted to wear one of these. ♡
But what's this for...?
Your lucky colors are red and yellow, and your lucky object is a dress!
We picked out an outfit to fit your cute personality!
Well...let's cut to the chase.
The only reason we brought you here was to...
...announce the result of the Exciting☆ Love Match Test!!!
Oh.
That's right.
TADA

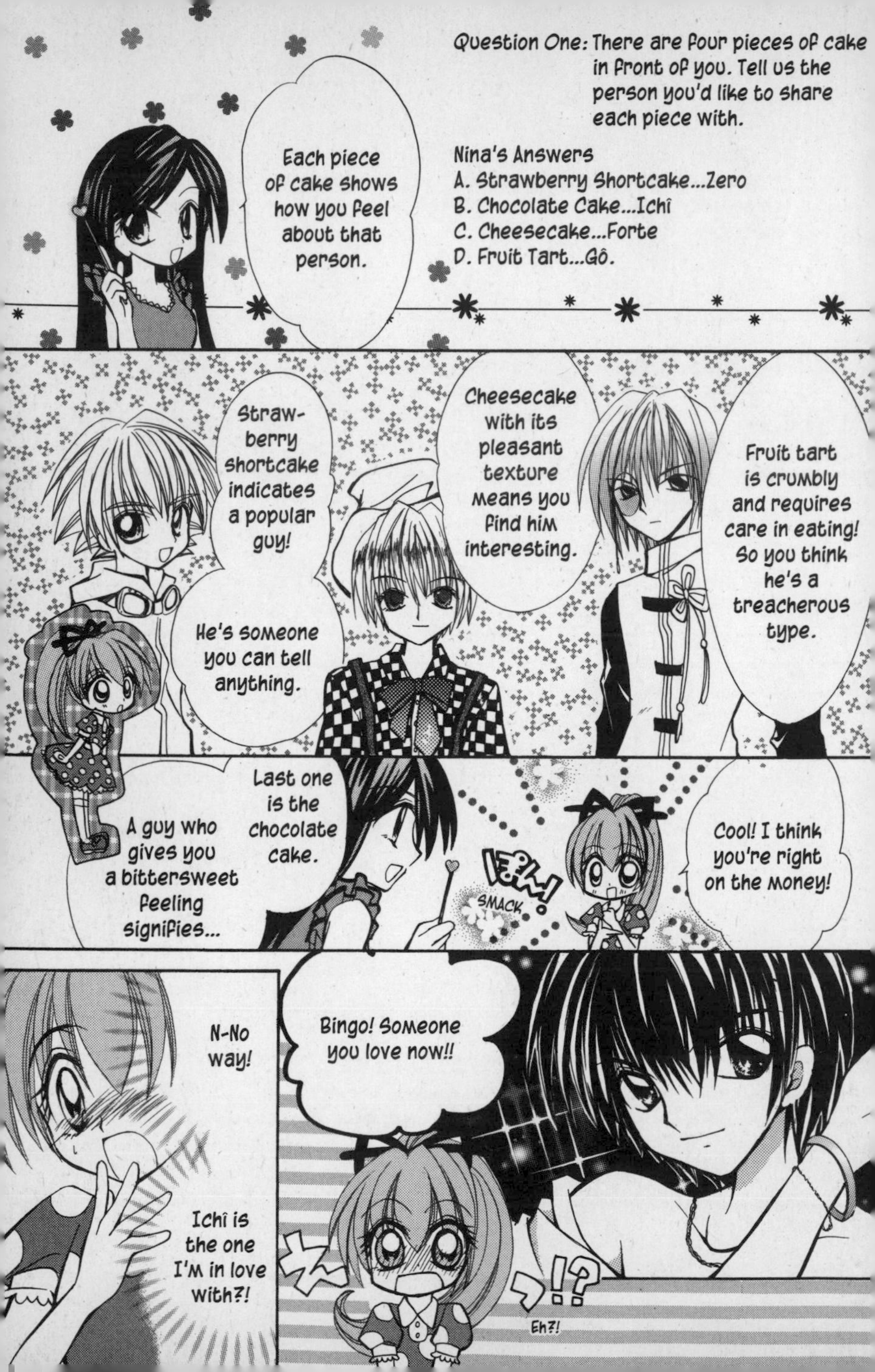
Question One: There are four pieces of cake in front of you. Tell us the person you'd like to share each piece with.
Nina's Answers
A. Strawberry Shortcake...Zero
B. Chocolate Cake...Ichî
C. Cheesecake...Forte
D. Fruit Tart...Gô.
Each piece of cake shows how you feel about that person.
Fruit tart is crumbly and requires care in eating! So you think he's a treacherous type.
Cheesecake with its pleasant texture means you find him interesting.
Straw-berry shortcake indicates a popular guy!
He's someone you can tell anything.
Cool! I think you're right on the money!
SMACK
Last one is the chocolate cake.
A guy who gives you a bittersweet feeling signifies...
Bingo! Someone you love now!!
!?
Eh?!
N-No way!
Ichî is the one I'm in love with?!

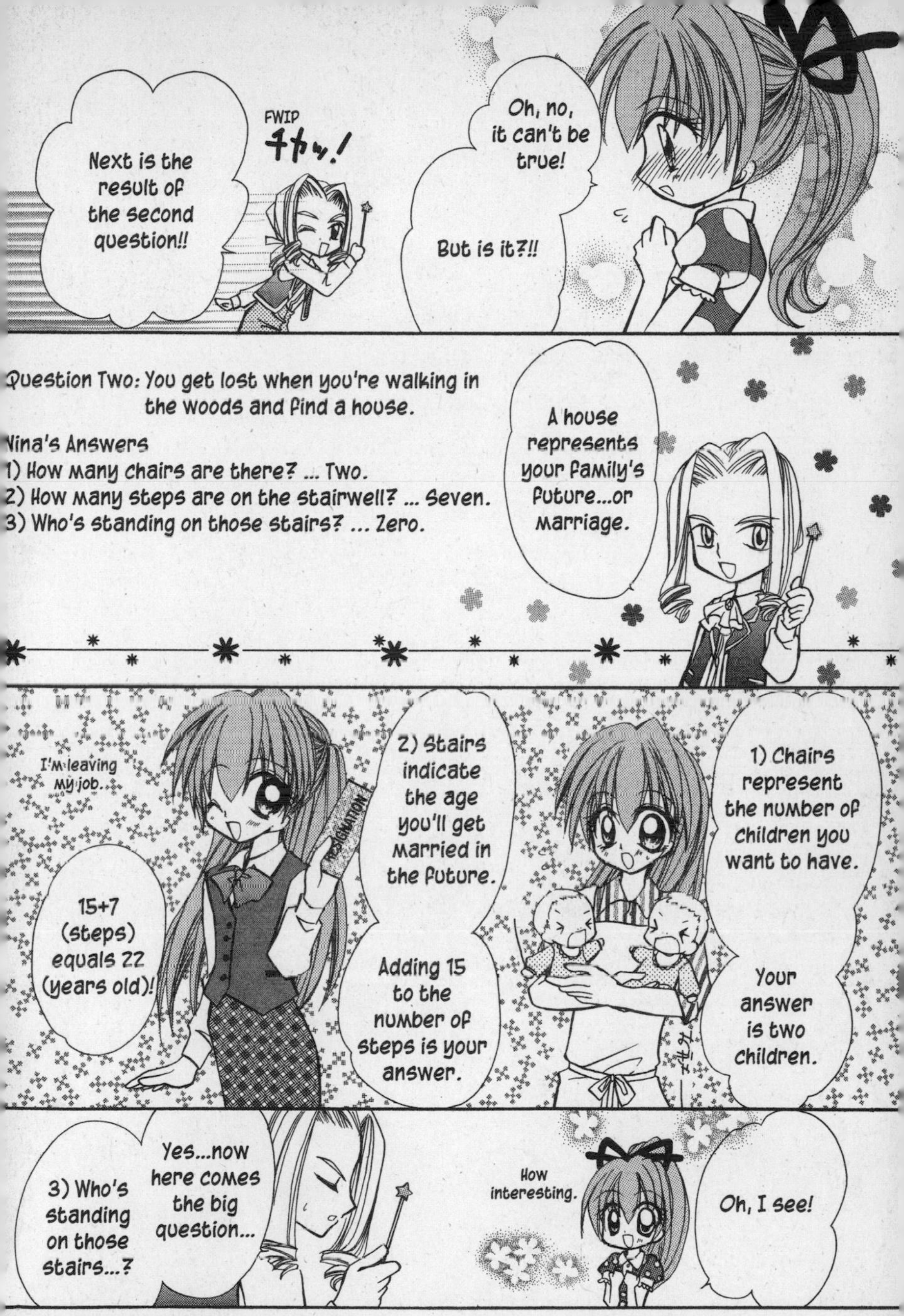

Oh, no, it can't be true!
But is it?!!
FWIP
チャッ!
Next is the result of the second question!!
A house represents your family's future...or marriage.
Question Two: You get lost when you're walking in the woods and find a house.
Nina's Answers
1) How many chairs are there? ... Two.
2) How many steps are on the stairwell? ... Seven.
3) Who's standing on those stairs? ... Zero.
1) Chairs represent the number of children you want to have.
Your answer is two children.
2) Stairs indicate the age you'll get married in the future.
Adding 15 to the number of steps is your answer.
I'm leaving my job.
RESIGNATION
15+7 (steps) equals 22 (years old)!
Oh, I see!
How interesting.
Yes...now here comes the big question...
3) Who's standing on those stairs...?

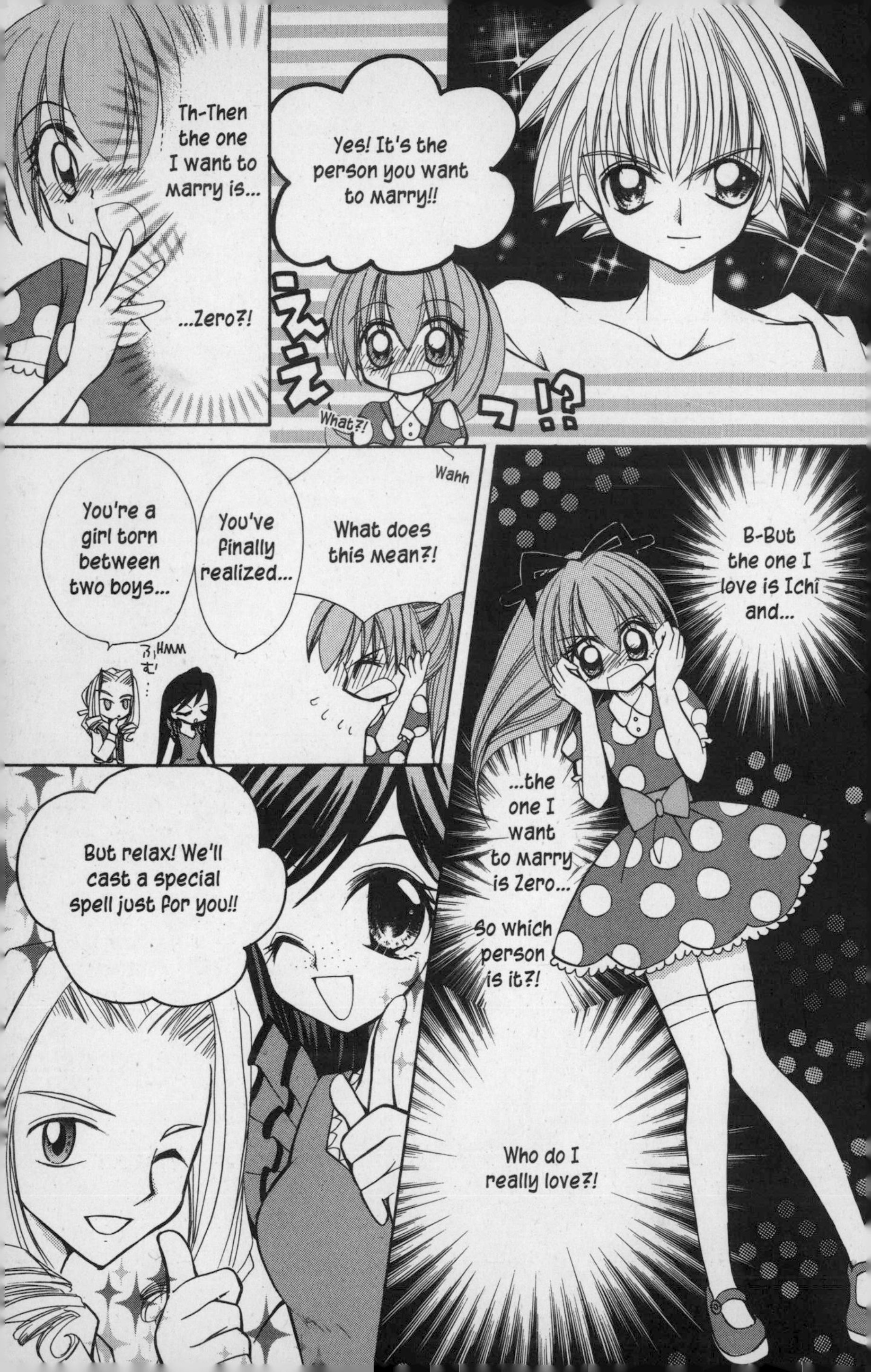
Yes! It's the person you want to marry!!
えぇ〜っ !?
What?!
Th-Then the one I want to marry is...
...Zero?!
B-But the one I love is Ichi and...
...the one I want to marry is Zero...
So which person is it?!
Who do I really love?!
Wahh
What does this mean?!
You've finally realized...
You're a girl torn between two boys...
ふむ HMM
But relax! We'll cast a special spell just for you!!

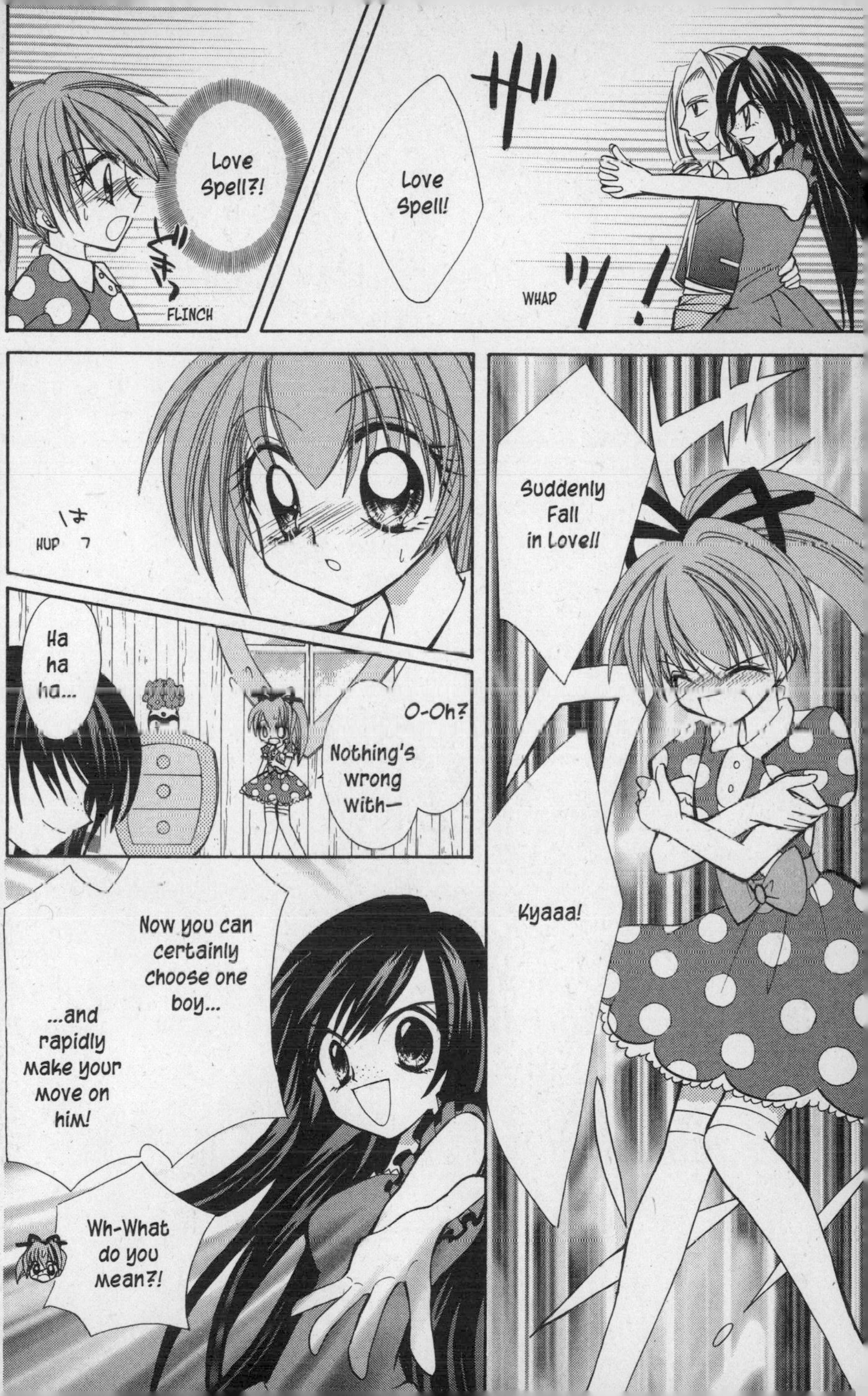

WHAP
Love Spell!
Love Spell?!
FLINCH
Suddenly Fall in Love!!
Kyaaa!
HUP
O-Oh? Nothing's wrong with—
Ha ha ha...
Now you can certainly choose one boy...
...and rapidly make your move on him!
Wh-What do you mean?!

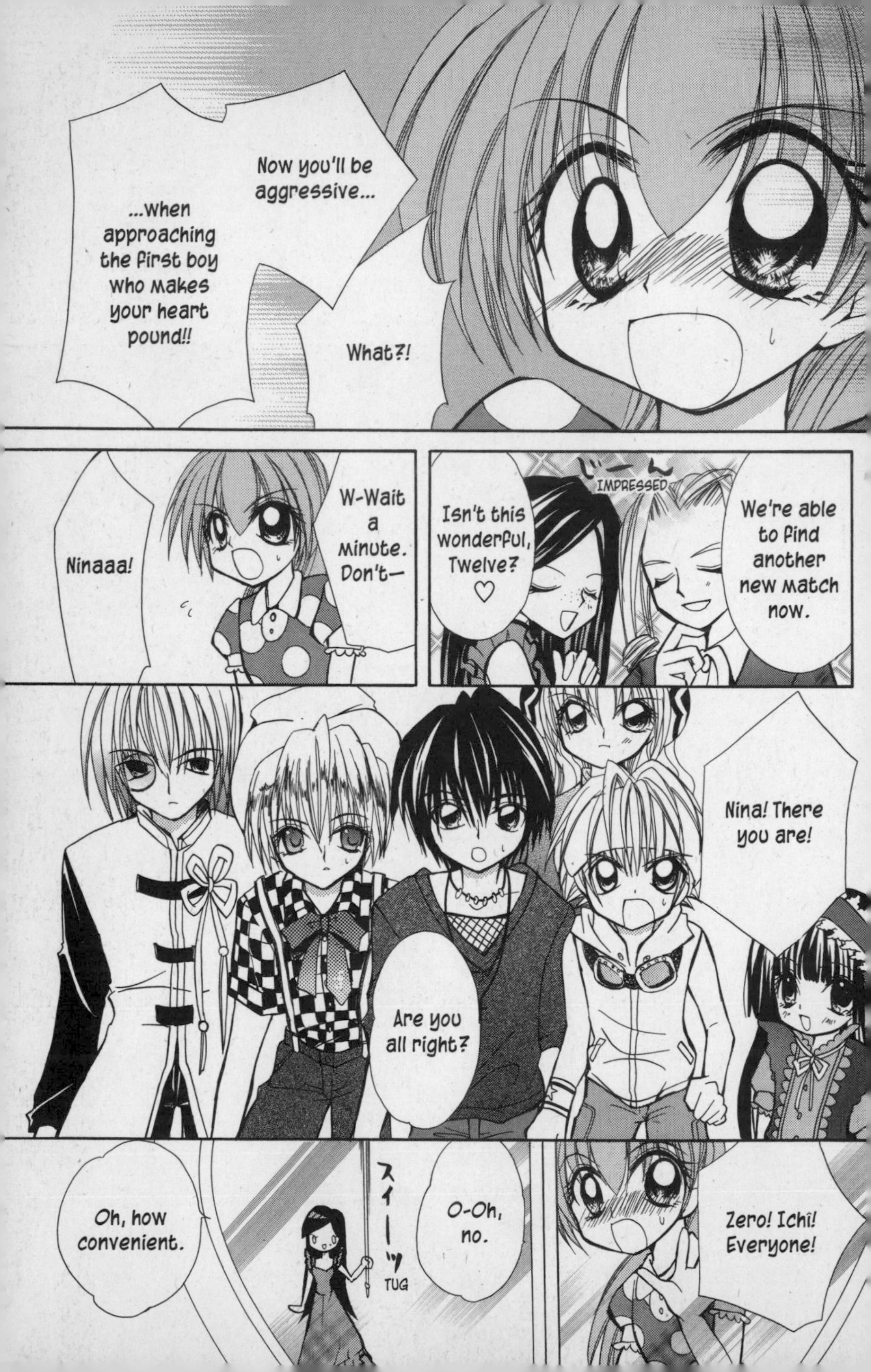
Now you'll be aggressive...
...when approaching the first boy who makes your heart pound!!
What?!
We're able to find another new match now.
じーん
IMPRESSED
Isn't this wonderful, Twelve? ♡
W-Wait a minute. Don't—
Ninaaa!
Nina! There you are!
Are you all right?
Zero! Ichi! Everyone!
O-Oh, no.
スイーッ
TUG
Oh, how convenient.

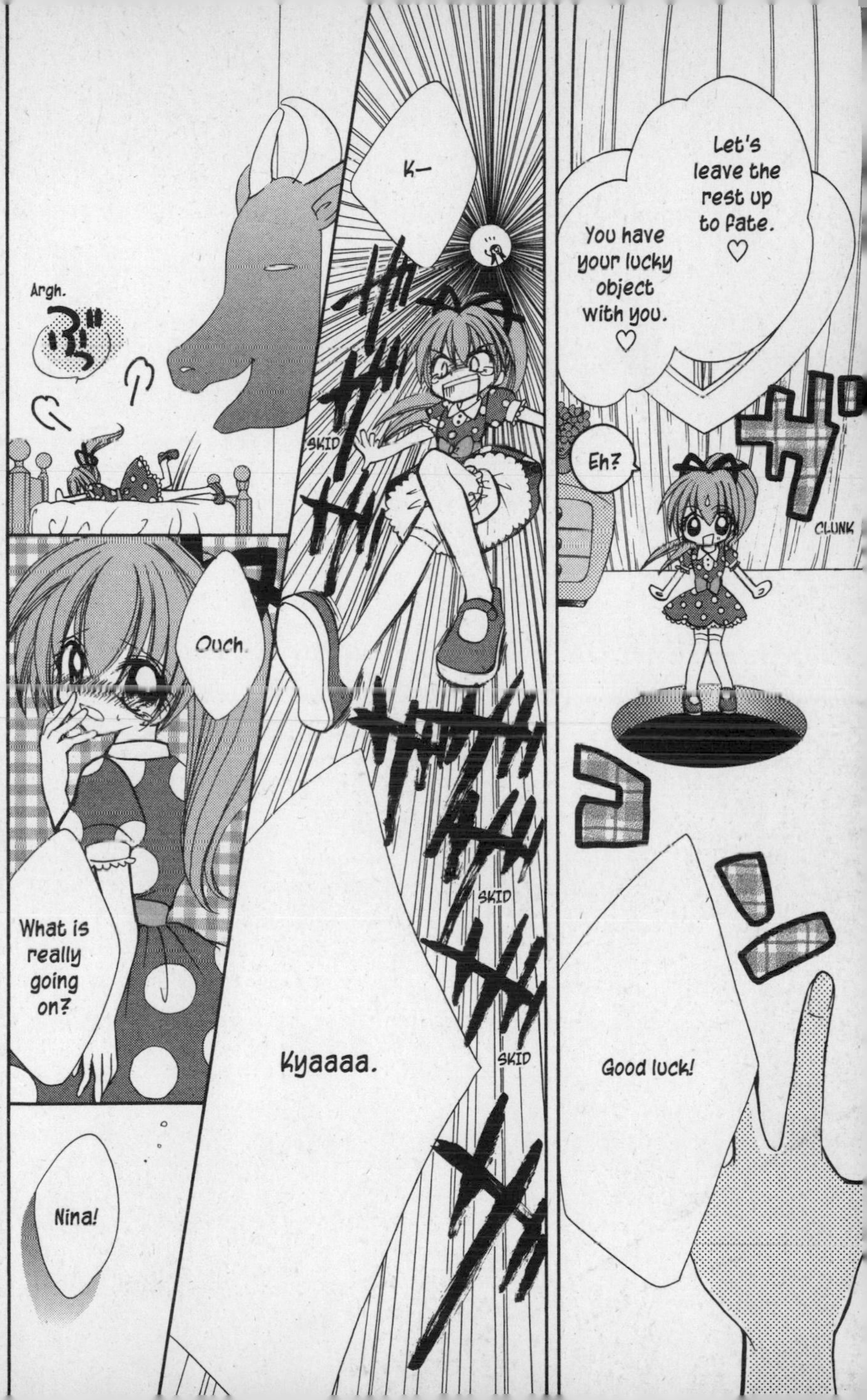
Let's leave the rest up to fate. ♡
You have your lucky object with you. ♡
Eh?
CLUNK
Good luck!
K—
SKID
SKID
SKID
Kyaaaa.
Argh.
Ouch.
What is really going on?
Nina!

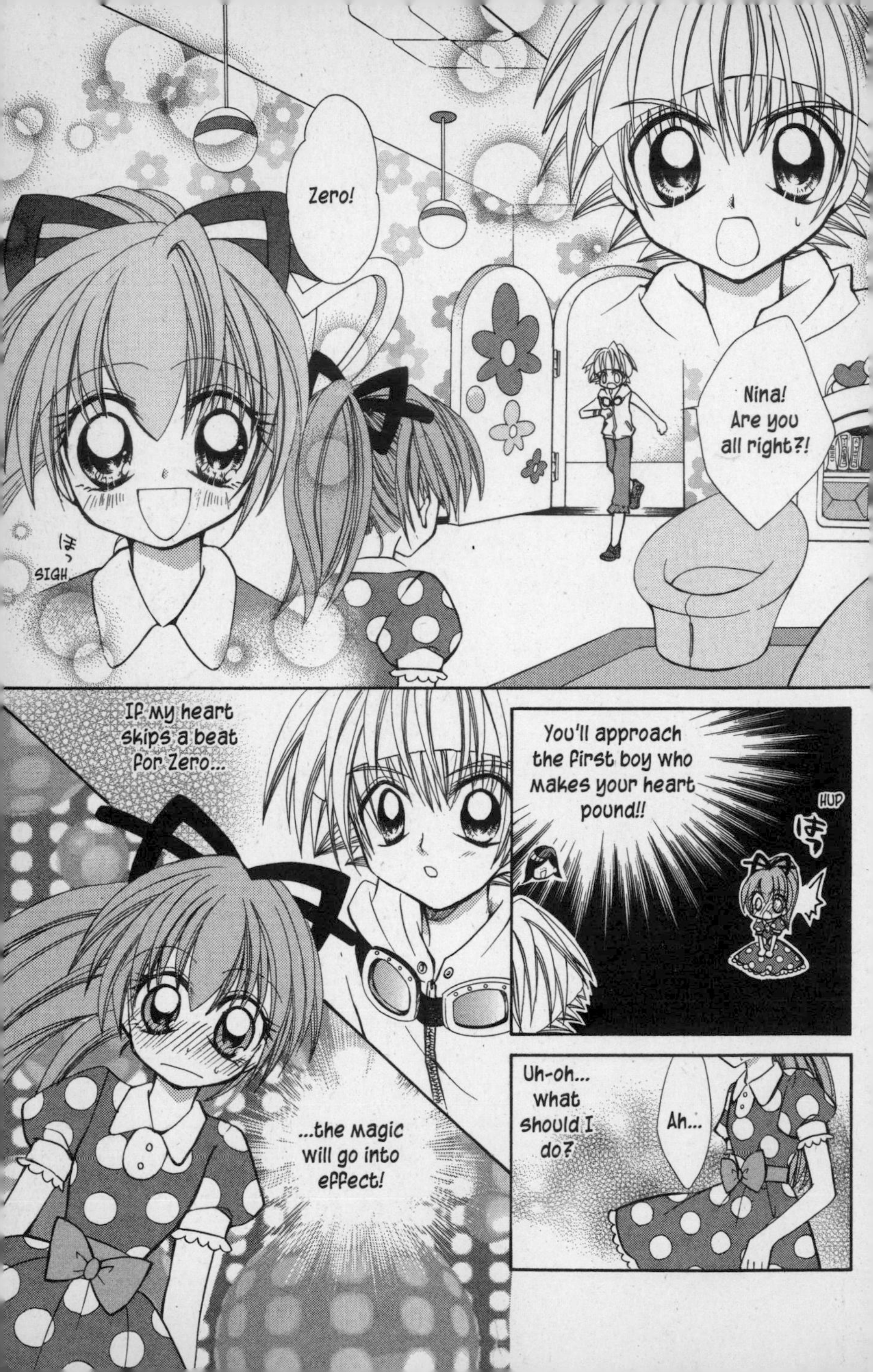
Nina! Are you all right?!
Zero!
ほっ
SIGH
You'll approach the first boy who makes your heart pound!!
HUP
ほっ
Ah...
Uh-oh... what should I do?
If my heart skips a beat for Zero...
...the magic will go into effect!

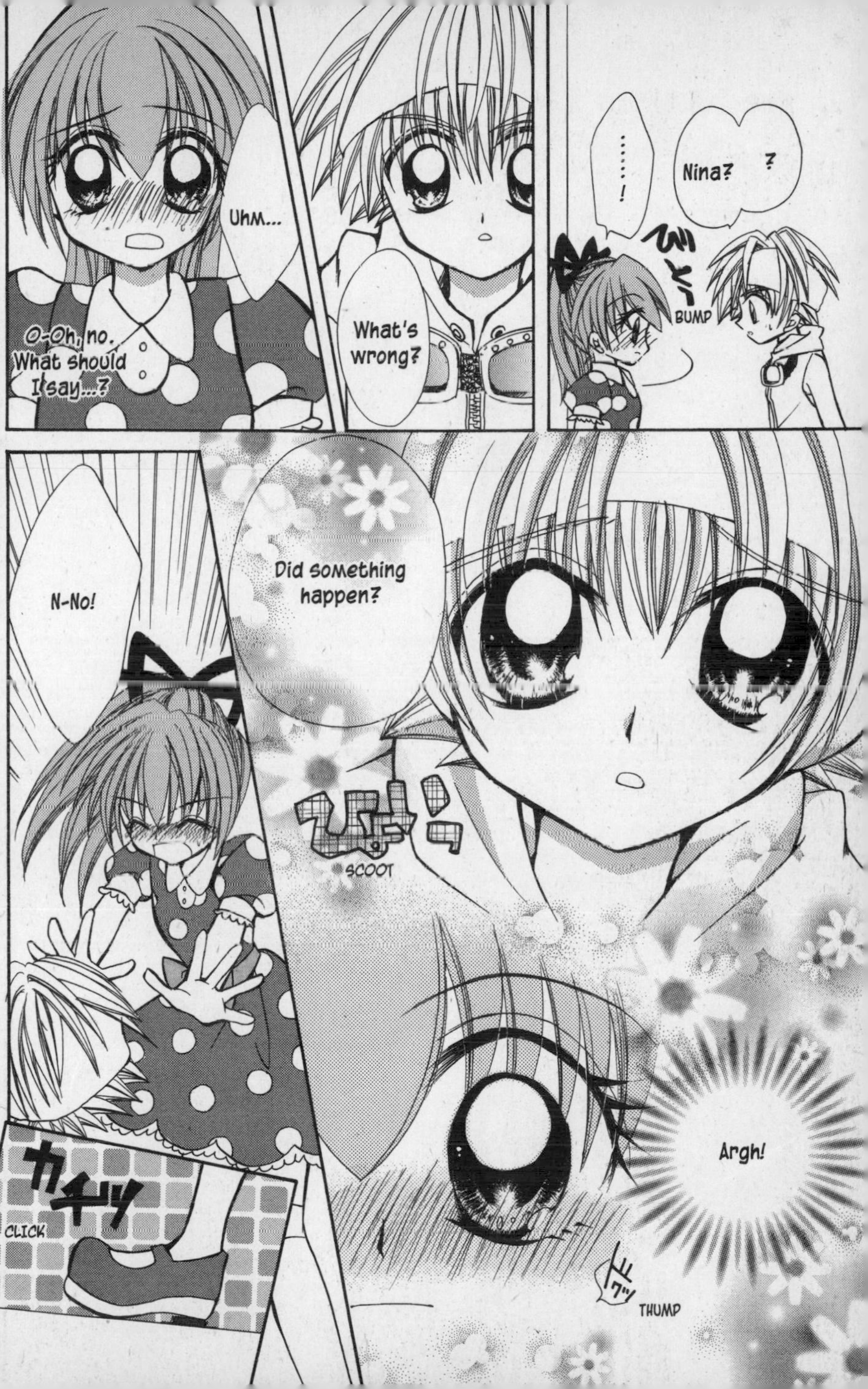
Nina?
?
......!
BUMP
What's wrong?
Uhm...
O-Oh, no. What should I say...?
Did something happen?
SCOOT
Argh!
THUMP
N-No!
CLICK

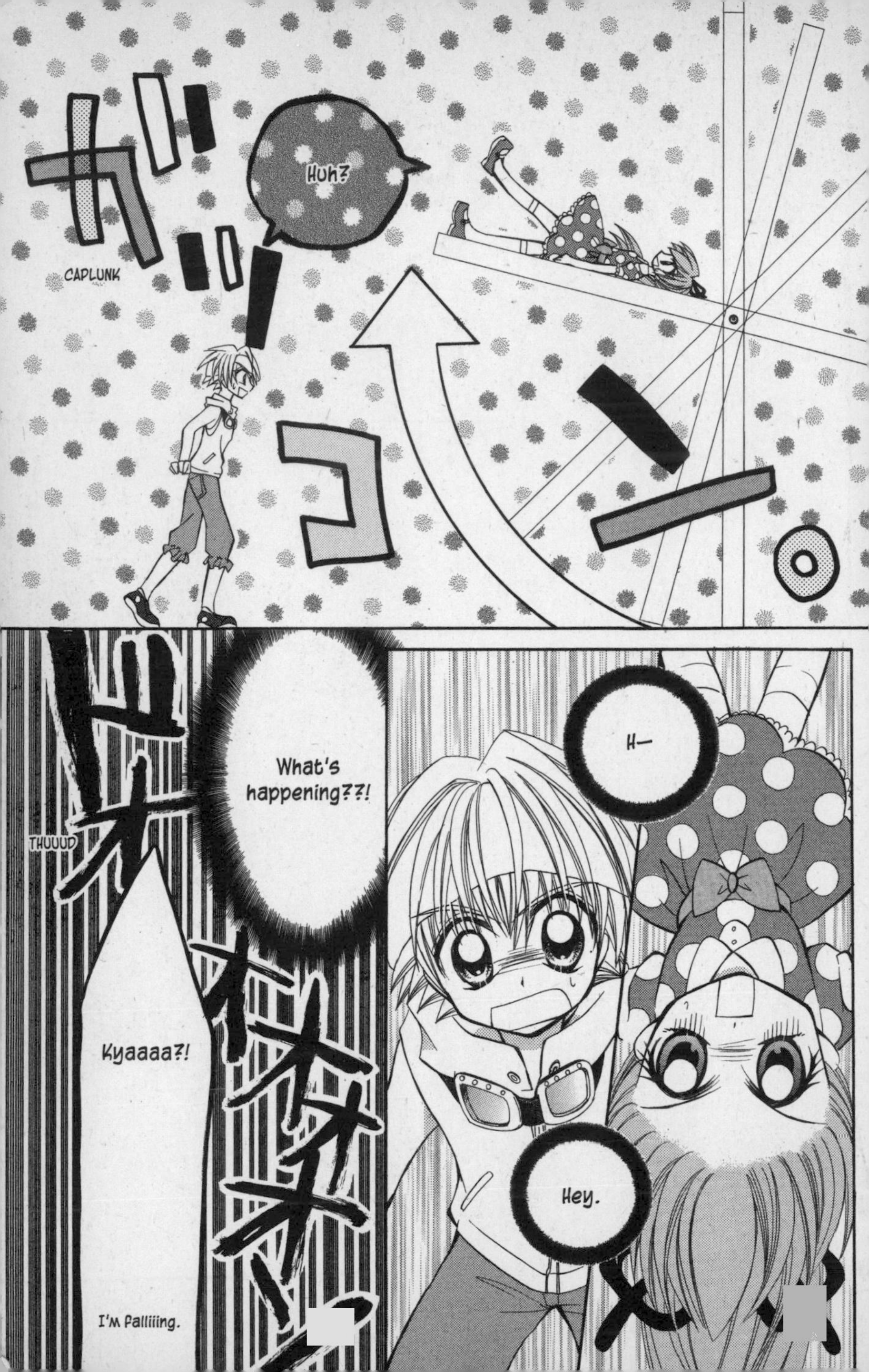
Huh?
CAPLUNK
H—
Hey.
What's happening??!
THUUUD
Kyaaaa?!
I'm falliiing.

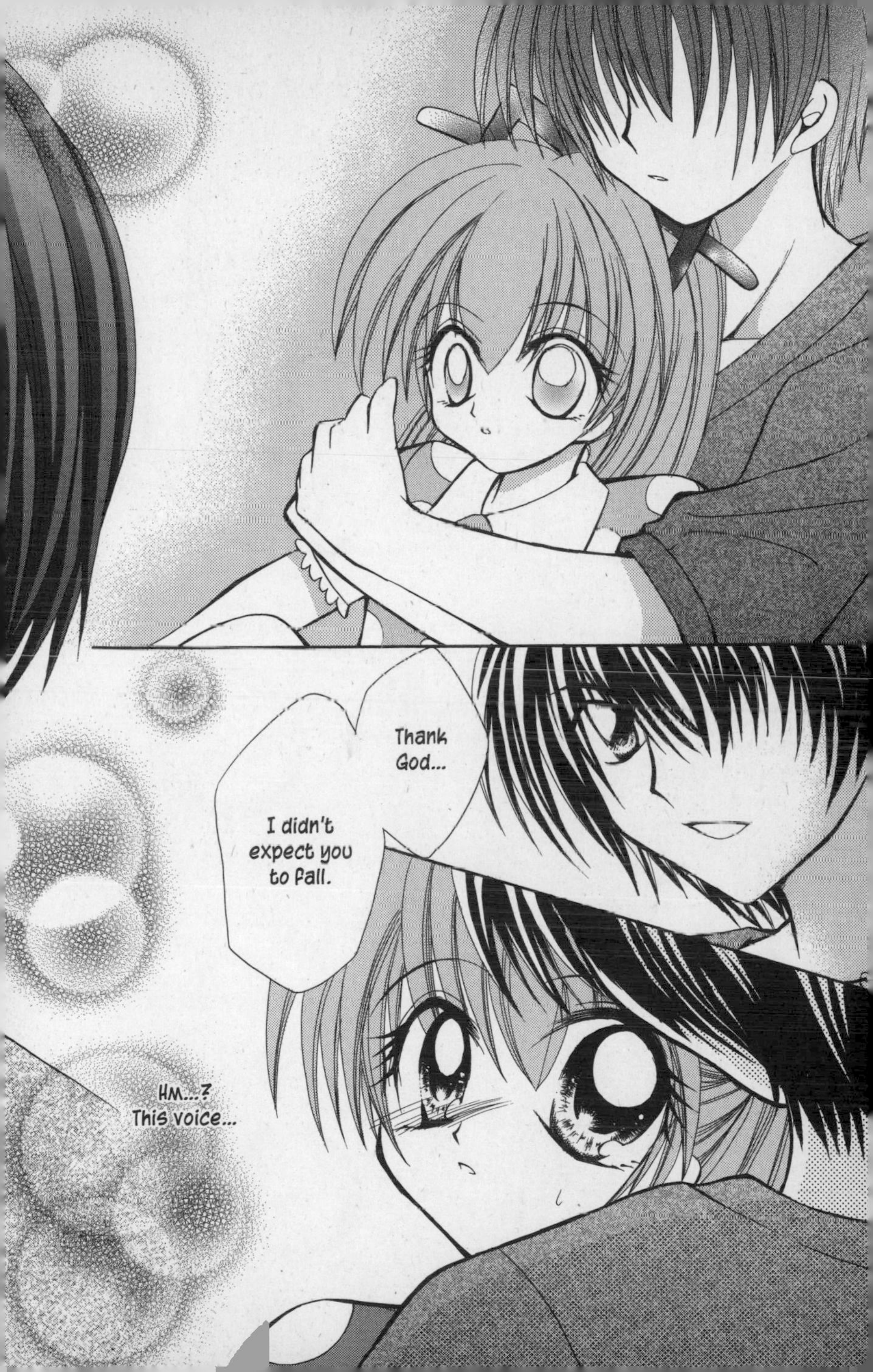
Thank God...
I didn't expect you to fall.
Hm...?
This voice...

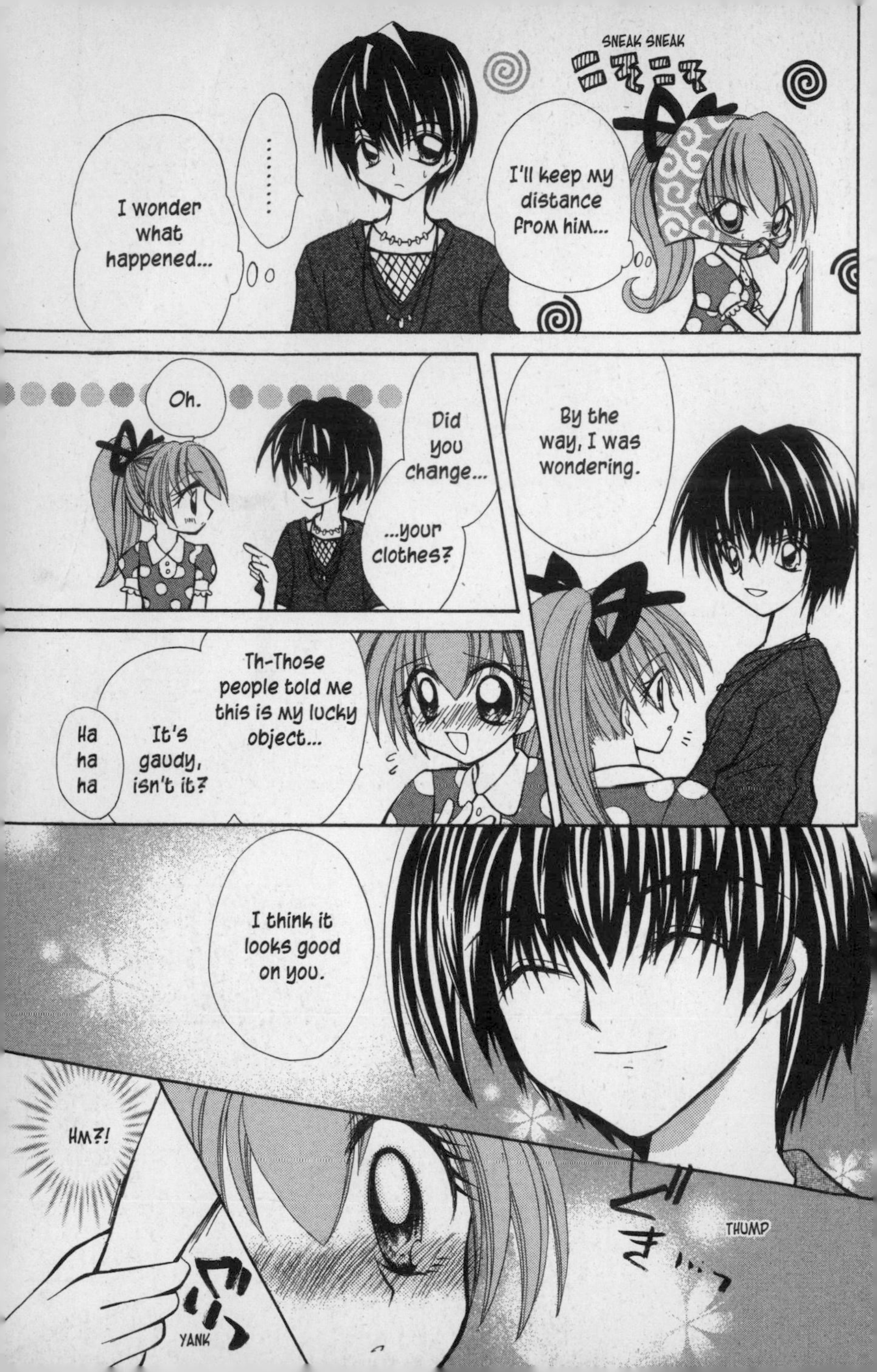
SNEAK SNEAK
I'll keep my distance from him...
......
I wonder what happened...
By the way, I was wondering.
Did you change...
...your clothes?
Oh.
Th-Those people told me this is my lucky object...
It's gaudy, isn't it?
Ha ha ha
I think it looks good on you.
THUMP
HM?!
YANK

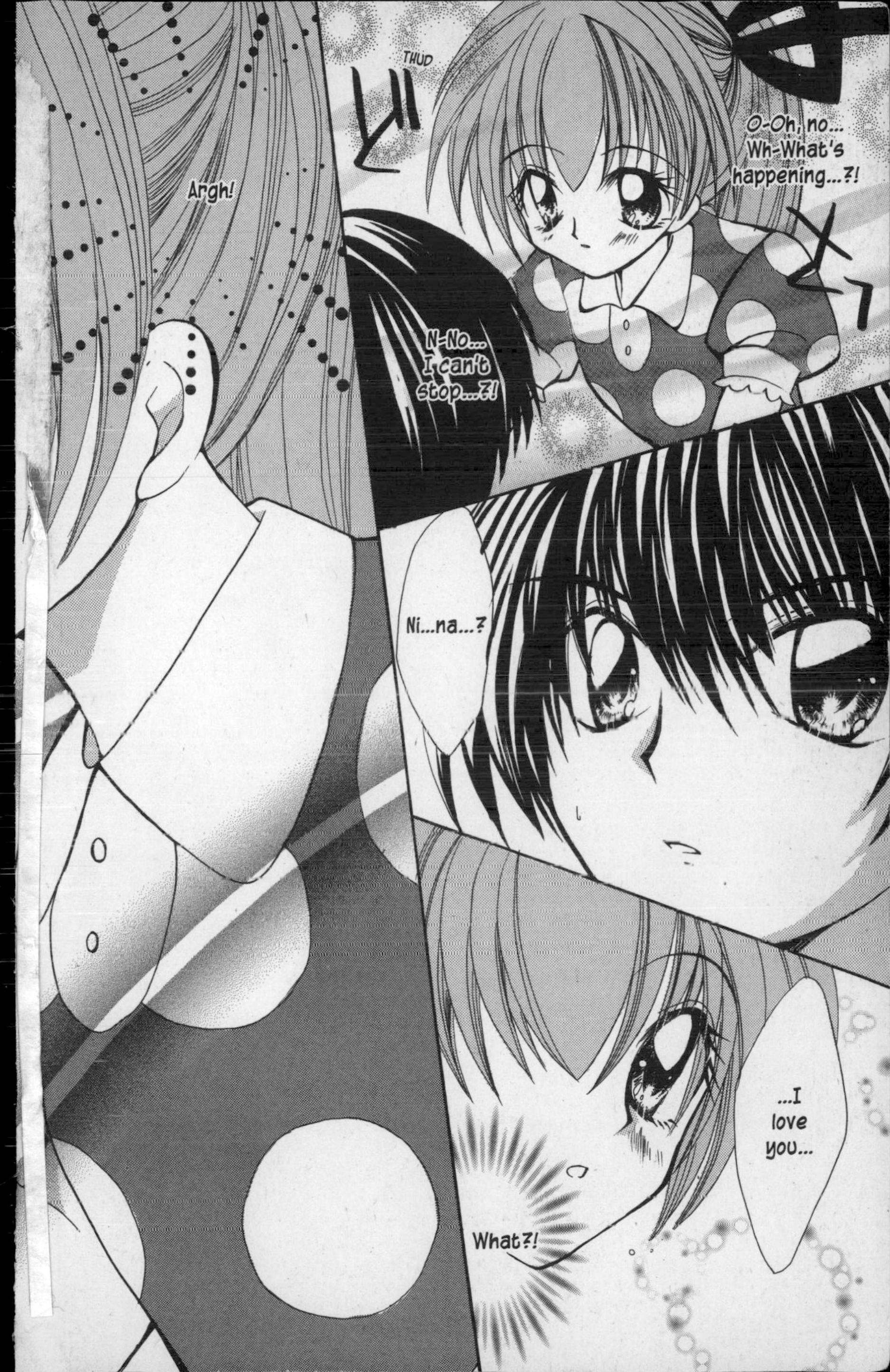

O-Oh, no... Wh-What's happening...?!
THUD
N-No... I can't stop...?!
Ni...na...?
...I love you...
What?!
Argh!

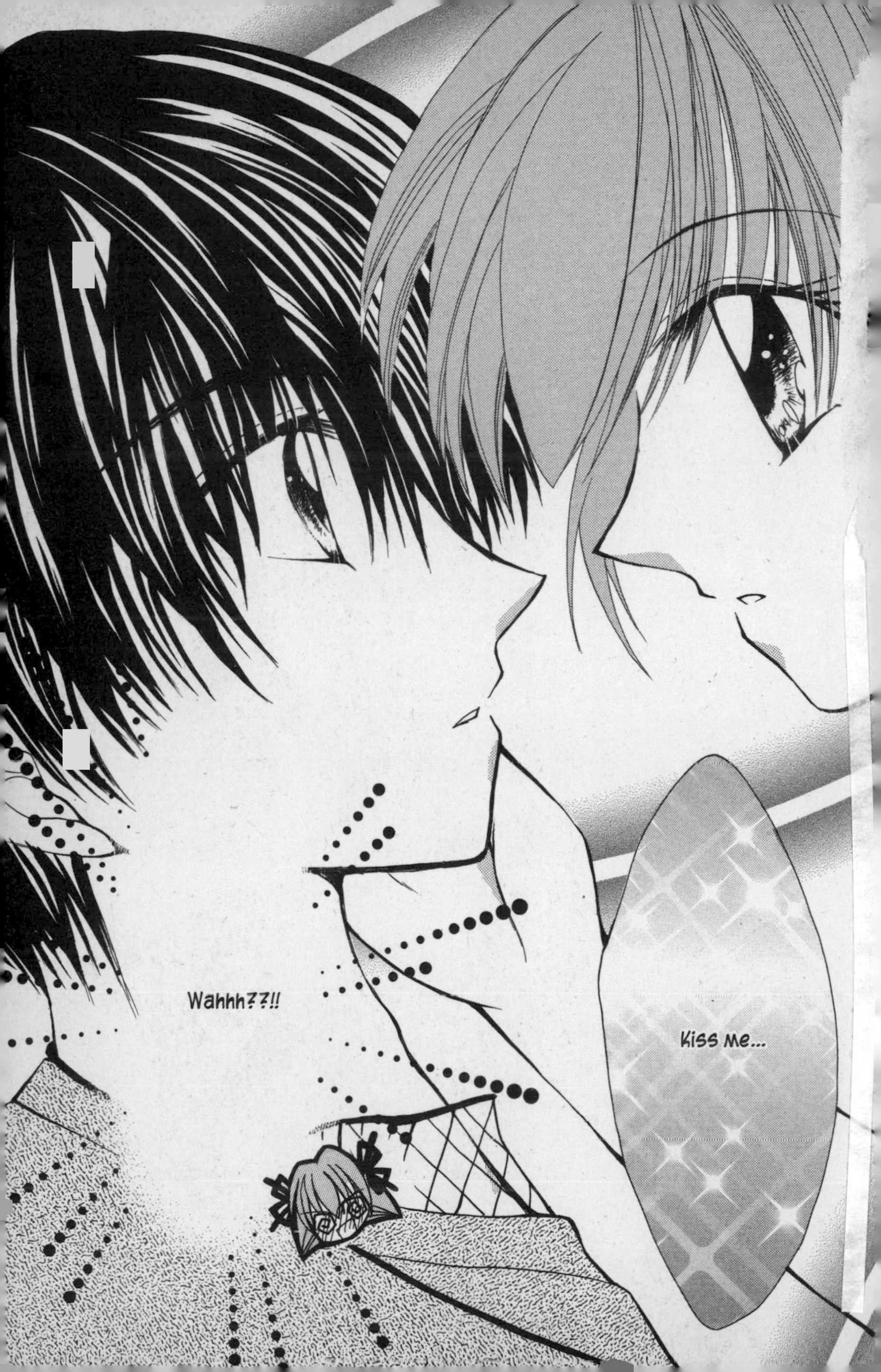
Kiss me...
Wahhh??!!

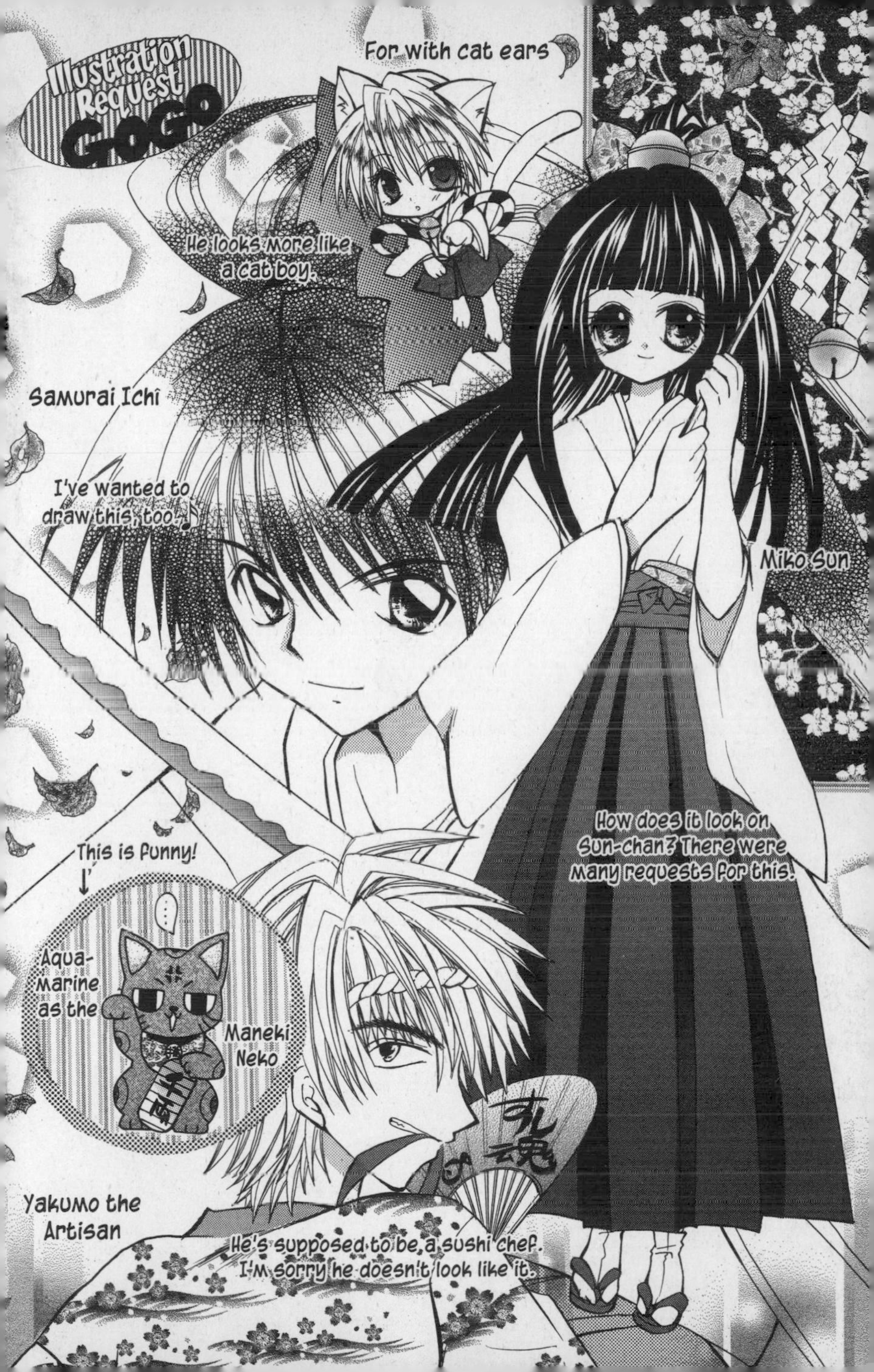
Illustration Request GoGo
For with cat ears
He looks more like a cat boy.
Samurai Ichi
I've wanted to draw this, too.♪
Miko Sun
How does it look on Sun-chan? There were many requests for this.
This is funny!
...
Aqua-marine as the
Maneki Neko
Yakumo the Artisan
He's supposed to be a sushi chef. I'm sorry he doesn't look like it.

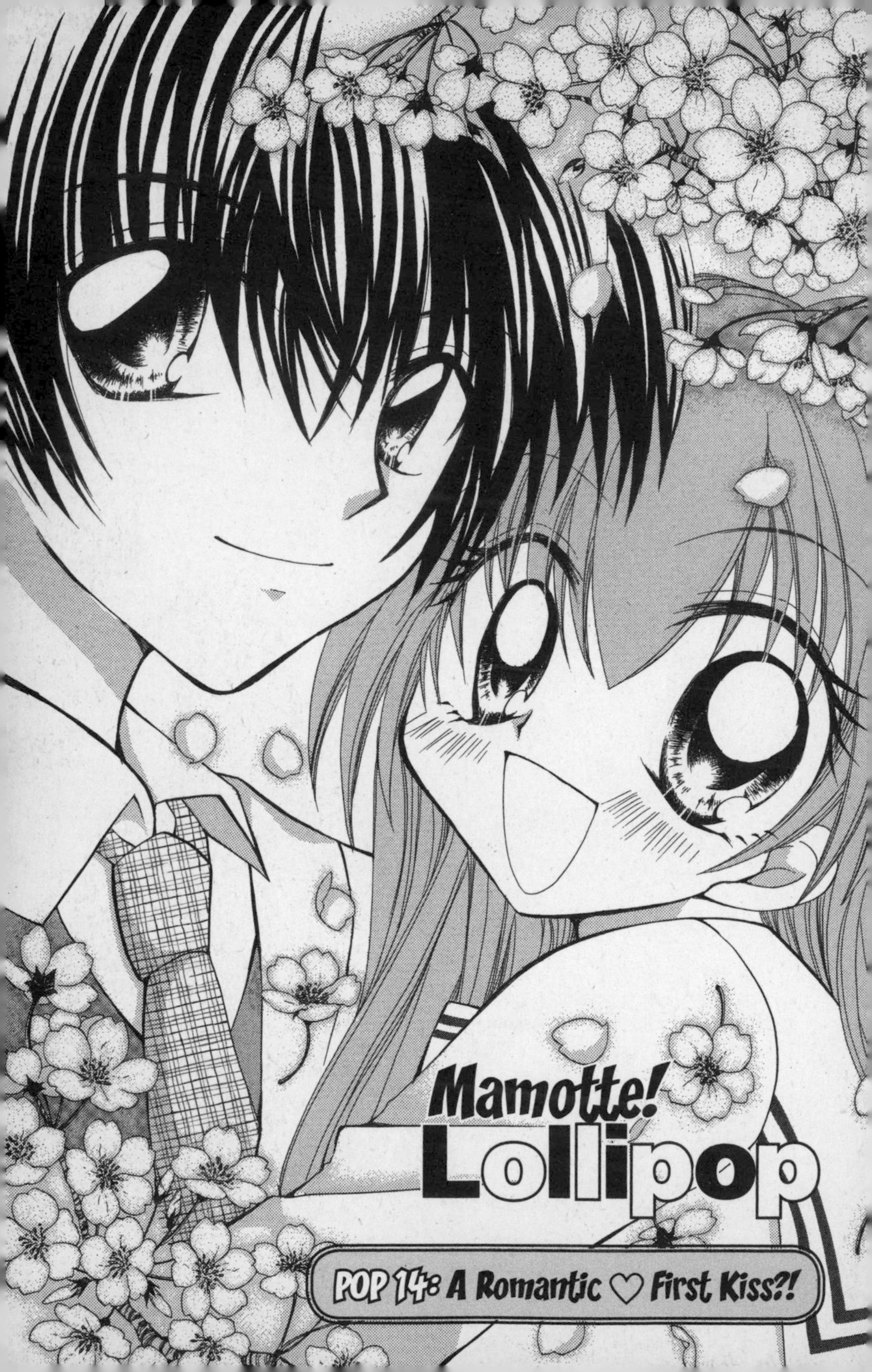
Mamotte! Lollipop
POP 14: A Romantic ♡ First Kiss?!

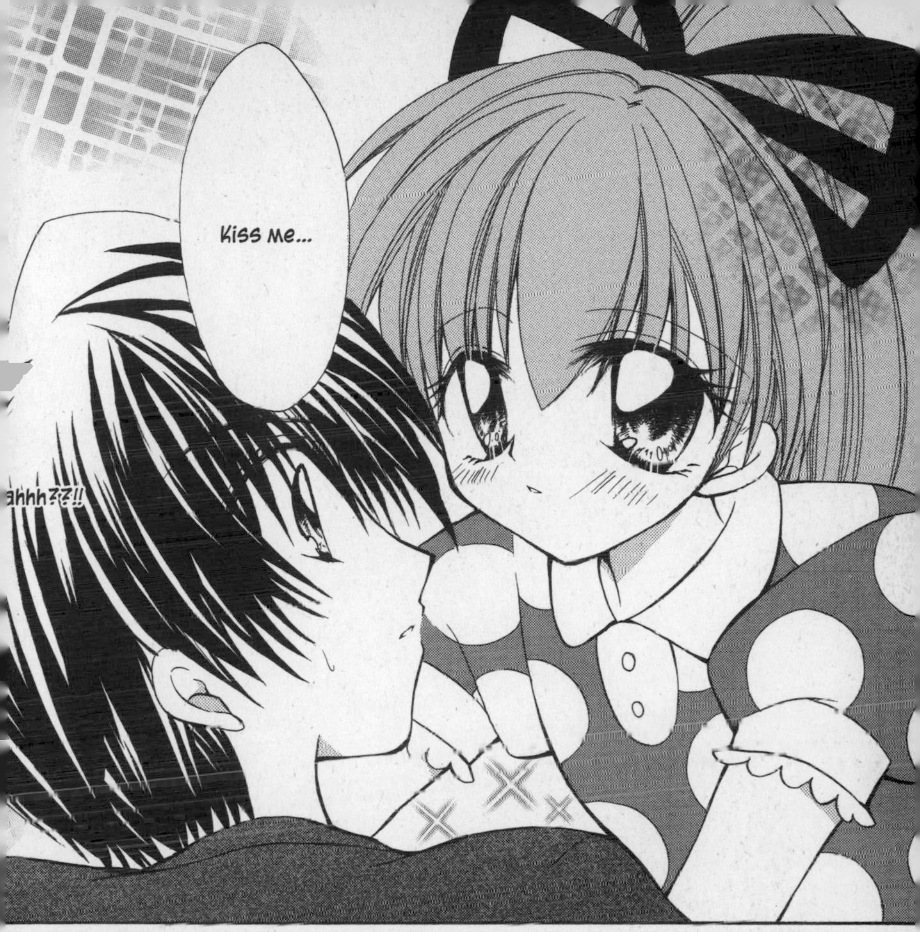
Kiss me...
ahhh??!!

Pop 14 A Romantic ♥ First Kiss?!

It's spring so I drew cherry blossoms! I love cherry blossoms! It's my favorite flower. This cover page was made to look like a school entrance ceremony. I wanted to draw a girl's white sailor-style uniform and a blazer jacket. I think Ichi and Zero both look good in blazer jackets.

There's been some progress in the love story, I think? It's hard to tell. I have no idea what will happen, either. I'm still improvising as I go along, so I almost wonder if this is fine. But on the other hand, it's probably better that we can't predict the story.

This time I chose the chapter title. I took Eleven's tactic name and used it. (Laugh)

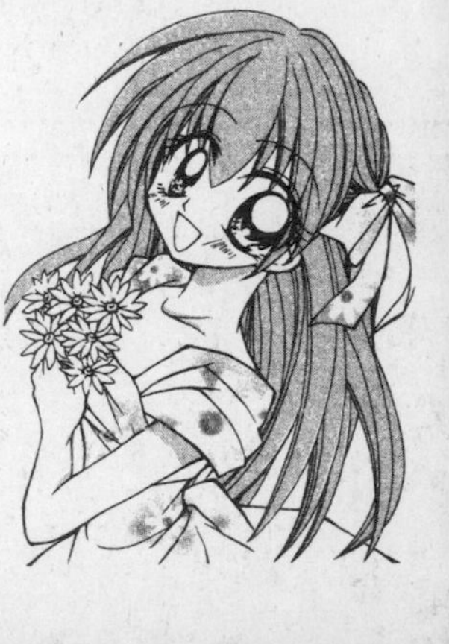

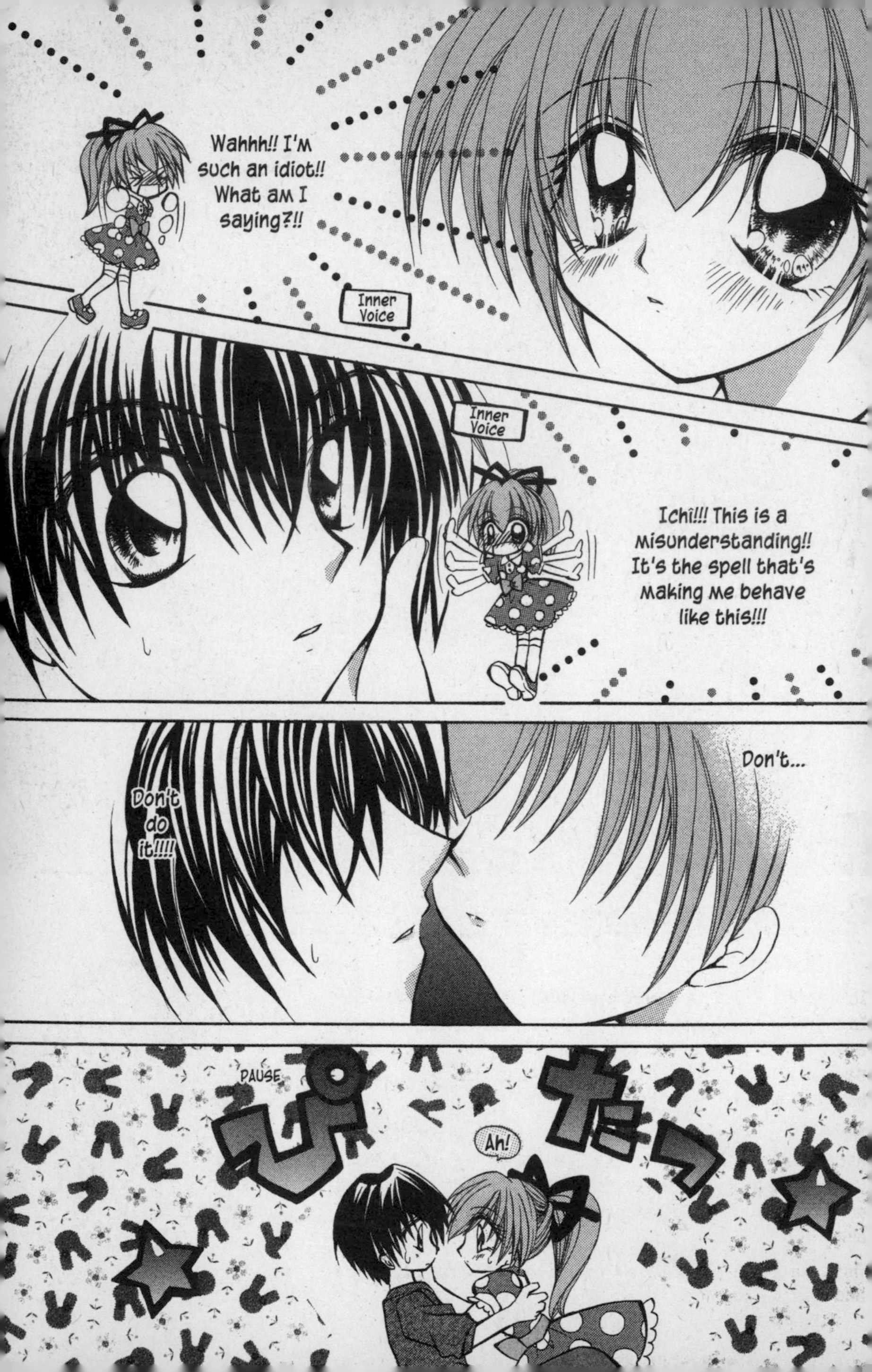
Wahhh!! I'm such an idiot!! What am I saying?!!
Inner Voice
Inner Voice
Ichi!!! This is a misunderstanding!! It's the spell that's making me behave like this!!!
Don't...
Don't do it!!!!
ぴたっ
PAUSE
Ah!

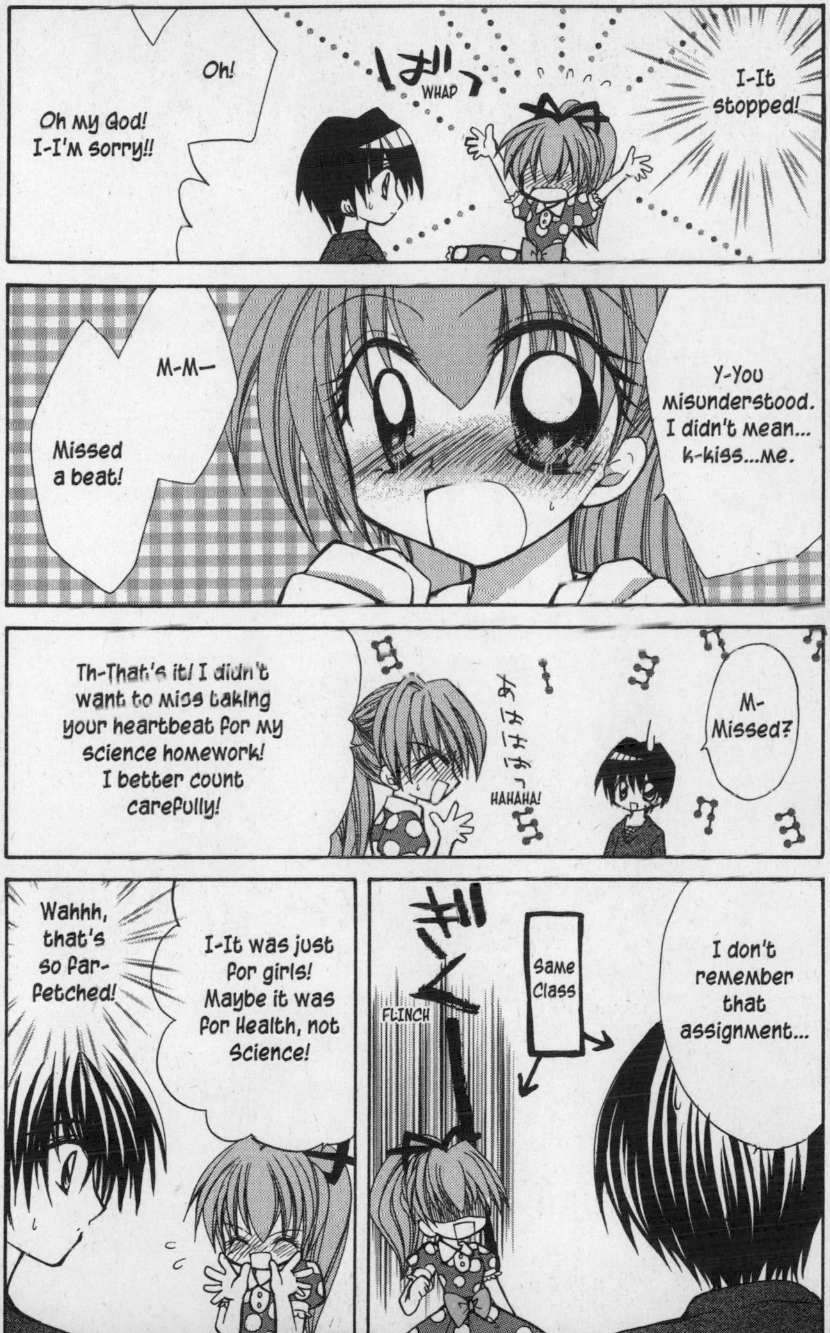
I-It stopped!
ばっ
WHAP
Oh!
Oh my God! I-I'm sorry!!
Y-You misunderstood. I didn't mean... k-kiss...me.
M-M—
Missed a beat!
M-Missed?
HAHAHA!
Th-That's it! I didn't want to miss taking your heartbeat for my science homework! I better count carefully!
I don't remember that assignment...
Same Class
FLINCH
I-It was just for girls! Maybe it was for Health, not Science!
Wahhh, that's so far-fetched!

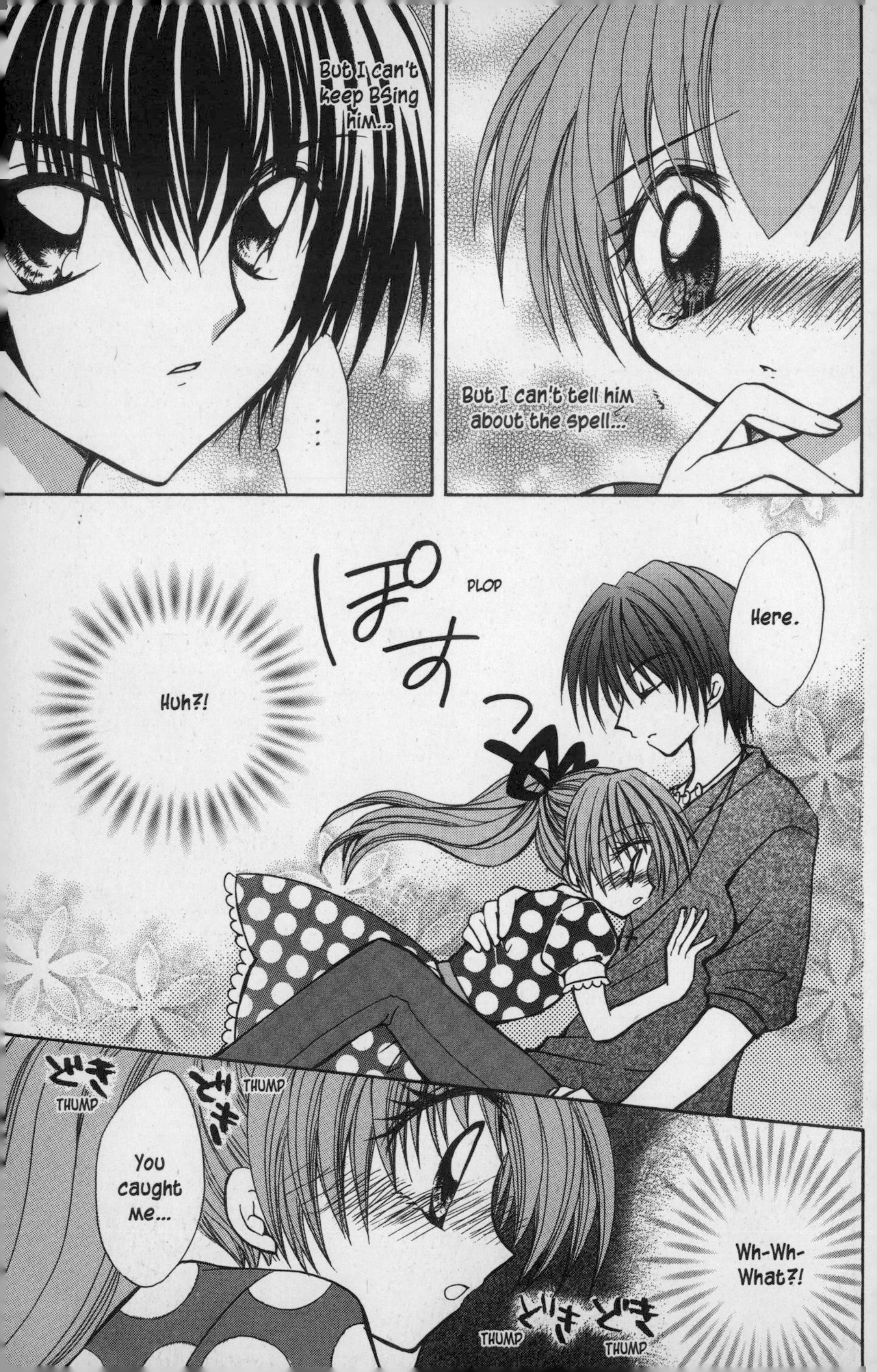
But I can't tell him about the spell...
But I can't keep BSing him...
...
Here.
ぽすっ
PLOP
Huh?!
Wh-Wh-What?!
どきどき
THUMP
THUMP
You caught me...
どき
THUMP
どき
THUMP

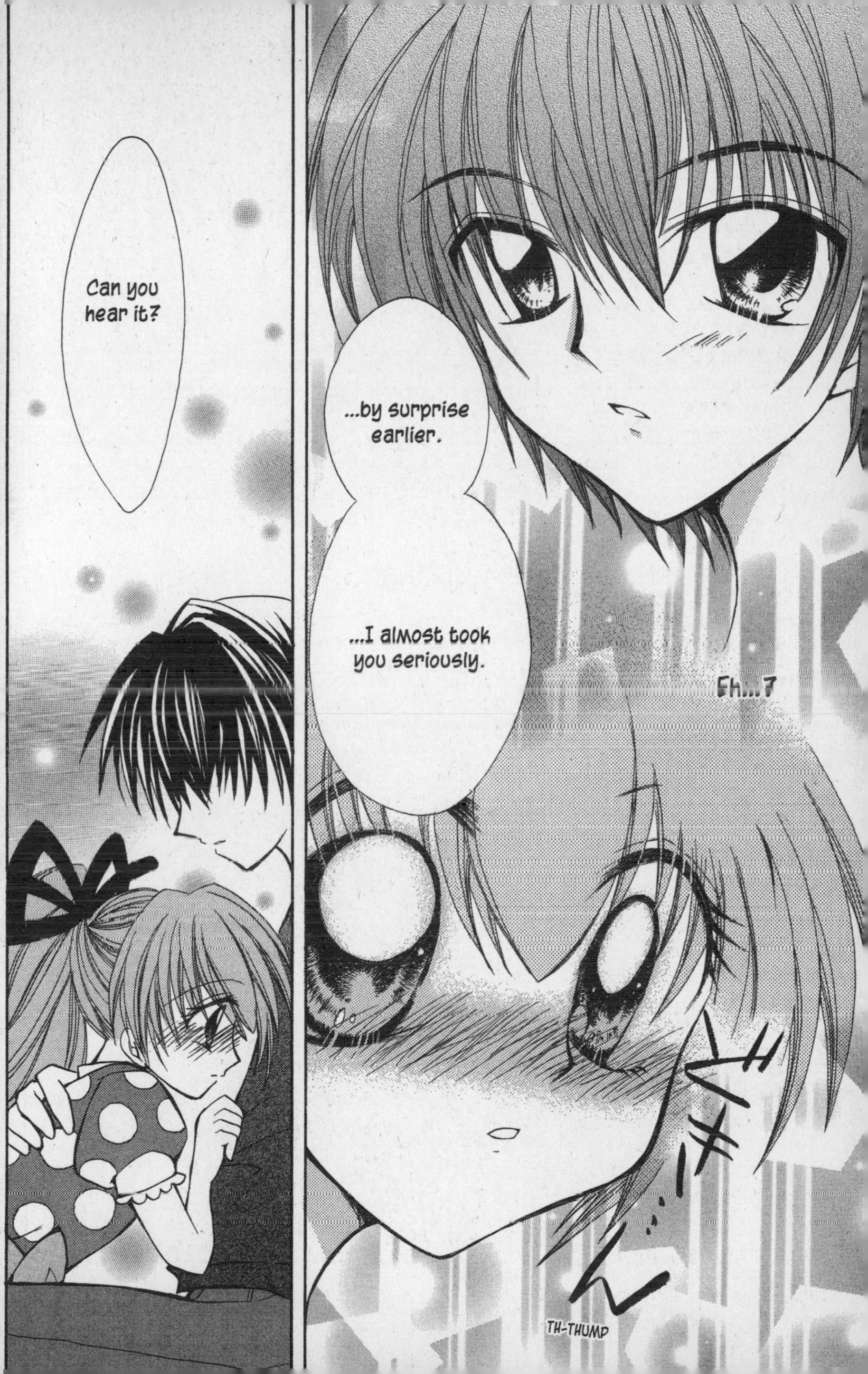
...by surprise earlier.
...I almost took you seriously.
Eh...?
TH-THUMP
Can you hear it?

Fan Letter

★ Thank you for always reading my work. I really get lots of comments and love stories from everyone. And there are people who send me key chains and other gifts. It's fun getting things that look like a lollipop, too! But you don't really need to do this for me.

★ We make reply inserts. Since we have a hard time with mailing addresses and stamps, it'll help us if you include a return envelope. We're sorry for the inconvenience we may have caused you.

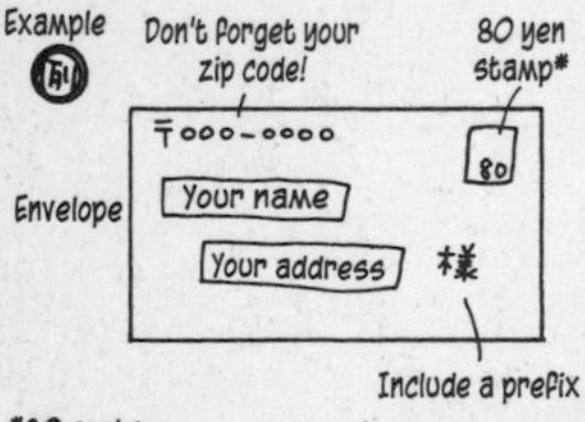
Example
Don't forget your zip code!
80 yen stamp*
〒000-0000
80
Envelope
Your name
Your address
様
Include a prefix

*80 cents

< Mailing Address for Fan Letters>

Nakayoshi Editorial Department
Michiyo Kikuta
P.O. Box 91
Akasaka Post Office
Tokyo, Japan 107-8652

<Official Website>

http://tokyo.cool.ne.jp/michiyo-k-miracle/

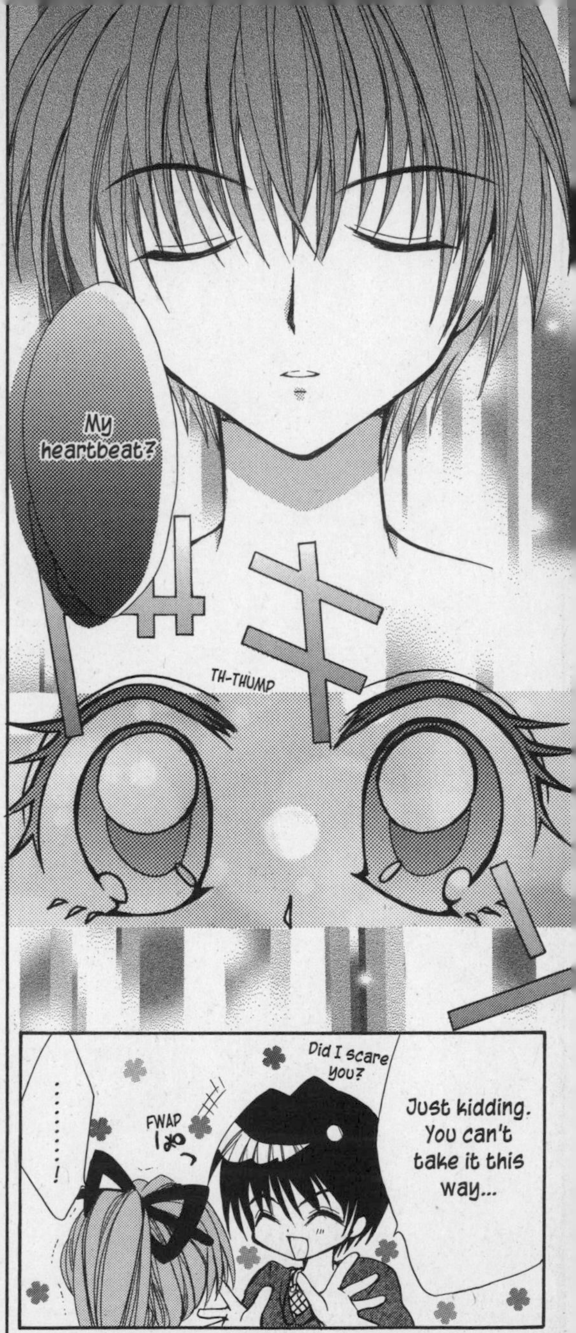
My heartbeat?
TH-THUMP
Just kidding. You can't take it this way...
Did I scare you?
FWAP
......!

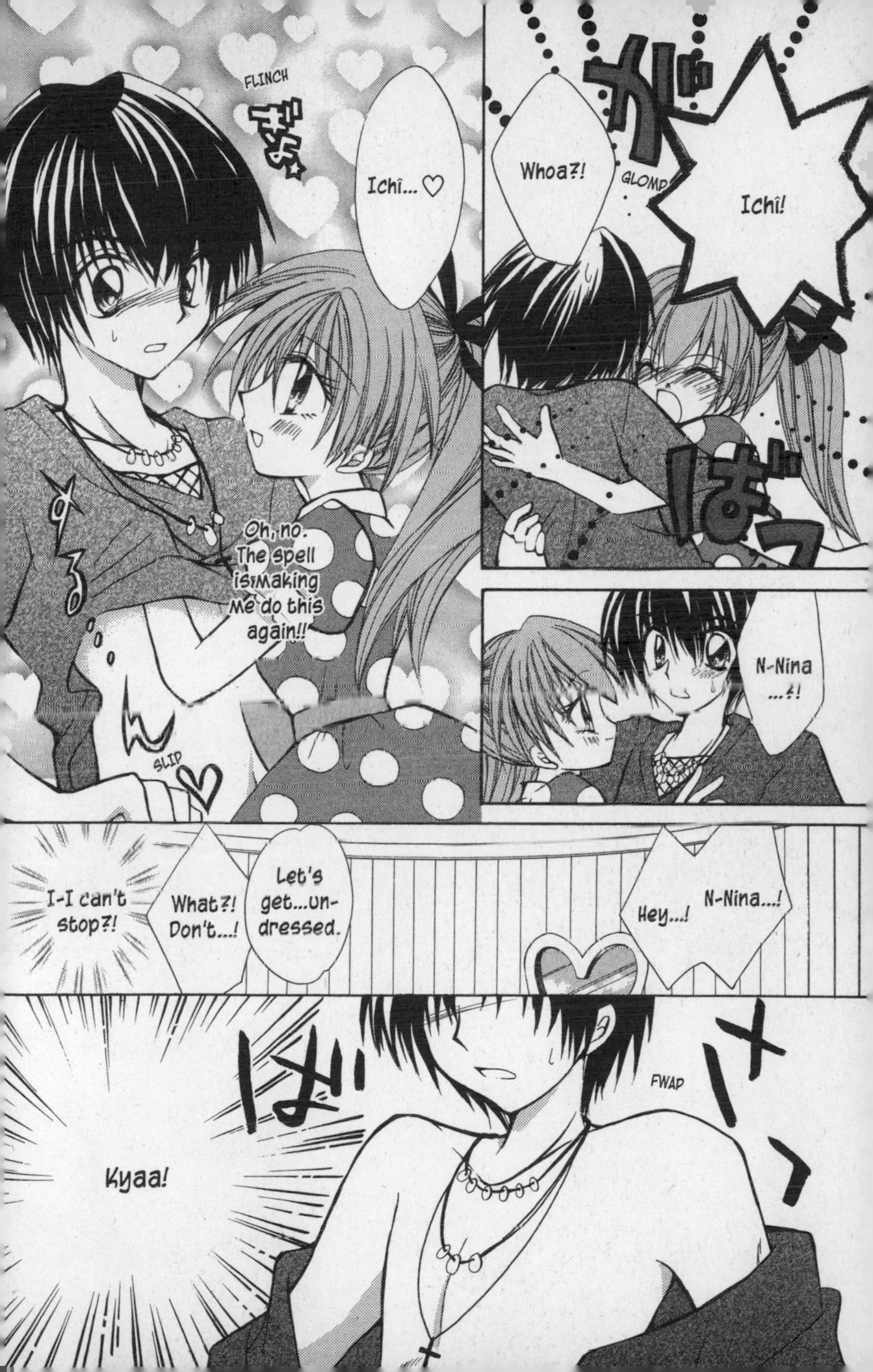
Ichî!
GLOMP
Whoa?!
N-Nina ...?!
Ichî... ♡
FLINCH
Oh, no. The spell is making me do this again!!
SLIP
N-Nina...!
Hey...!
Let's get...undressed.
What?! Don't...!
I-I can't stop?!
FWAP
Kyaa!

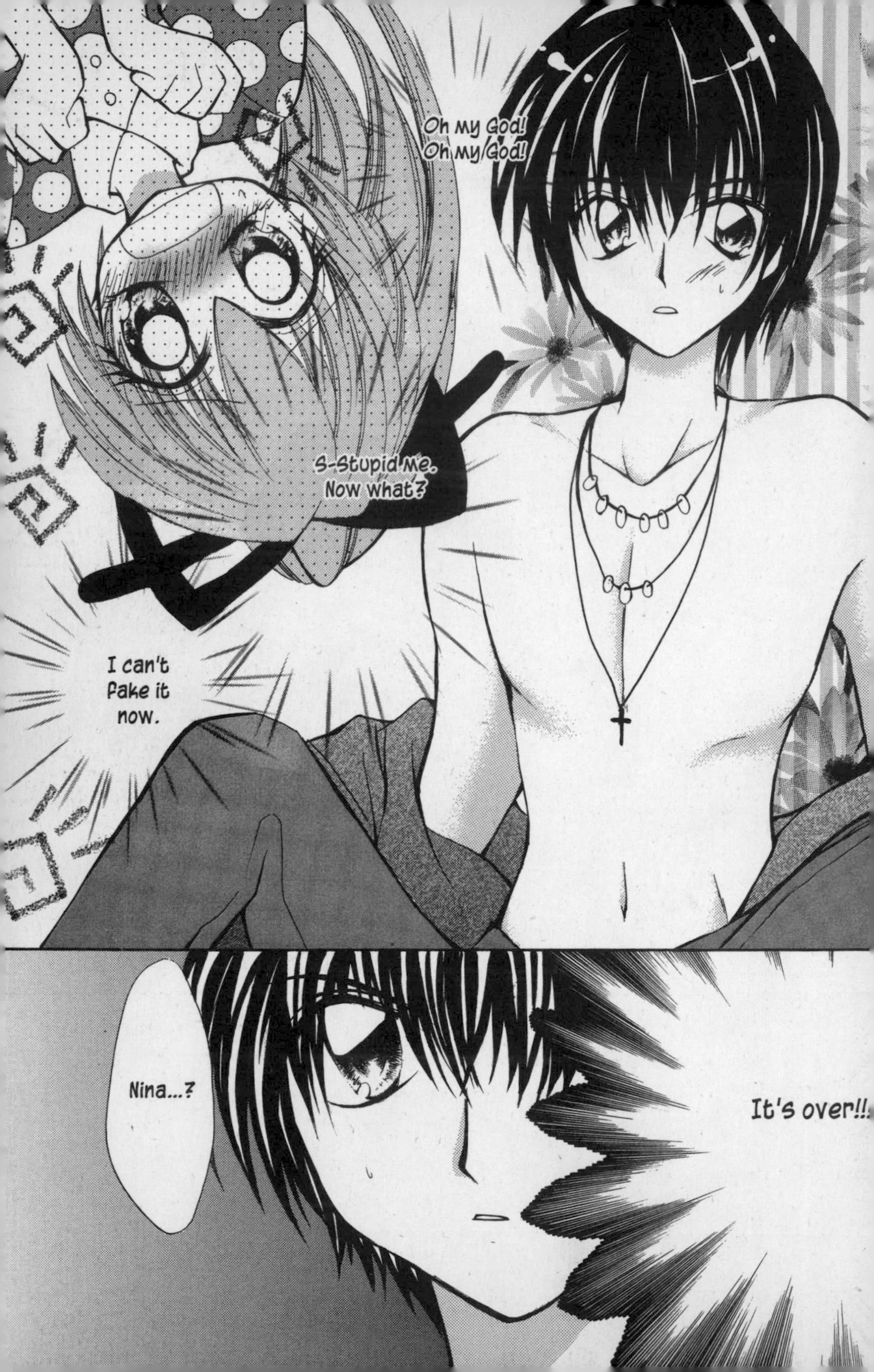
Oh my God! Oh my God!
S-Stupid me. Now what?
I can't fake it now.
It's over!!
Nina...?

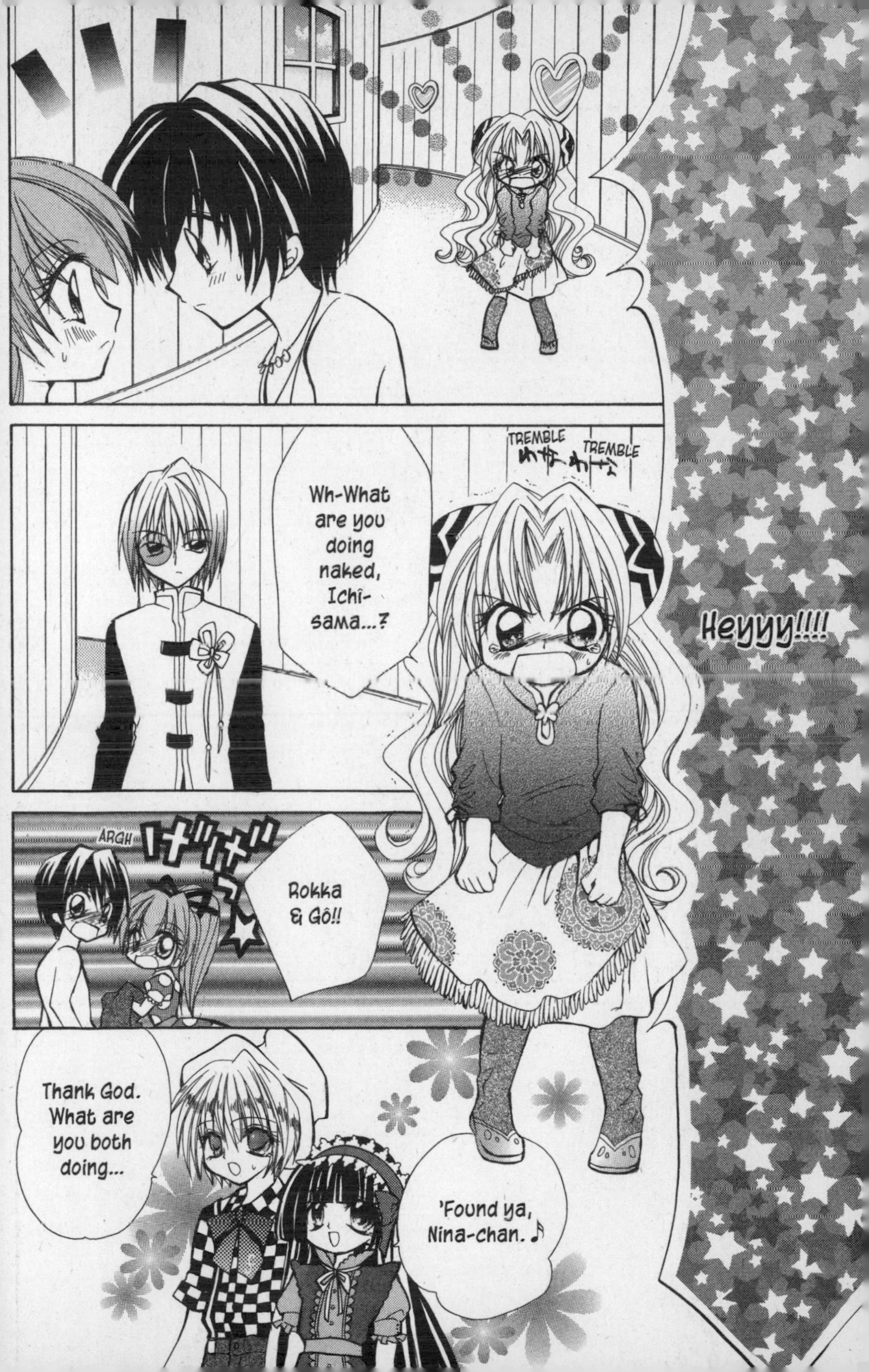
TREMBLE
TREMBLE
Heyyy!!!!
Wh-What are you doing naked, Ichî-sama...?
ARGH
Rokka & Gô!!
'Found ya, Nina-chan. ♪
Thank God. What are you both doing...

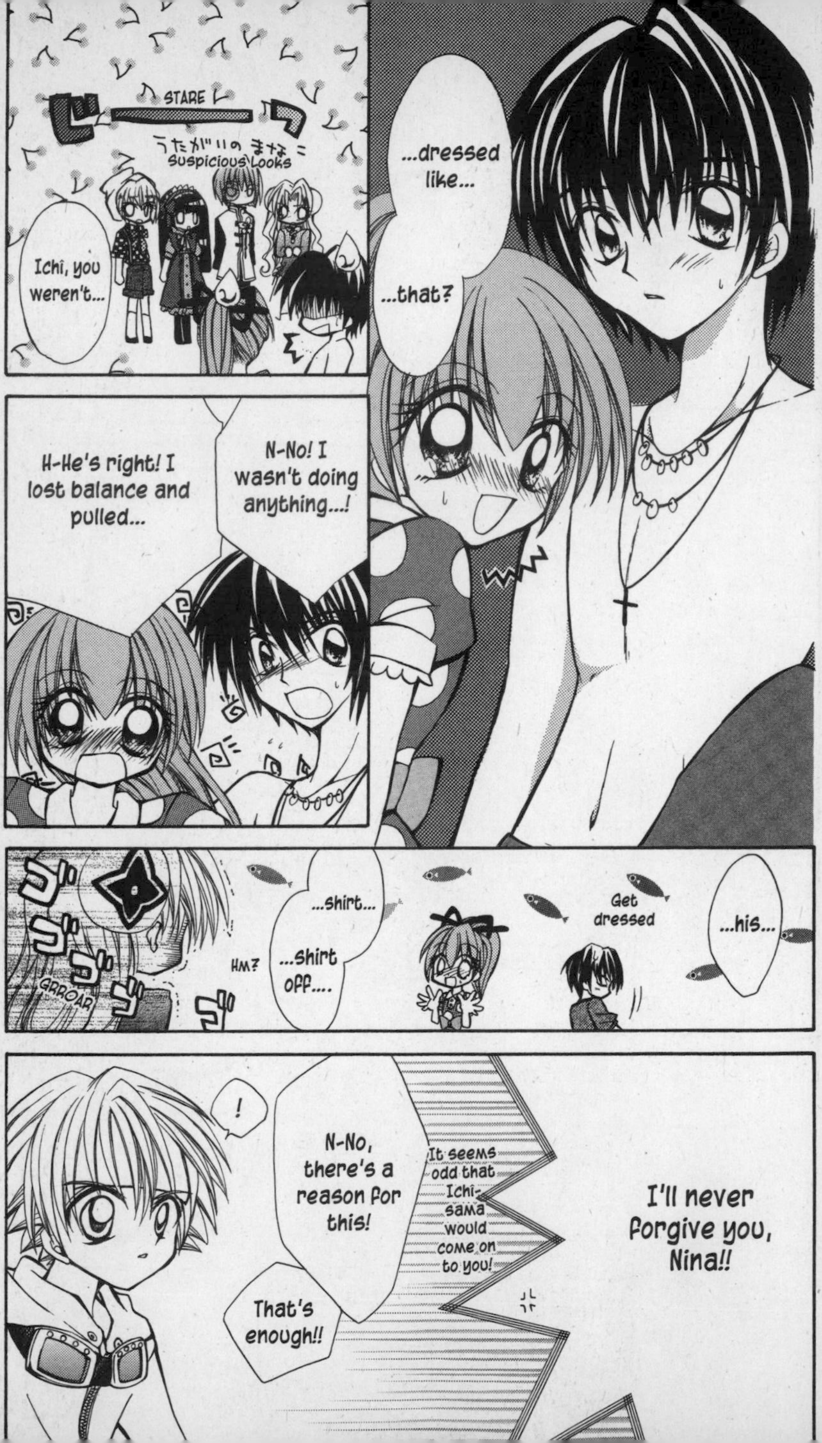
...dressed like...
...that?
STARE
うたがいのまなこ
Suspicious Looks
Ichi, you weren't...
N-No! I wasn't doing anything...!
H-He's right! I lost balance and pulled...
...his...
Get dressed
...shirt...
...shirt off....
HM?
GRROAR
I'll never forgive you, Nina!!
It seems odd that Ichi-sama would come on to you!
N-No, there's a reason for this!
!
That's enough!!

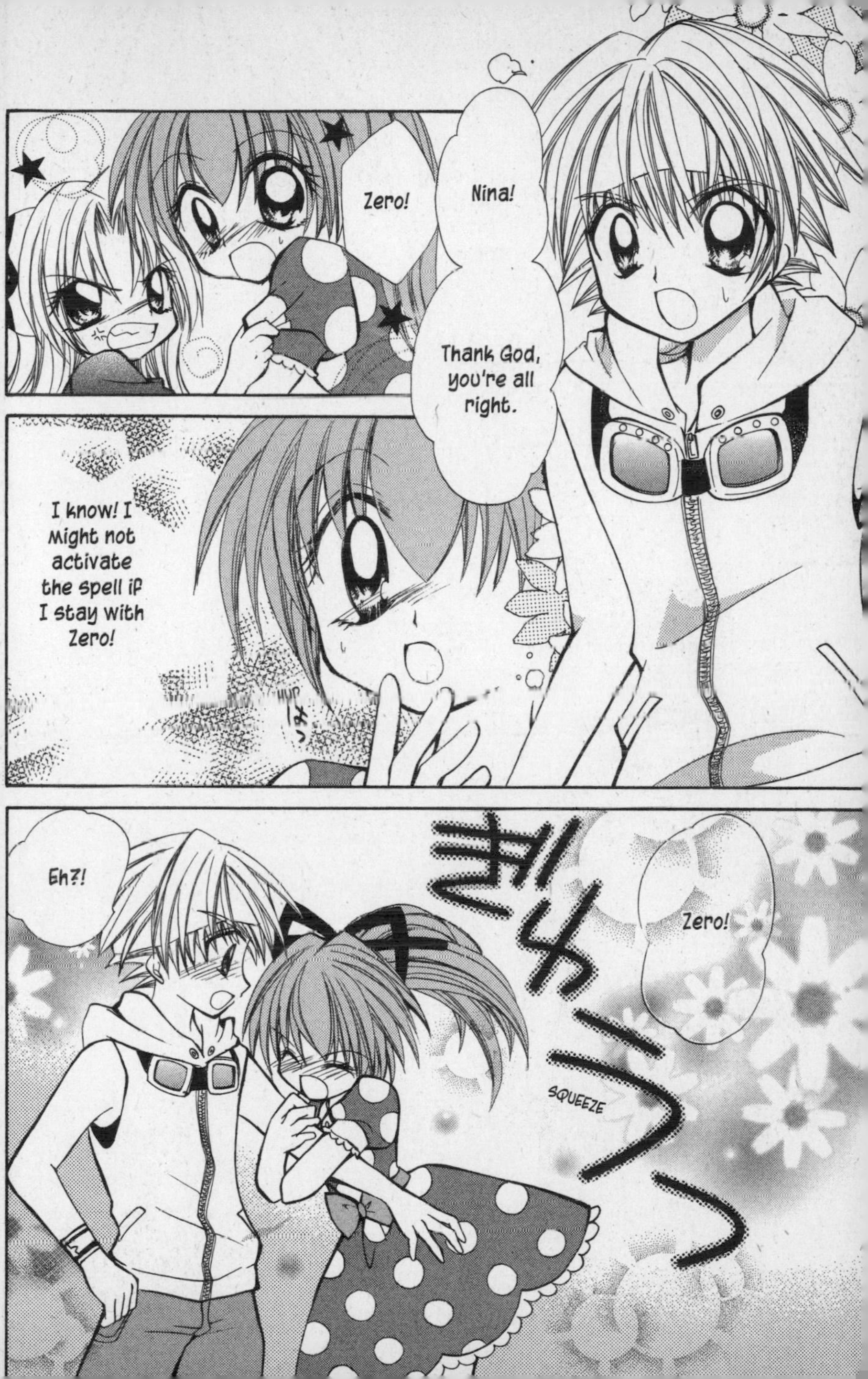
Nina!
Thank God, you're all right.
Zero!
I know! I might not activate the spell if I stay with Zero!
HUP
Zero!
SQUEEZE
Eh?!

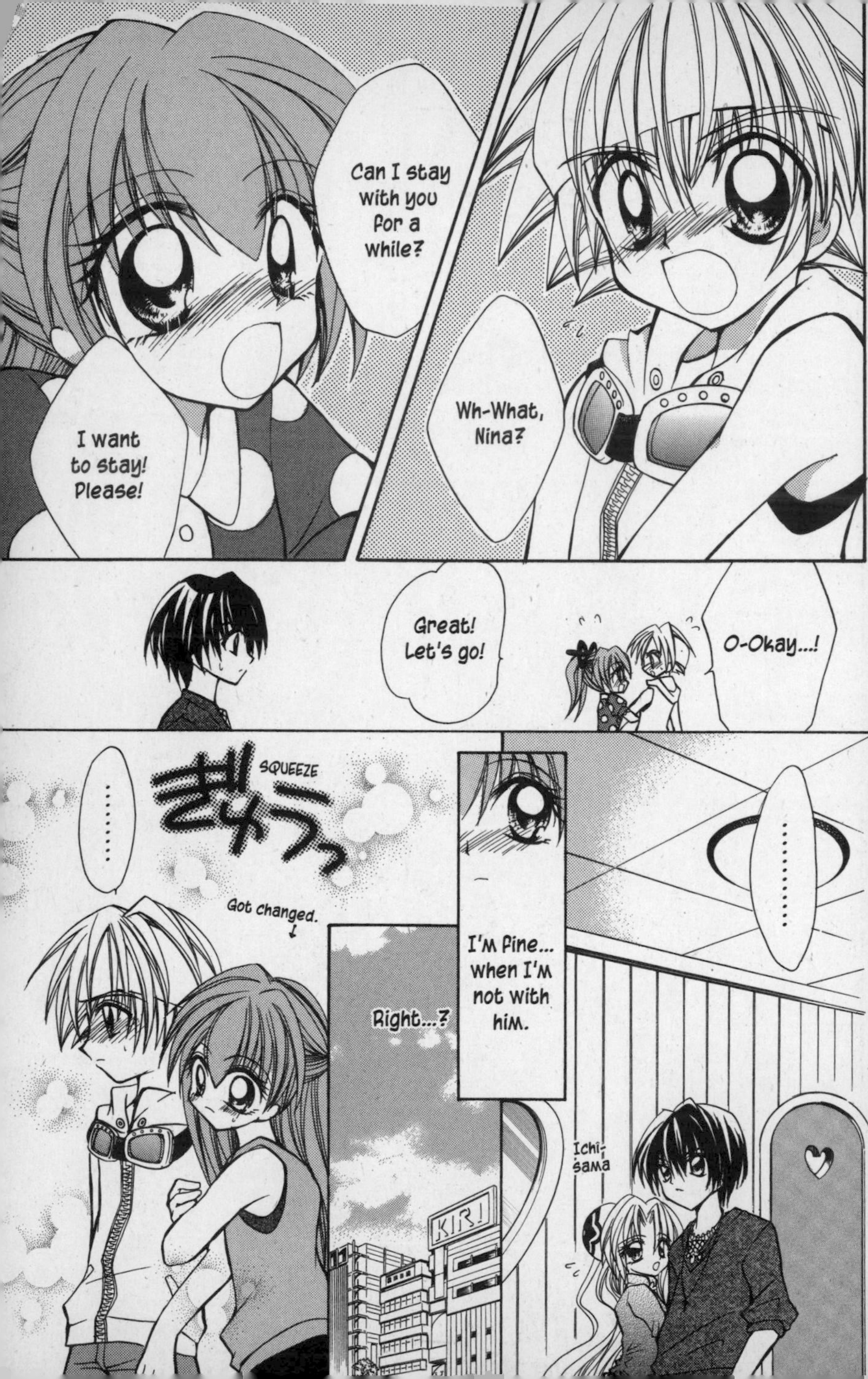
Wh-What, Nina?
Can I stay with you for a while?
I want to stay! Please!
O-Okay...!
Great! Let's go!
....
I'm fine... when I'm not with him.
Ichi-sama
Right...?
....
SQUEEZE
Got changed.

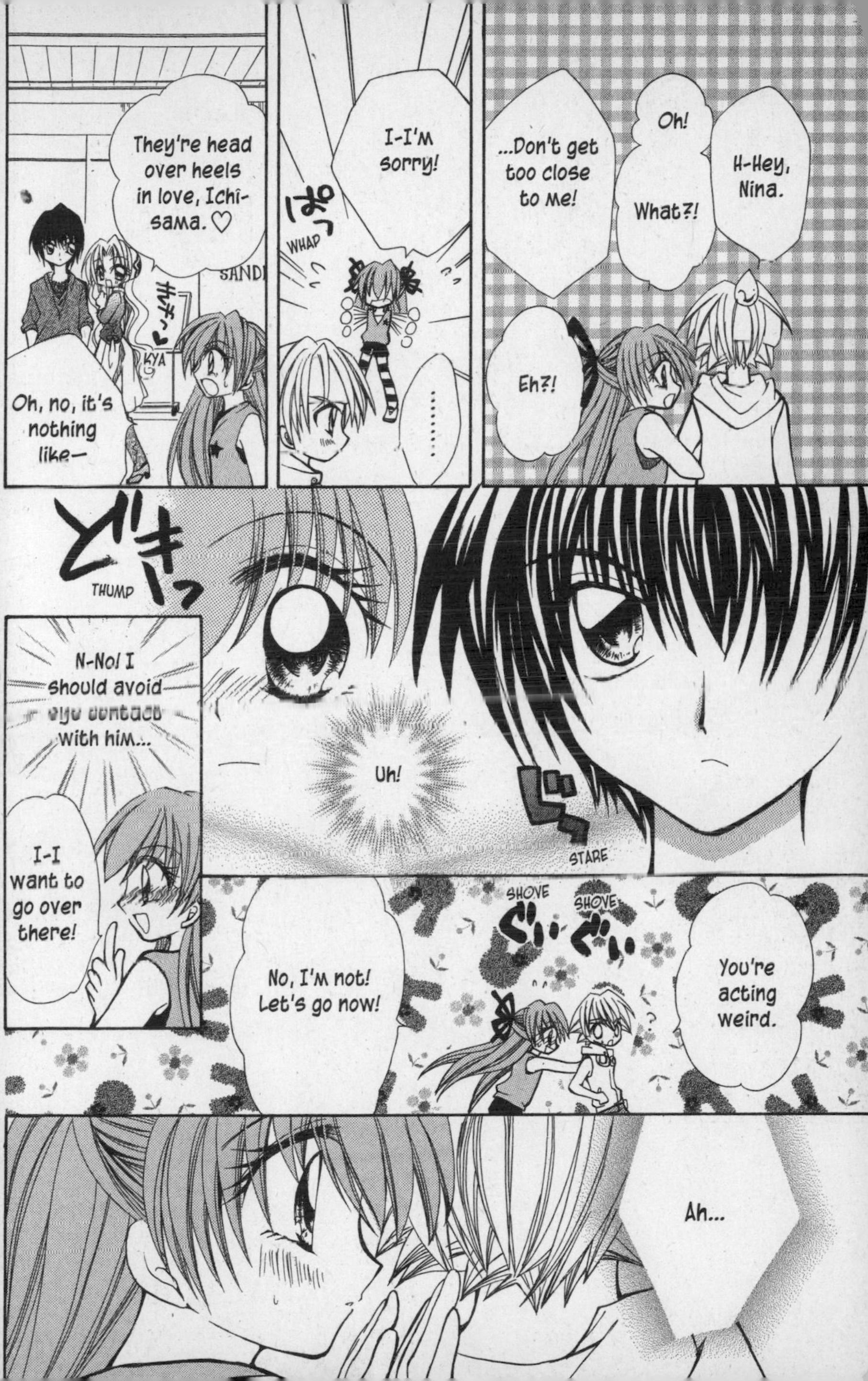
H-Hey, Nina.
Oh!
What?!
...Don't get too close to me!
Eh?!
I-I'm sorry!
ぱっ
WHAP
......
They're head over heels in love, Ichî-sama. ♡
きゃっ
KYA
SANDI
Oh, no, it's nothing like—
じっ
STARE
Uh!
どきっ
THUMP
N-No! I should avoid eye contact with him...
I-I want to go over there!
You're acting weird.
ぐいぐい
SHOVE
SHOVE
No, I'm not! Let's go now!
Ah...

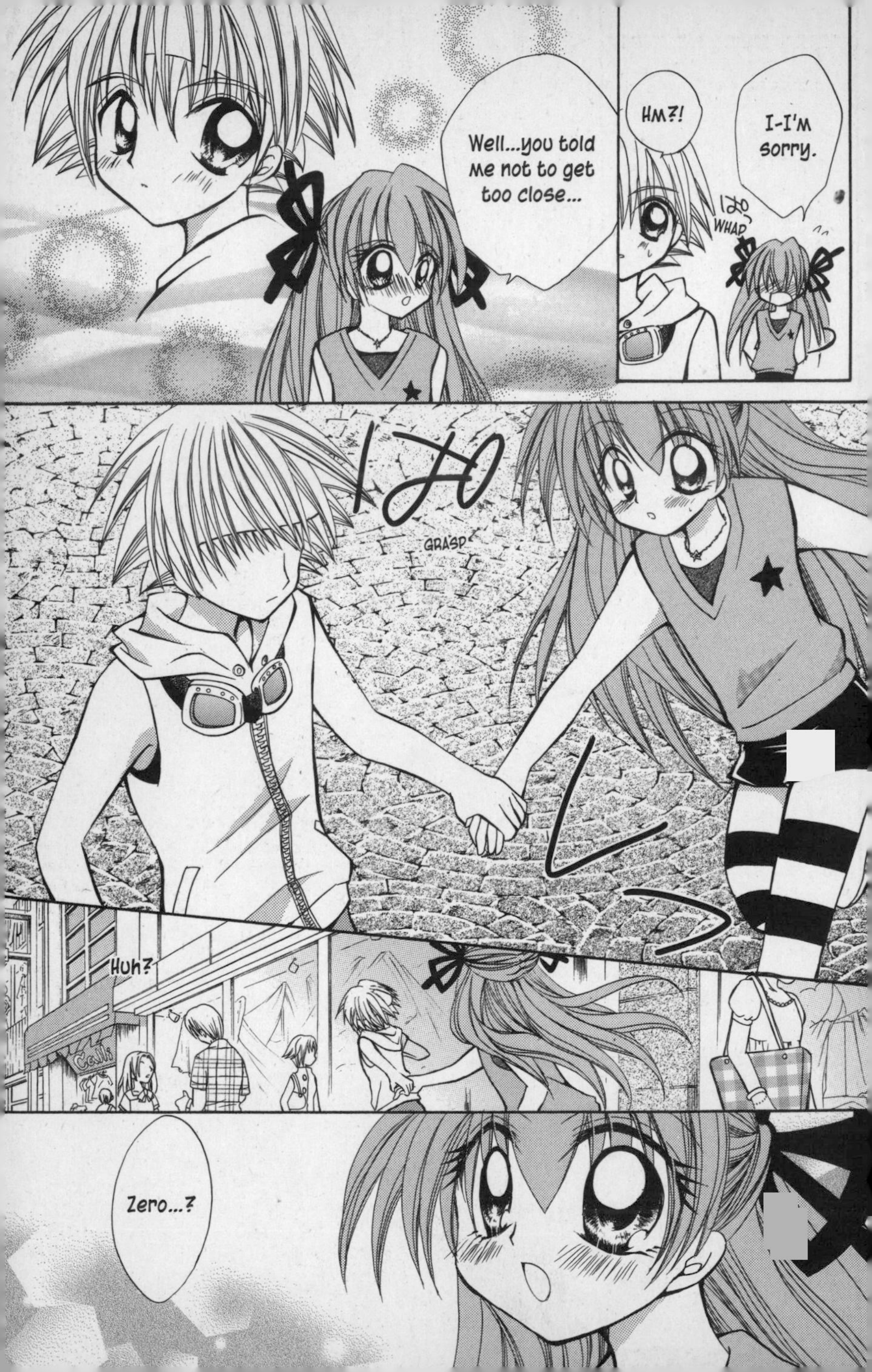
I-I'm sorry.
HM?!
WHAP
Well...you told me not to get too close...
GRASP
Huh?
Zero...?

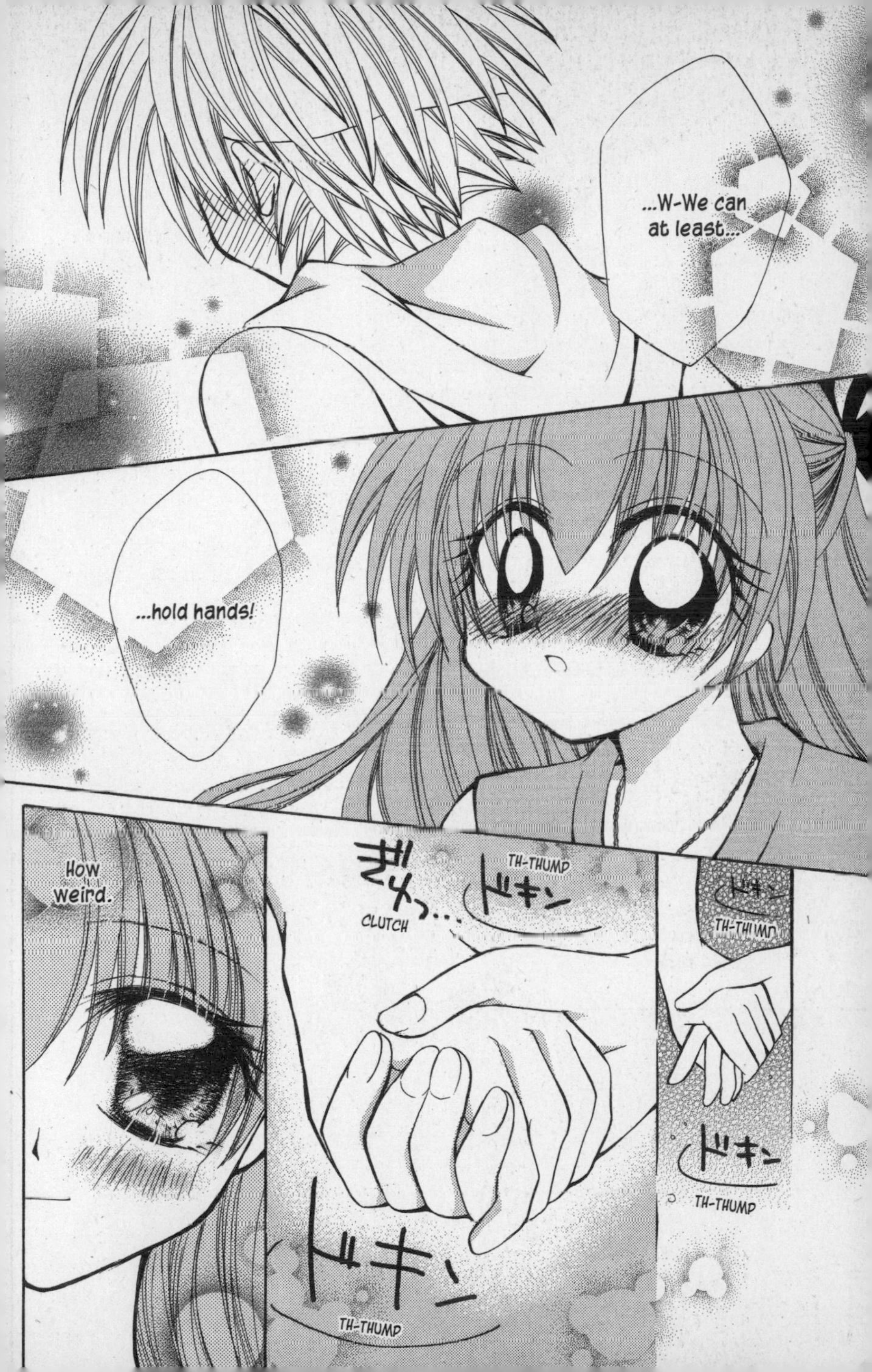
...W-We can at least...
...hold hands!
ドキン
TH-THUMP
ドキン
TH-THUMP
ぎゅっ…
CLUTCH
ドキン
TH-THUMP
ドキン
TH-THUMP
How weird.

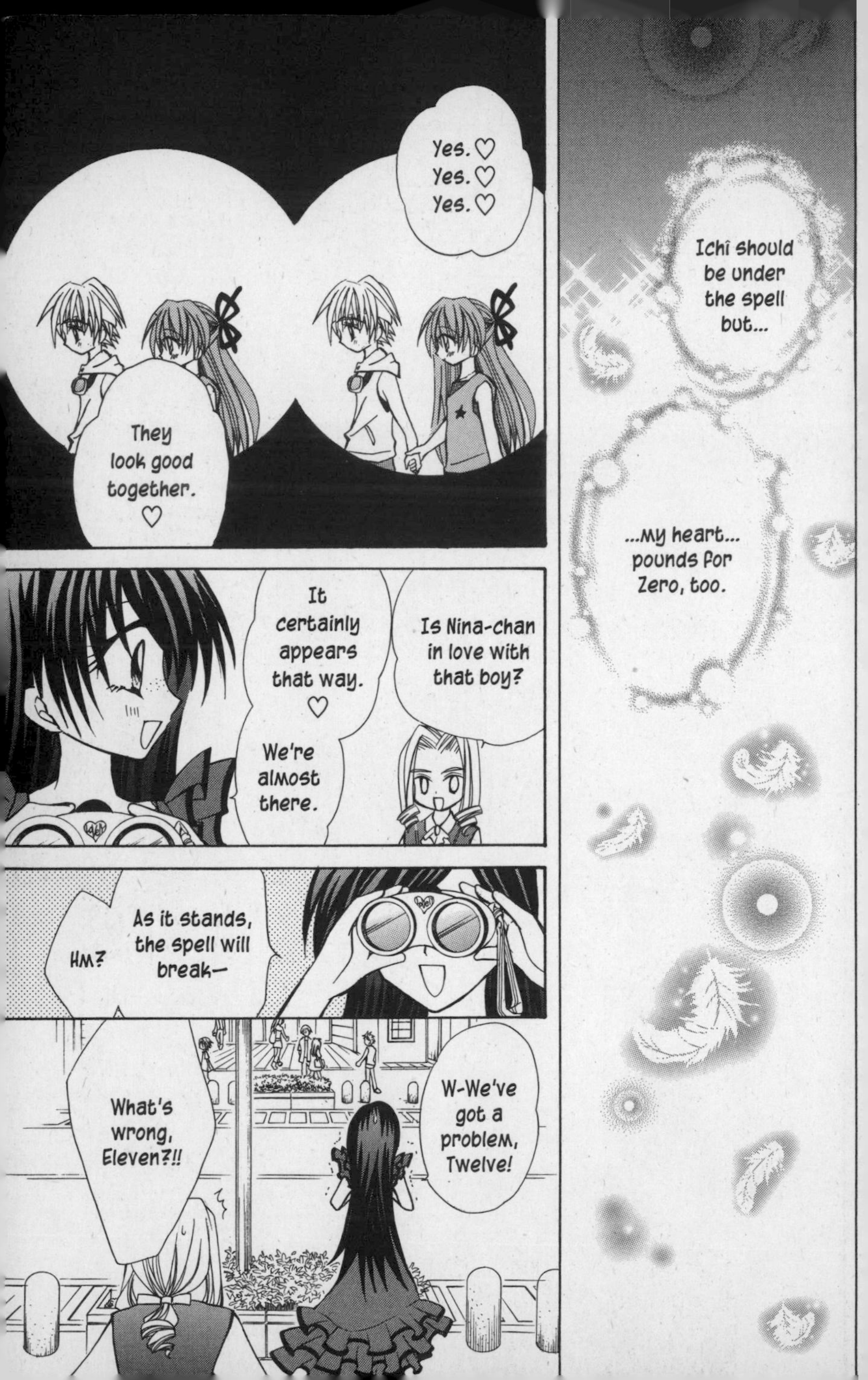
Ichi should be under the spell but...
...my heart... pounds for Zero, too.
Yes. ♡ Yes. ♡ Yes. ♡
They look good together. ♡
Is Nina-chan in love with that boy?
It certainly appears that way. ♡
We're almost there.
As it stands, the spell will break—
Hm?
W-We've got a problem, Twelve!
What's wrong, Eleven?!!

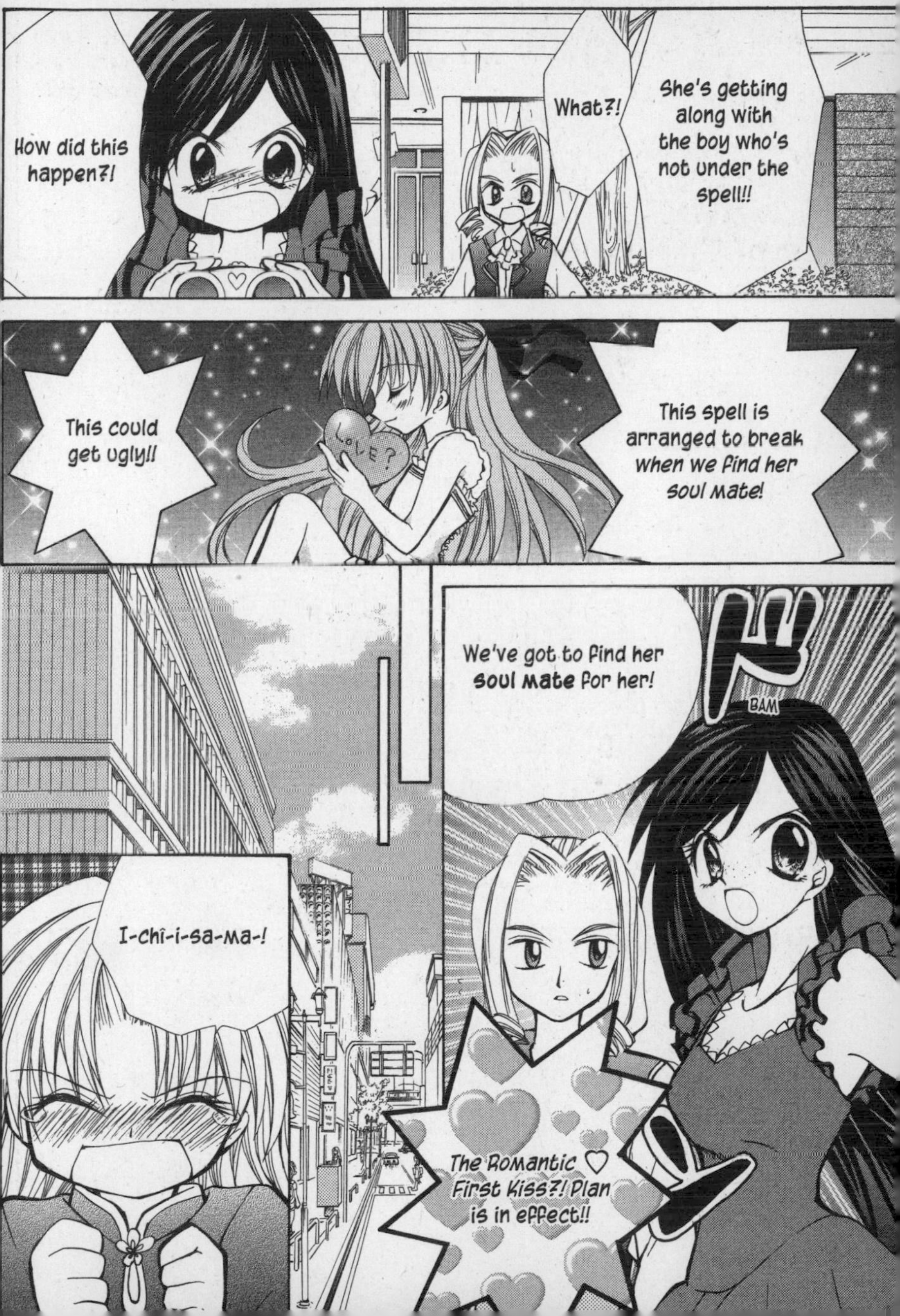
She's getting along with the boy who's not under the spell!!
What?!
How did this happen?!
This spell is arranged to break when we find her soul mate!
This could get ugly!!
We've got to find her **soul mate** for her!
BAM
The Romantic ♡ First Kiss?! Plan is in effect!!
I-chî-i-sa-ma-!

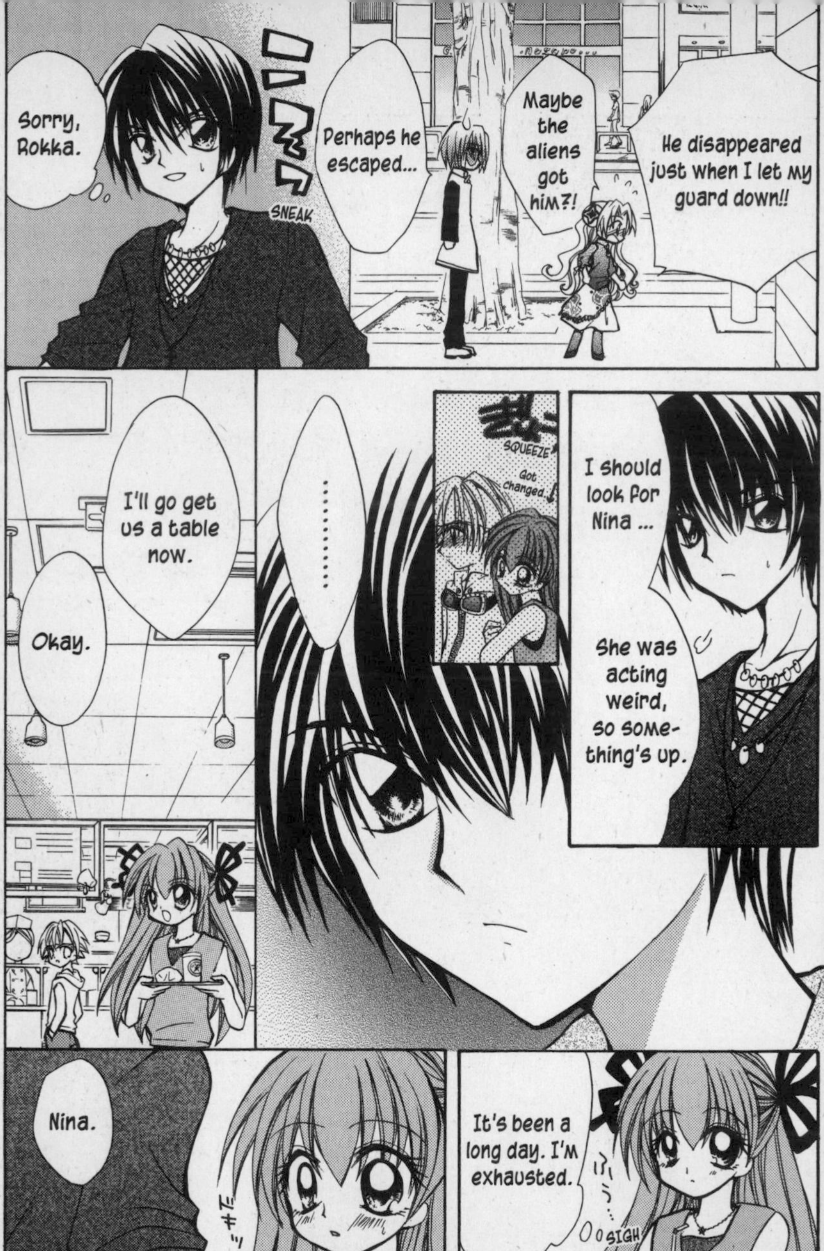
He disappeared just when I let my guard down!!
Maybe the aliens got him?!
Perhaps he escaped...
SNEAK
Sorry, Rokka.
I should look for Nina ...
She was acting weird, so something's up.
SQUEEZE
Got changed.
......
I'll go get us a table now.
Okay.
It's been a long day. I'm exhausted.
SIGH
FLINCH
Nina.

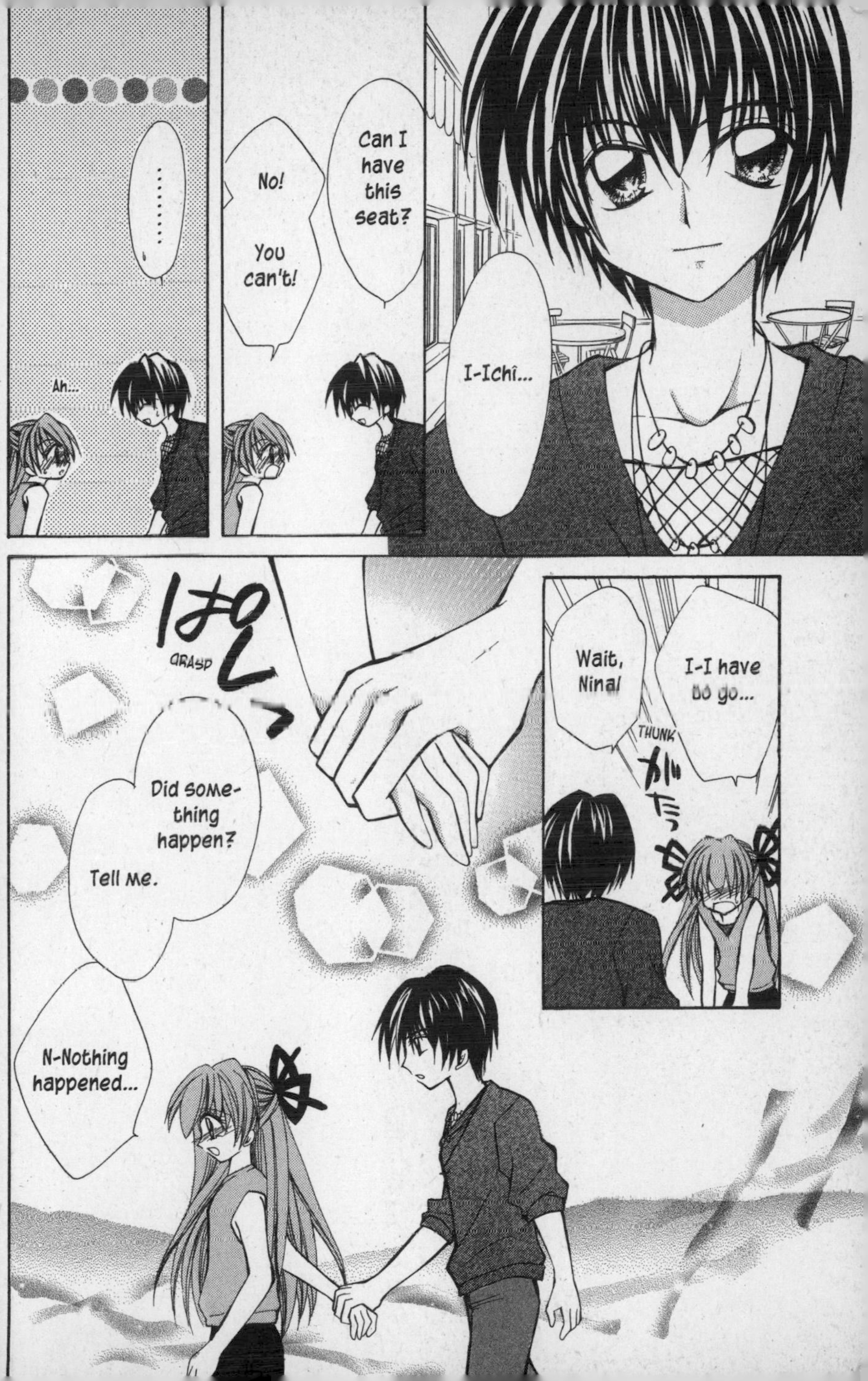
I-Ichi...
Can I have this seat?
No! You can't!
......
Ah...
I-I have to go...
Wait, Nina!
THUNK
GRASP
Did some-thing happen? Tell me.
N-Nothing happened...

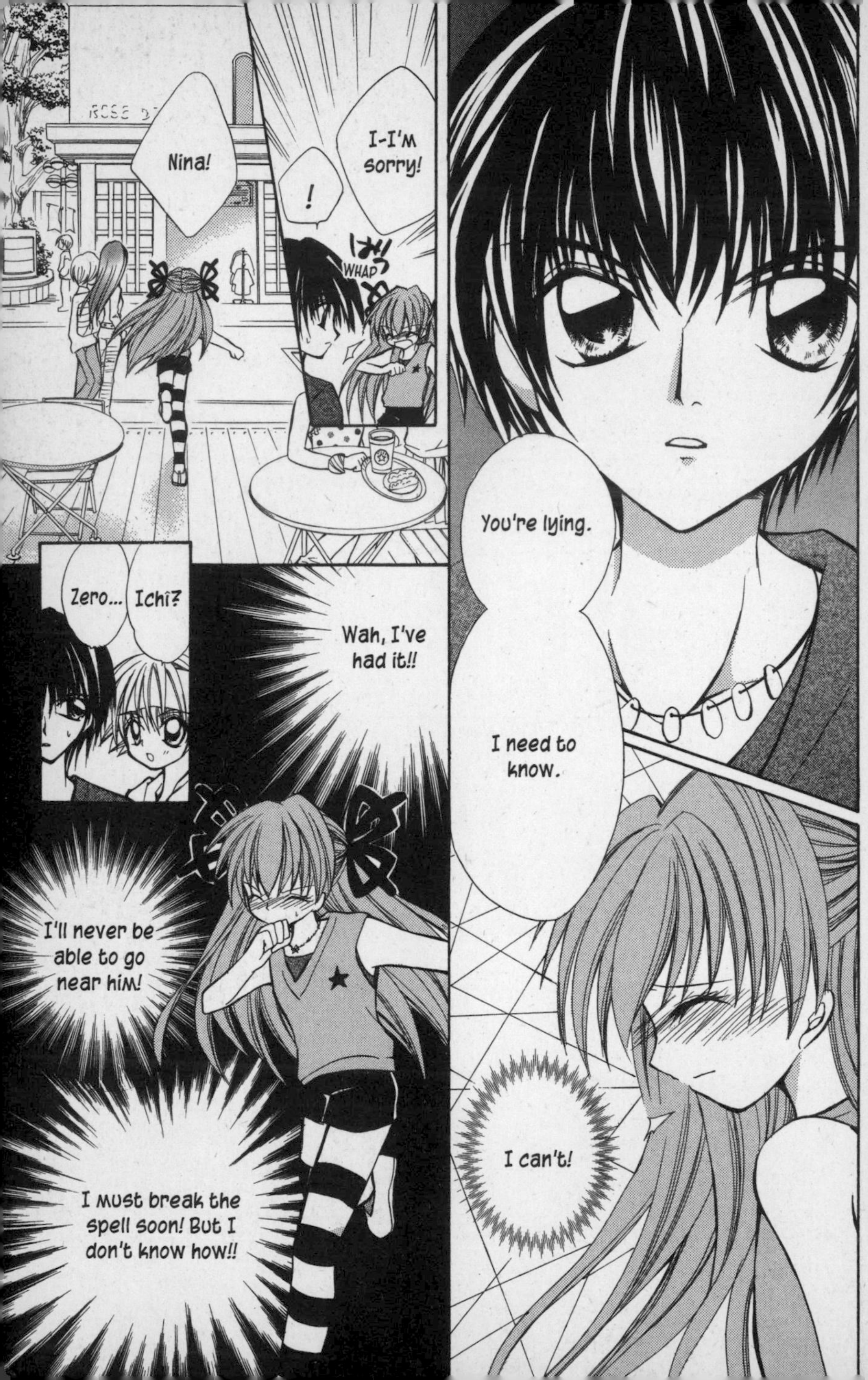
You're lying.
I need to know.
I can't!
I-I'm sorry!
!
WHAP
Nina!
Zero...
Ichi?
Wah, I've had it!!
I'll never be able to go near him!
I must break the spell soon! But I don't know how!!

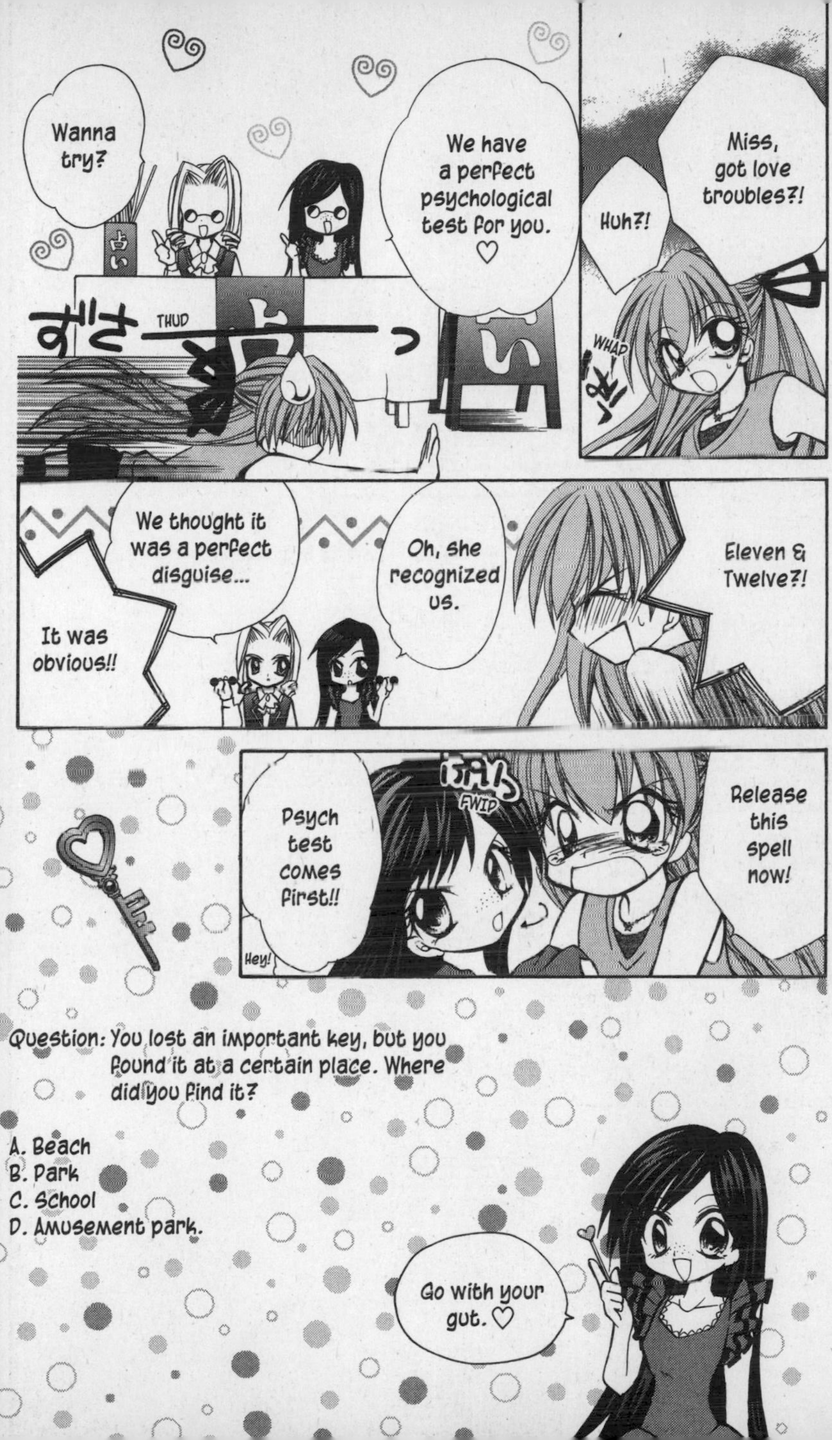
Miss, got love troubles?!
Huh?!
WHAP
We have a perfect psychological test for you. ♡
Wanna try?
THUD
Eleven & Twelve?!
Oh, she recognized us.
We thought it was a perfect disguise...
It was obvious!!
Release this spell now!
FWIP
Psych test comes first!!
Hey!
Question: You lost an important key, but you found it at a certain place. Where did you find it?
A. Beach
B. Park
C. School
D. Amusement park.
Go with your gut. ♡

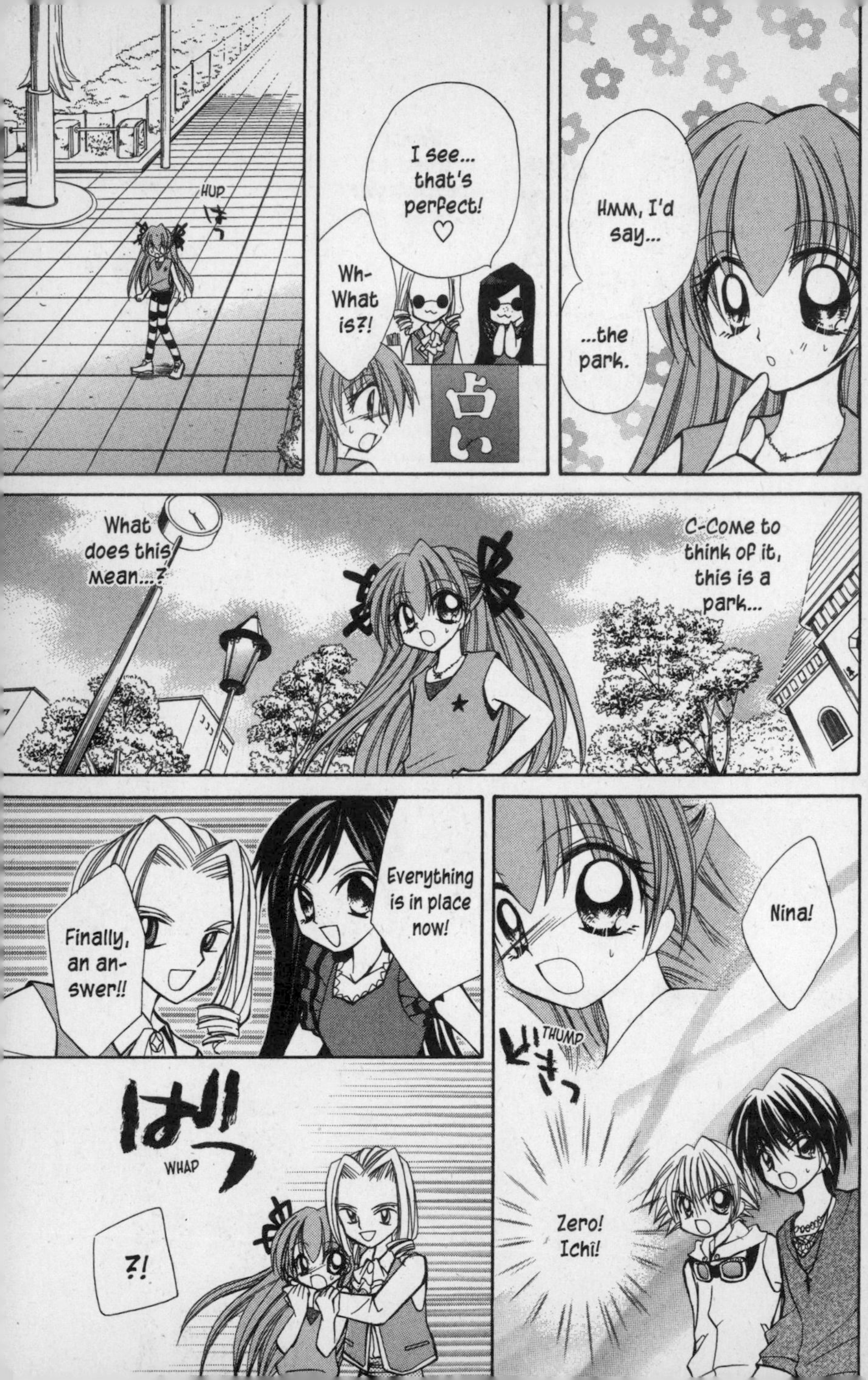

Hmm, I'd say...
...the park.
I see... that's perfect! ♡
Wh- What is?!
占い
HUP
はっ
C-Come to think of it, this is a park...
What does this mean...?
Nina!
THUMP
どきっ
Zero! Ichi!
Everything is in place now!
Finally, an answer!!
ぱっ
WHAP
?!

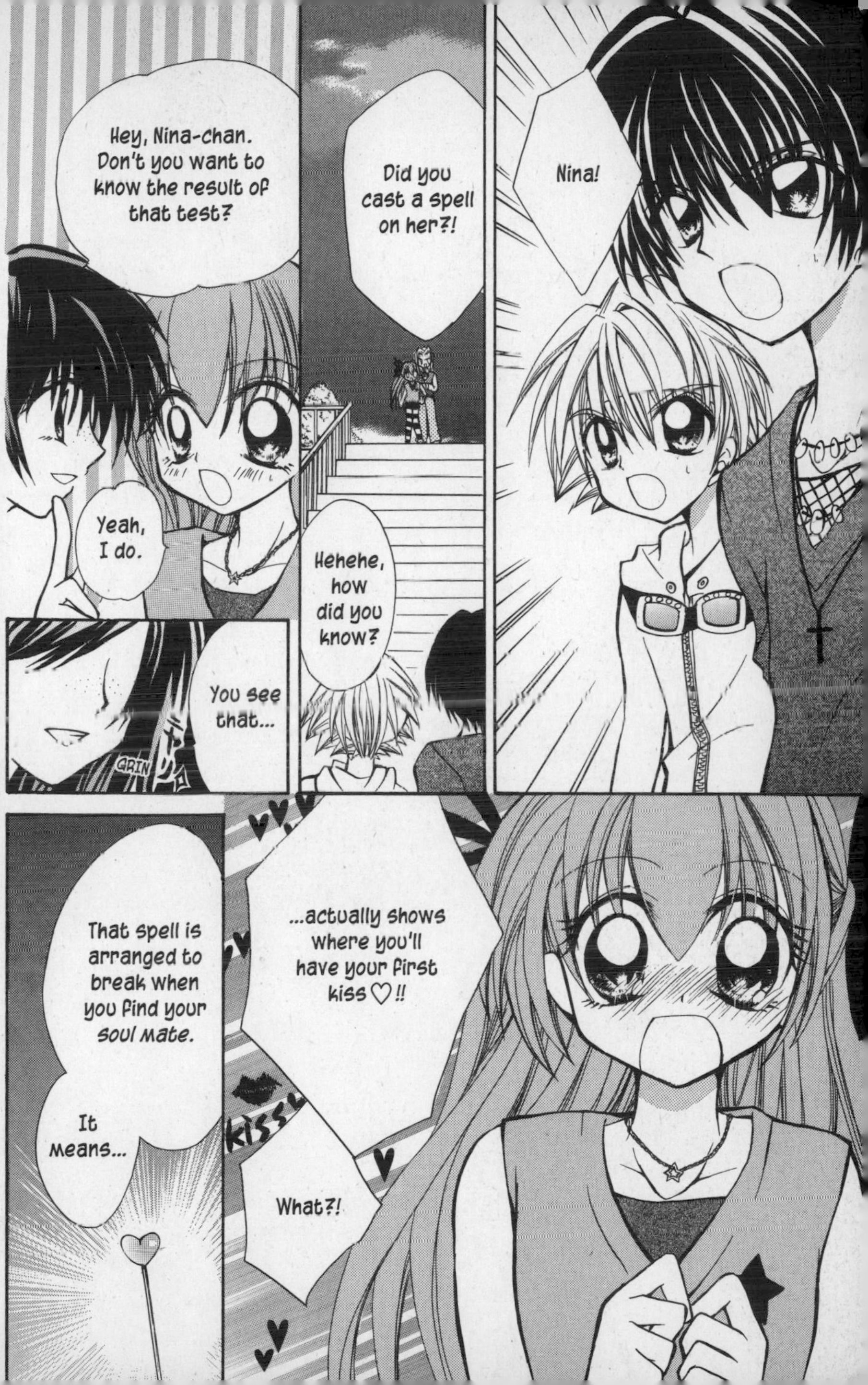
Nina!
Did you cast a spell on her?!
Hehehe, how did you know?
Hey, Nina-chan. Don't you want to know the result of that test?
Yeah, I do.
You see that...
GRIN
...actually shows where you'll have your first kiss♡!!
kiss
What?!
That spell is arranged to break when you find your soul mate.
It means...

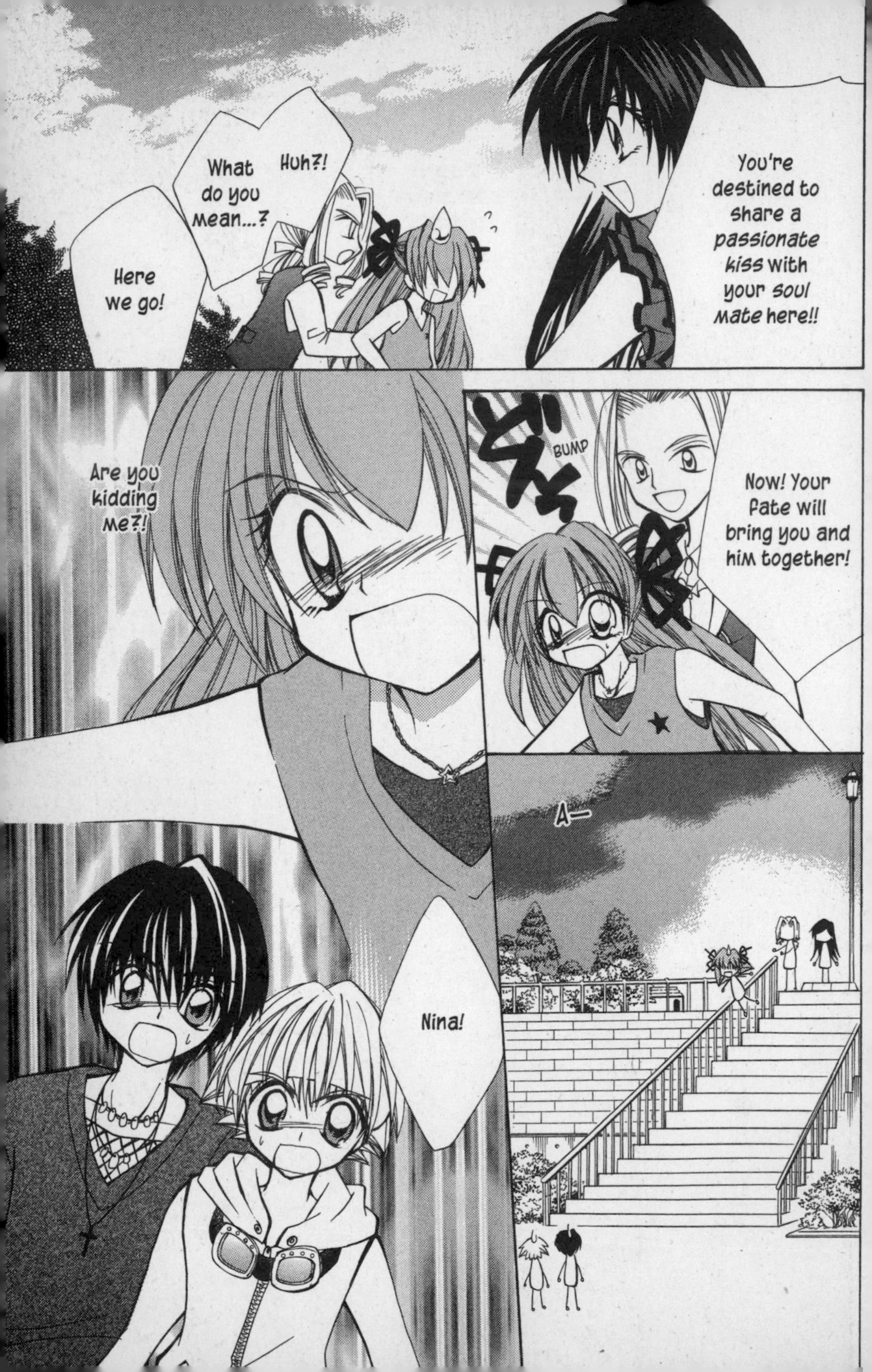
You're destined to share a passionate kiss with your soul mate here!!
Huh?!
What do you mean...?
Here we go!
BUMP
Now! Your fate will bring you and him together!
A—
Are you kidding me?!
Nina!

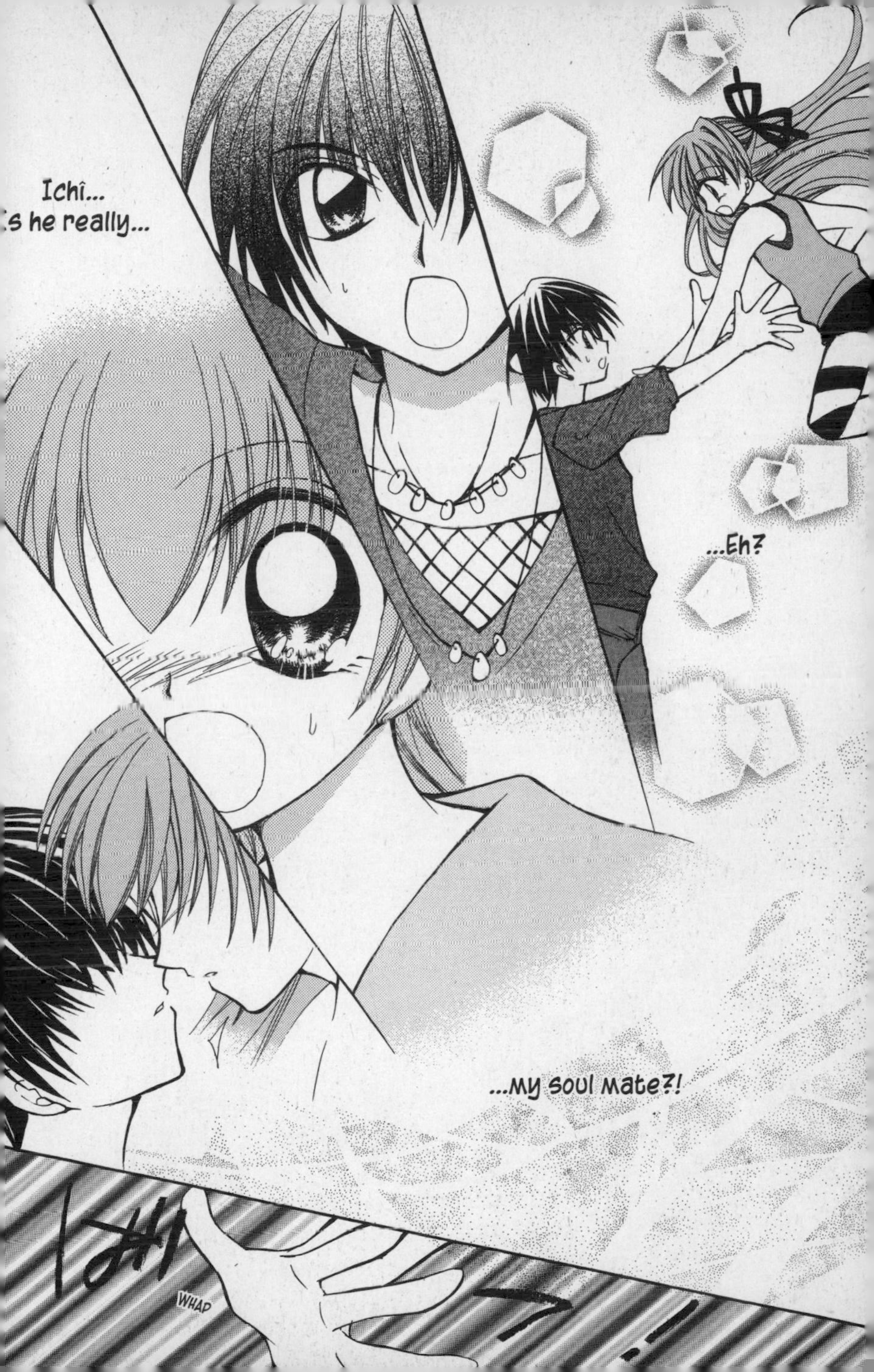
...Eh?
Ichî...
s he really...
...my soul mate?!
WHAP

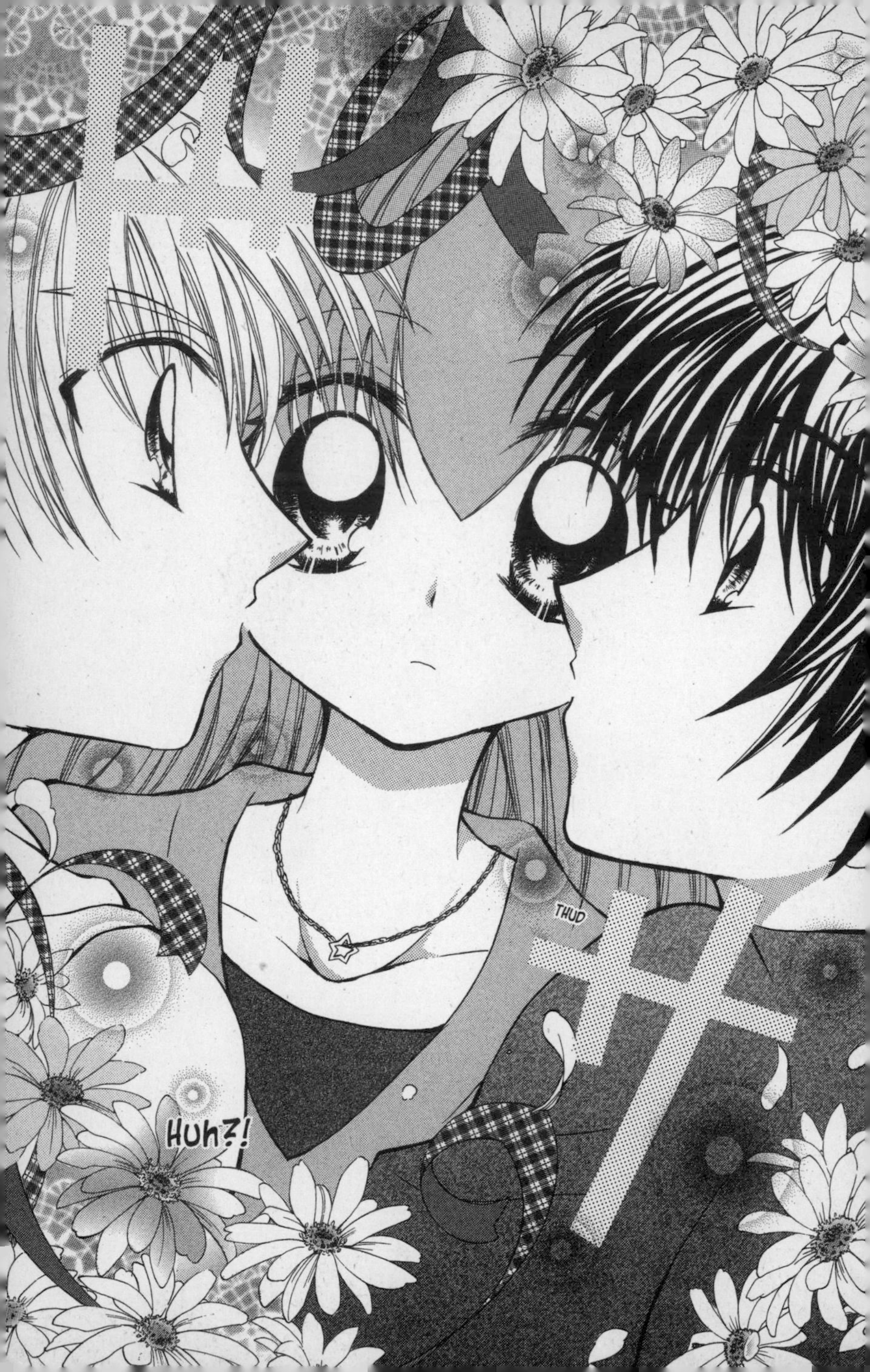
THUD
HUH?!

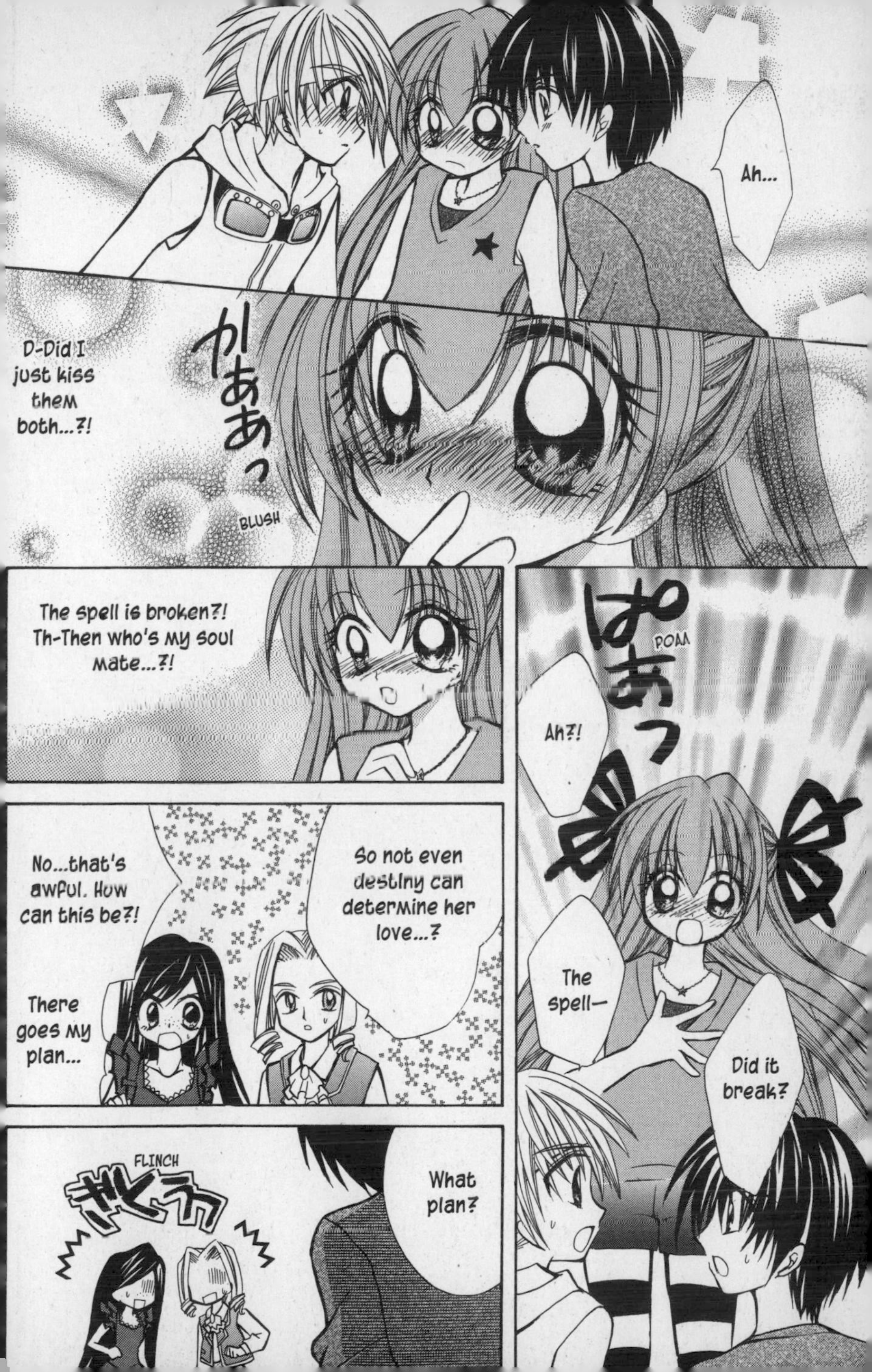

Ah...
かああっ
BLUSH
D-Did I just kiss them both...?!
ぱあっ
POAA
Ah?!
The spell—
Did it break?
The spell is broken?! Th-Then who's my soul mate...?!
So not even destiny can determine her love...?
No...that's awful. How can this be?!
There goes my plan...
What plan?
ぎくっ
FLINCH

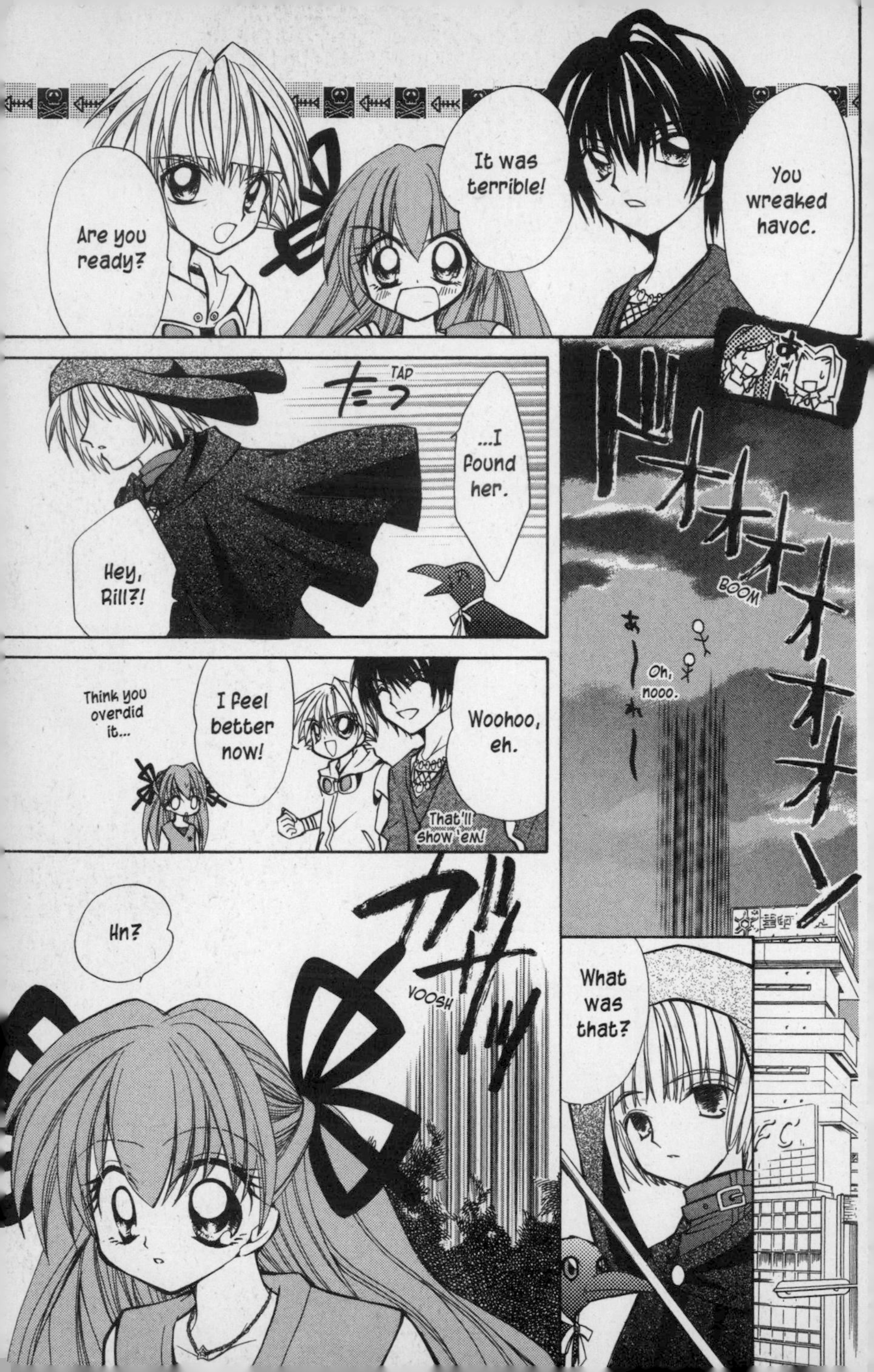
You wreaked havoc.
It was terrible!
Are you ready?
Ah
BOOM
Oh, nooo.
TAP
...I found her.
Hey, Rill?!
Woohoo, eh.
That'll show 'em!
I feel better now!
Think you overdid it...
What was that?
VOOSH
Hn?

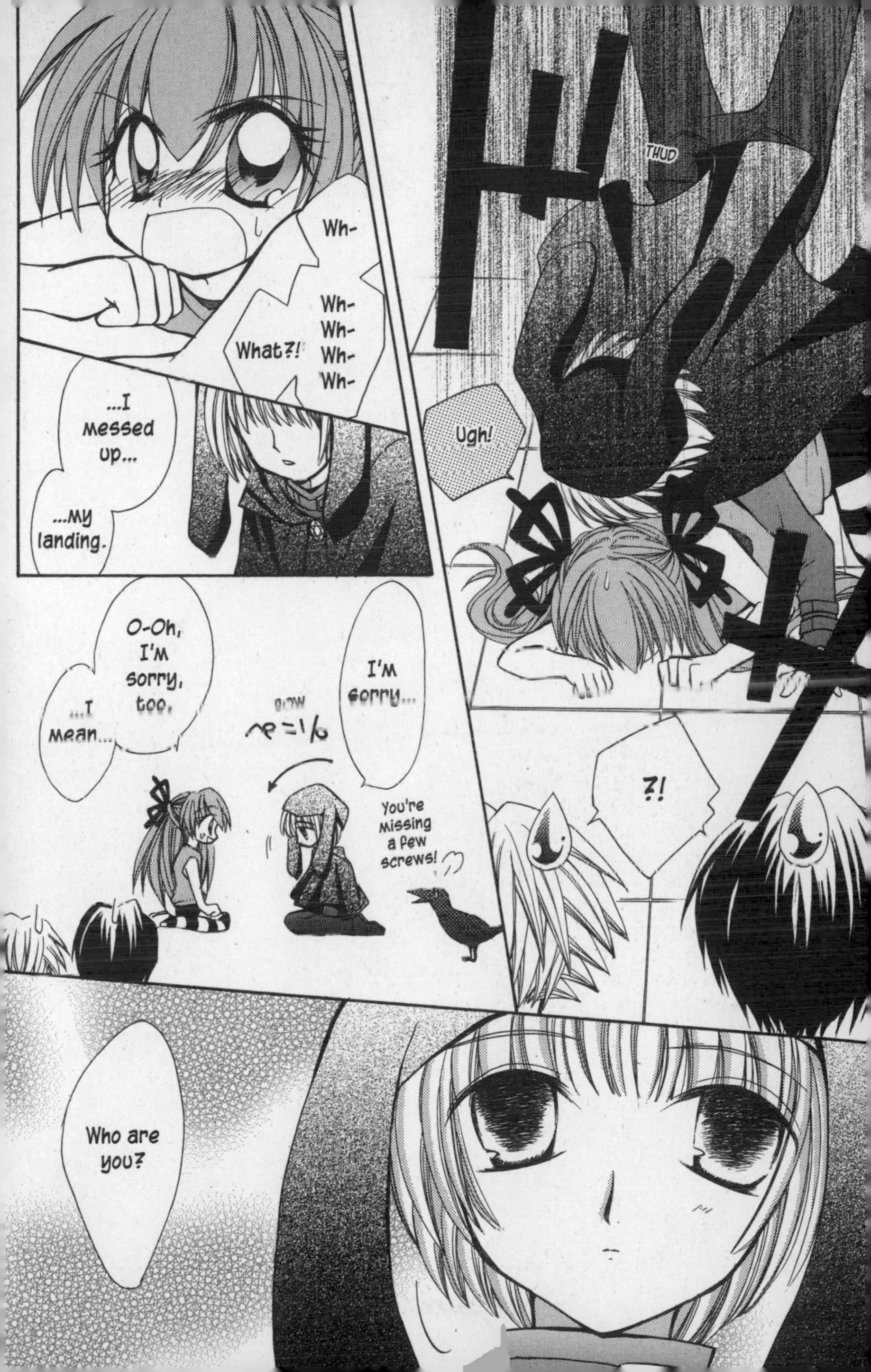
THUD
Ugh!
Wh-
Wh- Wh- Wh- Wh-
What?!
...I messed up...
...my landing.
?!
I'm sorry...
BOW
O-Oh, I'm sorry, too.
...I mean...
You're missing a few screws!
Who are you?

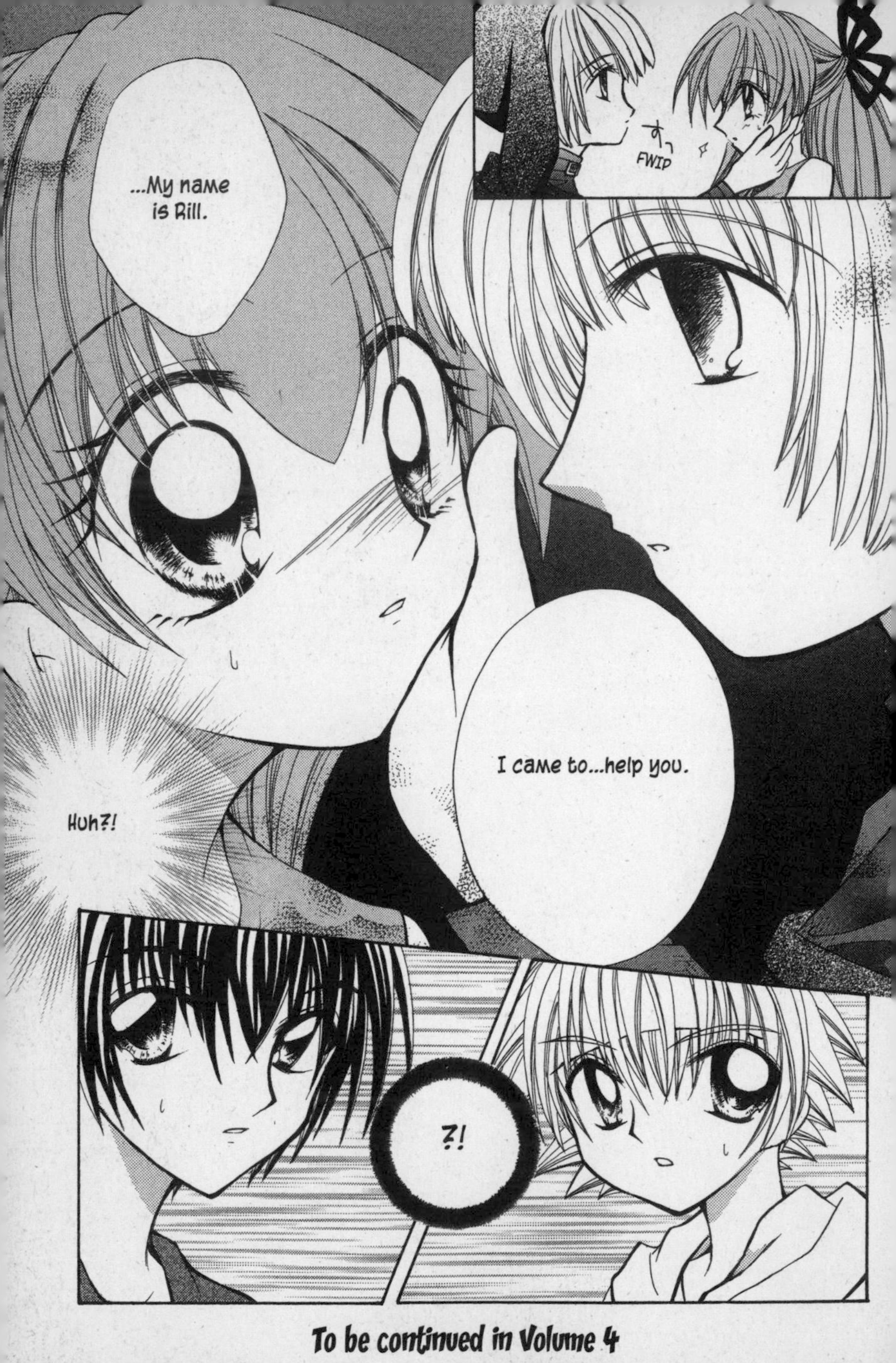
す
FWIP
...My name is Rill.
I came to...help you.
Huh?!
?!

To be continued in Volume 4

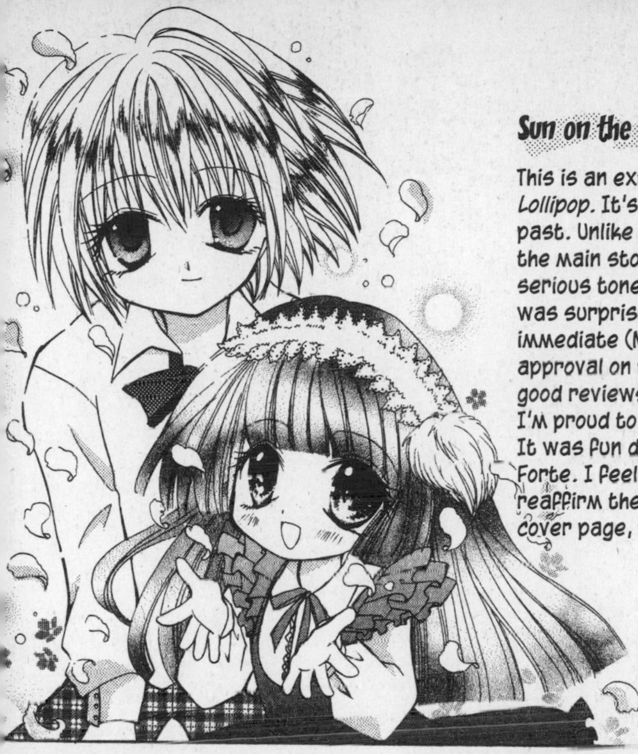

Sun on the 17th of July

This is an extra story for the *Lollipop.* It's about Sun and Forte's past. Unlike the slapstick style in the main story, this has a pretty serious tone. I love this manga. I was surprised that I got an immediate (No corrections needed!) approval on the storyboard! It got good reviews from everyone and I'm proud to have drawn it as well. It was fun drawing little Sun and Forte. I feel as if I was able to reaffirm their bond. And I like the cover page, too.

Chocolate and Vanilla Lollipop

This was an extra story that was published in *Nakayoshi Lovely* in winter. It's like a skit . . . (Laugh) I had fun drawing it. Everyone is being so silly. The character to the right (Read this after you've become familiar with the story.) is another version of the joke. I drew it with the intention of using it in this story, but I was told it'd be too confusing and that I should forget it . . . Since I already drew it, I decided to insert it in this book. Well, this manga is of no significance! Don't think about it too hard. What Sun-chan is holding is Cake-kun who escaped. She must have wanted it . . . .

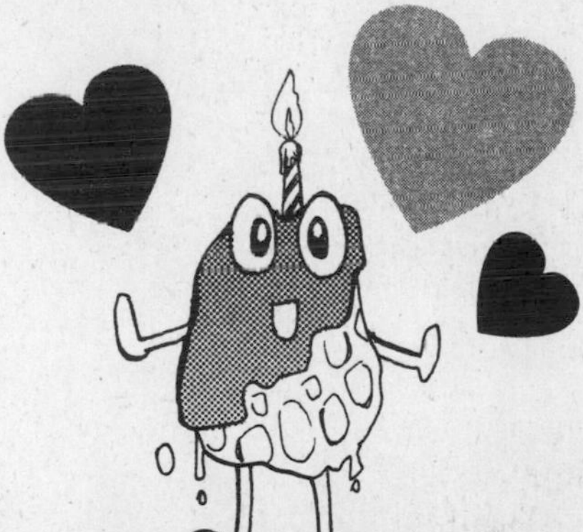

See the miracle of the silent night, Cake-kun, in action at page 197.★

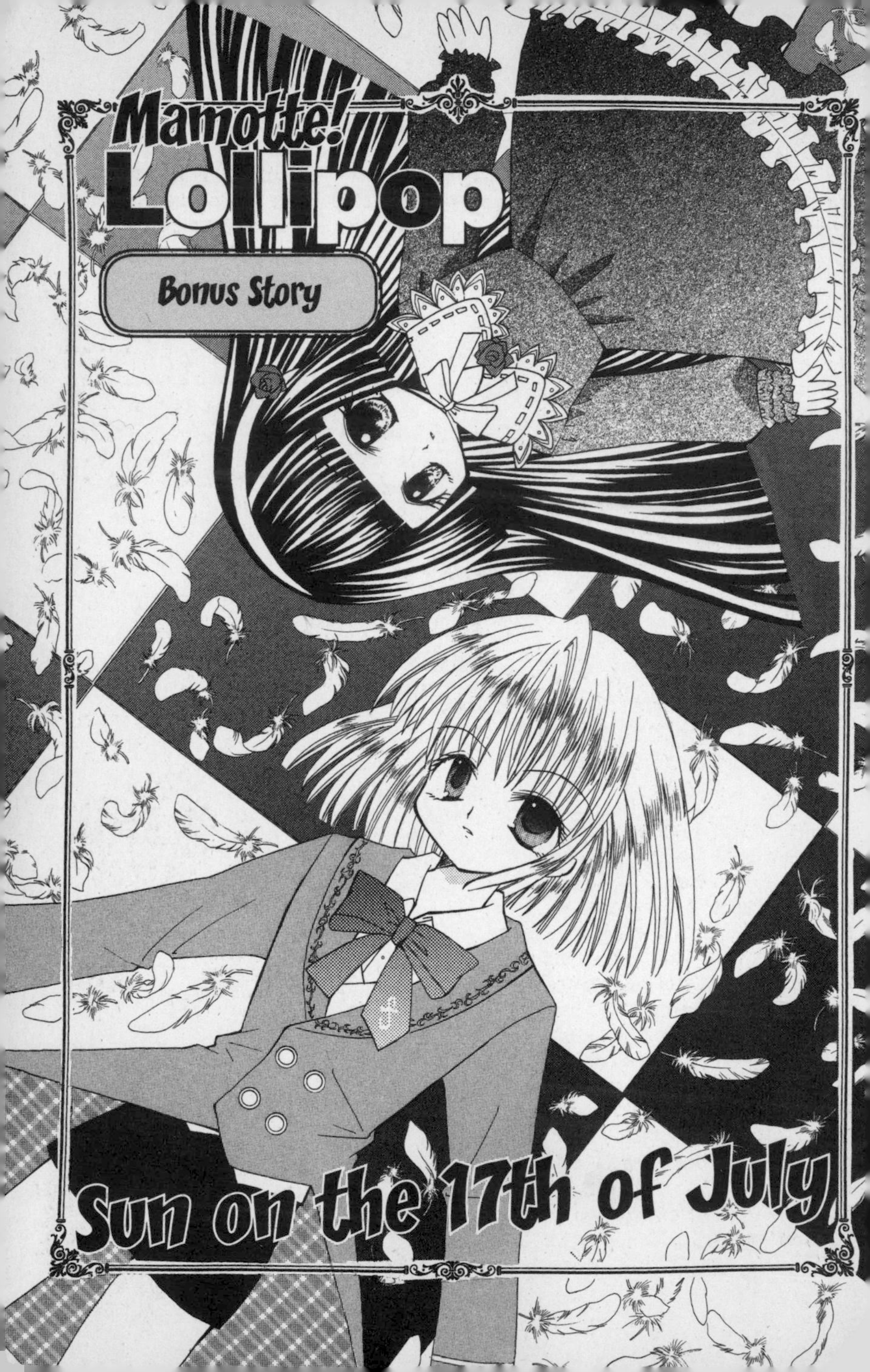
Mamotte! Lollipop
Bonus Story
Sun on the 17th of July

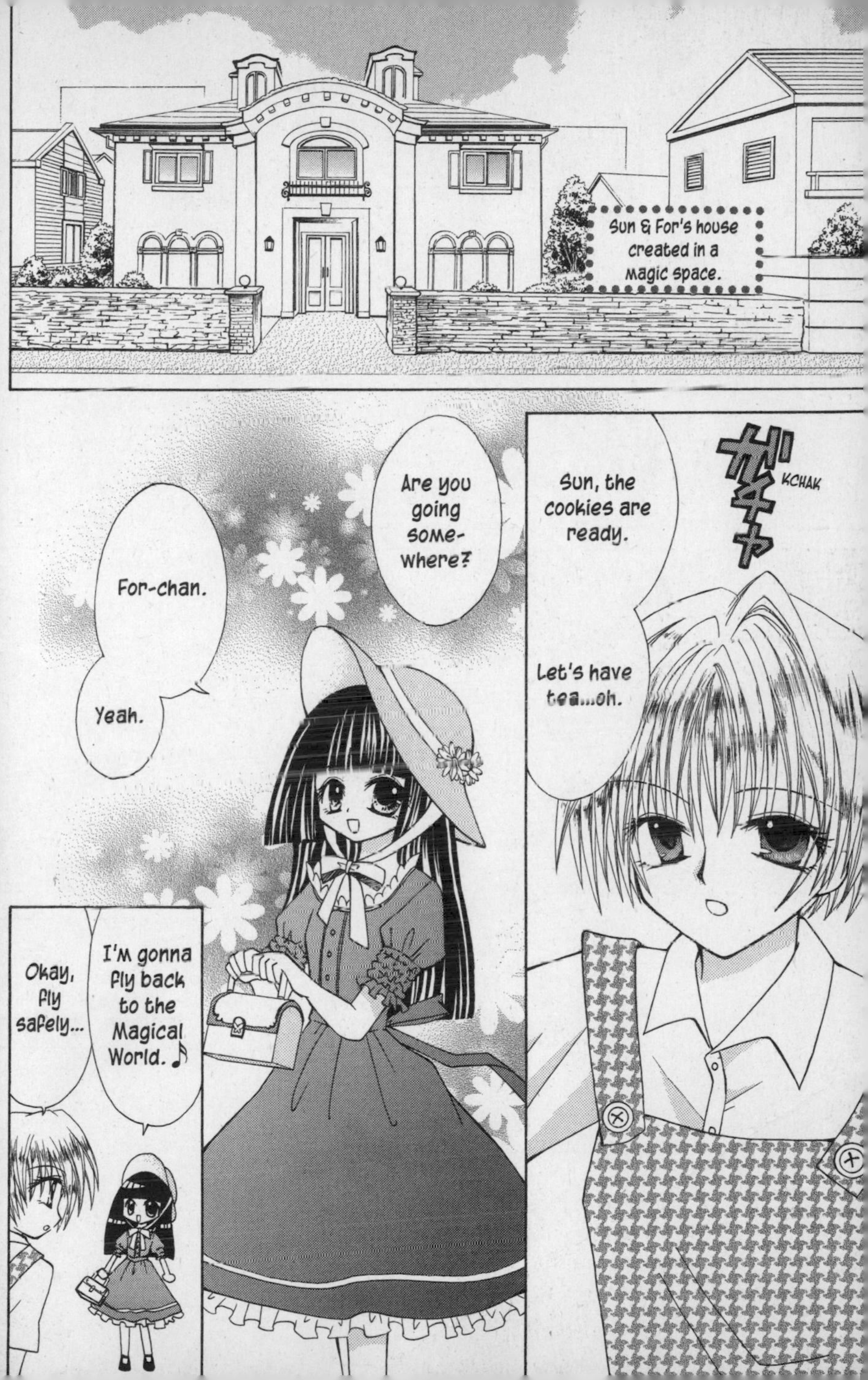
Sun & For's house created in a magic space.
ガチャ KCHAK
Sun, the cookies are ready.
Let's have tea...oh.
Are you going some-where?
For-chan.
Yeah.
I'm gonna fly back to the Magical World. ♪
Okay, fly safely...

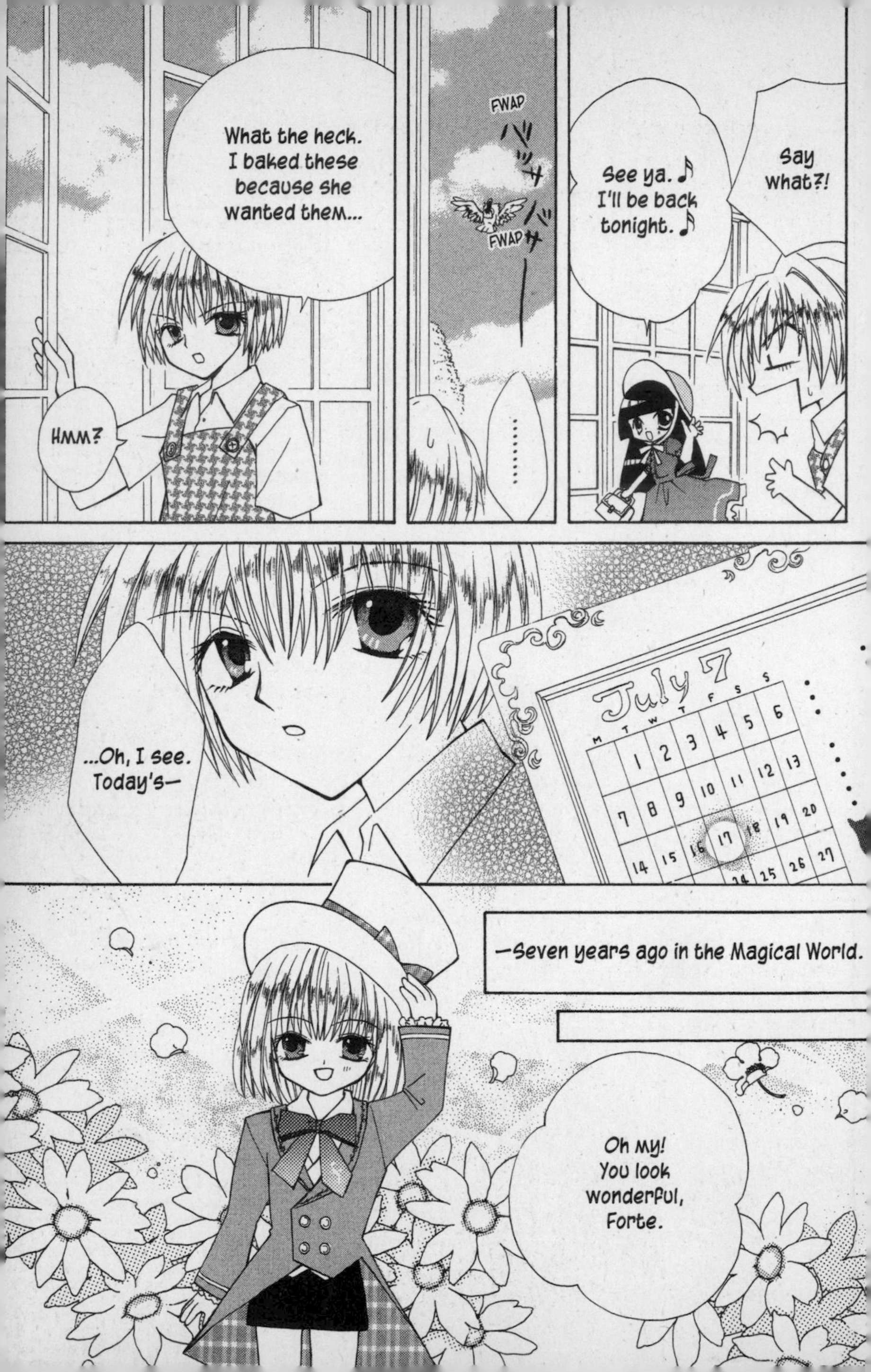
Say what?!
See ya. ♪ I'll be back tonight. ♪
FWAP
FWAP
......
What the heck. I baked these because she wanted them...
Hmm?
......
July
...Oh, I see. Today's—
—Seven years ago in the Magical World.
Oh my! You look wonderful, Forte.

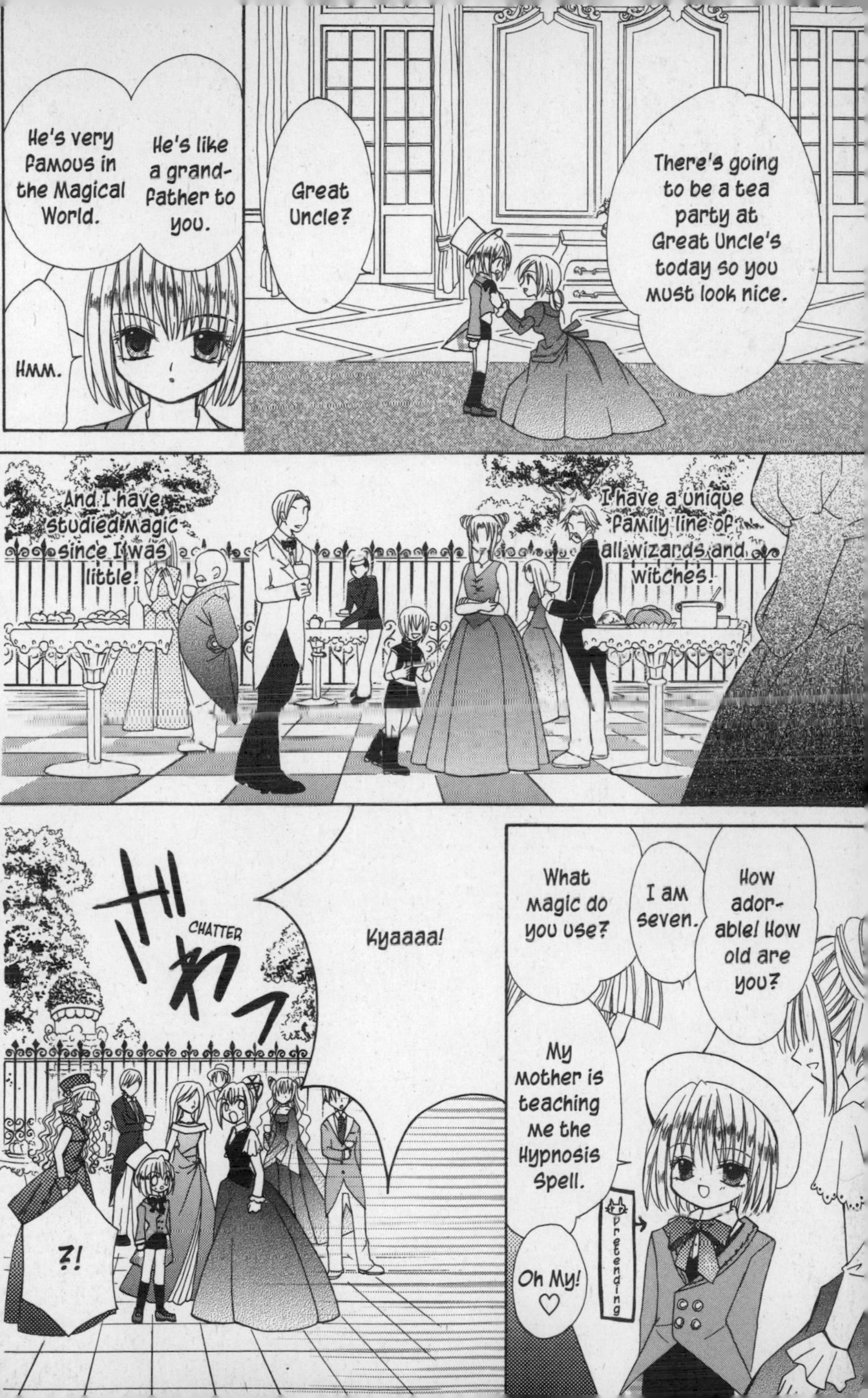
There's going to be a tea party at Great Uncle's today so you must look nice.
Great Uncle?
He's like a grandfather to you.
He's very famous in the Magical World.
Hmm.
I have a unique family line of all wizards and witches!
And I have studied magic since I was little!
How adorable! How old are you?
I am seven.
What magic do you use?
My mother is teaching me the Hypnosis Spell.
Pretending
Oh My! ♡
Kyaaaa!
CHATTER
?!

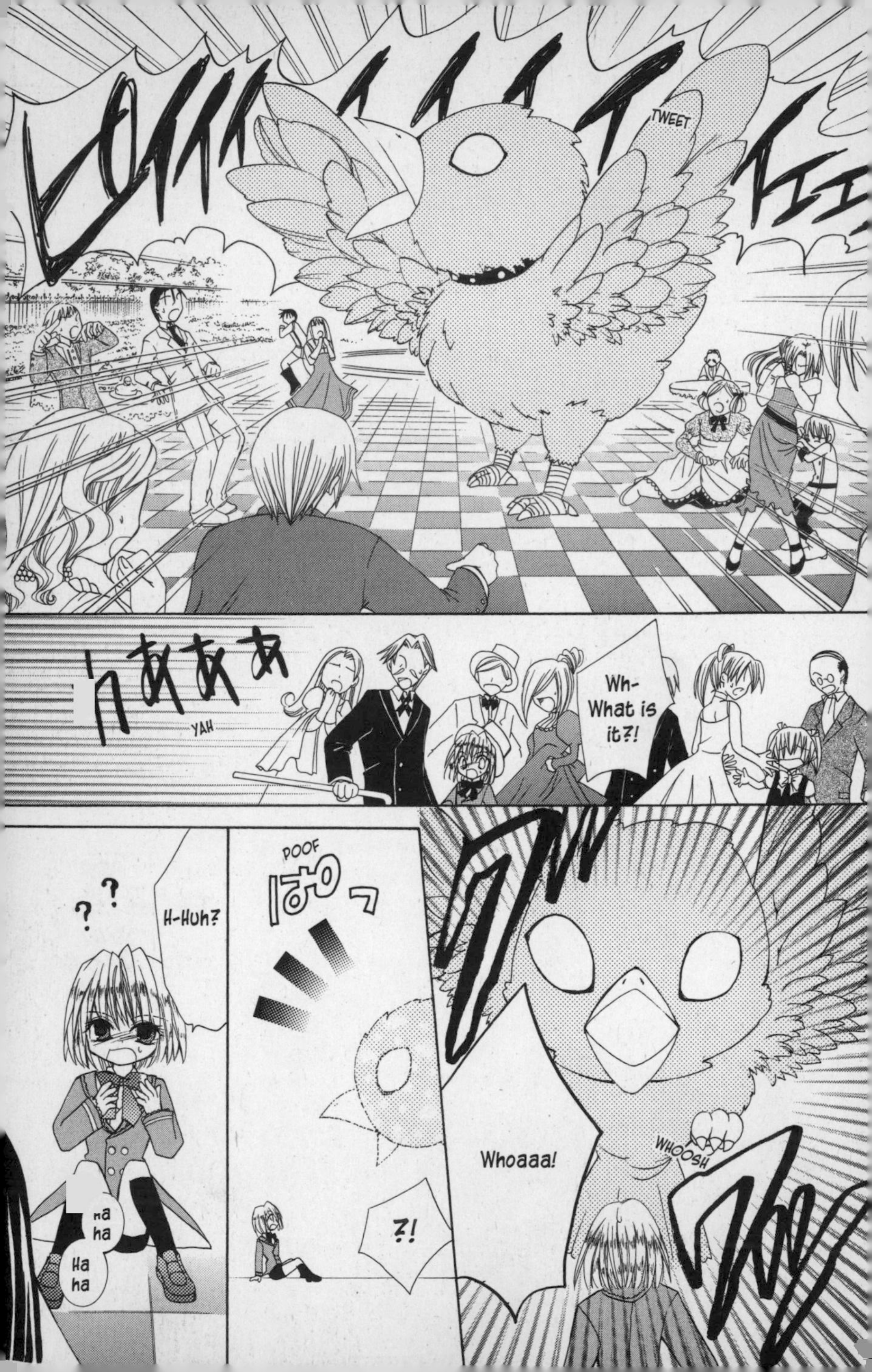
TWEET
Wh-
What is it?!
YAH
Whoaaa!
WHOOSH
POOF
?!
H-Huh?
Ha
ha
Ha
ha

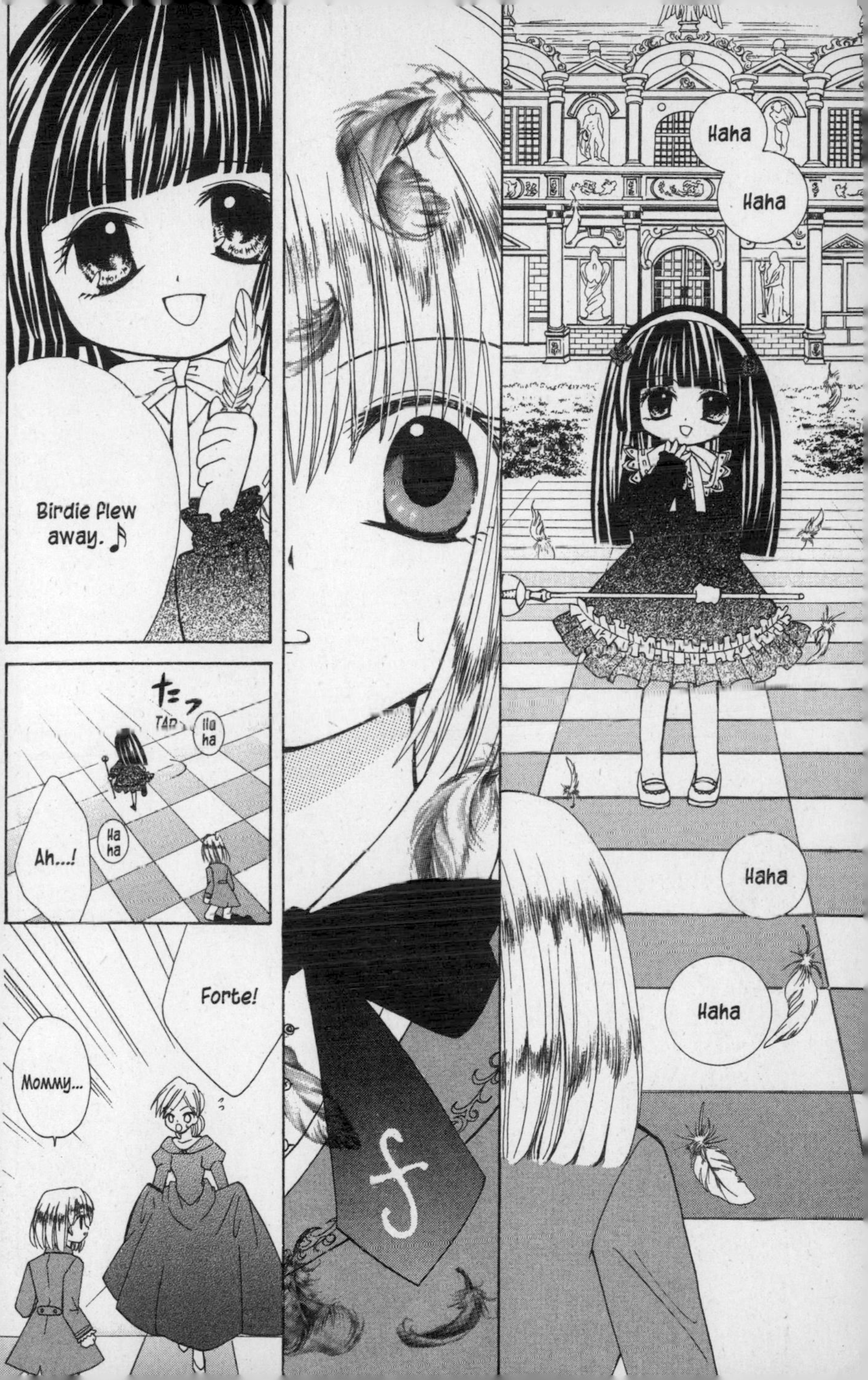
Haha
Haha
Haha
Haha
Birdie flew away. ♪
たっ
TAP
Ha ha
Ha ha
Ah...!
Forte!
Mommy...

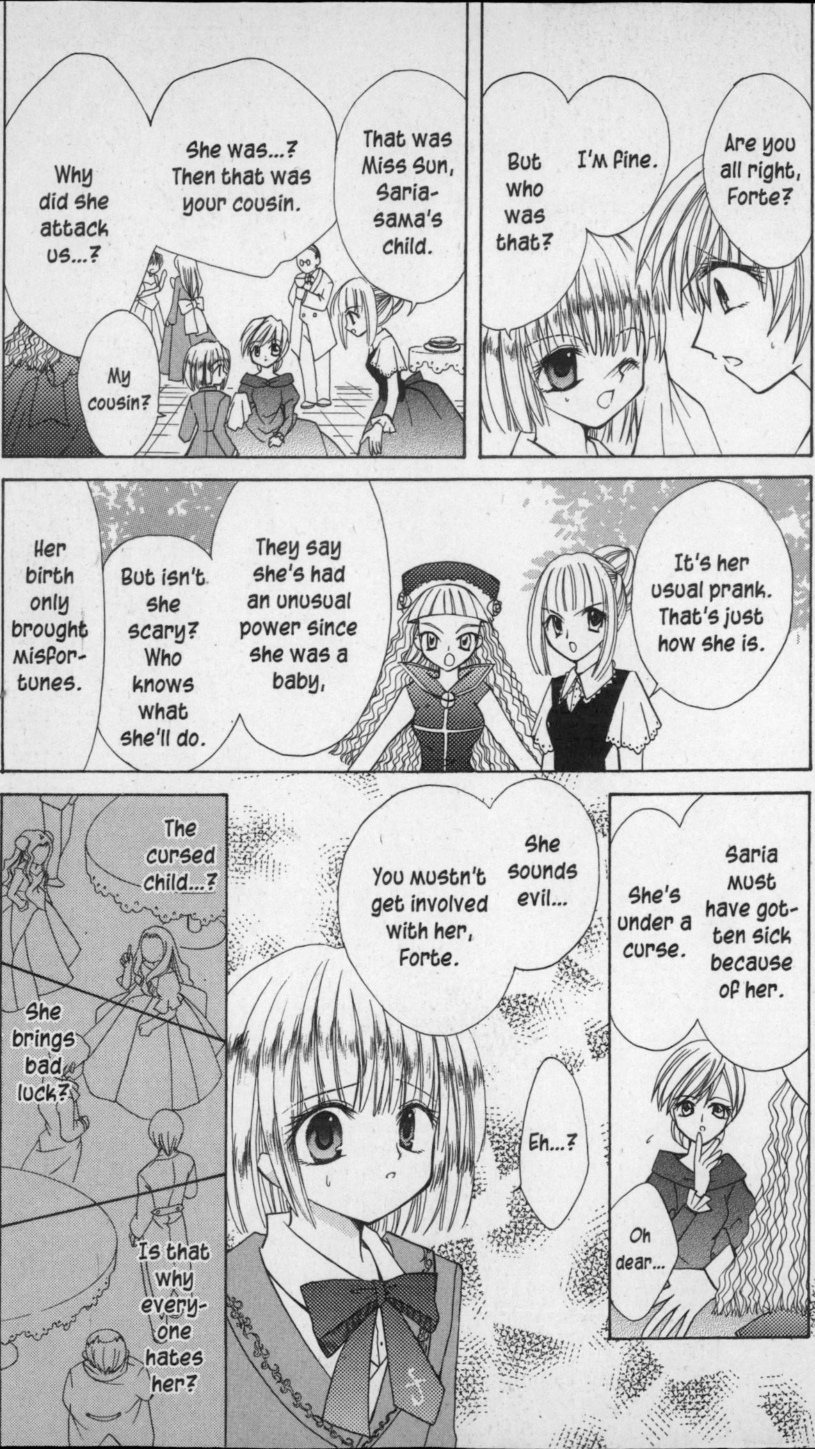
Are you all right, Forte?
I'm fine.
But who was that?
That was Miss Sun, Saria-sama's child.
She was...? Then that was your cousin.
Why did she attack us...?
My cousin?
It's her usual prank. That's just how she is.
They say she's had an unusual power since she was a baby,
But isn't she scary? Who knows what she'll do.
Her birth only brought misfortunes.
Saria must have gotten sick because of her.
She's under a curse.
Oh dear...
She sounds evil...
You mustn't get involved with her, Forte.
Eh...?
The cursed child...?
She brings bad luck?
Is that why everyone hates her?

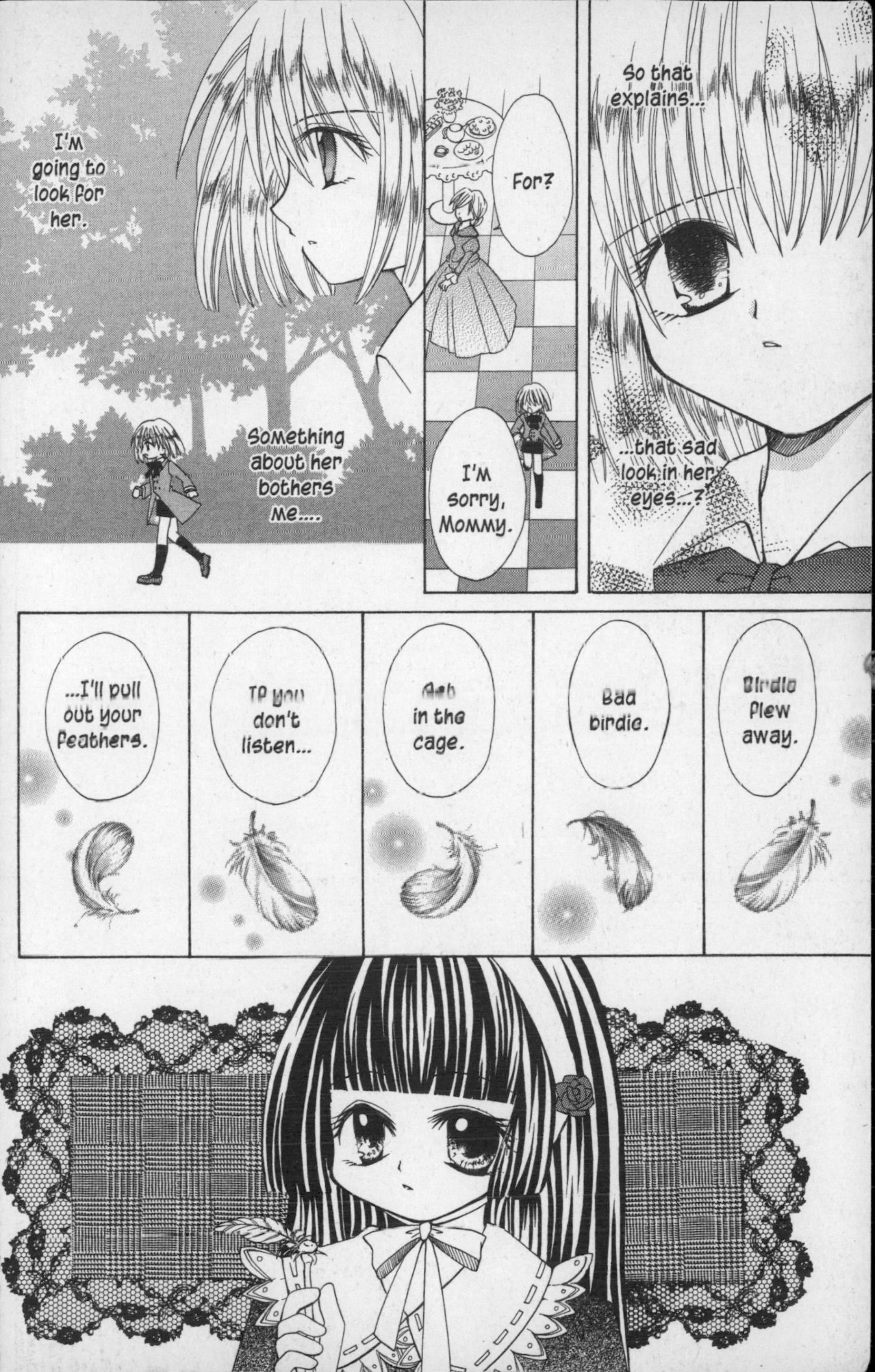
So that explains...
...that sad look in her eyes...?
For?
I'm sorry, Mommy.
I'm going to look for her.
Something about her bothers me....
Birdie flew away.
Bad birdie.
in the cage.
If you don't listen...
...I'll pull out your feathers.

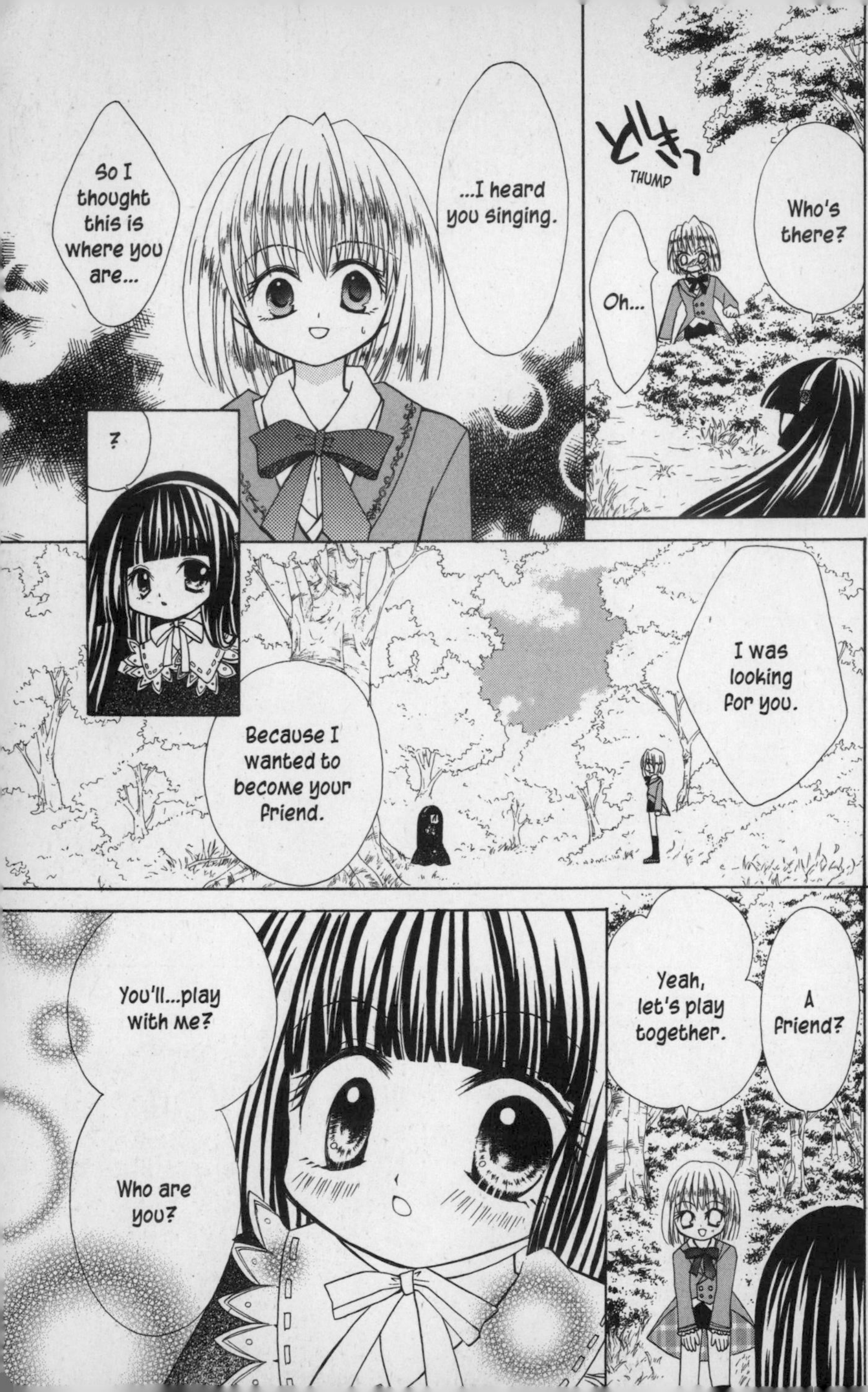
どきっ
THUMP
Who's there?
Oh...
...I heard you singing.
So I thought this is where you are...
?
I was looking for you.
Because I wanted to become your friend.
A friend?
Yeah, let's play together.
You'll...play with me?
Who are you?

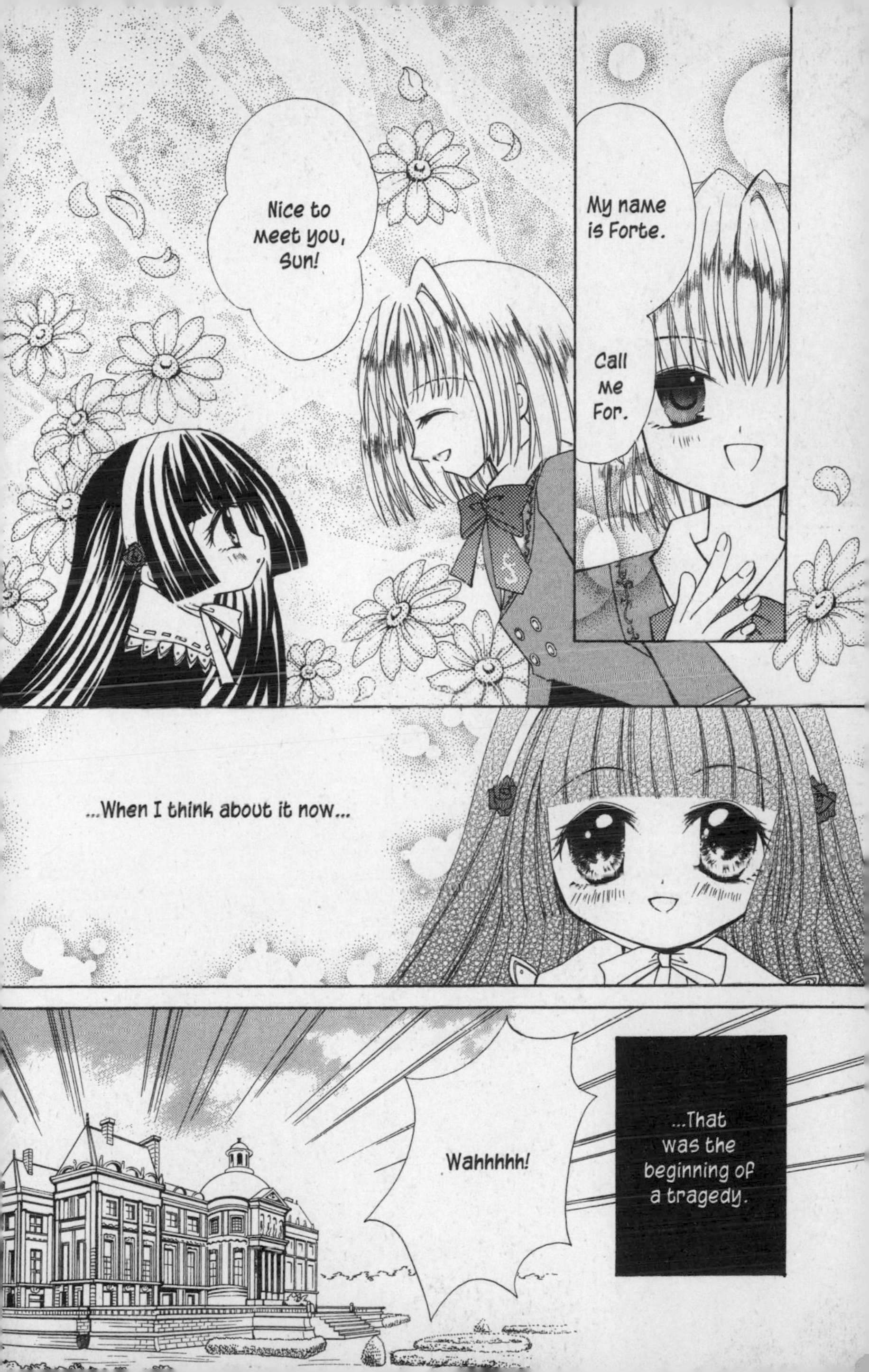
My name is Forte.
Call me For.
Nice to meet you, Sun!
...When I think about it now...
...That was the beginning of a tragedy.
Wahhhhh!

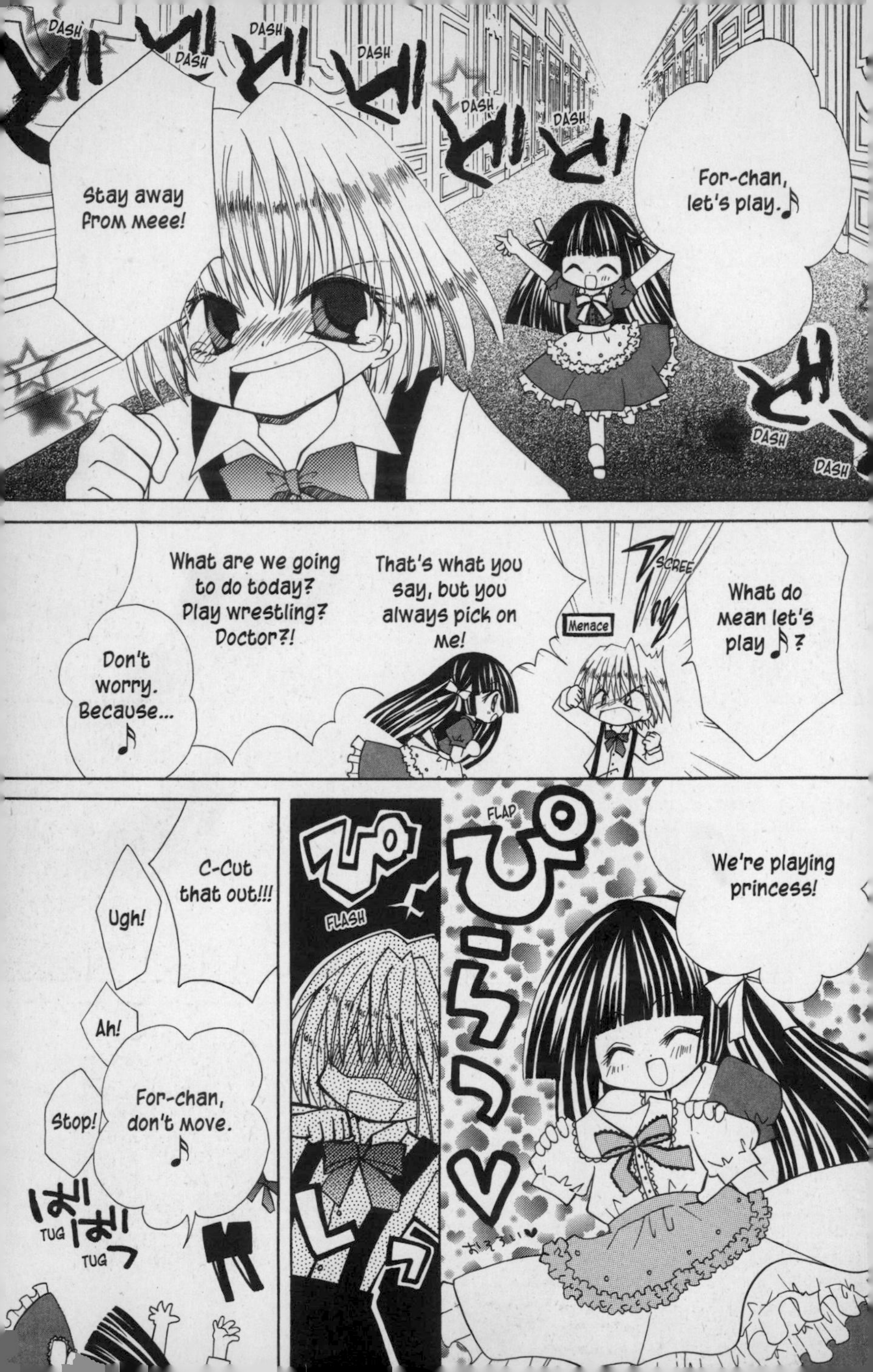
DASH DASH DASH DASH DASH DASH
For-chan, let's play.♪
DASH DASH
Stay away from meee!
What do mean let's play♪?
SCREE
Menace
That's what you say, but you always pick on me!
What are we going to do today? Play wrestling? Doctor?!
Don't worry. Because...♪
We're playing princess!
FLAP
FLASH
C-Cut that out!!!
Ugh!
Ah!
For-chan, don't move.♪
Stop!
TUG TUG

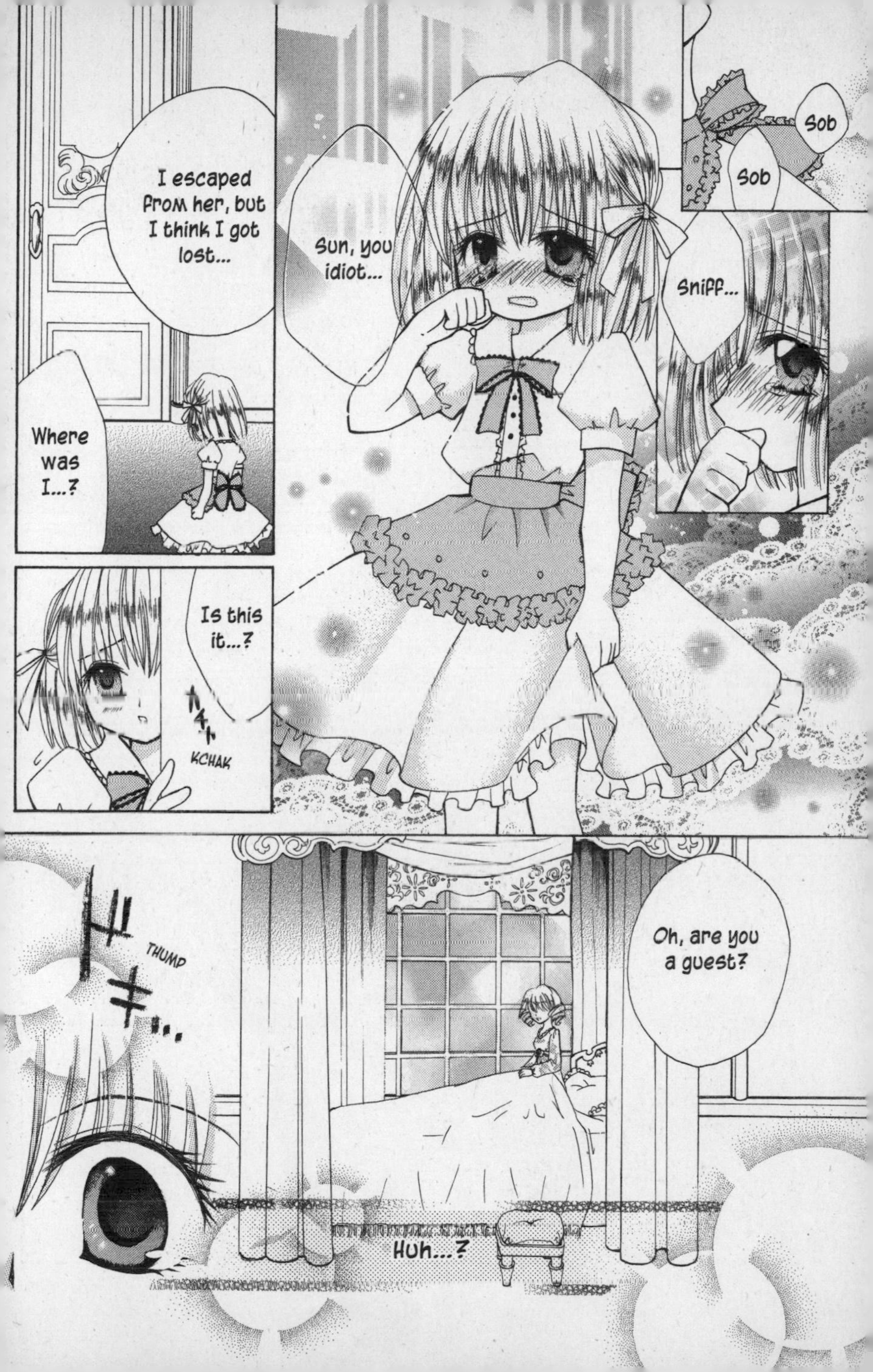
Sob
Sob
Sniff...
Sun, you idiot...
I escaped from her, but I think I got lost...
Where was I...?
Is this it...?
KCHAK
Oh, are you a guest?
Huh...?
THUMP

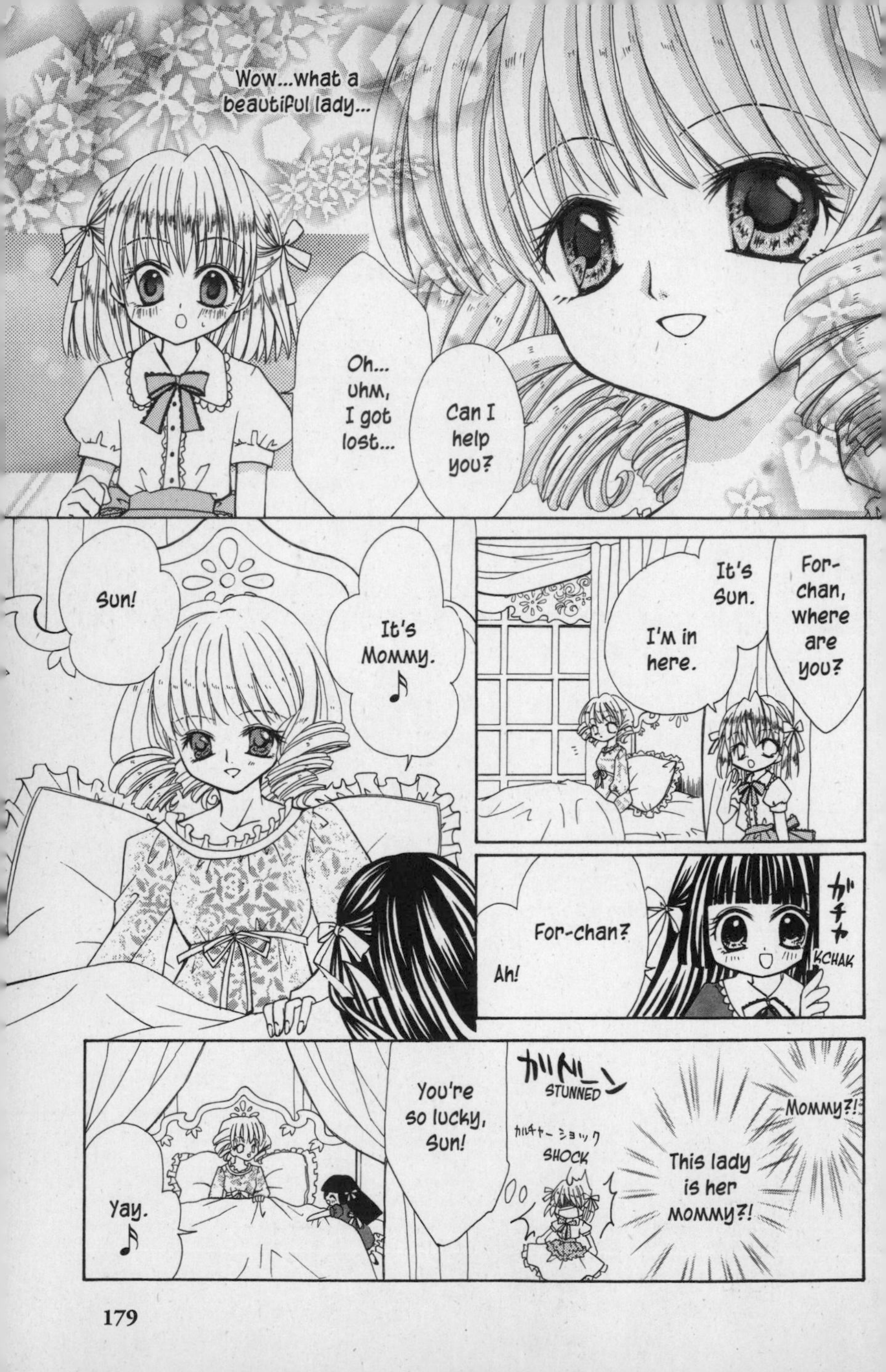
Wow...what a beautiful lady...
Can I help you?
Oh... uhm, I got lost...
For-chan, where are you?
It's Sun.
I'm in here.
ガチャ
KCHAK
For-chan?
Ah!
It's Mommy. ♪
Sun!
Mommy?!
This lady is her Mommy?!
カルチャーショック
SHOCK
STUNNED
You're so lucky, Sun!
Yay. ♪

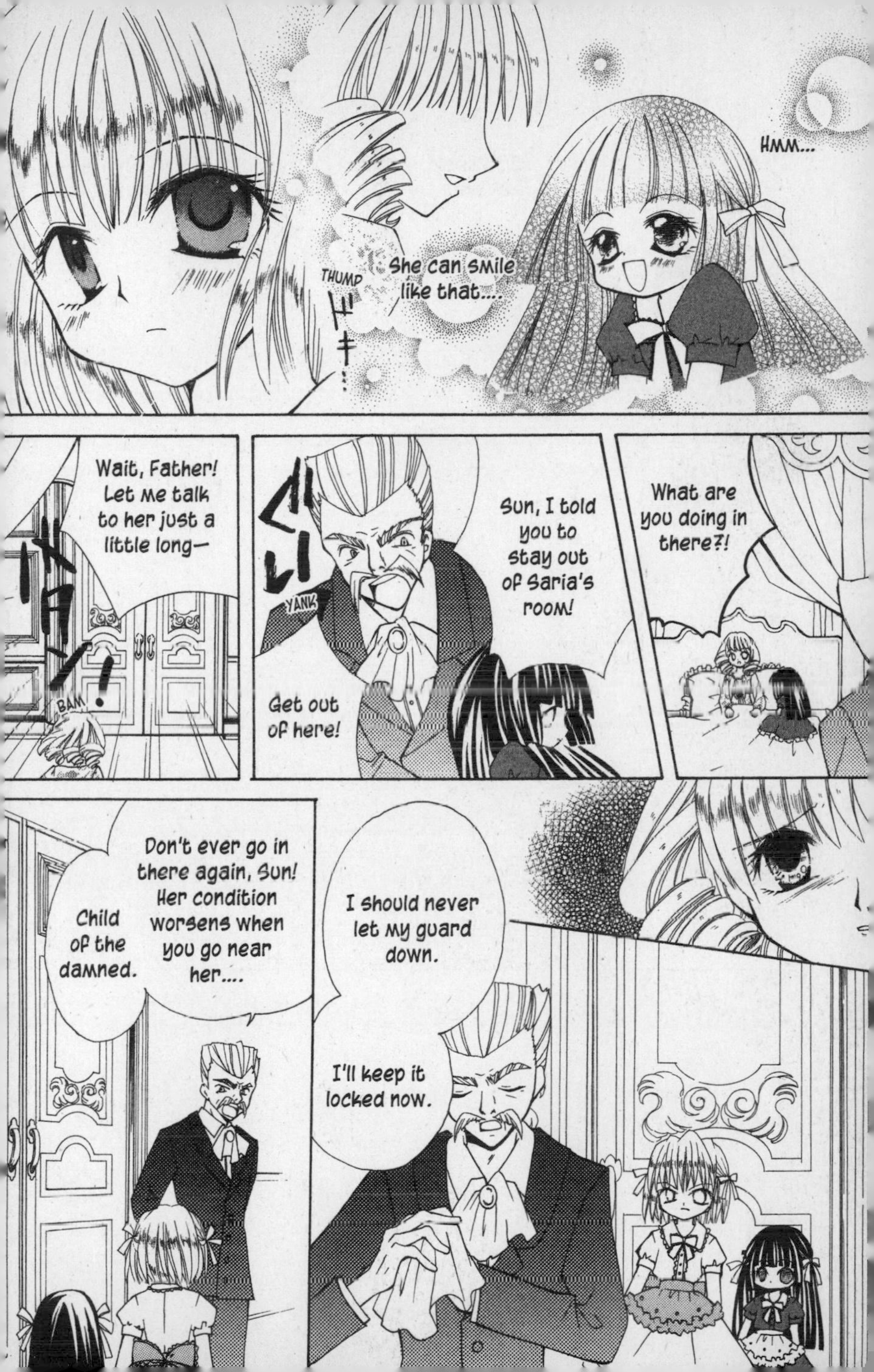
HMM...
She can smile like that....
THUMP
What are you doing in there?!
Sun, I told you to stay out of Saria's room!
YANK
Get out of here!
Wait, Father! Let me talk to her just a little long—
BAM
I should never let my guard down.
I'll keep it locked now.
Don't ever go in there again, Sun! Her condition worsens when you go near her....
Child of the damned.

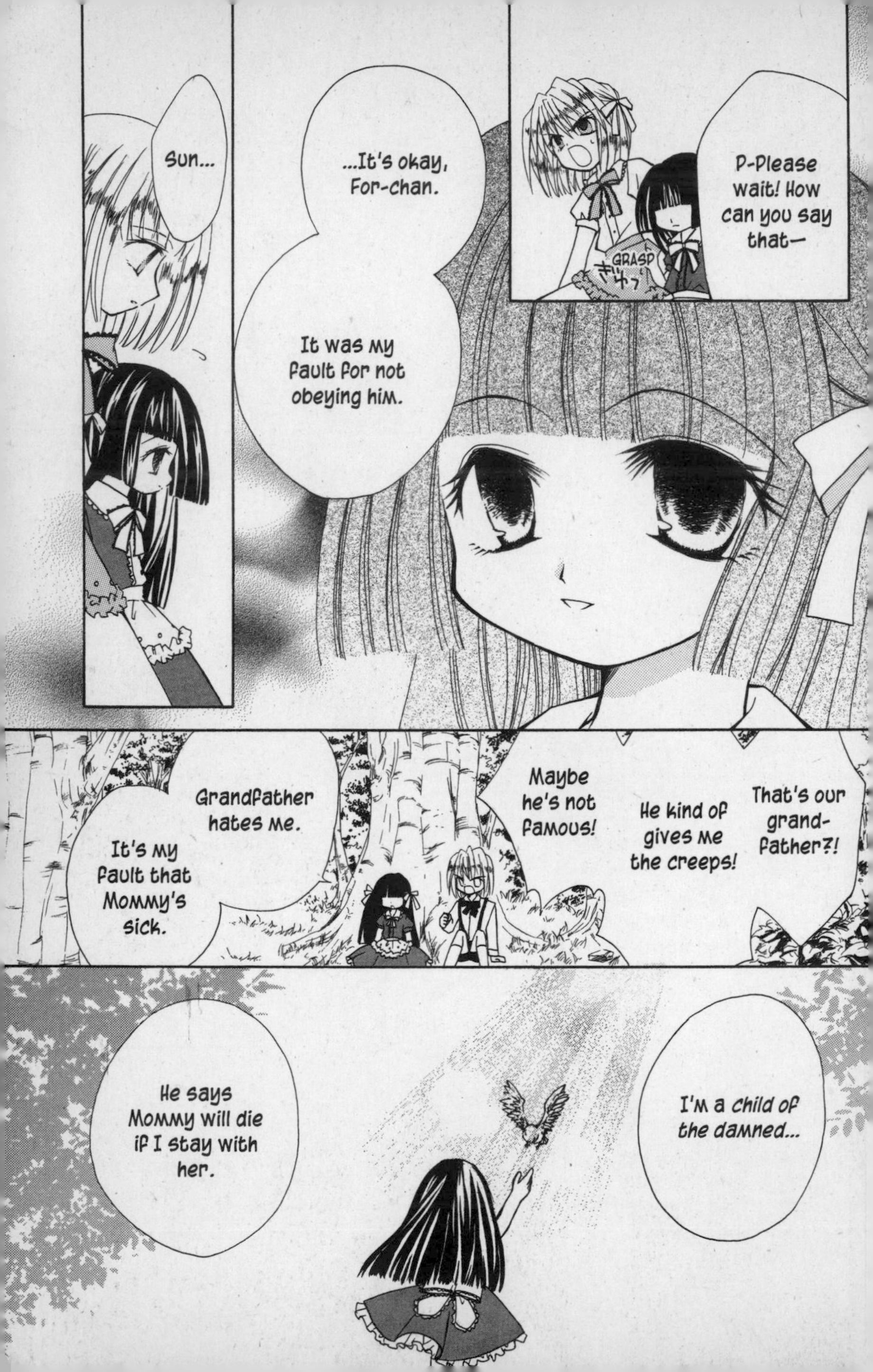

P-Please wait! How can you say that—
GRASP
ぎゅっ
...It's okay, For-chan.
It was my fault for not obeying him.
Sun...
That's our grand-father?!
He kind of gives me the creeps!
Maybe he's not famous!
Grandfather hates me.
It's my fault that Mommy's sick.
I'm a child of the damned...
He says Mommy will die if I stay with her.

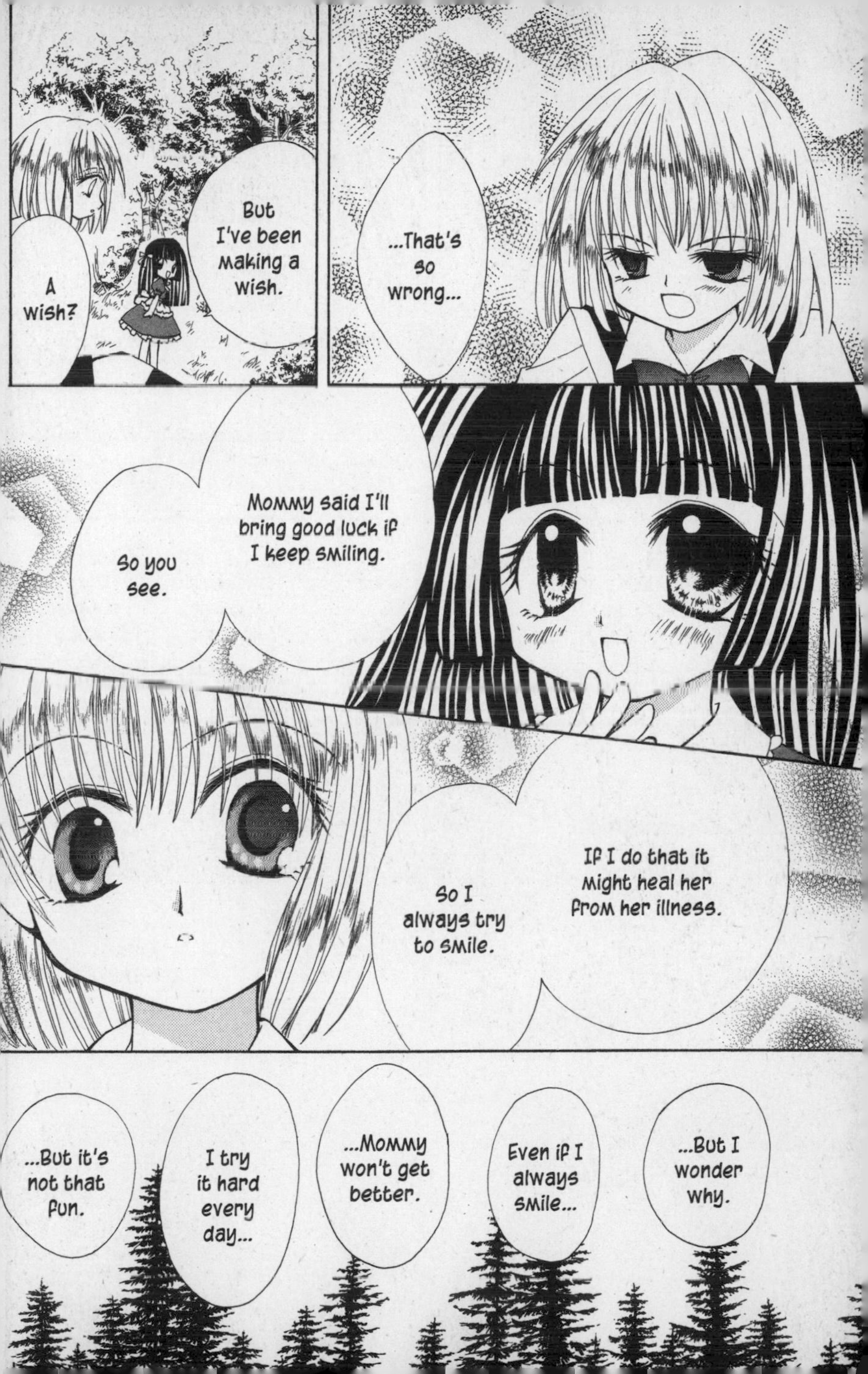
...That's so wrong...
But I've been making a wish.
A wish?
Mommy said I'll bring good luck if I keep smiling.
So you see.
If I do that it might heal her from her illness.
So I always try to smile.
...But I wonder why.
Even if I always smile...
...Mommy won't get better.
I try it hard every day...
...But it's not that fun.

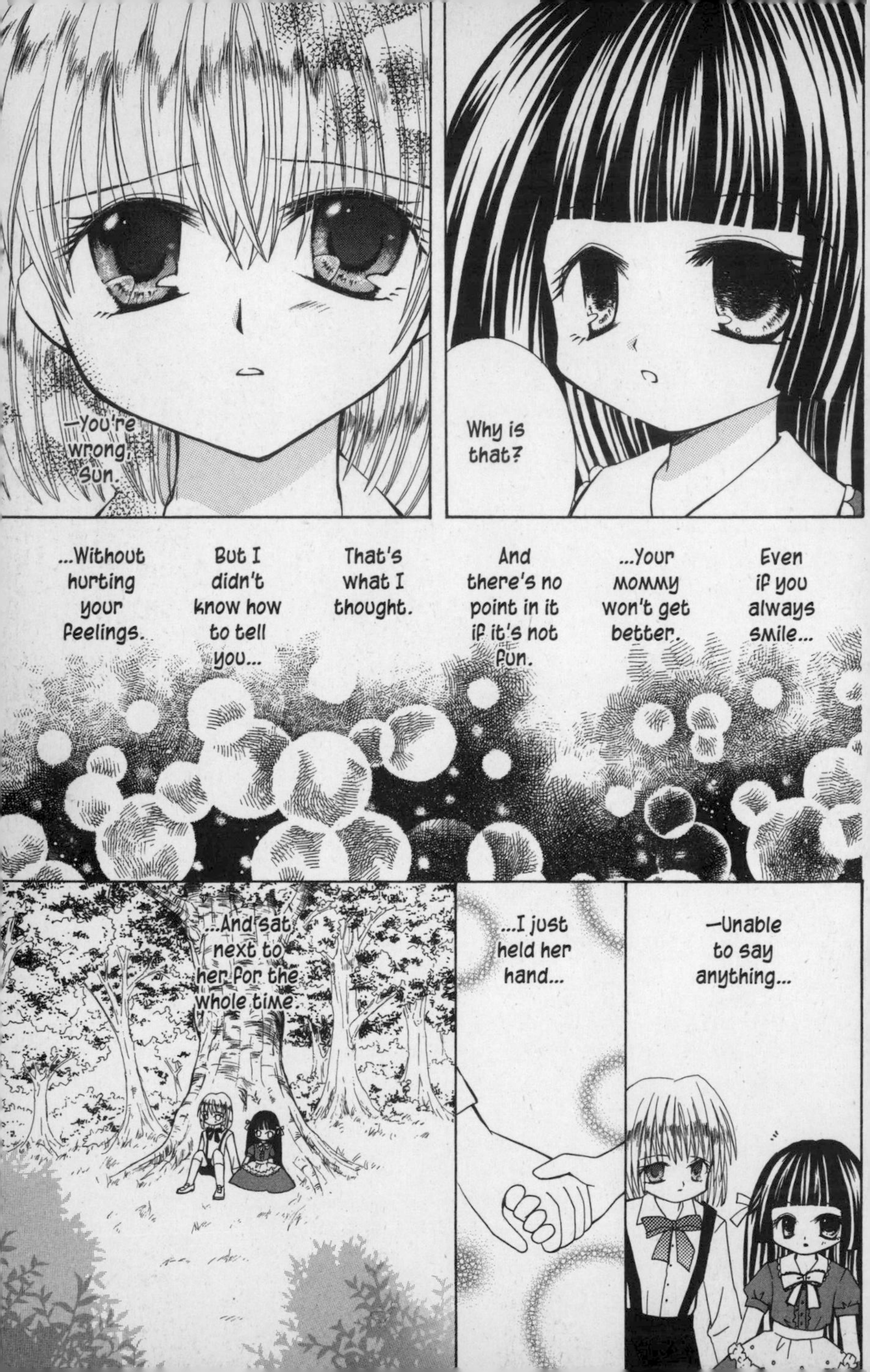
Why is that?
—You're wrong, Sun.
Even if you always smile...
...Your mommy won't get better.
And there's no point in it if it's not fun.
That's what I thought.
But I didn't know how to tell you...
...Without hurting your feelings.
—Unable to say anything...
...I just held her hand...
...And sat next to her for the whole time.

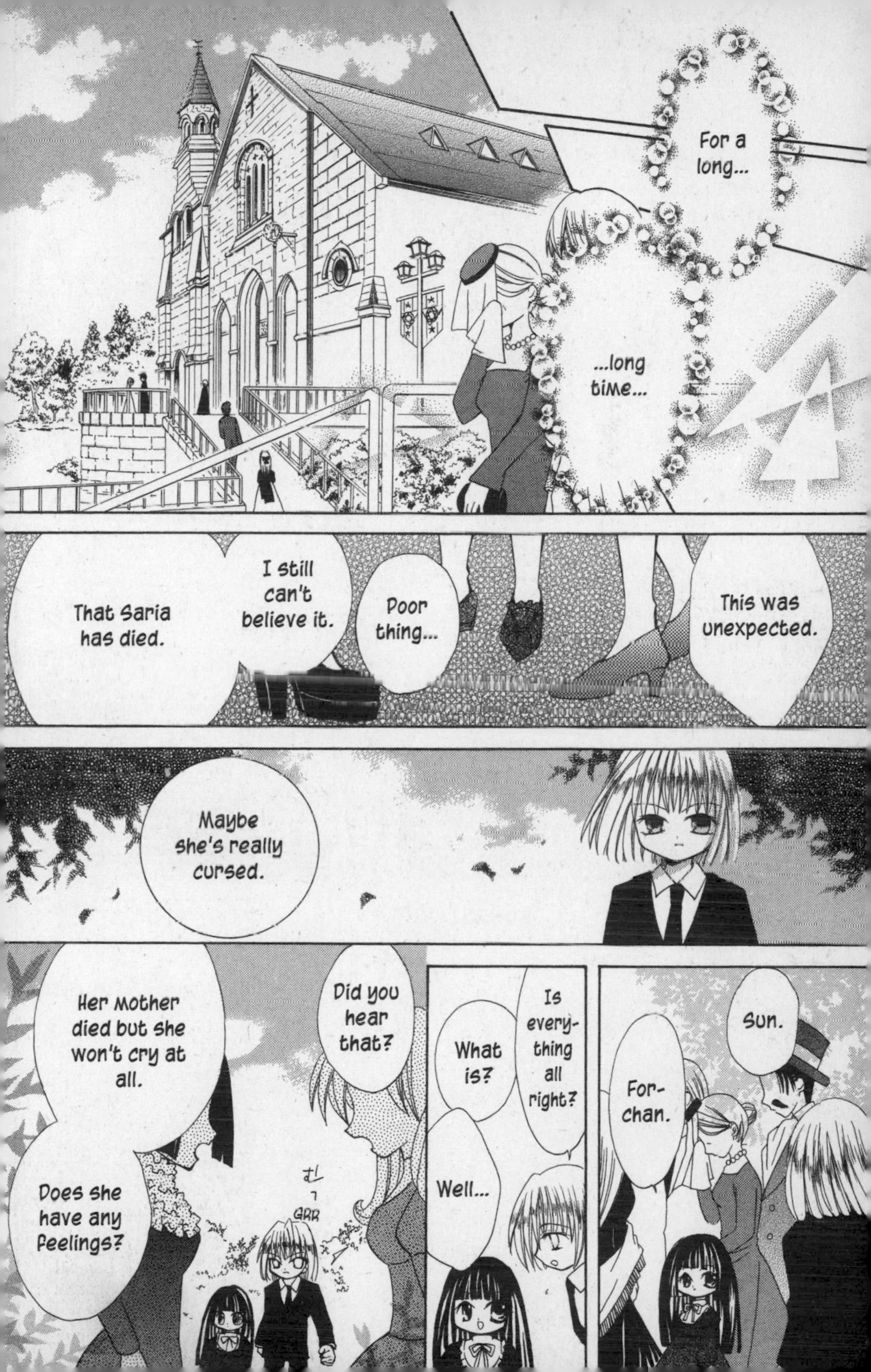
For a long...
...long time...
This was unexpected.
Poor thing...
I still can't believe it.
That Saria has died.
Maybe she's really cursed.
Sun.
For-chan.
Is every-thing all right?
What is?
Well...
Did you hear that?
Her mother died but she won't cry at all.
Does she have any feelings?
GRR

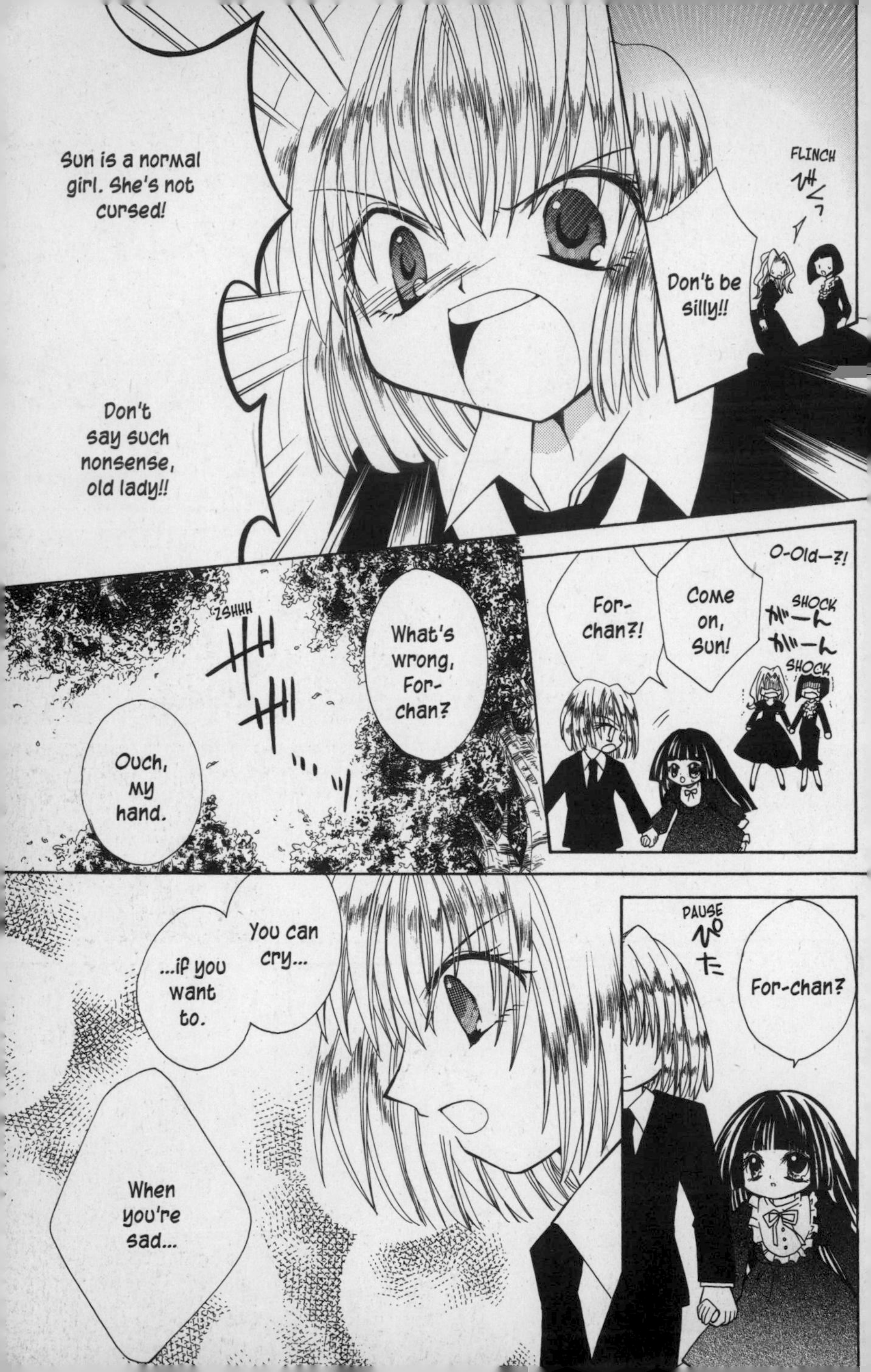
FLINCH
ビクッ
Don't be silly!!
Sun is a normal girl. She's not cursed!
Don't say such nonsense, old lady!!
O-Old—?!
SHOCK
がーん
がーん
SHOCK
Come on, Sun!
For-chan?!
What's wrong, For-chan?
ZSHHH
Ouch, my hand.
PAUSE
ぴた
For-chan?
You can cry...
...if you want to.
When you're sad...

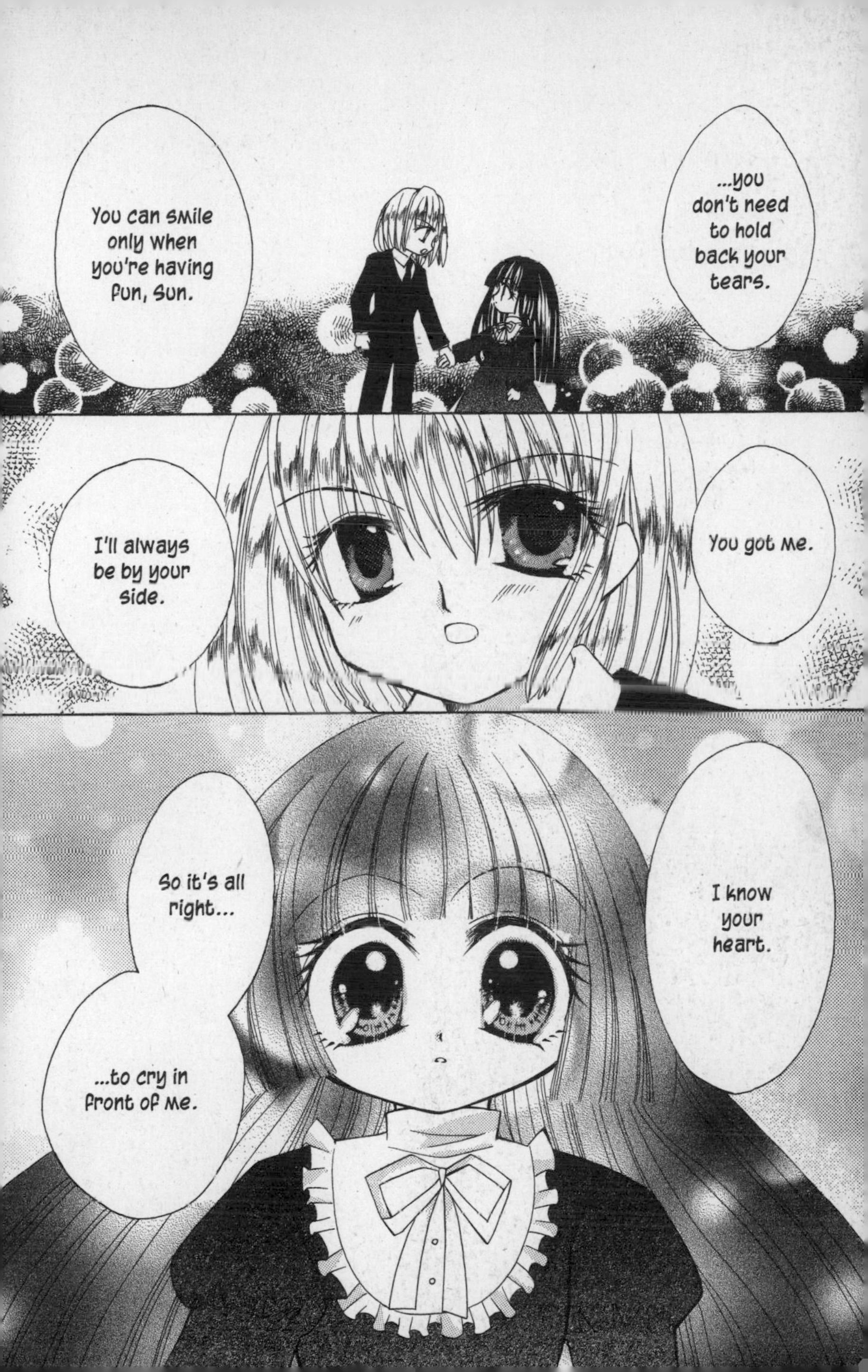
...you don't need to hold back your tears.
You can smile only when you're having fun, Sun.
You got me.
I'll always be by your side.
I know your heart.
So it's all right...
...to cry in front of me.

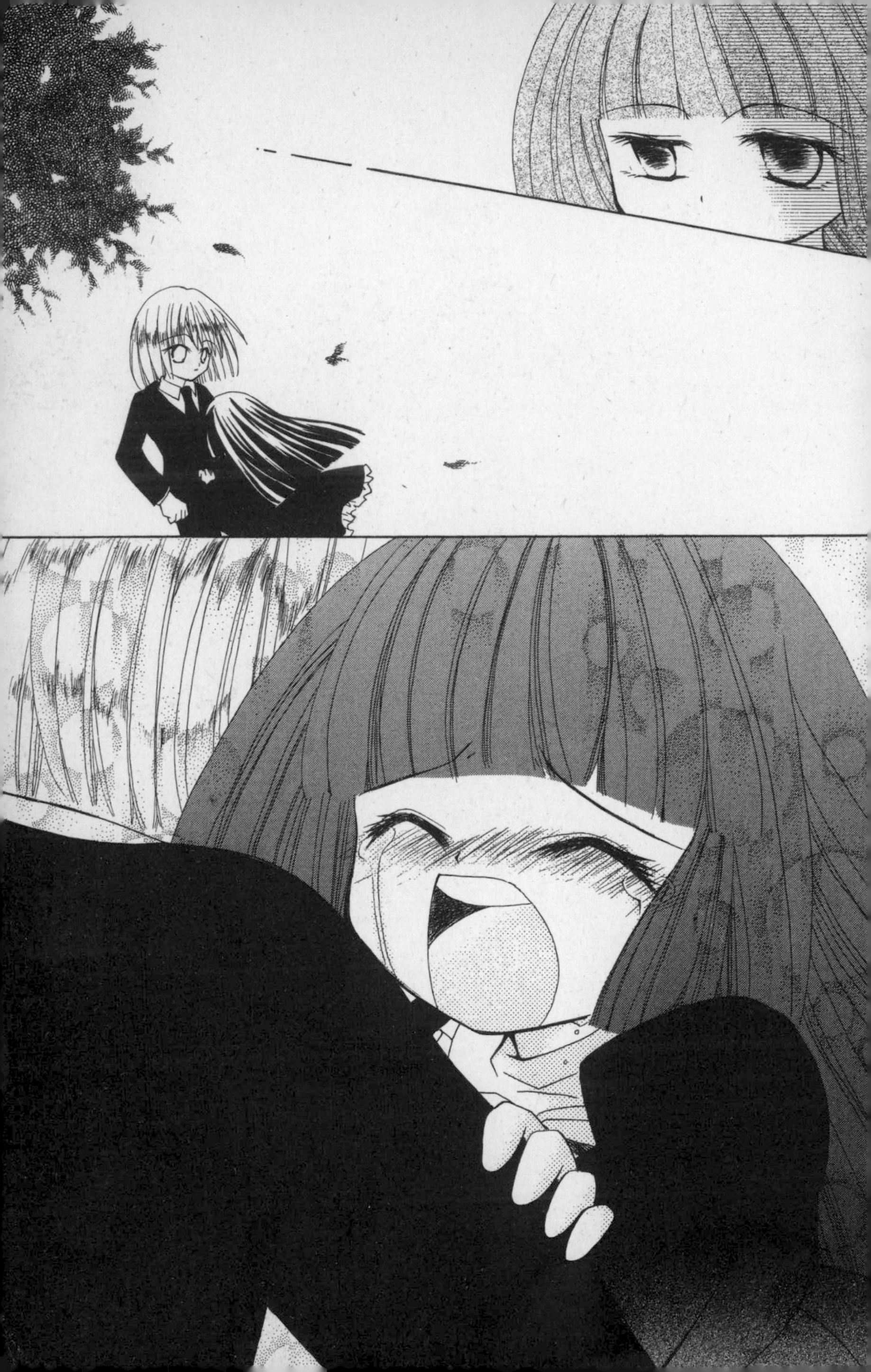

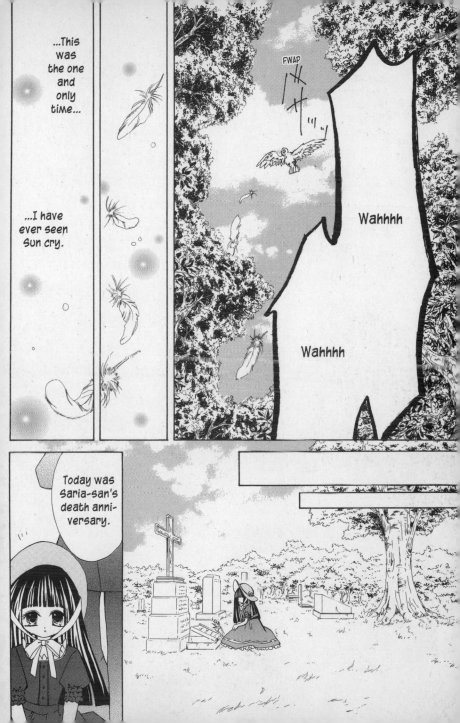

...This was the one and only time...

...I have ever seen Sun cry.

FWAP

Wahhhh

Wahhhh

Today was Saria-san's death anniversary.

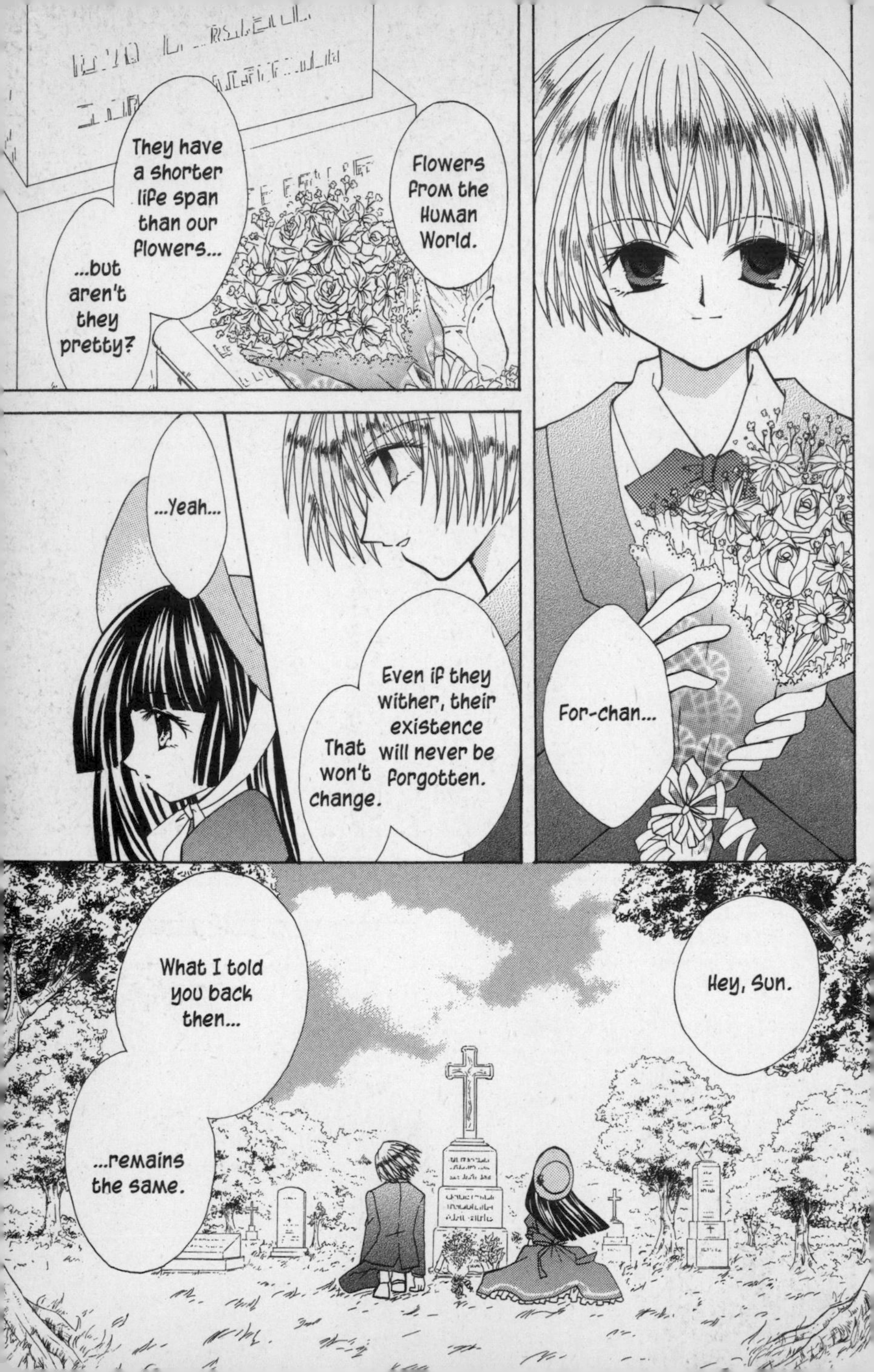
For-chan...
Flowers from the Human World.
They have a shorter life span than our flowers...
...but aren't they pretty?
...Yeah...
Even if they wither, their existence will never be forgotten.
That won't change.
Hey, Sun.
What I told you back then...
...remains the same.

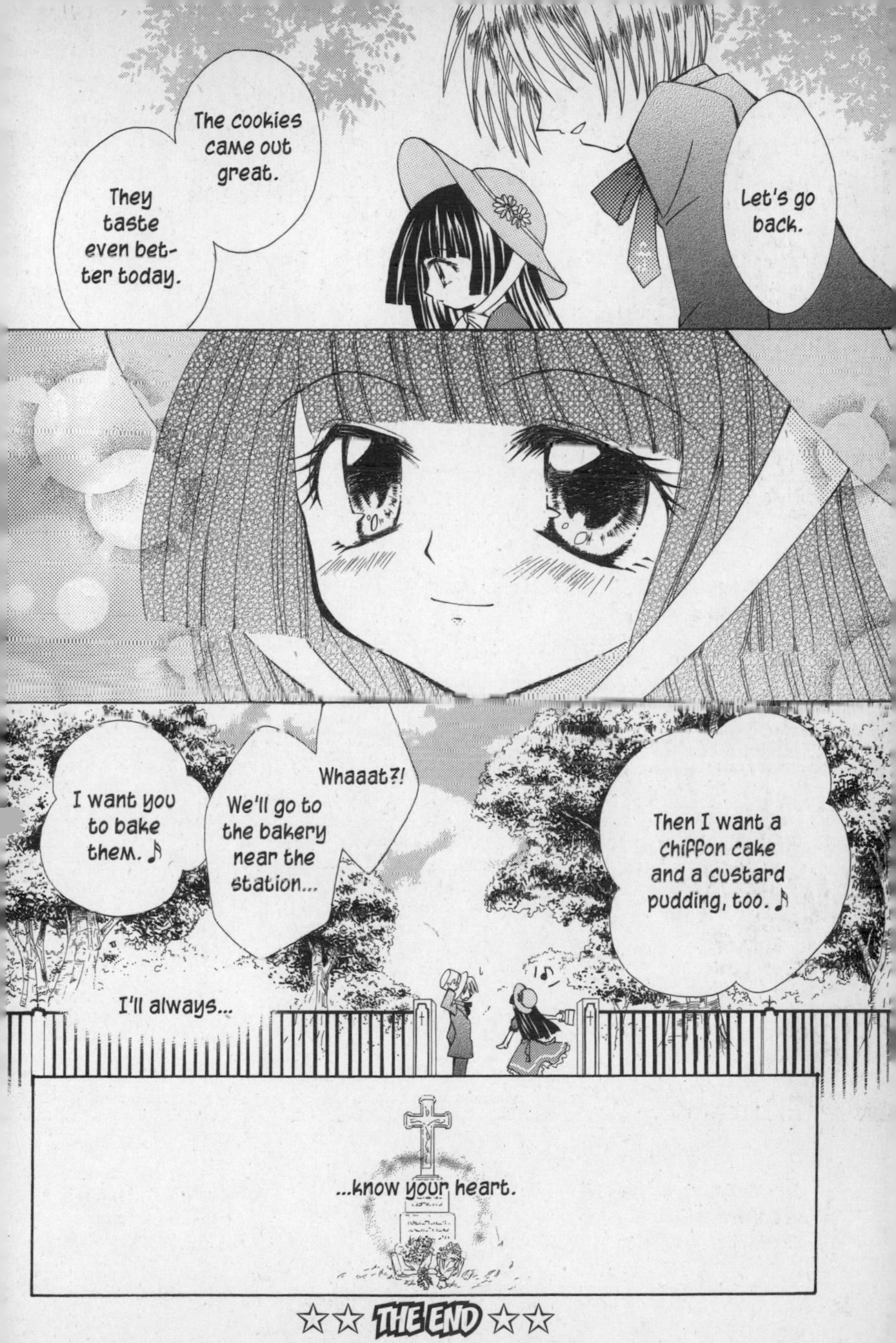
Let's go back.
The cookies came out great.
They taste even better today.
Then I want a chiffon cake and a custard pudding, too. ♪
Whaaat?!
We'll go to the bakery near the station...
I want you to bake them. ♪
I'll always...
...know your heart.
☆☆ THE END ☆☆

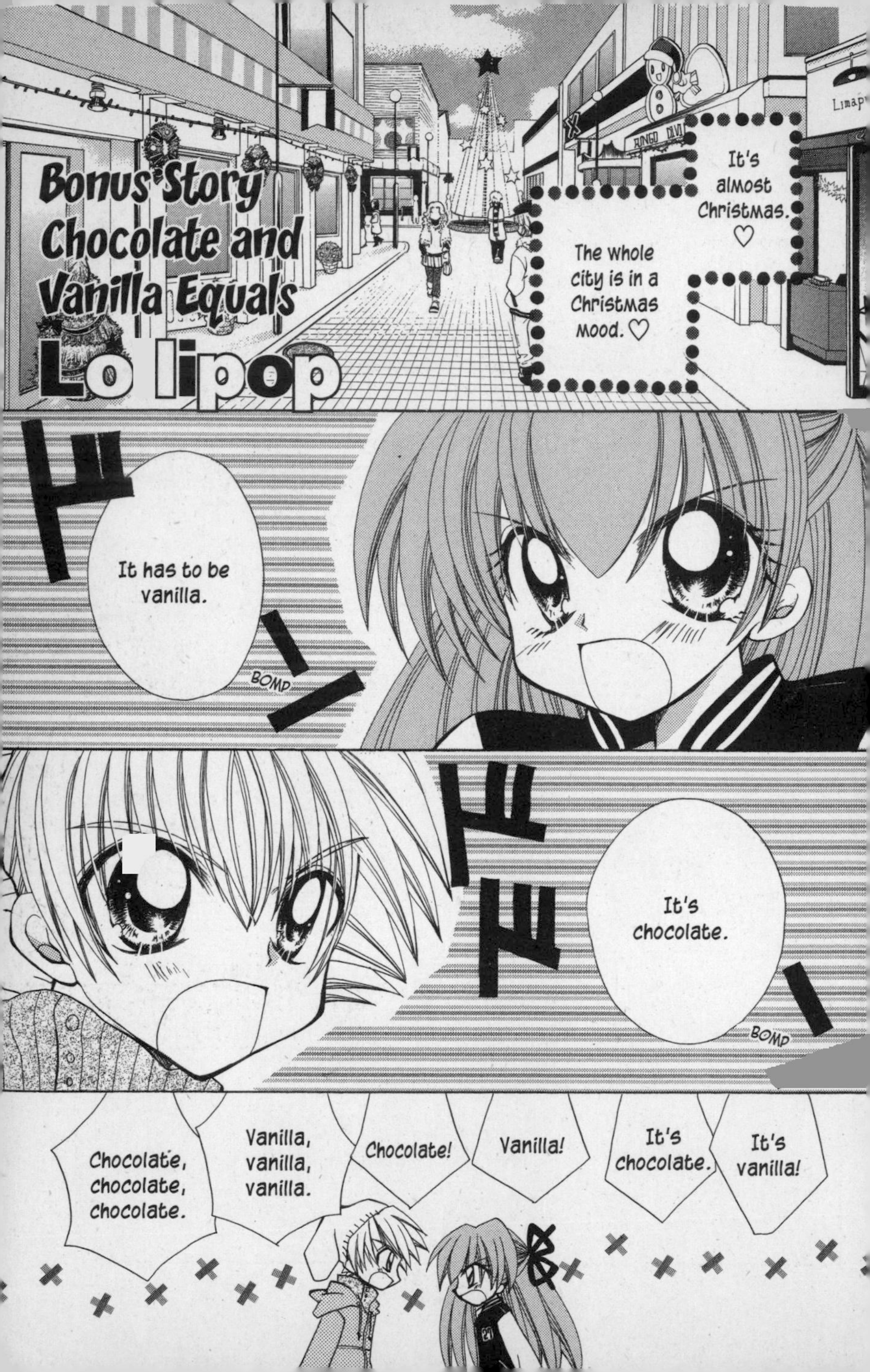
It's almost Christmas. ♡
The whole city is in a Christmas mood. ♡
Bonus Story
Chocolate and Vanilla Equals
Lollipop
It has to be vanilla.
BOMP
It's chocolate.
BOMP
It's vanilla!
It's chocolate.
Vanilla!
Chocolate!
Vanilla, vanilla, vanilla.
Chocolate, chocolate, chocolate.

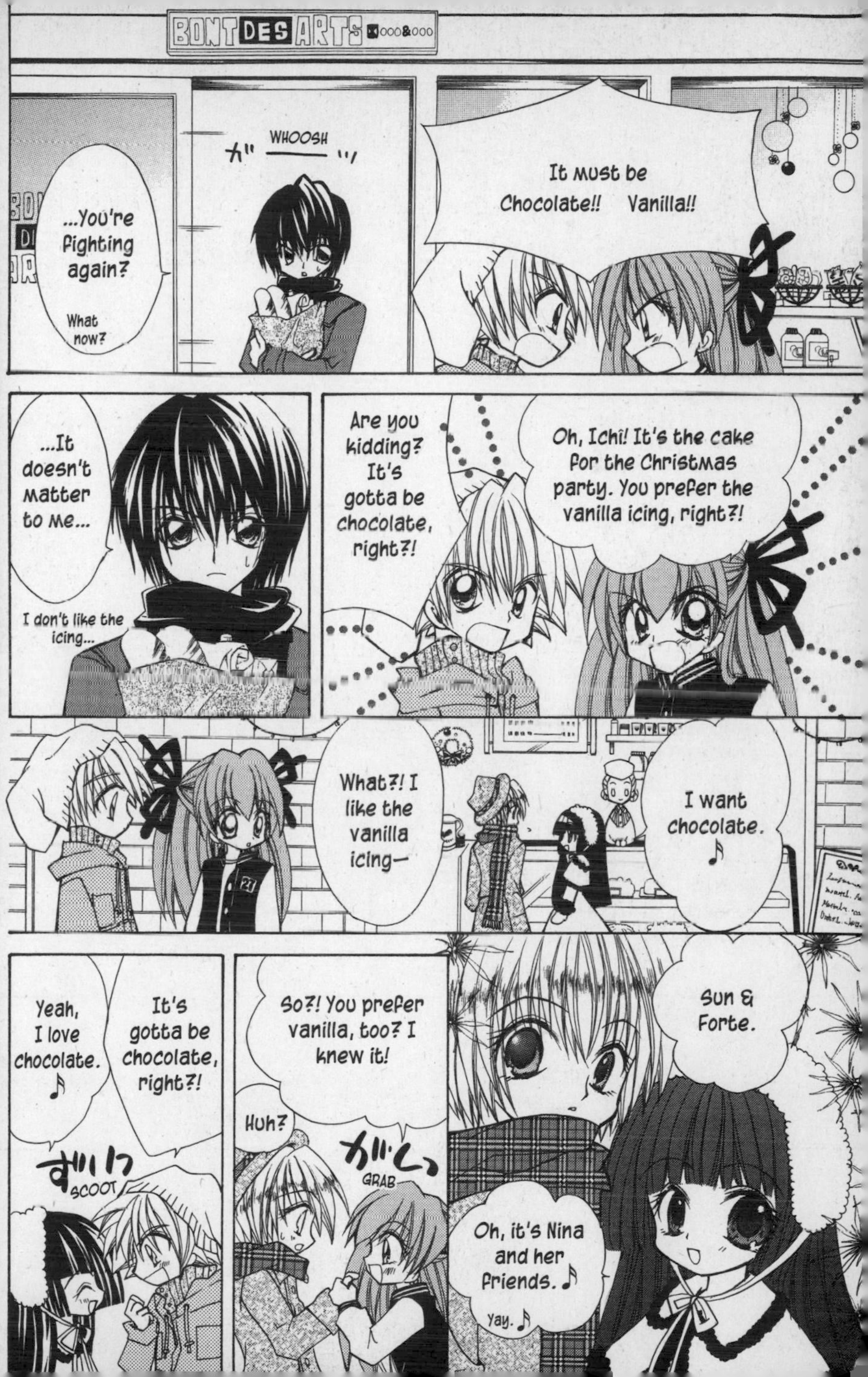
BONT DES ARTS
It must be Chocolate!! Vanilla!!
WHOOSH
...You're fighting again?
What now?
Oh, Ichi! It's the cake for the Christmas party. You prefer the vanilla icing, right?!
Are you kidding? It's gotta be chocolate, right?!
...It doesn't matter to me...
I don't like the icing...
I want chocolate. ♪
What?! I like the vanilla icing—
Sun & Forte.
Oh, it's Nina and her friends. ♪
Yay. ♪
So?! You prefer vanilla, too? I knew it!
Huh?
GRAB
It's gotta be chocolate, right?!
Yeah, I love chocolate. ♪
SCOOT

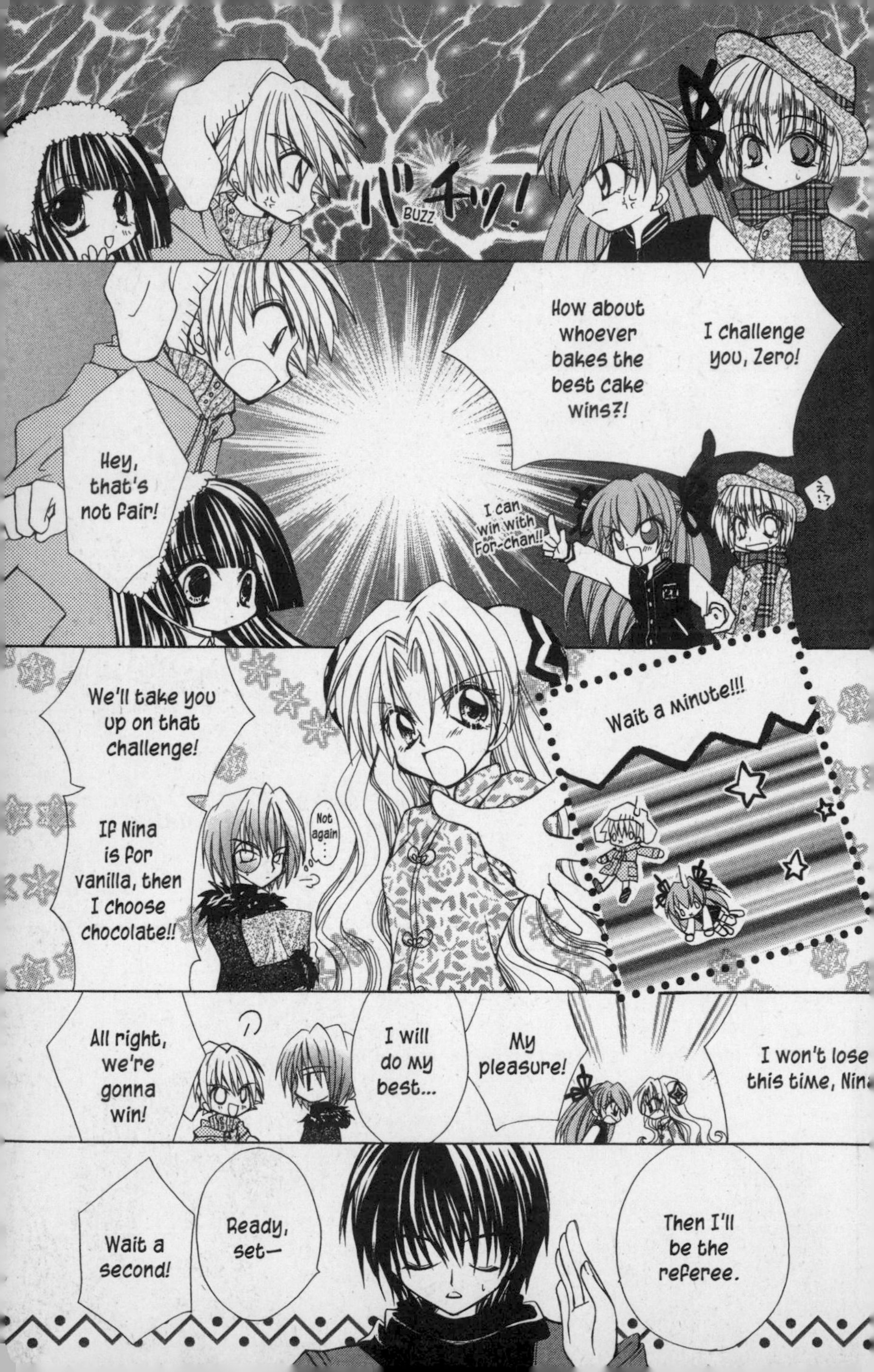
バチッ!
BUZZ
I challenge you, Zero!
How about whoever bakes the best cake wins?!
I can win with For-chan!!
え!?
Hey, that's not fair!
Wait a minute!!!
We'll take you up on that challenge!
If Nina is for vanilla, then I choose chocolate!!
Not again...
I won't lose this time, Nina
My pleasure!
I will do my best...
All right, we're gonna win!
Then I'll be the referee.
Ready, set—
Wait a second!

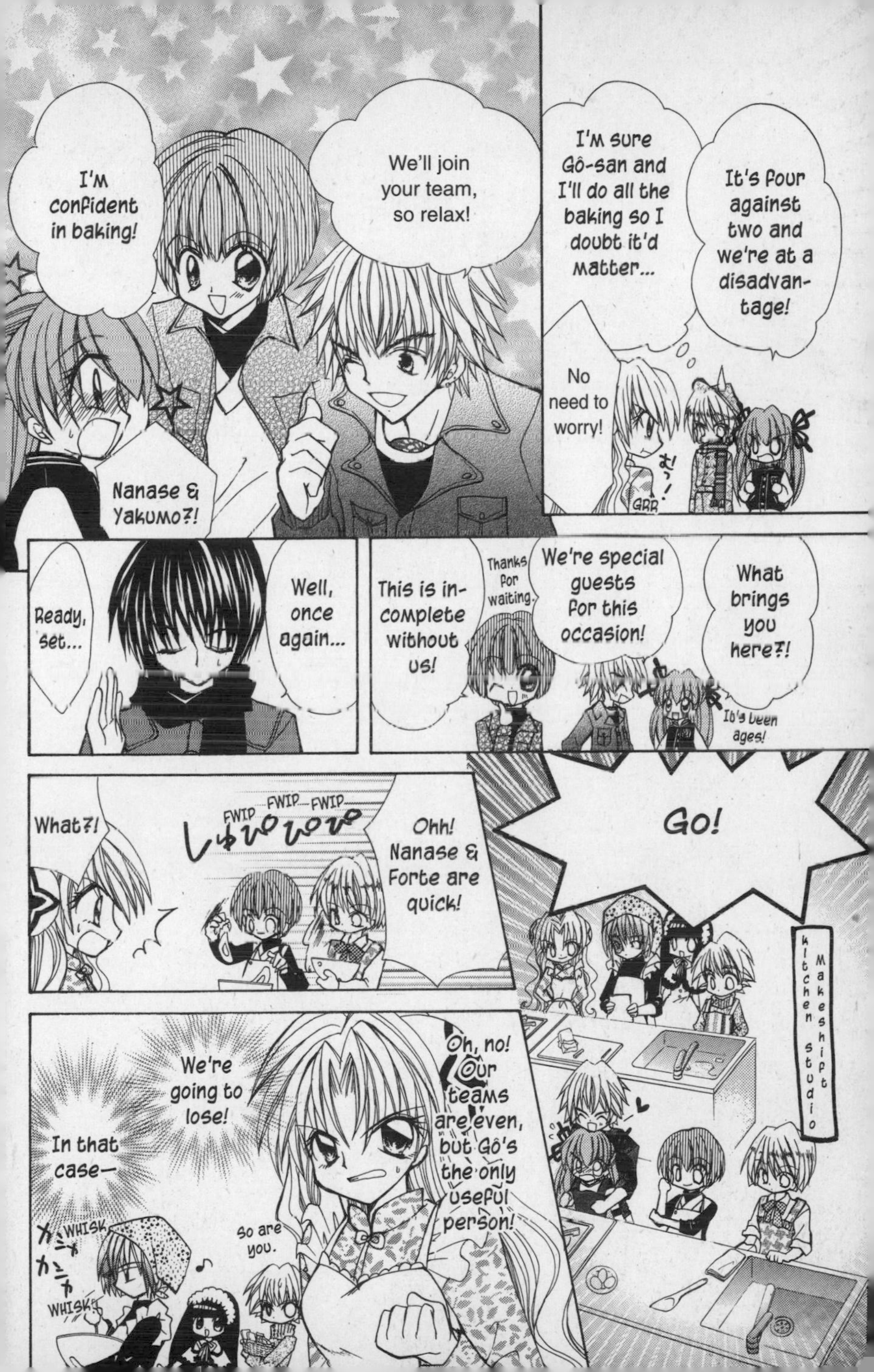
It's four against two and we're at a disadvantage!
I'm sure Gô-san and I'll do all the baking so I doubt it'd matter...
No need to worry!
GRR
We'll join your team, so relax!
I'm confident in baking!
Nanase & Yakumo?!
What brings you here?!
It's been ages!
We're special guests for this occasion!
Thanks for waiting.
This is in-complete without us!
Well, once again...
Ready, set...
GO!
Makeshift kitchen studio
Ohh! Nanase & Forte are quick!
FWIP FWIP FWIP
What?!
Oh, no! Our teams are even, but Gô's the only useful person!
We're going to lose!
In that case—
So are you.
WHISK
WHISK

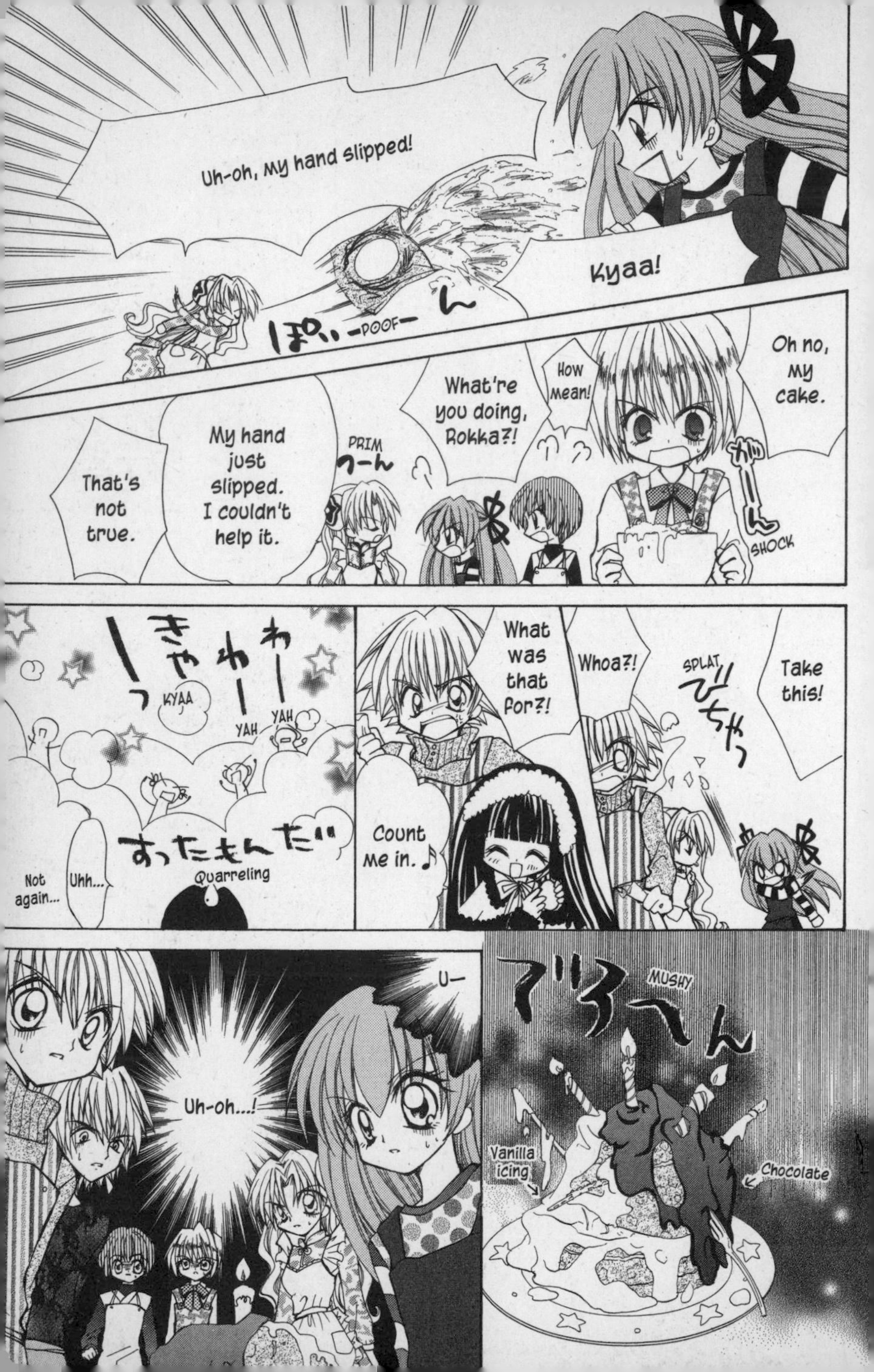
Uh-oh, my hand slipped!
Kyaa!
-POOF-
Oh no, my cake.
SHOCK
How mean!
What're you doing, Rokka?!
PRIM
My hand just slipped. I couldn't help it.
That's not true.
Take this!
SPLAT
Whoa?!
What was that for?!
Count me in.♪
KYAA
YAH
YAH
Quarreling
Uhh...
Not again...
MUSHY
Chocolate
Vanilla icing
U—
Uh-oh...!

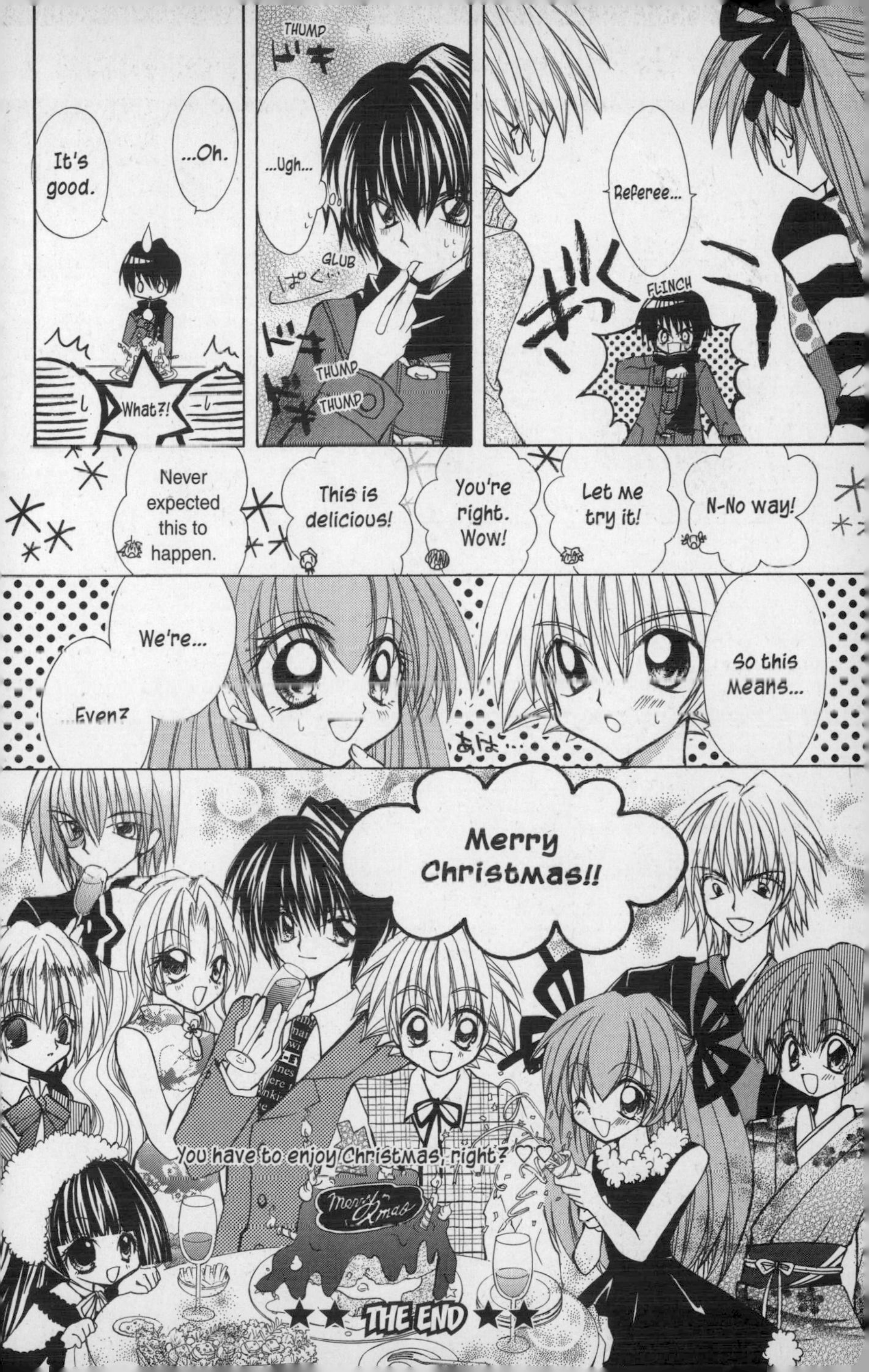
Referee...
FLINCH
ぎっく
THUMP
ドキ
...Ugh...
GLUB
ぱく…
ドキ
THUMP
THUMP
...Oh.
It's good.
What?!
N-No way!
Let me try it!
You're right. Wow!
This is delicious!
Never expected this to happen.
So this Means...
あは…
We're...
...Even?
Merry Christmas!!
You have to enjoy Christmas, right? ♡♡
Merry Xmas
★★ THE END ★★

Confidential: The Shocking End?! Here's the Cake-kun Version. ↓

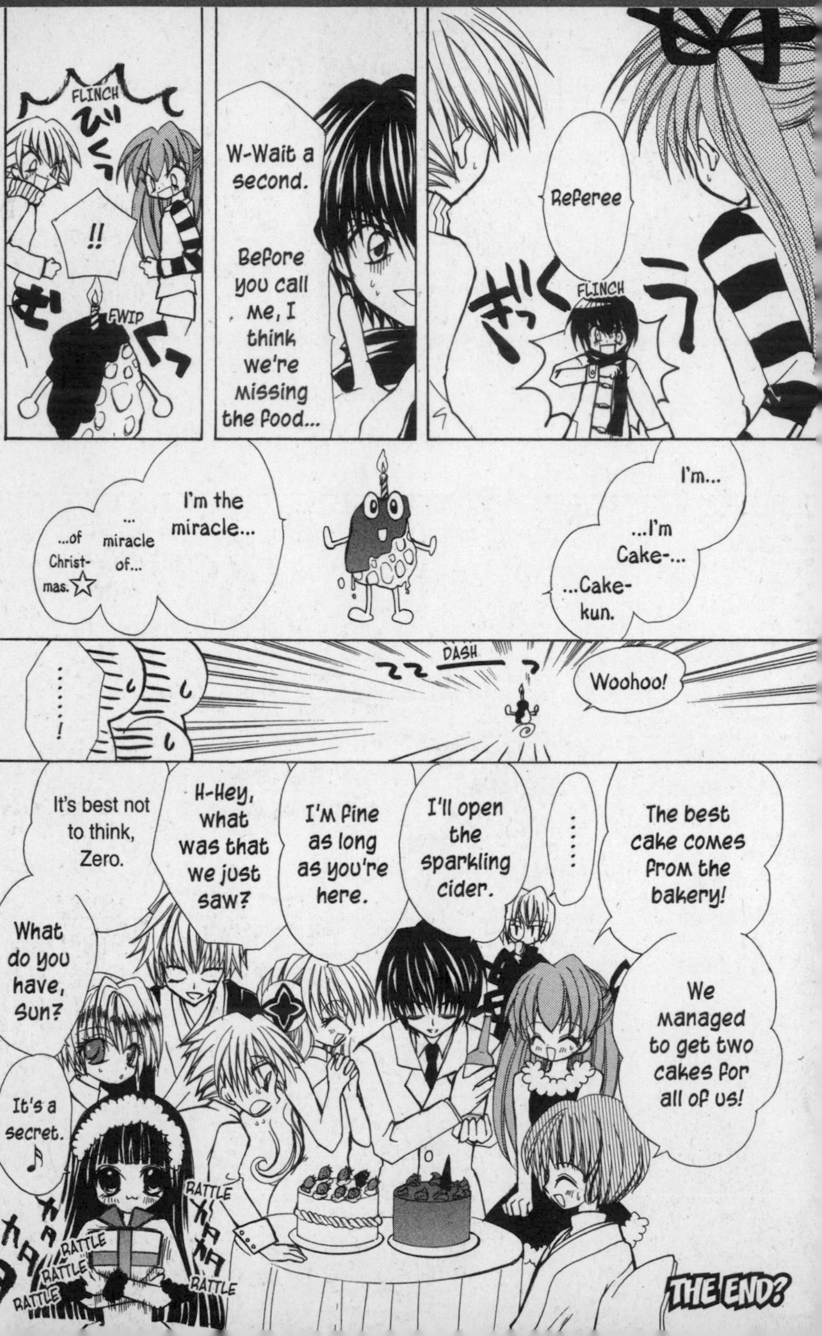
Referee
FLINCH
W-Wait a second.
Before you call me, I think we're missing the food...
FLINCH
!!
FWIP
I'm...
...I'm Cake-...
...Cake-kun.
I'm the miracle...
...miracle of...
...of Christmas.☆
Woohoo!
DASH
......!
The best cake comes from the bakery!
We managed to get two cakes for all of us!
......
I'll open the sparkling cider.
I'm fine as long as you're here.
H-Hey, what was that we just saw?
It's best not to think, Zero.
What do you have, Sun?
It's a secret. ♪
RATTLE
RATTLE
RATTLE
RATTLE
RATTLE
RATTLE
THE END?

Announcing the Results of the First Mamotte! Lollipop Character Popularity Poll!

11,653 legitimate votes

Where did your favorite character place in the ranking?!

Rank	Character	Votes
1	Nina	3,035 votes
2	Zero	2,670 votes
3	Ichî	2,415 votes
4	Sun	979 votes
5	Sarasa	375 votes

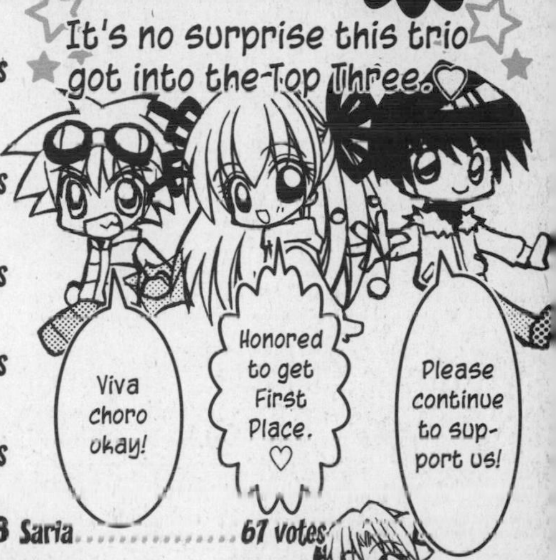
It's no surprise this trio got into the Top Three.♡
Viva choro okay!
Honored to get First Place. ♡
Please continue to support us!

Rank	Character	Votes	Rank	Character	Votes
6	Rukka	325 votes	16	Saria	67 votes
7	Forte	277 votes	16	Eleven	67 votes
8	Aquamarine	266 votes	18	Twelve	58 votes
9	Nanase	236 votes	19	Jeff	57 votes
10	Gô	142 votes	20	Sekiya Ijûin-sensei	56 votes
11	Kuku	102 votes	21	Ruby	49 votes
12	Hatsuka	95 votes	22	Yôka	43 votes
13	Yakumo	94 votes	23	Toto	40 votes
14	Rill	89 votes	24	Guy	19 votes
15	Will	70 votes	25	Gomez	9 votes

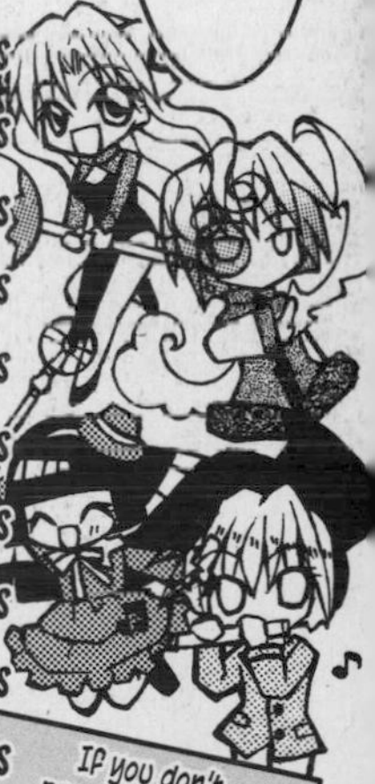

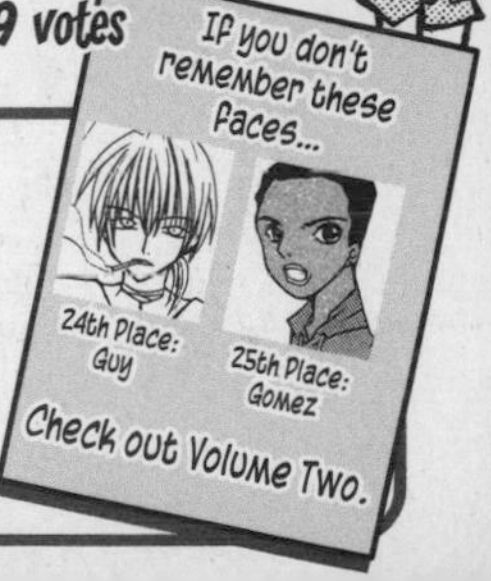
If you don't remember these faces...
24th Place: Guy
25th Place: Gomez
Check out Volume Two.

Thanks for participating in the poll!!

Mamotte! Lollipop is getting even more powered up after receiving everyone's ♡!
Please continue to support the series!
Look forward to the Second Poll. ☆

Bye-Bye ★

We're at the last page now. Thank you very much for reading all the way to the end. Can you believe we're at volume three now? Volume four is next!! We're getting to the most interesting part of the story and it'll probably pick up with more speed now. I can't wait to draw it. It's amazing that it's become ordinary to draw manga every month after starting the series over a year ago. I didn't think I could handle a serialization at first, though . . .(laugh)

I feel like the environment around me is gradually changing. It's natural for things to change over time, but it's kind of sad. I want to try something new. I'd like to learn to use a computer. There are so many things I want to try! But I'm so busy that I can't do some of them . . .

It's because I enjoy drawing manga and I have many readers that I can give my best effort! Check out volume four, too.

See ya!

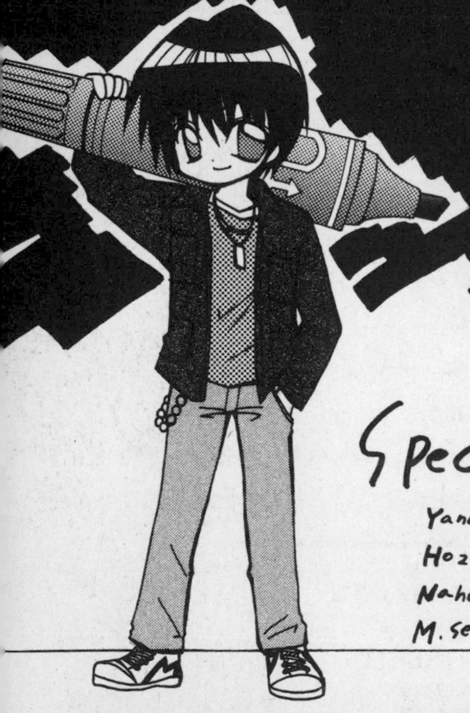

2004 3.19

Special thanks!

Yanomichi . Neginegi . Yunori morie
Hozumix . Kumi katuoka . Mai sukou
Nahoru mita . and special guest
M. sekiya .... and you!

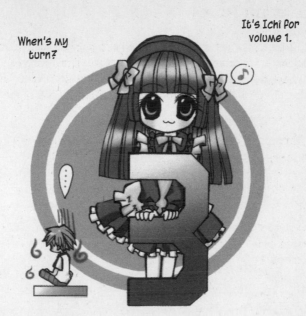

When's my turn?

It's Ichi for volume 1.

About the Creator

Michiyo Kikuta

Born in Ibaraki Prefecture on February 10. Aquarius, blood type B. She entered and won second place in the 31st Nakayoshi New Faces Manga Award with the manga *Giniro Moyô* in the year 2000, which then made its debut in *Nakayoshi Haru-yasumi Land* (Nakayoshi Spring Break Land) in 2001. Her featured works are *Mamotte! Lollipop* and *Medical Magical*. She enjoys clothes shopping and loves sweets.

Translation Notes

Japanese is a tricky language for most Westerners, and translation is often more art than science. For your edification and reading pleasure, here are notes on some of the places where we could have gone in a different direction in our translation of the work, or where a Japanese cultural reference is used.

Title: *Mamotte! Lollipop*

Mamotte means to protect and Lollipop, as we later come to know, is a tool that will help save the heroine from danger.

Names

The characters in *Mamotte! Lollipop* have names based on Japanese numbers. For example, Zero for *zero* (zero); Ichî for *ichi* (one), Nina for *ni* (two), and Sun for *san* (three).

Kyaa and *Gyaa*

Kyaa is a girlish scream. Though it sometimes indicates fright or surprise, it's usually a scream of delight. *Gyaa*, on the other hand, nearly always indicates real fright, embarrassment, or pain.

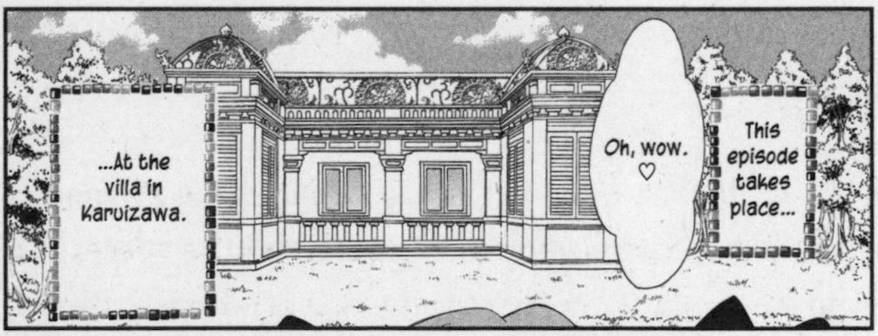
This episode takes place...
Oh, wow. ♡
...At the villa in Karuizawa.

Karuizawa, page 5

Karuizawa is an upscale mountain resort in Japan. Many wealthy people keep vacation homes here where they can escape from the summer heat.

NHK, page 5

NHK stands for Nippon Hôsô Kyôkai, which is a broadcasting corporation in Japan. It is known for its quality educational programs.

Let's dig in, page 11

Itadakimasu or "thank you for this meal," literally translated, is the customary phrase to use before beginning a meal in Japan. Since English has no satisfactory equivalent in English, "Let's dig in" was used in its place.

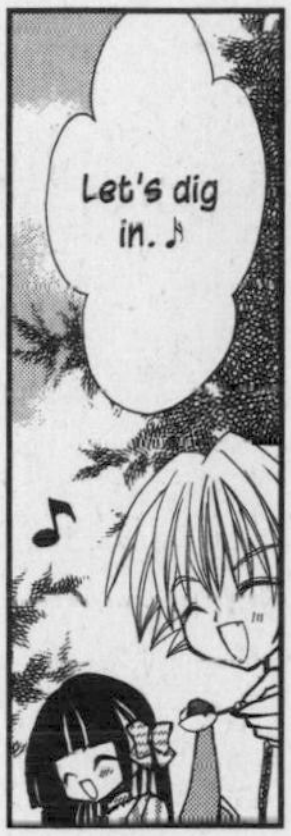
Let's dig in. ♪

Tanuki, page 27

A *tanuki* is a dog that looks just like your ordinary, garden-variety dog. It is also known as the "raccoon dog."

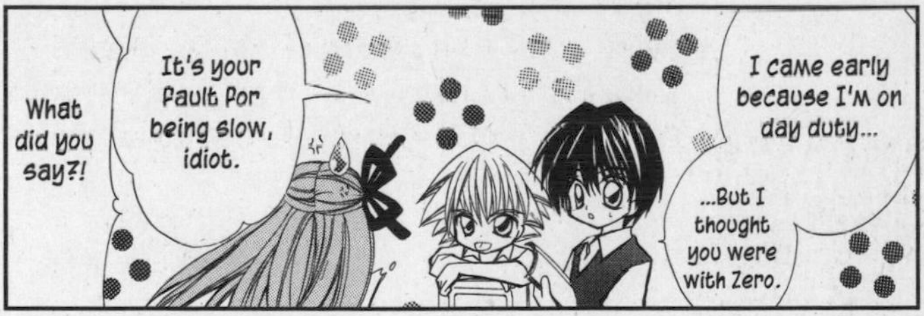
I came early because I'm on day duty...
...But I thought you were with Zero.
It's your fault for being slow, idiot.
What did you say?!

Day duty, page 41

In Japanese schools, a student is assigned to lead the class's routine tasks for a day. This includes taking attendance, cleaning the classrooms, and keeping the class journal.

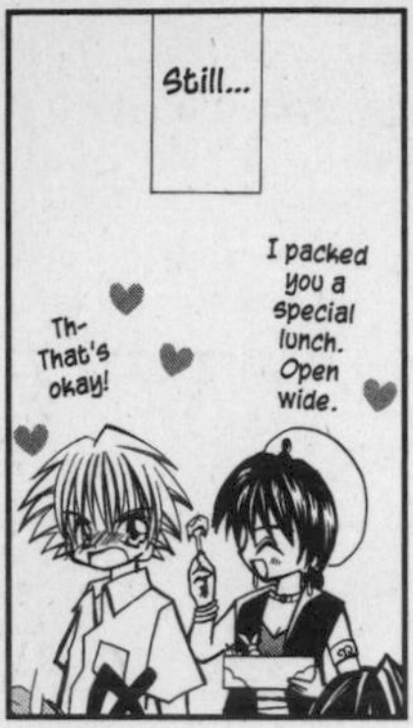
Still...
I packed you a special lunch. Open wide.
Th-That's okay!

Special lunch, page 49

Kuku is actually saying *aizuma bentô,* which, literally translated, means "sweetheart lunch box." An *aizuma bentô* is a lunch box packed by a wife for her husband with love.

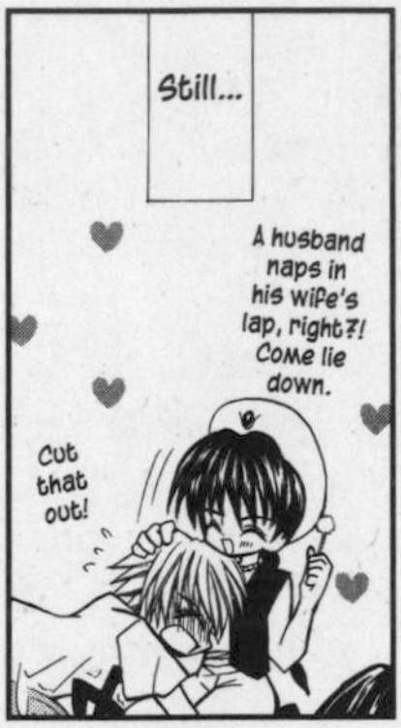
Still...
A husband naps in his wife's lap, right?! Come lie down.
Cut that out!

A husband napping in his wife's lap, page 49

What Kuku is offering to do is clean his ears, which is traditionally a family activity in Japan. It is common to find a family member laying his or her head on another member's lap for ear cleaning.

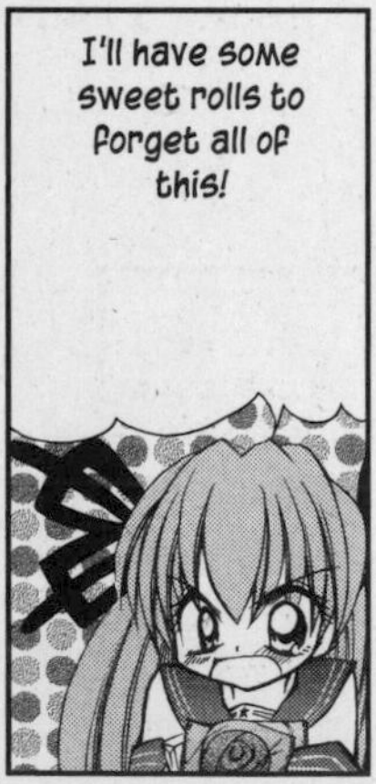
I'll have some sweet rolls to forget all of this!

Sweet rolls, page 52

Nina is actually shouting names of the sweet rolls—Special Butter Cream Sandwich and Maple Syrup and Orange Roll—she got from the school store.

KC, page 68

KC stands for Kodansha Comics, which is the imprint under which this manga was published in Japan.

New Year's greeting card, page 70

Preparing and sending New Year's greeting cards, in a postcard form, to friends, families, and acquaintances is a New Year's custom in Japan.

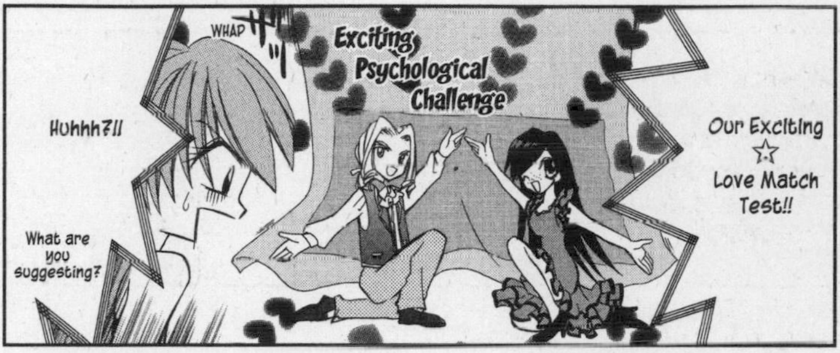
Our Exciting
☆
Love Match
Test!!
Exciting
Psychological
Challenge
WHAP
Huhhh?!!
What are
you
suggesting?

The Exciting ☆ Love Match Test, page 111

Eleven is actually saying *Dokidoki Shinri Test,* which means the "Exciting Psychological Test." Since a love quiz is what is being conducted, we felt this name worked a little better in English

Miko, page 134

Miko are young female attendants at Shinto shrines and temples.

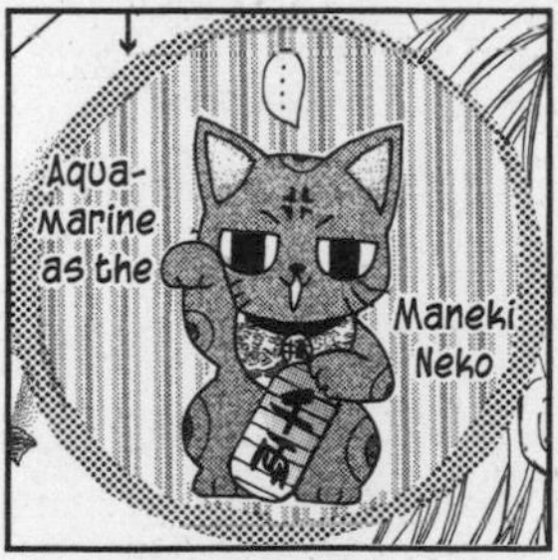
...
Aqua-
marine
as the
Maneki
Neko

Maneki Neko, page 134

Maneki Neko, literally translated as the "Beckoning Cat," is a Japanese porcelain or ceramic sculpture often displayed in the retail businesses in Japan. It is known as the "Lucky Cat" or the "Fortune Cat," and is believed to bring good luck to the owner.

School entrance ceremony and cherry blossoms, page 136

Spring is when the school year starts in Japan and school entrance ceremonies are held for incoming students. It also coincides with the cherry blossom season.

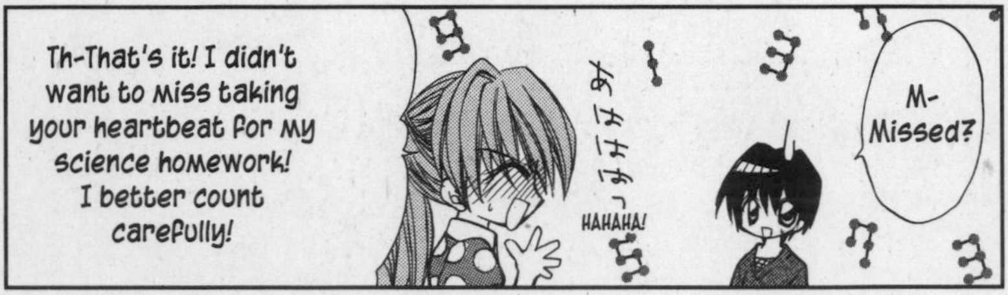

M-
Missed?
HAHAHA!
Th-That's it! I didn't want to miss taking your heartbeat for my science homework! I better count carefully!

Missed a heartbeat, page 138

This chapter opens with Nina actually saying *kiss shite,* and now she tries to convince Ichî that she meant *kisû shite.* The former means "kiss me" when the latter literally translates to "to have an odd number." Apparently, these two words have no connection and Nina has created a rhyme in a sense. It was difficult to replicate this play on words in English, so we went with "missed a beat" for a similar effect.

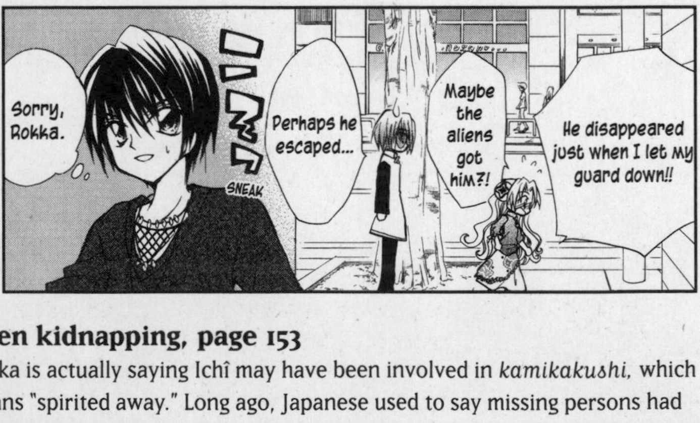

He disappeared just when I let my guard down!!
Maybe the aliens got him?!
Perhaps he escaped...
SNEAK
Sorry, Rokka.

Alien kidnapping, page 153

Rokka is actually saying Ichî may have been involved in *kamikakushi,* which means "spirited away." Long ago, Japanese used to say missing persons had been taken away by a fairy or ghost, the same way Americans talk about being abducted by aliens.

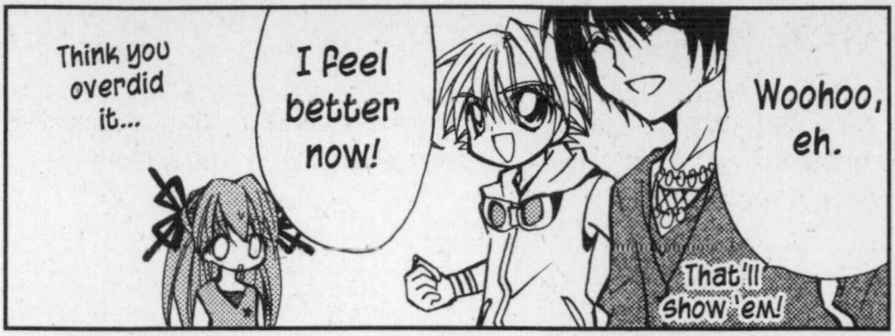
Woohoo, eh.
That'll show 'em!
I feel better now!
Think you overdid it...

Woohoo, page 163

Ichî is actually saying *Tamaya,* which is what spectators shout at fireworks festivals. Some spectators also shout *Kagiya.* This custom began in the 1800s when the two major fireworks manufacturers, Tamaya and Kagiya, were in fierce competition against each other. We use "Woohoo" as an English equivalent here.

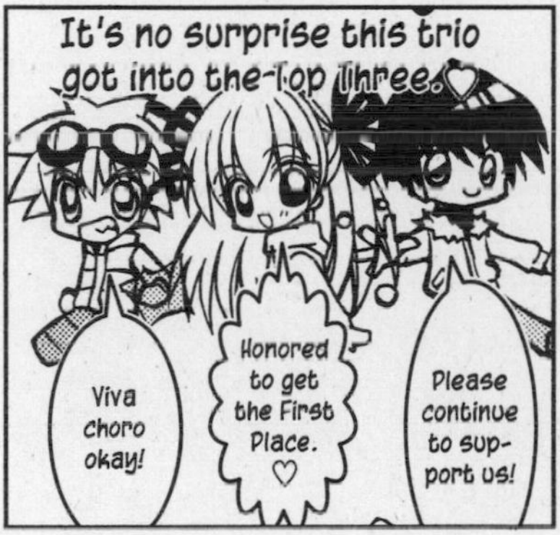
It's no surprise this trio got into the Top Three.♡
Please continue to sup-port us!
Honored to get the First Place. ♡
Viva choro okay!

Viva choro okay, page 198

This is a silly multi-lingual catchphrase Zero coined himself. He first used it in volume 1 of *Mamotte! Lollipop* and it's become something of a trademark for him. *Viva* is a Spanish exclamation, *choro* is from the Japanese word *choroi,* which literally means "easy," and "okay," is, well, exactly what it is.

Preview of Volume 4

We're pleased to present you a preview from volume 4. This volume will be available in English on August 28, 2007, but for now you'll have to make do with Japanese!

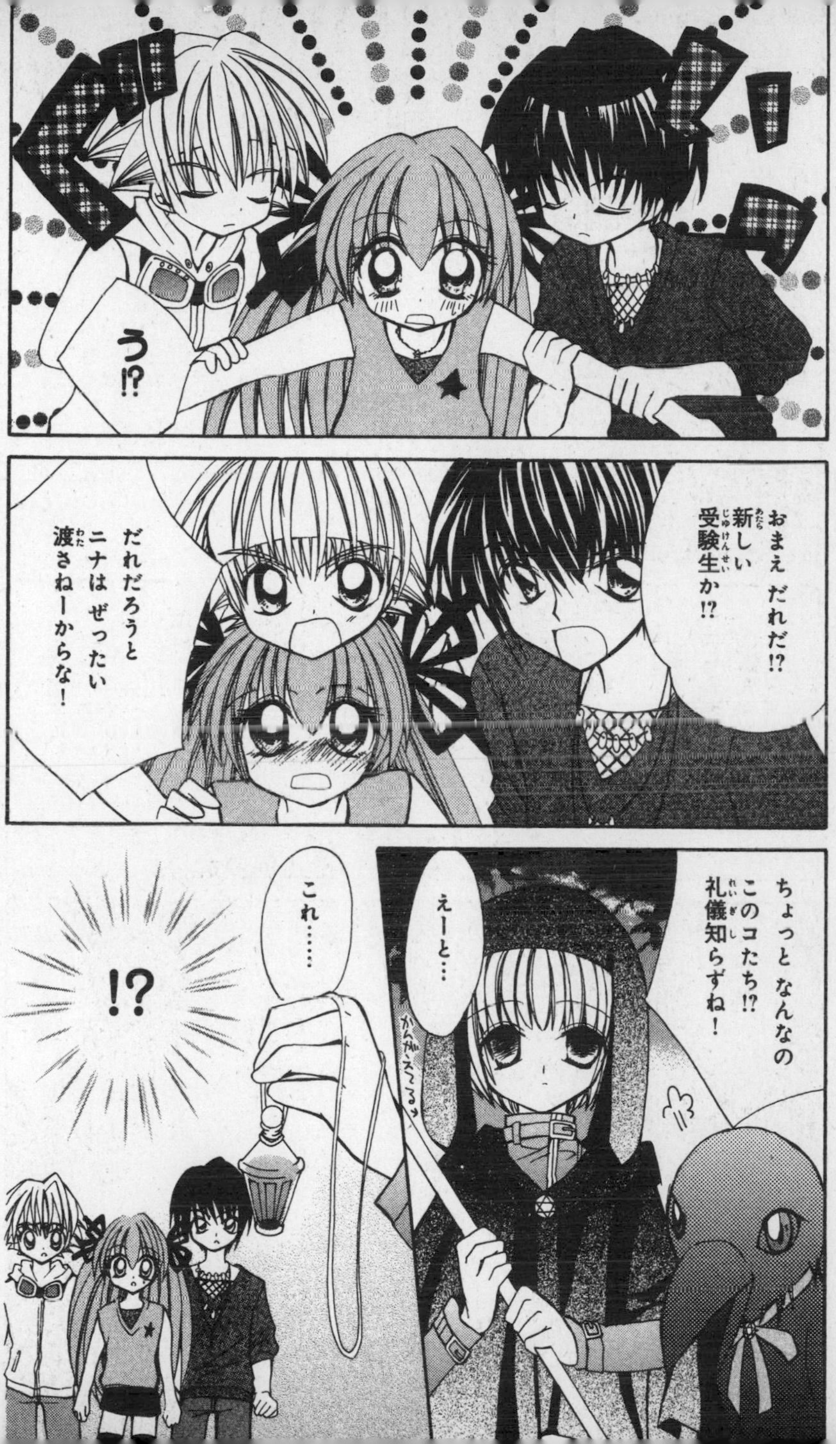
う!?
おまえ だれだ!? 新しい受験生か!?
だれだろうと ニナは ぜったい 渡さねーからな!
ちょっとなんなの このコたち!? 礼儀知らずね!
えーと…
かんちがえてる♪
これ……
!?

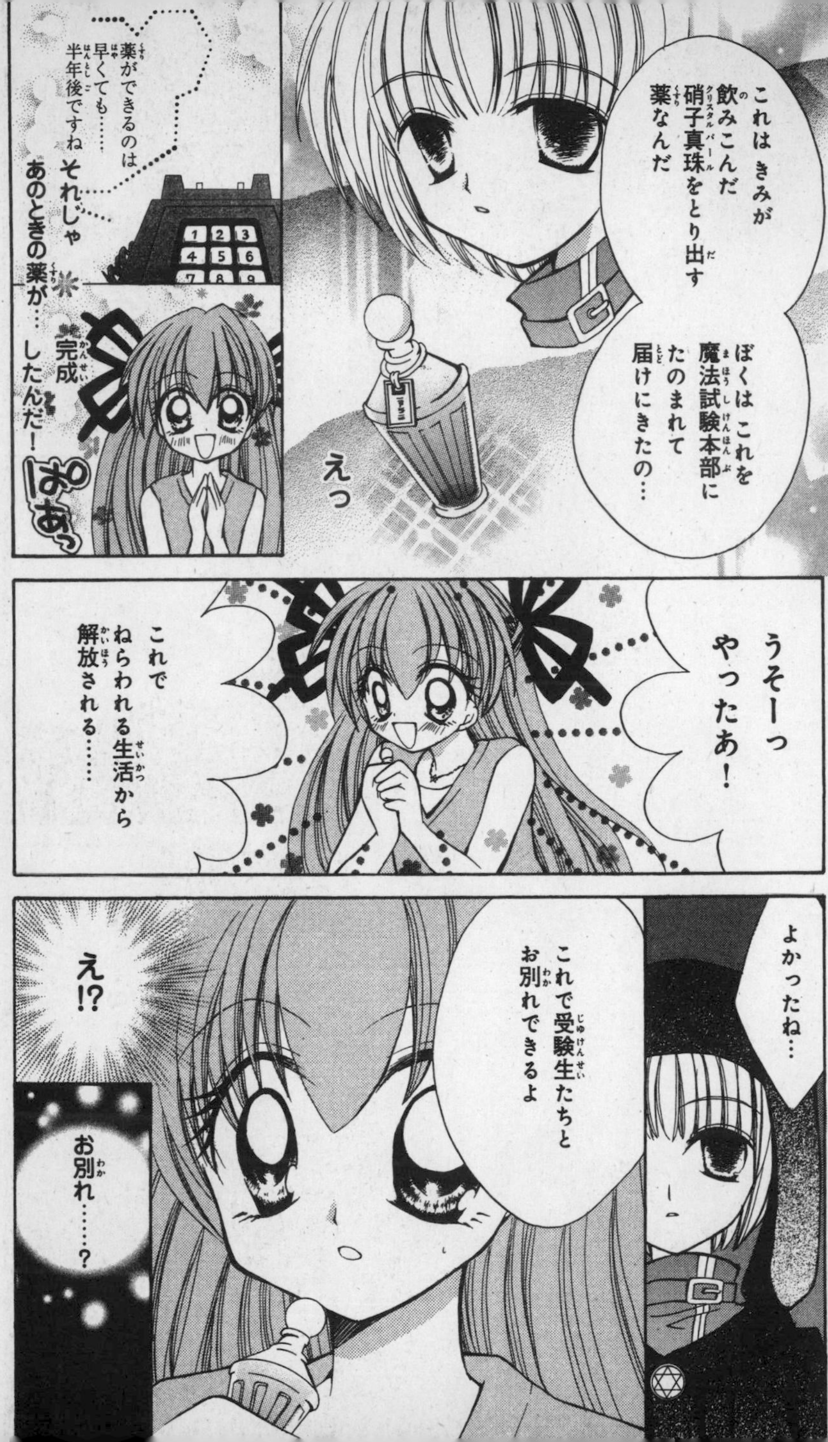
これは きみが飲みこんだ硝子真珠をとり出す薬なんだ
ぼくは これを魔法試験本部にたのまれて届けにきたの…
えっ
……薬ができるのは早くても……半年後ですね
それじゃあのときの薬が…
完成したんだ！
ぱあっ
うそーっやったあ！
これでねらわれる生活から解放される……
よかったね…
これで受験生たちとお別れできるよ
え!?
お別れ……？

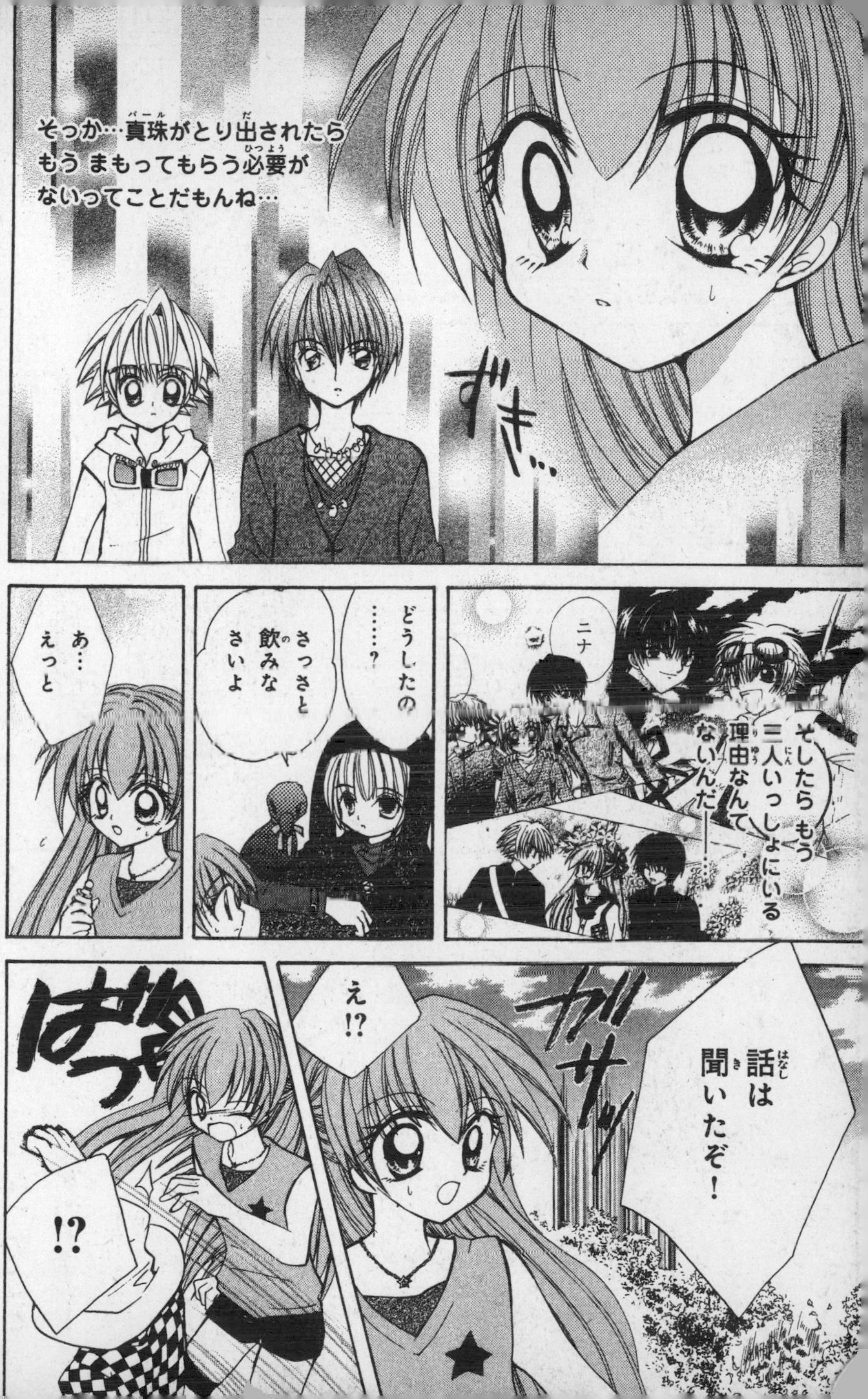
そっか…真珠がとり出されたら
もう まもってもらう必要が
ないってことだもんね…
ずき…
そしたら もう 三人いっしょにいる 理由なんて ないんだ——…
ニナ
どうしたの……?
さっさと飲みなさいよ
あ…えっと
話は聞いたぞ!
ガサッ
え!?
はっ
!?

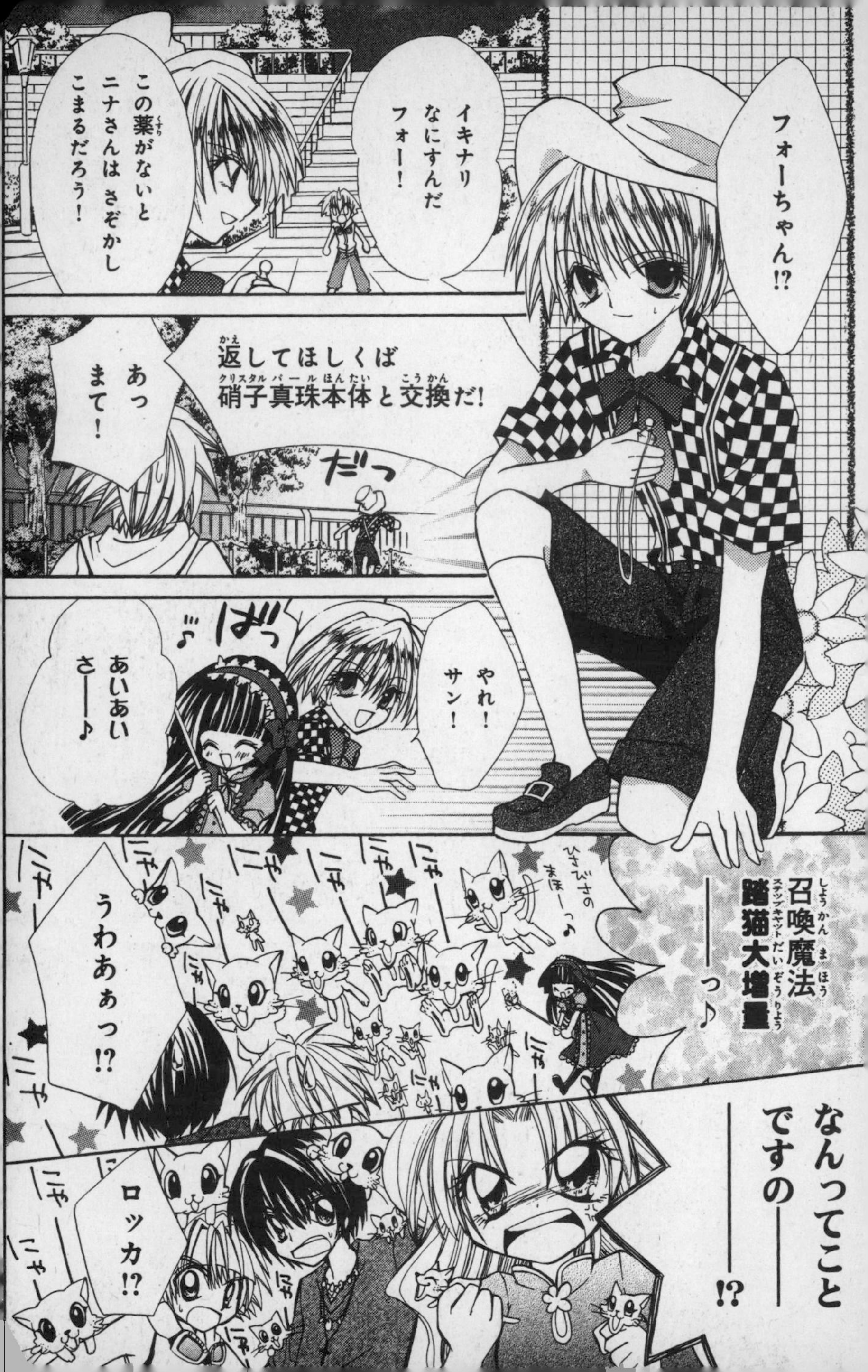
フォーちゃん!?
イキナリ なにすんだ フォー!
この薬がないと ニナさんは さぞかし こまるだろう!
返してほしくば 硝子真珠本体と交換だ!
あっ まて!
だっ
やれ! サン!
ぱっ
あいあい さー―♪
召喚魔法 踏猫大増量――っ♪
ひさびさの まほーっ♪
うわあぁっ!?
ニャー
なんてこと ですの―― ――!?
ロッカ!?

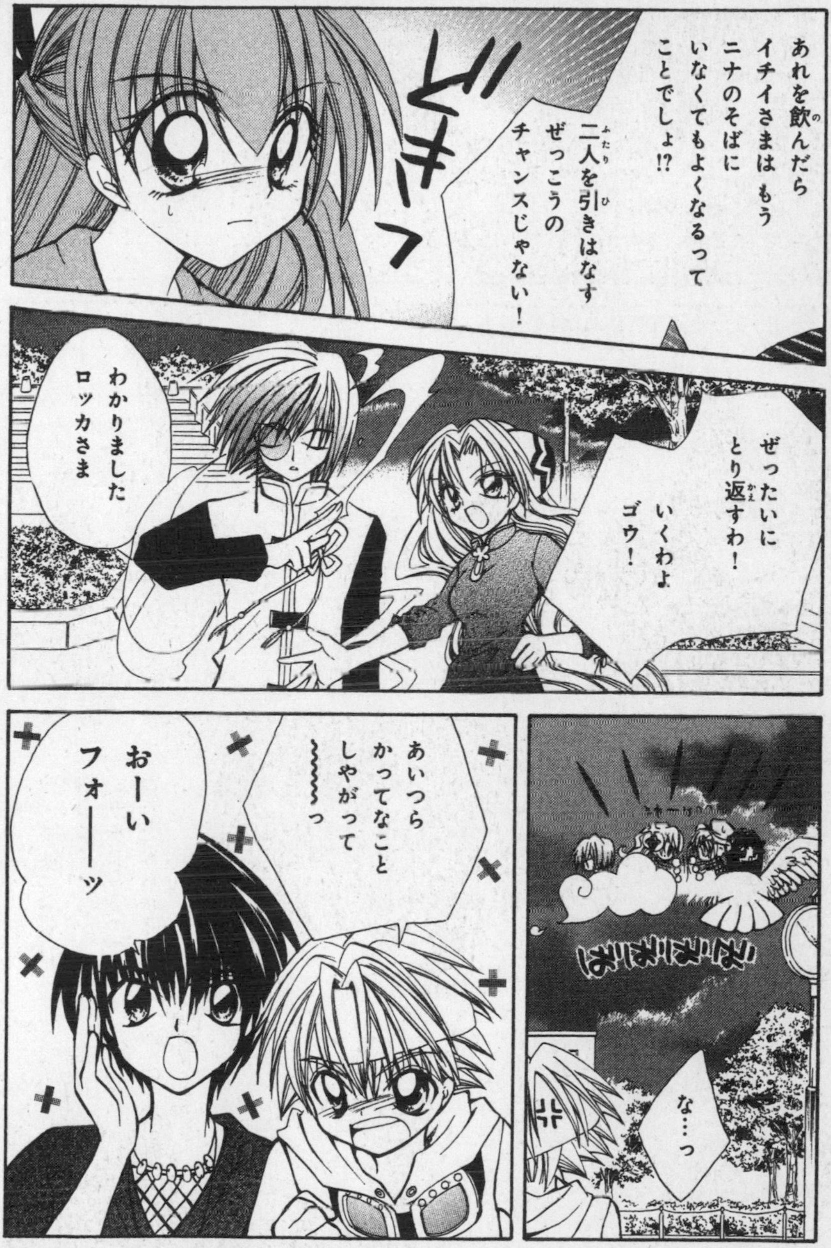
あれを飲んだらイチイさまはもうニナのそばにいなくてもよくなるってことでしょ!?
二人を引きはなすぜっこうのチャンスじゃない！
ぜったいにとり返すわ！
いくわよゴウ！
わかりましたロッカさま
な…っ
あいつらかってなことしやがって〜〜〜っ
おーいフォーーーッ

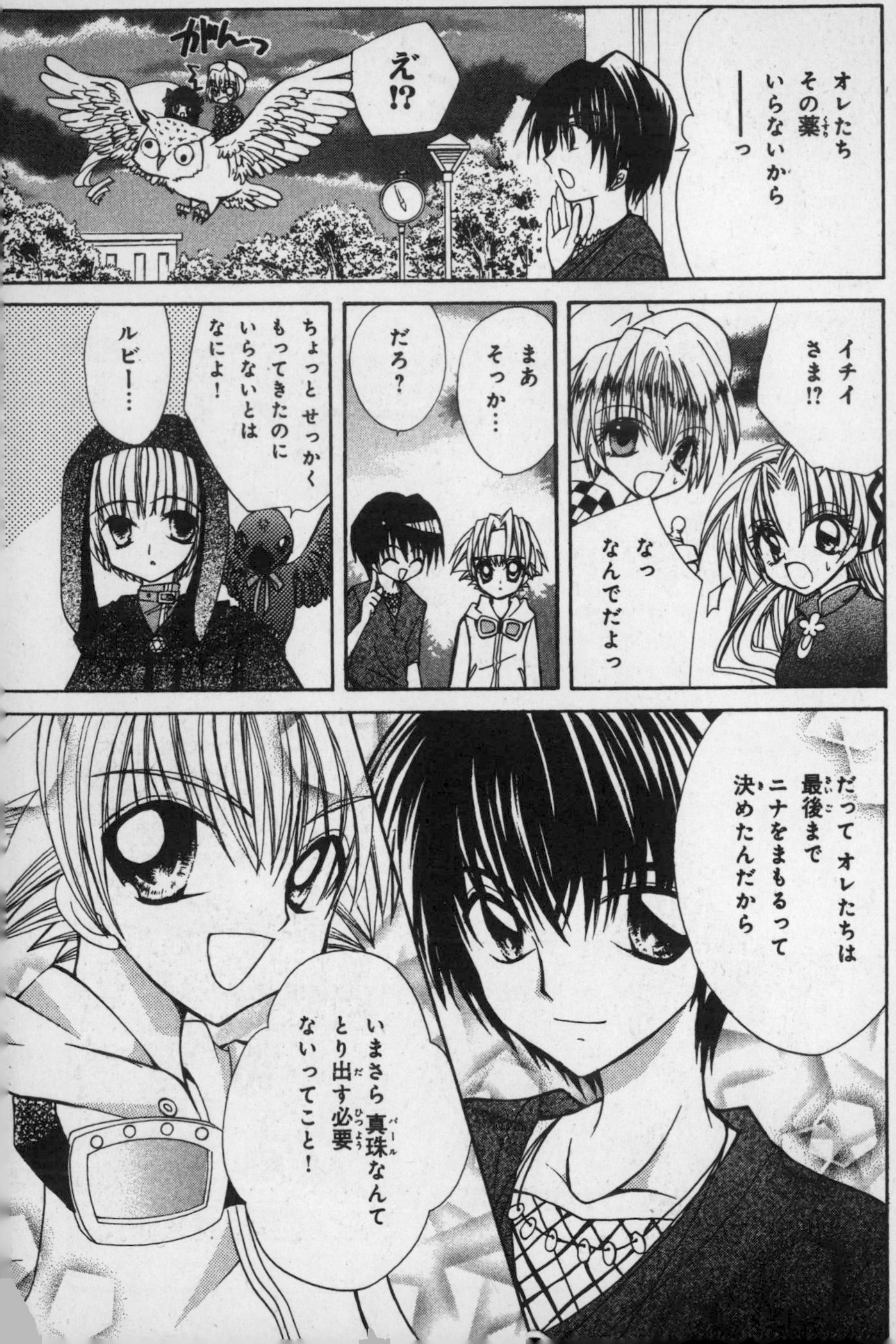
オレたち その薬 いらないから ——っ
え!?
がんーっ
イチイさま!?
なっ なんでだよっ
まあ そっか…
だろ?
ちょっと せっかく もってきたのに いらないとは なによ!
ルビー…
だって オレたちは 最後まで ニナをまもるって 決めたんだから
いまさら 真珠なんて とり出す必要 ないってこと!

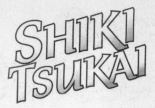
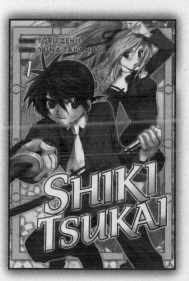
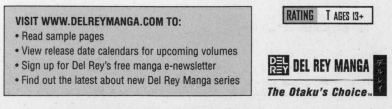

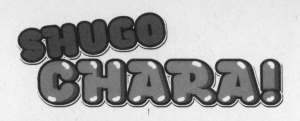

SHUGO CHARA!

PEACH-PIT

Creators of *Dears* and *Rozen Maiden*

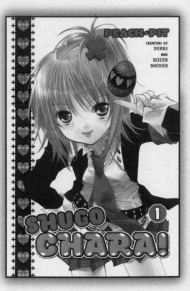

Everybody at Seiyo Elementary thinks that stylish and super-cool Amu has it all. But nobody knows the *real* Amu, a shy girl who wishes she had the courage to truly be herself. Changing Amu's life is going to take more than wishes and dreams—it's going to take a little magic! One morning, Amu finds a surprise in her bed: three strange little eggs. Each egg contains a Guardian Character, an angel-like being who can give her the power to be someone new. With the help of her Guardian Characters, Amu is about to discover that her true self is even more amazing than she ever dreamed.

Special extras in each volume! Read them all!

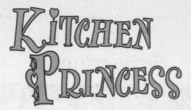

KITCHEN PRINCESS

STORY BY MIYUKI KOBAYASHI
MANGA BY NATSUMI ANDO
CREATOR OF ZODIAC P.I.

HUNGRY HEART

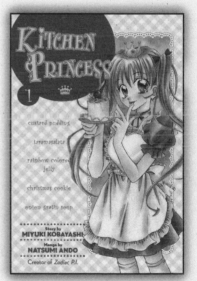

Najika is a great cook and likes to make meals for the people she loves. But something is missing from her life. When she was a child, she met a boy who touched her heart—and now Najika is determined to find him. The only clue she has is a silver spoon that leads her to the prestigious Seika Academy.

Attending Seika will be a challenge. Every kid at the school has a special talent, and the girls in Najika's class think she doesn't deserve to be there. But Sora and Daichi, two popular brothers who barely speak to each other, recognize Najika's cooking for what it is—magical. Could one of the boys be Najika's mysterious prince?

Special extras in each volume! Read them all!

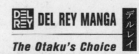

TOMA

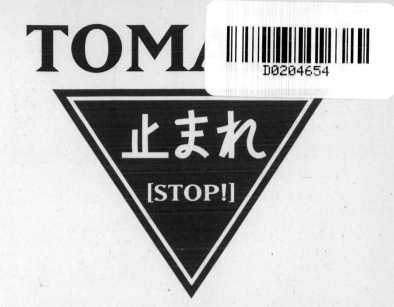

止まれ

[STOP!]

You're going the wrong way!

Manga is a completely different type of reading experience.

To start at the beginning, go to the end!

That's right! Authentic manga is read the traditional Japanese way— from right to left. Exactly the opposite of how American books are read. It's easy to follow: Just go to the other end of the book, and read each page—and each panel—from right side to left side, starting at the top right. Now you're experiencing manga as it was meant to be!